36 days

The Complete Chronicle of the 2000 Presidential Election Crisis

★ ★ ★ ★ ★

by correspondents of

The New York Times

★

Introduction by

DOUGLAS BRINKLEY

Times Books
Henry Holt and Company
New York

Times Books
Henry Holt and Company, LLC
Publishers since 1866
115 West 18th Street
New York, New York 10011

Henry Holt ® is a registered trademark of
Henry Holt and Company, LLC.

Published in Canada by Fitzhenry & Whiteside Ltd.,
195 Allstate Parkway, Markam, Ontario L3R 4T8.

Library of Congress Cataloging-in-Publication Data is available
ISBN: 0-8050-6850-3

Henry Holt books are available for special promotions and premiums.
For details contact: Director, Special Markets.

Acknowledgments

For **THE NEW YORK TIMES**: Thomas K. Carley, President, News Services; Mitchel Levitas, Editorial Director, Book Development. Special thanks to Jim Roberts, national political editor for the 2000 presidential campaign and special consultant on this book; Margaret O'Connor, picture editor, who selected the cover photographs; and Archie Tse, graphics editor.

Edited and Produced by **ELIZABETH PUBLISHING**:
General Editor: John W. Wright
Executive Editor: Alan Joyce
Writers and Editors: Alice Finer, David C. Major
Copyediting and proofreading: Jerold Kappes and Sue Mermelstein
Academic Adviser: Prof. Edward O'Donnell, Hunter College.

First Edition 2001

Book design by Virginia Norey

Printed in the United States of America
10 9 8 7 6 5 4 3 2 1

Please direct all comments to:
The New York Times, Publishing Dept.
122 East 42nd St., 14th Floor
New York, NY 10168

Contents

INTRODUCTION by Douglas Brinkley xi

day 1 ★

WEDNESDAY, NOVEMBER 8: **TOO CLOSE TO CALL**
OUTCOME HANGS ON CONTESTED FLORIDA VOTE 1
HOW GORE STOPPED SHORT ON HIS WAY TO CONCEDE 3
William Safire on "Snippy" 7
BUSH LEADS GORE BY 1,784 VOTES AS RECOUNT BEGINS 8
THE CASE OF THE "BUTTERFLY" BALLOT 10
A Case of Mistaken Identity 11
Measures of Elections Past 13

day 2 ★

THURSDAY, NOVEMBER 9: **CONFUSING BALLOTS, ANGRY VOTERS**
GORE VOWS COURT FIGHT OVER VOTE WITH FLORIDA'S OUTCOME STILL UP IN THE AIR 14
FOR DEMOCRATS, PROBLEMS ALL ACROSS FLORIDA 17
Street Protests Erupt in Palm Beach 20
Profile: Baker and Christopher 21
THE ELECTORAL COLLEGE REARS ITS UGLY HEAD 23
OpEd: Electoral College, Safeguard of Federalism 25
OpEd: The Electoral College, Unfair From Day One 26

day 3 ★

FRIDAY, NOVEMBER 10: **BUSH LEAD COLLAPSES**
AS BUSH LEAD SHRINKS TO 327 HE URGES GORE TO CONCEDE 28
DEMOCRATS SEEK MANUAL RECOUNTS 31
OVERVOTES AND UNDERVOTES 33
DEMOCRATS SPLIT OVER COURT FIGHT 35
AFRICAN-AMERICANS SEEK INQUIRY INTO FLORIDA VOTE 36

day 4 ★

SATURDAY, NOVEMBER 11: **BUSH GOES TO COURT**
BUSH SUES IN FEDERAL COURT TO STOP RECOUNT 39
Why the Republicans Went to Federal Court 42
HAGGLING OVER CHADS IN PALM BEACH COUNTY 43
Hanging Chads May Hold Key to Election 44

day 5 ★

SUNDAY, NOVEMBER 12:
AN UNPRECEDENTED RECOUNT BEGINS
PALM BEACH BOARD DOES THE UNTHINKABLE 48
Broward County Might Do Its Own Hand Recount 51
AWAITING COURT, BOTH SIDES SPIN HARD 53
WHAT NEXT? REPUBLICANS CORRECTED THOUSANDS OF ABSENTEE APPLICATIONS 54
SOME G.O.P. LEADERS QUESTION BUSH'S CAMPAIGN 56

day 6 ★

MONDAY, NOVEMBER 13: HARRIS TAKES CHARGE
DEMOCRATS SCRAMBLE OVER TUESDAY DEADLINE 60
FEDERAL JUDGE DEFERS TO STATE COURT 62
PALM BEACH COUNTY PREPARES TO RECOUNT VOTES 63
After Partial Recount, Broward Drops the Whole Idea 65
Volusia County's Recount Discovers 320 New Ballots 65
POLL: AMERICANS ARE DIVIDED BUT CALM 67

day 7 ★

TUESDAY, NOVEMBER 14: HARRIS UPS THE ANTE
DEMOCRATS DISPUTE FRIDAY DEADLINE 69
PALM BEACH PANEL VOTES TO RECOUNT 73
Broward Reconsiders Manual Countywide Recount 74
Profile: David Boies: Slayer of Microsoft Joins Gore Team 75
Florida Secretary of State's Statement 76

day 8 ★

WEDNESDAY, NOVEMBER 15:
PARTISAN TENSIONS RISE
HARRIS STYMIES GORE'S RECOUNT STRATEGY 77
Gore Speech Stuns Bush Team 79
Bush Sticks to the Script 80
GORE'S LAWYERS PUT PALM BEACH BALLOT IN THEIR SIGHTS 81
A MEMO FROM THE HOUSE WHIP 83

day 9 ★

THURSDAY, NOVEMBER 16: "THERE IS NO LEGAL IMPEDIMENT TO THE RECOUNTS"
FLORIDA COURT RULES FOR RECOUNTS AND BUSH GOES FEDERAL AGAIN 85
The Florida Supreme Court: A Democratic Oasis 87
PALM BEACH STARTS RECOUNT, FINALLY 88
Counting Chads 90
Palm Beach County Had Prior Complaints About Counts 90
Still Another County With the Ballot Blues 91

day 10 ★

FRIDAY, NOVEMBER 17:
FLORIDA HIGH COURT RESTARTS RECOUNTS

BUSH HAMMERED IN SEVERAL COURTS 94

JUDGE OKS CHADS, DIMPLED OR OTHERWISE 95

FUROR OVER ABSENTEE BALLOTS 96

Seminole County Absentee Dispute Goes to Court 98

day 11 ★

SATURDAY, NOVEMBER 18:
BUSH WINNING OVERSEAS COUNT

OVERSEAS BALLOTS BOOST BUSH LEAD TO 930 101

Rancor Prevails in Debate Over Military Votes 101

GORE LAWYERS BLAME HARRIS FOR...WELL, EVERYTHING 103

A Recount Moment: Eating the Chads 104

AN ACE IN THE HOLE FOR REPUBLICANS 106

day 12 ★

SUNDAY, NOVEMBER 19: THE COUNT DRAGS ON, THE LAWYERS FACE OFF

REPUBLICANS BLAST NEW RULES ABOUT DIMPLED CHADS 107

Legal Battle Lines Are Drawn 109

MILITARY BALLOTS MERIT A REVIEW, LIEBERMAN SAYS 111

Profile: Katherine Harris: Wicked Witch or Queen Esther? 113

day 13 ★

MONDAY, NOVEMBER 20: RECOUNT DEBATE REACHES FLORIDA SUPREME COURT

A SKEPTICAL FLORIDA SUPREME COURT ASKS TOUGH QUESTIONS 115

Seminole County Absentee Case Goes to Court 118

Judge Says He Can't Order Palm Beach Revote 118

PARTIES CLASH OVER RECOUNT STANDARDS 119

REPUBLICANS SEE A "MESS," DEMOCRATS SEE "SMOOTH" PROCESS 121

FLORIDA ATTORNEY GENERAL ORDERS 123
REVIEW OF MILITARY VOTES

OpEd: The Florida Court Should Boldly Take Charge 123

day 14 ★

TUESDAY, NOVEMBER 21: FLORIDA SUPREME COURT BACKS RECOUNTS—AGAIN

FLORIDA COURT UNANIMOUSLY AFFIRMS GORE'S CASE 125

Bush Camp Angrily Vows to Fight Ruling 127

DIMPLED VOTES ARE NEW HOPE FOR DEMOCRATS 128

Where the Three Counties Stand Now 130

OpEd: Florida's Justices Went Too Far 130

day 15 ★

WEDNESDAY, NOVEMBER 22:
MIAMI-DADE GIVES UP, G.O.P. MAKES THREATS
MIAMI-DADE HALTS RECOUNT 133
Chaotic Protest Influences Miami-Dade's Decision 134
CHENEY IN HOSPITAL WITH MILD HEART ATTACK 136
G.O.P. LAUNCHES MULTIPLE LEGAL ATTACKS 137
BUSH FILES SUIT TO RESTORE REJECTED MILITARY BALLOTS 138
FLORIDA LEGISLATORS CONSIDER OPTIONS TO AID BUSH 139
CONGRESSIONAL REPUBLICANS THREATEN TO CHALLENGE ELECTORS 141

day 16 ★

THURSDAY, NOVEMBER 23:
GORE PLANS TO CONTEST ELECTION
GORE LOSES MIAMI-DADE SUIT BUT PLANS FOR LEGAL CHALLENGE 142
GORE ASKS U.S. SUPREME COURT TO REJECT BUSH'S APPEAL 144
TEMPERS FLARE OVER BROWARD RECOUNT 145
POOR HANDWRITING AND MIX-UPS DISQUALIFIED ABSENTEE VOTES 146
DEMOCRATS FIGHT ON, BUT SOME LOSE HEART 147

day 17 ★

FRIDAY, NOVEMBER 24:
THE U.S. SUPREME COURT PLUNGES IN
HIGHEST COURT, SURPRISINGLY, AGREES TO HEAR BUSH'S APPEAL 149
GORE SET TO FIGHT ON MANY FRONTS 152
Democrats Prepare Broad Attack on Harris's Certification 153
FLORIDA LEGISLATURE PLANS TO BACK BUSH SUIT 154
MODEST GAINS FOR GORE IN BROWARD AS REPUBLICANS JEER 155
OpEd: The Right Moment for the Supreme Court 156

day 18 ★

SATURDAY, NOVEMBER 25:
CHECKING FOR DIMPLES AS DEADLINE NEARS
RECOUNTS GIVE GORE 466 VOTES 158
NEW DETAILS IN ABSENTEE BALLOT CASE 161
G.O.P. SUES OVER MILITARY ABSENTEE BALLOTS 162

day 19 ★

SUNDAY, NOVEMBER 26: HARRIS DECLARES BUSH THE WINNER

BUSH WINS YET AGAIN BUT GORE WON'T CONCEDE 164

Bush Quietly Claims Victory 166

A NEW YORK TIMES INTERVIEW WITH AL GORE 168

GORE'S LAWYERS OUTLINE STRATEGY 170

HOW HARRIS REJECTED PALM BEACH RECOUNT 171

FUROR ERUPTS OVER 218 VOTES IN NASSAU COUNTY 173

Tracking Bush's Lead *174*

day 20 ★

MONDAY, NOVEMBER 27: GORE CONTESTS THE ELECTION

FLORIDA JUDGE ASKED TO DECLARE GORE THE WINNER 175

Bush Plans Transition As Gore Asks for Patience 178

Clinton Administration Denies Bush Team Money and Office for Transition 180

JEB BUSH REPORTEDLY READY TO SIGN BILL GIVING REPUBLICANS VICTORY 181

day 21 ★

TUESDAY, NOVEMBER 28: TIME IS OF THE ESSENCE

FLORIDA LAWMAKERS MOVE TO ASSURE BUSH VICTORY 183

STATE JUDGE REFUSES TO COUNT BALLOTS, SETS HEARING FOUR DAYS FROM NOW 186

ANOTHER ABSENTEE BALLOT CONTROVERSY 188

ERROR-PRONE MACHINES LOWERED MINORITY VOTE 189

Counting the Blanks *191*

day 22 ★

WEDNESDAY, NOVEMBER 29: GORE APPEALS FOR FASTER COUNT

GORE LOSING TIME AS BUSH LAWYERS STALL 192

JEB BUSH BACKS PLAN FOR LEGISLATURE TO BYPASS COURTS 195

day 23 ★

THURSDAY, NOVEMBER 30: G.O.P. CHALLENGES GORE, MOVES ON SPECIAL SESSION

REPUBLICANS ATTACK GORE'S SUIT 197

TV Follows Truck Carrying Ballots 200

LAWMAKERS MOVE CLOSER TO SPECIAL SESSION 201

OpEd: Florida Legislature Plays a Dangerous Game 203

day 24 ★

FRIDAY, DECEMBER 1: HISTORIC MOMENT AT THE SUPREME COURT

SHARP QUESTIONING REVEALS A DEEPLY DIVIDED COURT 206
Outside, a Loud Jury of Jeers 209
Excerpts from the Supreme Court Hearing 210
ARTICLE II AND SECTION 5: THE HEART OF THE MATTER? 211
Two Laws at Issue in Dispute before Supreme Court 214
TWO SETBACKS FOR GORE IN FLORIDA COURTS 215
Profile: Laurence H. Tribe 217
Profile: Theodore B. Olson 218

day 25 ★

SATURDAY, DECEMBER 2: "EVERY DAY, EVERY HOUR MATTERS"

GORE'S TRIAL IN FLORIDA BOGS DOWN 221
A Ponderous Day at Trial 225
JUDGE SAULS WEIGHS COMPETING LEGAL STANDARDS 225

day 26 ★

SUNDAY, DECEMBER 3: A 14-HOUR DAY IN COURT

IN LEON COUNTY, LAWYERS WRAP UP ARGUMENTS 228
GORE DIGS IN 232
CHENEY CALLS FOR GORE CONCESSION 233

day 27 ★

MONDAY, DECEMBER 4: A MAJOR SETBACK FOR GORE, BUSH GETS NO HELP

FLORIDA JUDGE HANDS GORE A MAJOR DEFEAT 235
Pessimism on the Vice President's Team 238
Bush Takes Restrained Tone 239
U.S. JUSTICES SEND CASE BACK TO FLORIDA HIGH COURT 240

day 28 ★

TUESDAY, DECEMBER 5: AL GORE, OPTIMIST

COURT DEFEAT LEAVES GORE UNBOWED 242
Democrats See Hope in Absentee Ballot Application Trials 244
FLORIDA SUPREME COURT MOVES QUICKLY TO HEAR GORE CONTEST OF THE ELECTION 246
BUSH LAWYERS AGAIN URGE FEDERAL COURT TO REJECT FLORIDA RECOUNTS 247

day 29 ★
WEDNESDAY, DECEMBER 6: FLORIDA LEGISLATURE DIMS GORE'S HOPES
LEGISLATORS MOVE ON ELECTORS, COURT SET TO HEAR APPEAL 249
Bitter Disagreements over Lawmakers' Action 251
24,000 VOTES AT STAKE IN ABSENTEE BALLOT TRIALS 253
FEDERAL COURT REJECTS BUSH REQUEST TO BAR RECOUNTS 255

day 30 ★
THURSDAY, DECEMBER 7: FLORIDA HIGH COURT AGAIN HEARS GORE APPEAL
FLORIDA JUSTICES ASK POINTED QUESTIONS 256
SAULS'S DIFFICULT HISTORY WITH FLORIDA HIGH COURT 259
WHO'S FUNDING THE RECOUNT FIGHT? 263

day 31 ★
FRIDAY, DECEMBER 8: FLORIDA SUPREME COURT BACKS RECOUNT
BUSH'S LEAD BELOW 200 AS FLORIDA SUPREME COURT ORDERS MANUAL RECOUNT 264
Angry Republicans Vow Bitter Fight 268
Ruling Fuels G.O.P. Resolve to Appoint Electors 270
GORE LOSES BOTH ABSENTEE BALLOT SUITS 271
Statement by the Supreme Court of Florida 272
OpEd: The Chaos a Recount Could Bring 273
Tracking Bush's Lead 274

day 32 ★
SATURDAY, DECEMBER 9: U.S. SUPREME COURT HALTS THE RECOUNT
BITTERLY DIVIDED HIGH COURT SUDDENLY STEPS IN 276
Federal Court Had Just Voted for Recount 278
Text of Supreme Court's Decision 279
STUNNED DEMOCRATS ATTACK COURT'S DECISION 281
COUNTING STOPPED COLD BY SUPREME COURT ORDER 282
Florida's Undervote 285

day 33 ★
SUNDAY, DECEMBER 10: BUSH V. GORE
THE BRIEFS ARE FILED 287
The Bush Argument 287
The Gore Argument 288
THE COURT'S CREDIBILITY IS AT RISK 289
OpEd: Supreme Court's Incursion Was Not Needed 291

day 34 ★

MONDAY, DECEMBER 11:
SUPREME COURT II: SOBER, INTENSE
HARD AND FAST QUESTIONS FROM THE HIGHEST COURT 294
Justices' Queries Reveal Their Chief Concerns 297
MEANWHILE, FLORIDA
SUPREME COURT REWRITES OPINION 299
Legislature Prepares to Appoint Electors 300
Those Other Lawsuits Are Still Going On 301
A Laugh Always Helps 302

day 35 ★

TUESDAY, DECEMBER 12:
U.S. SUPREME COURT ENDS RECOUNTS
A DEEPLY-DIVIDED COURT ENDS THE STRUGGLE 304
Gore Still Doesn't Concede 307
Bush Plays the Strong, Silent Role 308
GORE BACKERS LOSE IN FLORIDA SUPREME COURT 308

day 36 ★

WEDNESDAY, DECEMBER 13:
GORE FINALLY CONCEDES
GORE BOWS OUT AND URGES UNITY 310
BUSH VOWS TO BE PRESIDENT FOR "ONE NATION" 312
COURT'S ACTION BRINGS CONFUSION, NOT CLARITY 314
OpEd: Court May Have Expanded Voting Rights 316
OpEd: No Surprise, It's an Activist Court 317
A Popular Vote Edge for Gore... 319

POSTSCRIPTS: LOOKING BACK, LOOKING AHEAD
OpEd: This Election's Lesson: Win the Small States 321
INSIDE THE CAMPAIGN: GORE'S HARD STRATEGIC CALLS 322
GORE'S CRITICAL MISTAKE: FAILURE
TO ASK FOR A STATEWIDE RECOUNT 331
BOIES'S CONCESSION ON "DEADLINE" PROVED FATAL 334
INSIDE THE CAMPAIGN: G.O.P.'S DEPTH OUTDID GORE'S TEAM 336
ELECTION DISPUTE CASTS CLOUD ON JEB BUSH'S FUTURE 343
LEGAL SCHOLARS QUESTION SUPREME COURT'S ROLE 346
TWO MEDIA GROUPS MOVE TO EXAMINE FLORIDA VOTES 347

APPENDIX: TEXT OF SUPREME COURT RULING IN
BUSH V. GORE FLORIDA RECOUNT CASE 350

INDEX 375

Introduction

BY DOUGLAS BRINKLEY

—A presidential election is sometimes. . . a turning-point in history. In form it is nothing more than the choice of an administrator who cannot influence policy otherwise than by refusing his assent to bills. In reality it is the deliverance of the mind of the people upon all such questions as they feel able to decide.

—James Bryce, The American Commonwealth, 1888

Whenever U.S. politics turn too strange to quite grasp, as was so emphatically the case in the aftermath of the surreal presidential election of 2000, it is the wise citizen who reaches for Scotsman James Bryce's indispensable three-volume study *The American Commonwealth*, published in 1888 and deemed by both Theodore Roosevelt and Woodrow Wilson to put the more celebrated Frenchman Alexis de Tocqueville's 1835 opus *Democracy in America* to shame. Of course, Bryce's work came out the same year Republican Benjamin Harrison received 100,000 fewer popular votes than his Democratic opponent, Grover Cleveland, yet carried the Electoral College 233 to 168, prompting one Pennsylvania political boss to remark that Harrison would never know "how close a number of men were compelled to approach...the penitentiary to make him President."

The grand merit of *The American Commonwealth* lies in Bryce's up-close observations of our nation's political institutions at work, including the major political parties and actual municipal and state governments. Throughout his classic analysis, Bryce maintains that American presidential elections tend to be ridiculously melodramatic, and that the victor generally is the candidate with the better presentation rather than the more apparent wisdom. "Great men are not chosen President, firstly, because great men are rare in politics," he wrote; "secondly, because the method of choice does not bring them to the top; thirdly, because they are not, in quiet times, absolutely needed."

But one suspects that even this thoughtful Scot might have been baffled by the presidential election that ended the American Century — an election so close it took 36 days to figure out who would lead the United States into the next millennium. Perhaps even more surprising, in retrospect, is how scant the chances appeared at the beginning of the campaign that the election of 2000 would generate so much excitement, so much bitter controversy, and so many sweeping historical precedents. Not the least of these precedents, of course, is that the U.S. Supreme Court, for all intents and purposes, decided the next leader of the free world by one swing vote.

James Bryce is no longer around to share his sagacity, so it is fortunate to have a first-rate source of analysis like the book at hand, an account of the post-election coverage by the New York Times' team of political reporters. The story begins in the summer of 1999, when some dozen Republicans, a couple of Democrats, and a smattering of third-party aspirants declared themselves for the U.S. presidency in 2000 — a group most remarkable, perhaps, for its diversity, ranging from Patrick J. Buchanan on the far right to Ralph Nader on the left. Later, many Americans griped that although each tried to distinguish himself from his rival, there wasn't much of a choice between the two final candidates, Vice President Al Gore and George W. Bush, Governor of Texas. Both were fiftysomething white males with Ivy League bachelor's degrees and politically prominent fathers, Gore's a former U.S. senator and Bush's a former president.

Given the general lack of enthusiasm for either candidate, it's a wonder that voter turnout in 2000 topped the 49.08 percent of eligible Americans who cast their ballots for president in 1996. In hindsight, however, a great many more people probably wished they had voted — and that, as much as anything, is what affords this election its lasting, historical significance. For in the waning weeks of the year just ended, we as a nation went through a political science class that few Americans will soon forget, and from which, with any luck, most will have learned something.

Among the great fallacies in politics is that history repeats itself. Every national election has a tone and tenor all its own; despite the frequent analogies made in the aftermath of the 2000 election to the Samuel Tilden-Rutherford B. Hayes squeaker of 1876, this one was different from any presidential contest that came before it. And this is not only because the Supreme Court ended the Florida vote recount and decided the election. Voters, enjoying the twin pleasures of peace and prosperity, and expecting little of its politicians, rendered not just one but several split decisions: Gore and Bush finished in a virtual dead heat; the U.S. Senate wound up dead even between the two major parties for the first time since 1880, and the U.S. House of Representatives came closer to parity than at any time in the last half-century, with the Republicans holding the advantage by only nine seats.

So how did we get to this strange balance in our political makeup, and what does it mean for the United States and its people? Democratic political consultant James Carville may have got it right in 1992 and '96, but in 2000 it wasn't the economy, stupid. Any number of pocketbook-based academic models of likely voter behavior indicated that Gore would win easily at various points throughout the last campaign, including at the end; what's more, exit polls showed that the vast majority of American voters considered the U.S. economy "excellent," or at least "good." After all, when Bill Clinton took office in 1992, the nation was staggering under the largest budget deficit in its history; as Clinton left, the federal budget showed a surplus for the first time in decades.

In the most recent election, the old rules simply did not seem to apply. The states did not line up by party quite the way they used to. Shifting expectations changed the definition of victory in the candidates' debates. And although the contest did not hinge on the economy this time, the incumbent vice president would have been wise to campaign full-out on the nation's prosperity, and with no apologies for any failings on the part of the fellow at the top of the ticket. It was he, after all, who put Gore in the catbird seat for his own run at the White House.

Indeed, many polls over the last two years showed that Bill Clinton, despite his impeachment by the U.S. House of Representatives over the Monica Lewinsky scandal, would have been reelected handily if the Constitution had permitted him to run again. That Al Gore refused to cash in on that popularity, or at least on the longest economic expansion in the nation's history, in fear of some moralistic voter backlash was not only curious, but fatal to his own hopes. Had the vice president let Clinton campaign for him, say in Florida, the difference might have proved enough even for him to win.

> *— The ordinary American voter does not object to mediocrity. He has a lower conception of the qualities requisite to make a statesman than those who direct public opinion in Europe have. He likes his candidate to be sensible, vigorous, and, above all, what he calls 'magnetic,' and does not value, because he sees no need for, originality or profundity, a fine culture or a wide knowledge.*
>
> *—James Bryce, The American Commonwealth, 1888*

On the eve of New Hampshire's first-in-the-nation presidential primary on Tuesday, February 1, 2000, polls showed Arizona's Vietnam War hero, Republican Senator John McCain, leading Bush by 10 percentage points, with Gore up 6 points over Democratic challenger Bill Bradley, despite the former senator from New Jersey's harsh attacks on the vice president's record, as well as his charge that it was "about time to tell the people what was the truth" about what Bradley dubbed Gore's "misrepresentations."

"The people of New Hampshire are not going to be fooled by Senator Bradley's last-minute, manipulative, negative, politics-as-usual campaign," the vice president responded.

Appearing on NBC's *Today* show that Monday morning, George W. Bush confided that his opponents' and the media's personal attacks regarding his intelligence "don't bother me much," and that "I'd rather be underestimated than feared." He got his wish: the next day, Gore and McCain captured New Hampshire's primaries; on February 22 McCain won GOP contests in Arizona and Michigan as well, running on the claim that his firm views on campaign finance reform made him the only Republican who could "beat Al Gore like a drum" in the general election. By March 7, however, Bush had effectively countered with an attractive five-year tax-cut plan and the charge that McCain, like Al Gore, would rather keep the people's money in Washington than give it back to those who earned it. Bush thus joined Gore in sweeping his party's Super Tuesday primary states, and on March 9 both John McCain and Democratic challenger Bill Bradley withdrew from the race, with McCain immediately endorsing Bush.

Members of the moderate Democratic Leadership Council that had done so much to put Bill Clinton in the White House pleaded with Gore to follow the same center-left path that had worked so well for the incumbent, but the candidate opted to reject this "New Democrat" approach in favor of old-fashioned populism. The vice president never seemed quite at ease, however, with the shirtsleeves-and-shouting approach to politicking. The most the Democrats appeared to gain from their candidate's new podium-pounding style was that the AFL-CIO, for the first time in the labor organization's 45-year history, wangled its workers a paid Election Day holiday; union members responded by turning out to vote overwhelmingly for Gore in the hotly contested states of Pennsylvania and Michigan.

The year 2000 also marked the first presidential election campaign in decades in which the Republican nominee not only did not pander to but actually snubbed the right-wing Christian Coalition. George W. Bush addressed the group's summer meeting only via a three-minute videotape. Far bolder, the Republican candidate refused to vow to appoint only abortion opponents to the judiciary if elected, or to ban the RU-486 abortion pill, and his VP choice, former Secretary of Defense Dick Cheney, betrayed an open mind by declining to rule out same-sex marriages in favor of the states' rights approach to gay and lesbian issues. Clearly, this was not Ronald Reagan's Republican Party. The gambit of shying away from extremism worked in wooing moderates — including some who might have leaned Democratic had Gore not mounted such a traditional, populist liberal campaign — while the far right voiced barely a whimper of protest at being largely ignored.

While both parties' presidential nominees performed better than expected at their respective national conventions, Gore stumbled badly in all three of the candidates' televised one-on-one debates. In the first, he came across as downright rude for rolling his eyes and sighing loudly while Bush was speaking; in the second he overcorrected and looked smarmy in his eagerness to agree with his rival; in the third Gore made the fatal error of encroaching upon his opponent's personal space, leaving himself open to a devastatingly well delivered, dismissive little nod of derision from Bush. "The debates changed the dynamic of the race," according to Andrew Kohut, director of the nonpartisan Pew Research Center. "That was a surprise. It certainly wasn't Gore going in there and cleaning Bush's clock, as expected.... Instead, Bush seemed knowledgeable enough for the job, while Gore annoyed some viewers by seeming, perhaps, too smart for his own good."

The Republican campaign strategy could not have worked so well on a less cynical — or more interested — American electorate. In fact, as events would show, the election hung on the nation's growing number of swing voters. According to a January 2001 Gallup Organization poll, 33 percent of the citizens surveyed called themselves Democrats, and 31 percent Republicans. That indicates a substantial plurality of Americans — 35 percent — now identify themselves as independents. On Election Day, these swing voters split evenly between Bush, the "compassionate conservative," and Gore, the populist.

Election Night 2000 was a disaster for TV news. At 7:50 p.m. Tuesday, the networks began to project Al Gore as the winner in Florida, with its 25 electoral votes. This premature call that set the Republican camp seething on the grounds that Florida's panhandle lay in the Central Time Zone, which meant residents of the far western part of the state still had more than an hour to vote. By 2:16 a.m. Wednesday, anchormen on every channel were admitting that a terrible mistake had been made, and that Florida was in fact leaning toward George W. Bush.

Most Americans who were still paying attention went to bed at that point, only the hardiest few laying stake to the claim that they were watching live when around 4:30 a.m. the networks apologized again and withdrew Bush's projected victory, now saying that Florida remained "too close to call" — as it would through the next 36 days, marking one of the strangest episodes in the history of American presidential politics.

Some 65 million viewers tuned in for at least part of the television networks' election coverage, and many saw reason for concern. A post-election Gallup poll showed that 65 percent of those surveyed believed the news media couldn't be trusted to get even their basic facts straight. Yet the major news outlets immediately began racking up their best ratings since the O.J. Simpson trial, and just as quickly seemed to forget they had anything to act embarrassed about.

The larger question, of course, is why the contest was so close that the media botched calling the winner, not once, but twice. In part the answer lies in the increasing centrism of both major parties, a conscious appeal to the vast and growing number of political moderates in America today. After he lost the New Hampshire primary to John McCain, for instance, Bush carefully recast his campaign to rely not so much on his affable personality as on the slogan "A Reformer With Results" — as well as on his moderate views on issues like Social Security, Medicare, and education, which echoed Democrat Bill Clinton more than Republican President George H.W. Bush.

Even Ralph Nader failed to win even the minimum 5 percent of the national vote required to qualify his Green Party for public financing in 2004, although he may have drawn enough support from the far left to lose the election for Al Gore. The splintered Reform Party's nominee, Pat Buchanan, barely outran the little-known Libertarian candidate Harry Browne. Gore, incidentally, came out on top in the national popular vote, 50,996,064 to Bush's 50,456,167, and on November 8 the vice president led in the electoral vote by 266 to 249, with 270 needed to win.

What developed over the next 36 days is chronicled in this book in fascinating detail: the bizarre uncertainty over who won the White House after a razor-close finish in Florida; the allegations of fraud and other ballot "irregularities" in various counties; the resulting legal and public-relations skirmishing between the candidates and their parties for the state's 25 electoral votes, and how the outcome of the contest came to be determined by one vote on the U.S. Supreme Court. Whatever else can be said about the presidential election of 2000, it offered quite a civics lesson to countless Americans hitherto bored by the workings of their democracy. It is not a small thing—but a very good one for the country—that the public has had such a striking reminder that every vote, including their own, really does count.

Avid politics-watchers, naturally, will be talking about the election-turned-lawsuit for decades to come. Some of the issues raised have special resonance: not since Martin Luther King, Jr. led the voting rights march from Selma to Montgomery in 1965, for example, has the United States heard the charge of "disenfranchisement" uttered with such vehemence. Alas, times may not have changed as much as hoped: the day after the election, NAACP President Kweisi Mfume asked the U.S. Justice Department to investigate allegations of minority voter discrimination and other similar charges in Florida. "The NAACP is concerned about reported instances of disproportionate disqualifications of black voters and the failure to pick up at least one ballot box from a heavily black precinct," Mfume said. "We have grave concerns that these and other acts may violate the 15th Amendment to the Constitution and the Voting Rights Act of 1965." Calling on the federal government to conduct a recount of Florida's votes, Mfume added: "We are not suggesting foul play, but we are very much concerned that foul play can happen."

Indeed it can, and has been at least alleged to have taken place in every hotly contested presidential election in American history. In some cases, the charges of chicanery came only after the contest had already been thrown to the U.S. House of Representatives to decide — seemingly a distinct possibility on the bicentennial of the 1800 election, which the House resolved in Thomas Jefferson's favor after a tie in the electoral vote — on the 36th ballot. The crisis that year was bitter partisan division between Jefferson's pro-French, pro-agrarian supporters and his opponent Aaron Burr's anti-French, big-government backers. Similarly, in 1824 the House awarded the presidency to John Quincy Adams – prior to George W. Bush the only son of a former President to win the office — after Adams failed to win a majority in the Electoral College and lost the national popular vote to Andrew Jackson, who cried that "corruptions and intrigues" in the House had thwarted "the will of the people."

Then there was the aforementioned contest of 1876, eventually given to Republican Rutherford B. Hayes by one electoral vote despite his loss to Democrat Samuel Tilden by more than a quarter-million of some eight million popular votes cast. Although that election's passionate ideological battles, mostly over race issues, stretch comparison with the pallid politics of 2000, some parallels can be drawn. For example, Florida was a battleground then, too; its ballot counts, along with those of Louisiana and South Carolina, were considered so suspect— stemming from charges of fraud and violence against African-American voters—that Congress named a commission to resolve the matter. Five U.S. Supreme Court justices served on that commission, and its deciding vote for Hayes came from a Republican appointee. This history prompted a current Justice, Stephen Breyer, to write in his dissenting opinion in the case of George W. Bush et al. Petitioners v. Albert Gore, Jr., et al. that in 1876 the work of his predecessors "did not lend that process legitimacy.... Nor did it assure the public that the process had worked fairly, guided by the law. Rather, it simply embroiled members of the court in partisan conflict, thereby undermining respect for the judicial process." Of the other three Court members who dissented in the 2000 case, Justice John Paul Stevens offered the bluntest analysis: "Although we may never know with complete certainty the identity of the winner of this year's Presidential election," he wrote, "the identity of the loser is perfectly clear.... It is the Nation's confidence in the judge as an impartial guardian of the rule of law."

Yet the point of history is to remind us that our own times are not uniquely oppressive. America today is unified and strong; harsh partisan bickering is the hallmark of a healthy democracy. This is not like the 1960s, when assassinations, the Vietnam War, and the South's agonies over civil rights were ripping America apart at the seams. And in 1876, it took five months to select a president after the election. In 2000, we needed only five messy weeks.

Most historians agree that the race most comparable to the one just ended was in 1960, not so much because the outcome was so close but because John F. Kennedy and Richard Nixon had espoused similar positions on the issues. Throughout the campaign, Democrat and Republican alike advocated tax cuts, increased military spending, civil rights, and the battle against global communism. In the end, JFK bested Nixon by fewer than 200,000 popular votes, but won handily enough in the Electoral College — amid allegations that the election had been "stolen" by powerful Democrats, including Chicago Mayor Richard Daley and Kennedy's own running mate, Lyndon B. Johnson. In fact, JFK won Illinois by just 8,858 of 4.8 million votes, and Texas by 46,257 of 2.3 million cast — after some 100,000 residents of Johnson's home state apparently came out of nowhere to vote for the Democratic ticket. Nevertheless, when it was all over Nixon is said to have talked a New York Herald Tribune reporter out of writing a series of articles on election fraud, arguing that "Our country can't afford the agony of a constitutional crisis — and I damn well will not be a party to creating one, just to become president or anything else."

Somehow it seems anachronistic that perhaps the most remarked-upon issue raised by Election 2000 is the advisability of abolishing the Electoral College in favor of direct presidential elections by a simple plurality of the national popular vote. Critics, including Hillary Rodham Clinton, who shortly after Election Day called for the abolition of the Electoral College, maintain that the Founding Fathers' system for picking America's leaders has grown hopelessly outdated and awkward to the point of becoming dysfunctional. Ronald Dworkin put this sentiment more succinctly in a December 14, 2000 essay in the New York Review of Books: "The Constitution's authors did not trust the people to elect the president directly; they expected the members of the Electoral College to be distinguished and independent citizens who would make up their own minds, after collective deliberation, about who the president and vice president should be.... Now we embrace the very different principle that the point of elections — and particularly the election of a national president, the one office we elect all together — is to determine and reflect the people's will."

In fact, the United States needs its Electoral College now as much as ever, for the very reason its critics deny: the traditional system does not so much encourage as demand that presidential candidates campaign in as many states as possible, rather than in just the most populous ones with the biggest TV markets and electoral-vote clout. The system also continues to protect the interests of regional groups such as small farmers, whom Dworkin and company argue are no longer either so isolated or so helpless as their predecessors in the days of the Founding Fathers, meaning they no longer need special treatment even if they do grow our food. That may be true for the farm states' now-dominant large-scale agricultural interests, which can afford to send their own lobbyists to Washington, but abolishing the Electoral College would deny small-yield and family farmers the voice the process makes audible to the national candidates who come calling every four years.

That said, the only immediate benefit to be gained from this past election is what we can learn from it about the flaws in our electoral system. How, for instance, can the world's highest-tech culture be hamstrung by such low-tech bungling at the ballot box? The lesson is clear: the United States must institute precise national voting standards that apply scientific exactitude to the counting of ballots. In the absence of such standards, future elections could become even more muddled in the wake of the legal precedent set by the U.S. Supreme Court's ruling against the Florida recount: as Ronald Dworkin explained in his essay: "The Court's equal protection decision is surprising.... The one-person-one-vote principle applies not just to presidential elections but to elections for every federal and state office, major or minor, across the country. I do not know how many states use nothing more concrete than a 'clear intent of the voter' standard for manual recounts, but several do, and the Supreme Court has now declared that they have all been acting, no doubt for many decades, unconstitutionally. This ruling alone may require substantial changes in the nation's electoral laws, and the Supreme Court may well regret having made it."

Nevertheless, the healing process has already begun. Americans understand that this is not a time for despair, and that the nation must march onward. Optimism is America's great healing agent. After all, we don't call it "The Democratic Experiment" for nothing, and at least there's no shame in trying to get things right no matter how long it takes. It would be tragic if cynicism obscured the brightness of America's potential. As the 43rd President of the United States was inaugurated, James Bryce looked prescient once again: "The presidential election," he wrote in 1888, "occurring once in four years, throws the country for several months into a state of turmoil, for which there may be no occasion. Perhaps there are no serious party issues to be decided, perhaps the best thing would be that the existing Administration should pursue the even tenor of its way. The Constitution, however, requires an election to be held, so the whole costly and complicated machinery of agitation is put in motion; and if issues do not exist, they have to be created." The more things change, the more they really do seem to stay the same.

day 1

Wednesday, November 8th

★ ★ ★ ★ ★

Too Close To Call

In the days leading up to the presidential election, every poll and pundit was clear about only one thing: the race would be the closest in decades. By pushing his campaign into a round-the-clock frenzy, Al Gore had erased the narrow lead held by George W. Bush, whose final hours on the stump were, by contrast, almost leisurely. And in the early morning hours, long after the polls had closed, no one could say who had won. The television networks and many newspapers tried to declare a winner, but quickly had to admit they were wrong. The vice president actually called Bush to say he would concede, but then called back and retracted his statement when it became clear that the vote in Florida was so close that neither candidate could claim the state's 25 electoral votes. Even though Gore was narrowly winning the popular vote, neither he nor Bush had enough electoral votes to claim victory. As Wednesday dawned, all eyes turned to Florida, where out of six million votes cast, Bush had a lead of 1,700.

Outcome Hangs on Contested Florida Vote

The outcome of the presidential race between Gov. George W. Bush and Vice President Al Gore balanced early this morning on no more than a few thousand votes in the closely contested state of Florida.

Shortly after 2 a.m., Bush appeared to have won Florida, and several news organizations, including *The New York Times,* declared that he had captured the White House. Aides to Gore said he was preparing his concession speech, while Bush expected to announce his victory. But later in the morning, as the count in Florida neared an end, the narrow margin that Bush had achieved unexpectedly evaporated, and state officials said they might have to count the overseas absentee ballots before they could be certain of the result.

By 4 this morning, the candidates were separated by only the barest of margins in the popular and electoral votes as the electorate seemed agonizingly split between Gore and Bush. Bush swept the South and won a patchwork of states in the Middle West. Gore claimed the largest states on the two coasts but stopped just short of victory.

> *"I'm not worried about me getting through it."*
>
> *—George W. Bush*

All night long, there were signs of hope — and despair — for each candidate. At one point, surveys of voters leaving their polling places projected that Bush was one percentage point ahead in the popular vote; at another point, they had him one point behind. At still another point, all the major networks called Florida, a critical battleground, for Gore. But in a rare reversal, they declared two hours later that the state was too close to call.

The electoral map seemed to have been turned on its head, as were many of the assumptions about which states were safely in one camp or another. Gore was defeated in Tennessee, for example, becoming the first presidential contender to lose in his home state since George McGovern lost in South Dakota in 1972. The results in many states were so close that it was possible that Gore would contest the outcome in some of them.

Around 7 p.m. in Texas, less than an hour after Bush and his family, including his parents, arrived at an Austin restaurant for dinner, they aborted their plan to watch the returns from a suite in the adjacent Four Seasons hotel and retreated to the governor's mansion. The decision came about the time that the networks were declaring Gore the winner in Michigan and Florida.

Soon after, Bush told reporters that he questioned early projections that he had lost Florida, where his brother Jeb is governor, and Pennsylvania, where one of his staunchest backers, Tom Ridge, is governor. "The networks are calling this thing awfully early," Bush said. "The people counting the votes are coming in with a different perspective."

In an interview on CNN, Karl Rove, Bush's chief strategist, chastised the network for its initial call of Florida, telling the anchor, Bernard Shaw, "I do think that is one criteria you might want to think about changing because you called the state before the polls have closed in a considerable part of the state."

In their final hours of stumping, Gore seemed far less confident of the outcome than Bush. The vice president did not sleep at all on Monday night, his aides said, and for more than 33 hours dropped in at battleground states, particularly focusing on Florida. At 4 a.m. yesterday, for instance, Gore, 52, was sitting at a table with eight nurses at a cancer center in Tampa.

Bush had a much calmer schedule, saying he slept — in his own bed in Austin — four or five hours on Monday night. Asked yesterday how she felt, Bush's wife, Laura, put her hand on her stomach, as if indicating a churning there. She looked nervous. But then she said: "I feel good. We got a lot of sleep in our own bed, with our own animals."

As he watched the returns with his parents last night, Bush said he did not feel he had his entire future at stake. "Actually, my whole future isn't on the line," he said. "I'm not worried about me getting through it."

Nov. 8, 2000, Richard L. Berke
Final Edition

How Gore Stopped Short On His Way to Concede

"You don't have to be snippy about it."
– Al Gore to George W. Bush

★ ★ ★

When his limousine arrived at the War Memorial Plaza in Nashville, where a few thousand despondent, rain-soaked supporters awaited the concession, Vice President Al Gore assumed he had lost the election. He had called Gov. George W. Bush at the Governor's Mansion in Austin, Tex., and extended his congratulations. He had written a short and gracious speech about moving the country forward and cooperating with the victor.

But several vans back in the motorcade, an aide's Skytel pager vibrated with a message to call Michael Whouley, a top Gore strategist who was monitoring Florida results at Gore headquarters. What Whouley had to say, the aide, Michael B. Feldman, recalled, was that the Florida secretary of state's Web page had winnowed Bush's advantage of 50,000 votes to 6,000, with precincts still to tally.

That changed everything. About a half hour later, at 2:30 a.m. Central time, Gore placed his second call of the evening to Bush. From a holding room beneath the plaza, where he had gone to concede, Gore told his Republican rival that circumstances had changed in the last 45 minutes. The race, Gore said, was now too close to call, and there would be an automatic recount in Florida. He was going to wait it out.

"You mean to tell me, Mr. Vice President, you're retracting your concession?" Bush asked, his tone incredulous, one aide said. The Texas governor had already begun preparing his victory remarks.

"You don't have to be snippy about it," Gore responded, according to several of those who heard Gore's side of the conversation.

Bush told Gore that his brother Jeb, the governor of Florida, had just assured him that Florida was his, Gore aides said.

"Let me explain something," Gore said. "Your younger brother is not the ultimate authority on this."

The conversation drew quickly to a close. The election did not.

After two sleepless days of campaigning, after a gut-wrenching night in which they had been convinced that they had won and then devastated that they had not, Gore and his aides were back in the game. "I don't think there's ever been a night like this one," William M. Daley, the Gore campaign chairman, told the crowd at the plaza around 3:05 a.m.

No one in the Bush campaign would disagree with that assessment. Less than two hours earlier, around 1:15 a.m., when the television networks had called the election for Bush, he assumed he was the president-elect. In the upstairs living room of the Governor's Mansion, where he had passed the endless hours with his wife, his parents and Jeb Bush, family members hugged one another tight.

Watching and Waiting

In Nashville at that time, Gore and his running mate, Senator Joseph I. Lieberman of Connecticut, were watching CNN with a large group of aides in a seventh-floor suite at the Loews Vanderbilt Plaza hotel. The room grew silent. Donna Brazile, Gore's campaign manager, sent the vice president a message at 1:20 a.m. Central time on his Blackberry, an instant messaging pager: "Never surrender. It's not over yet."

But ultimately, most in the group concluded that the networks had to be right. "They were just so damn positive," said Gore's brother-in-law, Frank Hunger. "And they were talking about 50,000 votes, and we never dreamed they would be inaccurate."

Gore went to his ninth-floor suite to break the news to his wife, Tipper, and his children, some of whom were sleeping, and some of whom cried. At both the hotel and the campaign headquarters across town, depression took the place of the happier, more hopeful emotions that held sway six hours earlier, before the roller coaster of election night 2000 began screaming down the rails.

Around 7 p.m. Tuesday, the television networks put Florida, Michigan and Pennsylvania in the Gore victory column. With one more key tossup state, the deal would be sealed. Some top Gore advisers were feeling good enough that they took a break to eat dinner in the hotel's steakhouse, where they could not even watch television.

It was the opposite of what was going on in Austin. For Bush, his advisers and his friends, confidence had been reigning for days. He spent Monday in Tennessee, Gore's home state, and in Arkansas, President Clinton's home state, and carried himself with the swagger of a certain winner.

But around 7 p.m. Tuesday, their optimism began to falter. Bush was in a private dining room at the Shoreline Grill, a restaurant adjacent to the Four Seasons hotel in Austin, eating a dinner of parmesan-crusted chicken with his parents, his wife, his daughters and all of his siblings.

The news about Florida flashed on a nearby television set, casting a pall over the meal. Bush had once joked that it would be a chilly Thanksgiving for his younger brother Jeb if Florida did not tip into the Bush column. And now it had tipped in the other direction.

Joe and Jan O'Neill, two close friends of the governor who were dining in another section of the restaurant, said the brothers shared an emotional moment. "I heard that Jeb hugged George, literally in tears," Mr. O'Neill said. Mrs. O'Neill added that the Florida governor told his brother he was sorry, which Jeb Bush confirmed yesterday. Then he left the room.

The Texas governor, his wife and his parents also left, heading back to the Governor's Mansion. They had intended to watch the returns with a group of relatives, friends and senior advisers in two suites on the ninth floor of the Four Seasons. But now, several of Bush's aides said, he wanted peace and quiet. Several aides said Bush had always kept open the possibility of going home. But Mr. O'Neill said that his change of plans was "not only last-minute, it was spur of the moment."

On the ninth floor of the Four Seasons and at the campaign headquarters, people channeled their tenuous hopes along two tracks. They wondered if Bush could win so many smaller states that he could reach the magic number of 270 electoral votes without Florida, and they plotted the possibilities.

"Sometimes you could hear a pin drop in the room," said a family friend at the Four Seasons, "like when New Mexico was called for Gore. We all had our own written lists of the states he needed. We had all done our own electoral calculations."

Several blocks away, Bush's chief strategist, Karl Rove, and one of his deputies, Matthew Dowd, had done the same thing. "Karl had actually formulated a strategy where the linchpin was the extra vote in Maine," said Stuart Stevens, one of the campaign's media advisers, referring to that state's ability to split its four electoral votes.

At the same time, Rove, Dowd and other Bush aides focused on Florida, gleaning information from the Internet and panicked phone conversations, and growing more and more convinced that the outcome was unclear. Rove called several television networks to tell them they had acted early and perhaps erroneously and needed to amend their predictions.

Not everyone at the headquarters was convinced. "It's the kind of thing you always do in a campaign, you grasp for any ray of hope," said Mark McKinnon, the chief media adviser. "It seemed like a thin ray, but it was one of the only ones we had."

Bush clung to it, encouraged by advisers. Every few minutes they called him with the latest updates, the latest calculations. And around 9 p.m., in yet another twist, the networks announced that they were putting Florida back into the undecided column. Ecstatic shrieks filled the streets in front of the State Capitol, the halls of the Four Seasons and the campaign headquarters. "What do you call the things you put on a heart-attack victim?" McKinnon asked. "It was like the campaign had gotten those electric paddles to its heart."

A Celebration Cut Short

But if the Bush campaign felt revived, the Gore campaign did not yet feel moribund. They were also doing the arithmetic, and they were also sopping up all the information they could. The direction all of this was headed was ambiguous for a good long while.

For hours, there seemed to be plenty of room for hope. Bush had developed a lead in Florida, but it began to shrink. Near midnight, Gore huddled with his top aides to discuss what they should do and decided he should go to the plaza and tell his supporters that the result might not be known until Wednesday. Then they decided to hold off for just a bit.

And then, seemingly inexplicably, Bush's margin in Florida ballooned. Both in the seventh floor suite and at the campaign's headquarters downtown, depression set in. In the expansive white "boiler room" there, where aides had monitored returns, campaign workers began to cry. "A shock rippled through," one aide said.

They had worked down to the last minute. Only hours earlier, top-level strategists like Sarah Bianchi, a leading policy adviser, and Gene Sperling, the president's national economic adviser, on loan from the White House, had been making last-minute get-out-the-vote calls to Democrats on the West Coast.

"I felt so deflated," said Mark D. Fabiani, Gore's deputy campaign manager for communications. "It had been an evening where you won and then lost and winning felt a lot better than losing. You had been up and down and swung around and then dumped out on your head."

It had all come down to Florida, and advisers at the Bush campaign headquarters huddled over computer screens, clicking from one Internet site to another. They factored in the voting histories of the counties to be tallied and punched numbers into calculators, desperate for an accurate prediction. They called Republican officials in the state. The hours and minutes crept by.

Bush remained at the mansion, where aides said his brother Jeb also kept an eye on the Internet. In front of the State Capitol, various speakers took the microphone to try to enlist Bush supporters in what amounted to public prayers. "We want Florida!" shouted George P. Bush, Jeb's oldest son. "We want Florida!" But the crowd — rain-soaked, shivering and weary — had gone limp.

Then, it happened. Around 1:15 a.m., the enormous television screens they were watching flashed that Bush would win not only Florida, but also the presidency. The loudspeakers blared the song "Signed, Sealed, Delivered."

At the Four Seasons, they roared, then filed into the buses waiting to take them to the State Capitol, about 10 blocks away. At the headquarters, they sobbed, then marched toward the same destination.

And at the Governor's Mansion, Bush, Jeb Bush and their proud parents hugged one another tight.

McKinnon took a turn in front of the television cameras, telling Candy Crowley, a correspondent for CNN, "I'm going to go to bed tonight and have a stiff drink as quickly as I can get off your set." But then he saw another network correspondent waving frantically, trying to deliver a piece of news that would delay that drink.

The seesawing state of Florida was decided anew, and the waiting had just begun.

Nov. 9, 2000, Kevin Sack and Frank Bruni

William Safire on "Snippy"

The earliest definition, in Nathaniel Bailey's 1727 dictionary, is "parcimonious" (now spelled parsimonious and considered a bookish term for a cheapskate) and "niggardly" (now used less frequently because some confuse it with a racial slur). In John Bartlett's 1848 Dictionary of Americanisms, it is defined as a "woman's word" for "finical," probably rooted in the sense of fine as "small," which has now become finicky and is a derogation meaning "excessively meticulous."

That cannot be what Al Gore meant. Let's go back to basics: to snip, from the German snippen, originally meant "to snatch quickly" and came to mean "to clip or cut off, often with a scissors." (This produced a snippet, a tiny piece of a thing, later extended to a short bit of prose or, in Dryden's use, "some small snip of gain.") The action of clipping or cutting off small pieces led to snippety, "fragmentary, scrappy," with a temporary detour to sniptious, and finally to snippy, metaphorically cutting off pieces, thereby seeming "curt, supercilious, fault-finding, airish," its meaning influenced by the "irritable, tart, short-tempered" sense of snappish.

Snippy, like snappish, begins with the sneaky sn sound, characteristic of sniveling, snide and snarling.

Earlier generations might have taken snippy to mean "brassy, cheeky, saucy"; now the wide-ranging senses are expressed as "touchy, flip, smart-alecky, disrespectful, on your high horse, having an attitude."

From the *On Language* column, November 26, 2000

Bush Leads Gore by 1,784 Votes as Recount Begins

"We have just reached the twilight zone of American politics."
— Gore campaign official

★ ★ ★

For the first time in more than a century, the winner of a presidential election remained unknown a full day after the polls closed, as George W. Bush and Al Gore dispatched teams of lawyers to Florida to wrangle over the handful of votes upon which their White House dreams now rest.

The fate of the two rivals appeared to ride on the verdict in Florida, where an incomplete vote count had Bush leading by 1,784 votes, an extraordinarily narrow margin in a nationwide race in which more than 96 million people voted. His lead in Florida was three one-hundredths of 1 percent of the votes cast.

Florida Secretary of State Katherine Harris said she would probably declare a winner by the close of business today after a recount of nearly six million votes and the tallying of absentee ballots. But it was far from certain that the matter would be resolved swiftly.

With Gore clinging to the slimmest popular vote margin in modern times, and Bush grasping for a bare majority of electoral votes to pull him over the top, both candidates were no doubt wondering if, had they done things a bit differently, they might now be mulling over choices for their Cabinet, not mulling over their job prospects.

Officials in both campaigns described the extraordinary series of events since the election as nothing short of surreal. It thrust the American political system into a limbo of sorts, with Bush and Gore not knowing whether they should disband their campaigns, prepare to govern or retreat behind closed doors.

Bush and his running mate, Dick Cheney, stepped out of the governor's mansion in Austin, Tex., yesterday afternoon to reassure their supporters, and the nation. In brief remarks, Bush said he expected the recount in Florida to confirm his victory there. He announced that he had called upon James A. Baker III, the secretary of state in his father's administration, to travel to Tallahassee, Fla., to look after his interests.

In what had the ring of a truncated version of an acceptance speech, Bush thanked Gore's supporters and said, "Secretary Cheney and I will do everything in our power to unite the nation, to call upon the best, to bring people together after one of the most exciting elections in our nation's history." He said he hoped the matter was "finalized as quickly as possible and in a calm and thoughtful manner."

Later in the afternoon, Gore and his running mate, Senator Joseph I. Lieberman of Connecticut, appeared before a backdrop of American flags in

Nashville, where the vice president said the outcome should not be hastily determined.

"Because of what is at stake," Gore said, "this matter must be resolved expeditiously, but deliberately and without any rush to judgment." He added, "No matter what the outcome, America will make the transition to a new administration with dignity, with full respect for the freely expressed will of the people, and with pride in the democracy we are privileged to share."

While Bush sent James A. Baker III, secretary of state under Bush's father, Gore said he had asked another former secretary of state, Warren Christopher, to join the team of lawyers representing him in Florida.

Yet for all the words about cooperation, prominent Democrats made clear in private conservations that they had no intention of standing by if Bush claimed the White House on the slimmest of margins. Noting that Gore can be a scrappy street fighter, an official who is close to the campaign said, "The sense is we're going to play hardball."

Officials in both campaigns were trying to figure how the outcome in Florida might be affected by absentee ballots from residents who are abroad. To be counted, those ballots must have been postmarked by Election Day and must arrive by Nov. 17. There is no record of how many were requested, but four years ago, roughly 2,300 were cast.

Republicans contended that most of those ballots would come from military personnel, who typically vote Republican. But Democrats countered that many in the military are minorities who would support Gore.

The voting even led a bemused President Clinton to appear before reporters at the South Lawn of the White House to reassure the nation — and friends and foes abroad — that the muddied verdict did not amount to a national crisis. "No American will ever be able to seriously say again, 'My vote doesn't count,' " he said.

After congratulating Gore and Bush "on a vigorous, hard-fought, truly remarkable campaign," Clinton told reporters: "I was just like you last night. I was a fascinated observer."

Christopher, speaking at a news conference after Gore, tried to reassure the public of the Democrats' intentions. "Last night was an extraordinary night," Christopher said. "None of us have ever seen anything quite like it. But I don't have any reason to think we're on the edge of a constitutional crisis. And we don't intend to try to provoke a constitutional crisis."

Yet those very words suggested that there were deep and consequential implications in the aftermath of the election for both the government — and for the American political system.

Nov. 9, 2000, Richard L. Berke

The Case of the "Butterfly" Ballot

WEST PALM BEACH — Senior Democratic officials seized on disputed votes cast in Palm Beach County to challenge George W. Bush's slim lead for the state's 25 electoral votes, vowing to fight beyond Thursday's vote recount if the Texas Republican prevails.

The dispute centers on the peculiar layout of a presidential ballot in Palm Beach County that some Democratic voters say caused them to become confused and mistakenly vote for Patrick J. Buchanan when they had intended to vote for Al Gore.

After the final tally, with Gore trailing Bush by just 1,784 votes in Florida, several senior Democratic officials said if the ballot had not flummoxed their supporters, Gore would have won enough votes to win Florida and the presidency.

Even though he never made even one campaign stop in Palm Beach County, Buchanan, the Reform Party candidate, finished with 3,704 votes in the staunchly Democratic county — nearly 2,700 more than Buchanan received in any of Florida's other 66 counties. A lawsuit was filed in West Palm Beach challenging the county's election and seeking a repeat of the vote two weeks from now.

"Leading Democrats have become increasingly concerned about the ballot in Palm Beach County," said a senior Democratic Party official. "This issue threatens to become a focal point for us even after the recount."

More than 29,000 ballots in Palm Beach County were thrown out because they included votes for more than one presidential candidate or had no names punched, according to records released today by the county's Supervisor of Elections. Democratic aides and lawyers said the ballots that were thrown out — about 4 percent of the votes cast in the county — were compelling evidence that the ballot was too confusing and possibly illegal.

Late today, three angry Palm Beach County residents, who said they mistakenly voted for Buchanan when they intended to vote for Vice President Gore, filed a lawsuit in state circuit court in West Palm Beach challenging the validity of the Palm Beach County vote. Other lawsuits were also planned, Democratic officials here said. The legal challenges will most likely complicate and could delay the tense fight for Florida's all-important 25 electoral votes.

Between Tuesday and today, hundreds of voters went to the Board of Election office in West Palm Beach to complain that they were so confused by the ballot's boxy layout that they had mistakenly voted for Buchanan instead of Gore.

Congressional leaders, Democratic officials and Gore aides blamed the Palm Beach County election supervisor, Theresa LePore. LePore, who redesigned the county's ballot this year, said she had hoped to make it easier to read for the county's many elderly voters. LePore is a Democrat. In an interview on Tuesday with the *Sun-Sentinel* of Fort Lauderdale, LePore said she did not

A Case of Mistaken Identity?

Some voters in Palm Beach County, Fla., claim they were confused by the punch-card ballot, one of several voting methods used in Florida. The ballot requires voters to punch a hole corresponding to their choice. But some voters have said that the positioning of the holes and the alignment of the candidates may have led some supporters of Al Gore to vote instead for Patrick J. Buchanan, who received more votes in Palm Beach than in any other Florida county.

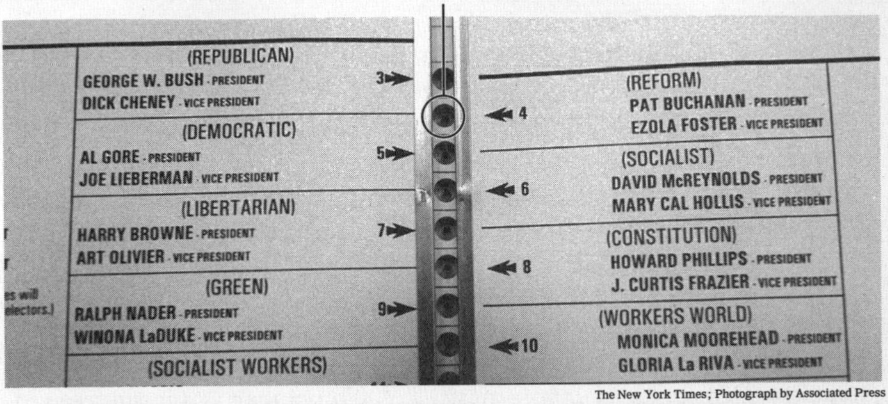

The New York Times; Photograph by Associated Press

think the ballot was confusing. "I was trying to make the print bigger so elderly people in Palm Beach County can read it," she said. "If I'd made it small, they would've said we made the print too small."

The Palm Beach design was not used in any other Florida county.

Instead of helping elderly readers, the redesigned ballot apparently confused many voters. Gore's name was the second one listed on the left side of the ballot, almost directly across from Buchanan's name, which was the first name on the right side of the ballot. In the ballot's center margin, near both candidates' names, were holes for voters to punch to vote for either candidate.

After numerous complaints were received on Tuesday morning, LePore issued this directive to the county's 106 precincts: "Attention all poll workers. Please remind all voters coming in that they are to vote only for one (1) presidential candidate and that they are to punch the hole next to the arrow next to the number next to the candidate they wish to vote for. Thank you!" Voters said that they were afraid they had mistakenly punched the second hole, a vote for Buchanan, because it was near the arrow pointing to a third hole that constituted a vote for Gore.

"The big concern we have is this ballot did not comply with what the law required," said Ronald G. Meyer, a Tallahassee lawyer who is preparing Democratic challenges to the vote in Palm Beach County that address the order of the listing of the candidates. "And as a result, we have 20,000 voters being disenfranchised, and we think that is a major, major breakdown in the electoral process."

Three voters who described themselves as flummoxed by the ballot filed a lawsuit in state circuit court in West Palm Beach. The three plaintiffs are a Del Ray Beach city commissioner, a Del Ray Beach chiropractor and a West Palm

Beach homemaker. In their lawsuit they allege that the ballot "format had never before been used in a presidential election," and that the design violated state law. The lawsuit asks a judge to order a new presidential vote in the county.

In the presidential election in Florida, there has never been a successful legal challenge of the results based on allegations of ballot irregularities, state election law experts said. There have been such challenges in races for lesser offices, in which election results have been overturned, the officials said.

Robert Weisman, the Palm Beach County administrator, said this afternoon that approximately 19,000 ballots included two or more votes for president, and that many included votes for both Gore and Buchanan. He said it was evidence that many voters were confused. Democrats quickly seized on that statistic, saying if Gore had received just 10 percent of those votes, he would have had enough to defeat Bush in Florida and win its precious 25 electoral votes, needed to win the presidency.

Clay Roberts, the Republican appointed director of the state division of elections, has said there is nothing wrong with the Palm Beach ballots.

Election officials who use punch card systems similar to the one in Palm Beach County expect that a certain number of ballots will have more than one hole punched in a given race, a practice called "overvoting." But they said the usual numbers were nowhere near as many as apparently were double–punched in Palm Beach County. "I would say that's an unusually large number," said Jack Gerbel, president of Unilect Corporation, a maker of punch card voting machines in California.

Ernest Hawkins, registrar of voters in Sacramento, Calif., and president of the National Association of County Clerks, Recorders and Election Officials, said he had only 1,147 "overvotes" out of 400,000 ballots in the presidential race in his county this year, and 5,148 ballots with no vote for president. Sacramento uses a punch card system similar to the one in use in Florida.

Hawkins said many election officials who use the punch card systems try to avoid the practice of putting names on facing pages, but sometimes it's impossible to avoid. "We don't use facing pages in Sacramento because it can be confusing, but we have in the past because of space issues," he said.

Outside the Board of Elections office in West Palm Beach today, several people held up signs saying, "Honk for Revote." Jeanette Lixey, a 32-year-old restaurant manager in Royal Palm Beach, Fla., said that her husband, a carpenter, later realized he had punched the wrong hole in the ballot and had voted for Buchanan. "He can't believe it, and I can't believe it," Lixey said.

County Commissioner Burt Aaronson, a Democrat, said he was especially struck by the fact that 37 people in Kings Point, a Democratic retiree stronghold of Delray Beach, had voted for Buchanan. "We know that certain precincts are totally Democratic," Aaronson said. "You can knock on every door in Kings Point, and you wouldn't find 10 votes for Buchanan.

Buchanan's 3,704 votes in Palm Beach County was by far his strongest showing in any county in Florida, and was 20 percent of his vote total in Florida of 17,358. His second best showing was 1,012 votes in Pinellas County, site of his campaign's Florida headquarters. He received only 561 votes in Miami-Dade and 789 in Broward County, which both have considerably higher populations than Palm Beach County.

LePore declined to be interviewed today. But her office issued a press release, saying that she would conduct a thorough recount of the county's ballots and would release the results upon its completion. "The supervisor of elections office in Palm Beach County has an unblemished record of public trust," the release said, "and we remain committed to protecting this reputation."

Nov. 9, 2000, Don Van Natta Jr. and Dana Canedy

Measures of Elections Past

Comparisons in presidential races dating to 1864, when the two-party system essentially developed.

Largest Popular Vote Totals

YEAR	CANDIDATE	TOTAL VOTES	PCT. OF VOTING-AGE POPULATION	PCT. OF VOTES CAST
1984	Ronald Reagan	54,455,075	31.21%	58.77%
2000	Al Gore	50,996,116	24.78	48.69
2000	George W. Bush	50,456,169	24.52	48.18
1988	George Bush	48,886,097	26.77	53.37
1996	Bill Clinton	47,402,357	24.12	49.23
1972	Richard M. Nixon	47,169,911	33.51	60.77

Closest Races by Electoral Vote

YEAR	LOSING CANDIDATE	ELECTORAL VOTES: NO. EARNED	ELECTORAL VOTES: SHORT OF VICTORY	WINNING CANDIDATE
1876*	Samuel J. Tilden	184	1	Rutherford B. Hayes
1916	Charles E. Hughes	254	12	Woodrow Wilson
1884	James G. Blaine	182	19	Grover Cleveland
1976	Gerald R. Ford	240	30	Jimmy Carter
1880	Winfield S. Hancock	155	30	James Garfield
1888*	Grover Cleveland	168	33	Benjamin Harrison

Closest Races by Popular Vote

YEAR	WINNING CANDIDATE	LOSING CANDIDATE	VOTE MARGIN	PCT. DIFF.
1876*	Rutherford B. Hayes	Samuel J. Tilden	–254,235	–3.02%
1888*	Benjamin Harrison	Grover Cleveland	–90,596	–0.80
1880	Chester A. Arthur	Winfield S. Hancock	1,898	0.02
1884	Grover Cleveland	James G. Blaine	25,685	0.25
1960	John F. Kennedy	Richard M. Nixon	118,574	0.17

*Race where losing candidate won the popular vote

Source: Dave Leip, Atlas of U.S. Presidential Elections

The New York Times

day

2

THURSDAY,
NOVEMBER 9TH

★ ★ ★ ★ ★

CONFUSING BALLOTS, ANGRY VOTERS

As more returns come in from around the country, Gore takes a clear-cut lead in the popular vote. As the required recount continues in Florida, he appears to be gaining on Bush, but he vows a court fight over the Palm Beach County ballot if necessary. Democrats are worried that the presidency will be decided by the Electoral College and that Florida's 25 votes hold the key to the election, so they are quick to publicize the many complaints about the design of ballots and the inadequacies of old voting machines, thereby setting the stage and defining the terms for the debate that will soon occupy all of the nation's major political and judicial institutions.

GORE VOWS COURT FIGHT OVER VOTE WITH FLORIDA'S OUTCOME STILL UP IN THE AIR

WASHINGTON — With the recount of Florida's votes still under way and George W. Bush clinging to a hairbreadth lead, Al Gore's campaign vowed to back a court fight over questionable ballots in Palm Beach County even after the tabulation was complete. Mr. Bush's margin appeared to be eroding as the recount went on.

Florida's 25 electoral votes are the key to victory in Tuesday's tinglingly close presidential election, because they would give one candidate or the other more than 270 votes, a majority in the Electoral College. With stakes of that magnitude, tempers began to fray today. In Austin, Nashville and Tallahassee, the two sides accused each other of politicizing the Florida situation and the Republicans threatened countermeasures in other states.

All this came at a difficult moment for the American political system. The transfer of power, especially after very close elections, is to democracies as knees are to football: the point of maximum vulnerability.

Both sides seemed to be improvising, and neither seemed to have decided how much to put the country through in its bid for victory. William M. Daley, Gore's campaign manager, said he had been "deeply troubled" by the confusing ballot used in Palm Beach County, and he contended that the Bush campaign had "put a demand for finality ahead of the pursuit of fairness."

> *"We do not want delay. What we do want, however, is democracy fulfilled."*
>
> *—William M. Daley, Gore's campaign manager*

Daley also accused the Bush camp of trying "to presumptively crown themselves the victors" by planning a transition team. Fearful that Bush and his strategists were winning the public relations battle by painting Gore as a sore loser, Daley said: "We do not want delay. What we do want, however, is democracy fulfilled."

In response, Karl Rove, Bush's chief strategist, discussed possible recounts in Iowa, New Mexico and Wisconsin, states Gore apparently carried by small margins. Karen P. Hughes, Bush's spokeswoman, described as "somewhat shrill" the language used by Gore campaign officials, and Donald L. Evans, the Bush campaign chairman, taunted Daley, saying:

"The Democrats who are politicizing and distorting these events risk doing so at the expense of our democracy. One of the options that they seem to be looking at is new elections. Our democratic process calls for a vote on Election Day. It does not call for us to continue voting until someone likes the outcome."

Bush remained in Austin; Gore returned to Washington from Nashville. Both seemed to hold themselves aloof from the public slugfest waged by their seconds, as if to avoid weakening prospects of unifying the nation when the moment arrives. No one suggested that a crisis was at hand, but a number of politicians warned against letting the situation drag on, unresolved, for weeks. Senator Robert G. Torricelli, Democrat of New Jersey, warned against getting mired in the courts. "I want Al Gore to win the election," Torricelli told reporters, "but more than that, I want somebody to win this election. There is going to have to be a very compelling case for anybody to take this into a court of law...It's a downward spiral. It may begin in Florida, but it can go to other states and ultimately the presidency of the United States should not be decided by a judge."

With people demonstrating in West Palm Beach against the ballot used only in that county — many seeking a new election in Palm Beach County — and politicians on both sides issuing rancorous statements, leaders of the Bush and Gore teams in Florida said they hoped to meet privately. People close to those leaders — James A. Baker III for the Bush camp and Warren Christopher representing Gore — said they hoped to keep tensions between the campaigns from boiling over. But there was no word tonight whether they had met or, if they had, what, if anything, they had agreed on.

Both men have served as the United States secretary of state. Asked to reflect on the effect of the controversy on the standing of the United States in the international community, Mr. Baker said, "Well, we cannot argue that it is good." But in the United States, he continued, "we resolve our disputes in a peaceful way."

Christopher said Baker had sought a meeting, and he warned that "cooperation cannot extend to the point of giving up justified legal challenges that are absolutely necessary to ensure the fairness of the process."

Katherine Harris, the Florida secretary of state, said late this afternoon that recount reports from 53 of 67 counties had been received. But Harris provided only overall vote totals recorded by her office, which gave Bush 2,909,661 votes and Gore 2,907,877 — a majority of 1,784 for the governor. Remarkably, that was the exact margin after the original tally, which lawyers for the two sides called a coincidence. An Associated Press survey, carried out by agency reporters in all 67 Florida counties, showed a different result. With the recount done in 66 counties, the news agency said, Bush's lead had shrunk to 229 votes. The missing county was Seminole, near Orlando; it went for Bush by a healthy margin in the original count.

Harris emphasized that her figures would remain unofficial until the remaining counties reported, for which the deadline is Tuesday. And she said ballots received from absentee voters overseas would be counted through Nov. 17, 10 days after Election Day. So a final Florida count will not be available until the end of next week, or possibly even later, if legal challenges filed in federal and state courts are still pending.

The Gore campaign is pressing for a recount by hand, as opposed to the electronic recount now taking place, in four of Florida's more populous counties: Miami-Dade; Broward, which includes Fort Lauderdale; Volusia, which includes Daytona Beach; and Palm Beach. Harris said that it was up to county election boards to decide whether to conduct these, but that if they took place, they would have to be completed by Tuesday. So far, officials in Volusia County have agreed, and Palm Beach officials agreed to a manual recount in three precincts.

If the legal issues in Florida have not been resolved by Dec. 18, a judge could conceivably grant an order restraining Gov. Jeb Bush, George W. Bush's younger brother, from issuing what is known as a Certificate of Ascertainment, identifying which slate of electors won on Nov. 7 — Republican or Democrat. Without that certificate, no Florida electors could vote in the electoral college ballot which is to take place that day. As things now stand, that would mean Gore would win since the 12th Amendment to the Constitution provides that a president is elected by "a majority of the whole number of electors appointed" — not an absolute majority of the 538 who are named in normal circumstances.

With the electoral votes of the other 49 states unofficially counted, Gore has 260, and Bush has 246. Of course, those totals could change if recounts or uncounted absentee ballots change the final tallies in other states where the finish was tight, especially in New Mexico, where thousands of absentee ballots from residents of Albuquerque were not yet counted.

Experts in election law said that Florida courts have the power to order new elections or change the results if they decide that voting problems have frustrated voters' intentions. But the courts have been reluctant to do so, especially in the absence of fraud and especially in weighty elections.

Here, said Terence J. Anderson, an election-law professor at the University of Miami, "We are travelling in totally uncharted water."

As for federal initiatives, Attorney General Janet Reno said today that the Justice Department would carefully review any complaints from Florida contending that federal election law had been violated. But so far, Ms. Reno added, she saw no reason to "jump in" on an issue governed mainly by state law.

Nov. 10, 2000, R.W. Apple Jr.

For Democrats, Problems All Across Florida

MIAMI — All over Florida today, Democratic officials and angry voters complained about Election Day irregularities, from confusing ballots, computer glitches and misplaced ballot boxes to accusations by some black voters that they were turned away from polling places. There was no trend to the accusations today, with some occurring in counties that favored Al Gore and some in counties favoring George W. Bush. But they all reflected the political chaos that seemed to descend on the state today.

The Broward County Democratic Committee today filed a letter with Judge Robert W. Lee of County Circuit Court asking for a manual recount of 6,686 ballots from which, they said, no presidential selection was tabulated by computers. The computers, the Democrats said, may not have picked up punch holes that were incompletely pressed, which, they say in their complaint, "should be obvious to the human eye."

A preliminary count of ballots in Broward County showed Gore leading

Bush by more than two to one with more than half a million votes cast. County election officials will meet on the 10th at 10 a.m. to consider a manual recount.

Today, officials in Volusia and Palm Beach counties agreed to perform manual recounts on Saturday. Palm Beach will count ballots in three precincts but Volusia officials will recount all their precincts. But throughout Florida there were complaints of problems typical of those that occur occasionally around the country that do not attract national attention. With the presidential election hanging on the outcome of the race for Florida's 25 electoral votes, though, each event here seemed momentarily monumental.

In Daytona Beach, the election supervisor's office was cordoned off by yellow crime-scene tape for nine hours on Wednesday after a judge ordered the office shut down following an accusation of election night improprieties that proved false. Lawyers around the state were busy collecting affidavits from hundreds of angry voters, a strong indication of lawsuits to come in the increasingly bitter struggle about the election's validity.

In response to the reports of problems, the Gore campaign chairman, William M. Daley, demanded a vote-by-vote manual recount in four counties — Palm Beach, Miami-Dade, Broward and Volusia — where about 30 percent of Florida's vote was cast. Democrats complained most loudly about the vote in Palm Beach County, where they said a ballot with a confusing layout had caused thousands of voters to mistakenly vote for Patrick J. Buchanan when they had intended to vote for Gore. In addition, 19,120 ballots were invalidated because voters in the county had mistakenly voted for two presidential candidates.

The recount in Palm Beach County gave Gore an extra 751 votes, and Bush an extra 108 votes. Election officials attributed this to two problems. First, about half the votes were discovered simply by running the punch cards through the card-reading machines once again. The officials could offer no explanation for why this occurred, but said they understood that other counties also recovered lost votes in this fashion. They said they had tested the vote-tabulation equipment both before and after the election and found it to be functioning properly. Second, an entire precinct was left uncounted. The precinct is made up largely of retirees, officials said.

"The person running the ballots through the card reader was supposed to hit the 'set' button," said Theresa LePore, the county elections supervisor who designed the disputed ballot. "They ran through the card reader with the 'clear' button hit instead of the 'set.' It was an operator error."

LePore said the mistake became apparent in the recount. The recounted precinct gave Gore 368 votes and Bush 23.

Election Night was perhaps most chaotic in Daytona Beach, which is in Volusia County. Judge Michael McDermott of Volusia County Court, chairman of the county canvassing board, ordered the election headquarters in Daytona Beach sealed from 3:45 a.m. to 1:15 p.m. on Wednesday after two Republican

Party officials said they had seen an election worker leaving the building with two black bags they said they believed contained ballots. About 4 a.m., sheriff's deputies stopped a car driven by Debbie Allen, an election office worker, near Daytona Beach, about 25 miles from the office, and searched the vehicle.

Allen and her brother, an election volunteer, were escorted back to the election office, where deputies searched the bags, which contained personal clothing and a sample ballot. "There was nothing inappropriate," said Gary Davidson, a spokesman for the sheriff's office.

Earlier, Volusia County election results were delayed several hours by a computer disk error that subtracted 16,000 votes from Gore and added hundreds to Bush in one precinct in Deland. It also gave the Socialist Workers Party candidate, James Harris, 9,888 votes. Employees of a software company determined that the disk was damaged. Elections officials said a new disk was installed and the correct results for the precinct appeared on the screen: Gore, 193; Bush, 22; Harris, 8.

Tonight, Volusia County election officials decided to conduct a manual recount after requests were received from leaders of both the Republican and Democratic parties. In the county, Gore received 97,063 votes and Bush 82,214 votes.

At 4 p.m. Wednesday, a Volusia County election worker, Gene Tracy, noticed that about 800 ballots that he had brought from a polling place to a location where they were to be picked up for delivery to county officials were still in the back seat of his car. He rushed them to election headquarters, but the voting results had already been transmitted electronically from the polling place on Tuesday night, said Tracy's wife, Mary, also a precinct worker. "He nearly had a stroke," she said.

Dozens of registered voters also complained that they were denied the right to vote because their names did not appear on voter logs. The voters, many of whom registered when they received their driver's license, complained to county election officials.

Like voters in Palm Beach County, some voters in Osceola County, south of Orlando, may have inadvertently voted for the wrong candidate. Voting cards failed to fit properly in the slots of some voting machines, election officials said, apparently giving more than 300 votes to the Libertarian Party candidate, Harry Browne. One hundred people who live in Osceola County are registered as Libertarian Party members.

In Broward and Miami-Dade Counties, elected officials said today that dozens of black voters had been unfairly turned away from the polls. Representative Carrie Meek, a Democrat, said her office had received numerous complaints by African-American and Haitian-American voters who tried to vote but were turned away. Some were told they did not have valid identification; some said they felt intimidated by poll workers.

Democratic lawyers said they were gathering affidavits from black voters and were considering a federal Voting Rights Act lawsuit.

"They are frustrated black people worked so hard for the right to vote, they died for the right to vote," Meek said. "And we have seen a presidential election here where people had that right denied, through intimidation. Some Haitians are saying this is worse than an election in Haiti. What kind of superpower has an election like this?"

The National Association for the Advancement of Colored People also said there had been efforts to stop blacks from voting in several areas of the state. At Bethune-Cookman College in Daytona Beach, many students reported being turned away from the polls even though they had brought photo identification cards and voter registration cards.

In Pinellas County on Florida's west coast, election workers conducted a second recount today after the first recount produced an increase of more than 400 votes for Gore. Some votes had been "overlooked" by a clerk on election night, said Debbie Clark, the supervisor of elections. "The clerk apparently thought some cards had been counted when they weren't," Clark said.

Clark said that most people in the elections office were Republicans, "professionals first and party people second." Gore won the county by about 15,000 votes.

In Pensacola, the state attorney began a criminal inquiry of voter fraud after a forged ballot was found. A prosecutor said he was trying to determine if the ballot was part of a larger scheme to redirect mailed ballots to someone who filled them out and forged voters' signatures.

Nov. 10, 2000, Don Van Natta Jr.

Street Protests Erupt in Palm Beach

WEST PALM BEACH — As lawyers and election workers hovered gravely over disputed ballots inside Palm Beach County's government center, the scene outside dissolved into a debate over intelligence: one side ridiculed a candidate, the other side, the voters.

And so it went across the chasm of Olive Street, the usually quiet thoroughfare that cuts through downtown. On one side of the road supporters of Al Gore gathered to demand a new vote across the entire county to undo the effects of the county's now-notorious ballots. The Gore crowd chanted, "Re-vote! Re-vote!" and denounced Theresa LePore, the county supervisor of elections, who had approved the design of the ballots. The crowd swelled to several hundred by midday, when the Rev. Jesse Jackson stopped by to decry what he said was the denial of voting rights to many across Palm Beach County.

"There was a misalignment in the process," Jackson said. "If you drive your car down the road in a little car and your wheels are not aligned, you have a wreck. That was a wreck in West Palm."

But for many who came to demonstrate, the issue was less about the confusion of the ballots than about the presumed lack of intelligence on the part of George W. Bush. Many demonstrators waved signs that read, "Bush is too dumb to be president." Others talked of how the country's economy would slide if Bush entered the White House.

On the other side of Olive Street, the Republicans denounced those who complained about the ballots. They laughed at the Democratic demonstrators across the road and at those who had failed to figure out the ballot's instructions.

"I wasn't confused," several placards read.

Jack Rampriester, a mortgage broker from Boca Raton, said, "All you had to do was read the directions. Why is that only Democrats are complaining about the ballot language? Are they too dumb to read?"

Like many of those who marched and chanted outside the government center, Rampriester said he had decided to join the demonstration when he saw it on television at work. He and a friend, Pat Shanahan, put together a pair of homemade signs and jumped in their cars.

"Somebody had to come down here and tell the truth," Shanahan said. "The Democrats are talking a lot of nonsense. There wasn't anything wrong with those ballots."

Meanwhile, inside the government center, the woman everyone wanted to talk to — LePore — made her only public appearance at a press conference. And through her lawyer, Bruce Rogow, she declined a request for an interview.

"Hindsight is 20-20," *The Palm Beach Post* quoted LePore as saying, "But I'll never do it again."

While many people here said they respected LePore, some voters voiced their suspicions about the ballot design, spinning out theories of a conspiracy to throw the vote to Bush and the Republicans.

"She is the one who created this problem," Edna Bookspan, who was playing bridge at the Fountains Condominium Complex, said of LePore, a Democrat. "I don't know why she did it, but I think ultimately Bush's people were behind it."

Nov. 10, 2000, Dexter Filkins

Profile: BAKER AND CHRISTOPHER
TWO CORPORATE LAWYERS READY FOR BATTLE

WASHINGTON — Warren Christopher drinks a chardonnay from his favorite Sonoma Valley winery, wears suits custom-stitched by his Beverly Hills tailor, jogs judiciously and prides himself on his verbal politesse. James A. Baker III drinks Dr Pepper, wears finely stitched cowboy boots (sometimes), hunts wild game and engages audiences with his salty one-liners.

But the two former secretaries of state are also steely corporate lawyers, deliberate negotiators and battle-scarred veterans of public service who are fiercely devoted to their parties, fiercely attentive to detail and fiercely loyal to their clients. So it made perfect sense that Vice President Al Gore turned to Christopher and that Gov. George W. Bush turned to Baker to represent their respective interests in helping supervise the Florida recount that could determine the presidency.

After just one day on the job, the two former chief American diplomats did battle in separate news conferences, as Baker suggested that the Gore campaign's challenge to the Florida vote would prolong the absence of a clear victor, and that could weaken America's standing in the world. Christopher offered assurances that the country was in safe hands.

"The presidential election, of course, is on hold, and that affects the position of the United States in a number of different ways, particularly internationally," Baker said.

Asked about the remark at a later news conference, Christopher dismissed Baker's comments as a "self-serving myth," bluntly adding, "Let me assure you that the presidency goes on until Jan. 20 in a vigorous way, and none of our allies are in any doubt as to who's in charge of the government until Jan. 20."

Baker, who said that "we need to back off here a bit about filing lawsuits and hurling charges," also spoke warmly of Christopher, saying, "We're actually good friends." Christopher, by contrast, withheld any warm remarks about his predecessor. Instead, Christopher said that the Gore team had "come to believe that there are serious and substantial irregularities resulting from the ballot used only in one county, that that ballot was confusing and illegal, and that arising out of this is the need for redress, in order to make sure that the will of the people can be properly honored in this situation."

Despite their time in Washington and their involvement in political campaigns over the years, the two men have rarely intersected professionally. People who have worked with both of them say that there is a mutual respect between them; they do not describe them as friends.

The choice of Christopher came as no surprise. The 75-year-old most senior partner at the law firm of O'Melveny & Myers, in Los Angeles, has served as a sort of national wise man in other times of crisis. He was vice chairman of the inquiry in the Johnson administration into the Watts riots in Los Angeles in 1965, and in 1991 headed the independent commission that investigated widespread accusations of brutality and racism in the wake the videotaped beating of Rodney G. King, a black motorist, by white police officers.

As deputy secretary of state in the Carter administration, Christopher negotiated the release of 52 Americans held hostage in the United States Embassy in Iran. He oversaw the process that chose Gore as President Clinton's running mate in 1992 and served as head of Clinton's transition team. Christopher also headed the selection committee for Gore's running mate earlier this year and was widely credited with the choice of Joseph I. Lieberman.

Bush's choice of Baker was less predictable. The 70-year-old senior partner at the family law firm of Baker & Botts in Houston also serves as senior counselor to The Carlyle Group, a merchant banking firm in Washington, and as the United Nations' negotiator for resolving the conflict in the Western Sahara.

Although Baker's close associates insist he has played a behind-the-scenes advisory role to the Bush campaign, Baker has never hidden his displeasure with President George Bush's decision in the summer of 1992 to wrest him from his role as the country's chief diplomat to manage the Bush re-election campaign. He was widely blamed for a half-hearted performance. In choosing Baker, Governor Bush set aside whatever residue of ill will that may still linger over his father's defeat in 1992, and Baker's outsider status during the campaign may turn out to be a plus in this instance.

He is "a man of impeccable credentials and integrity," Bush said in explaining his choice. Baker is also a master strategist of presidential politics, having been chief of staff in the Reagan administration and having led presidential campaigns for five consecutive presidential elections from 1976 to 1992.

"These are two quintessential professionals," a former official who has worked with both men said. "They are perfectionists who master their talking points and their briefs, and they can sit through hours and hours of negotiations. They are the two chief grown-ups."

Nov. 10, 2000, Elaine Sciolino

The Electoral College Rears Its Ugly Head

Suddenly, the debate over the Electoral College got real. For years, many scholars had predicted that this 18th-century institution was, as Laurence H. Tribe, an expert in constitutional law at Harvard Law School, puts it, "a train wreck waiting to happen." How would the voters react, scholars asked, if the Electoral College awarded the presidency to a candidate who did not, in fact, carry the popular vote?

Some scholars argued that a country that has come to revere majority rule and the principle of one-person, one-vote, was bound to chafe at an institution created by men who were deeply suspicious of too much direct power in the hands of the voters. Those constitutional what-ifs became very real, with George W. Bush on the brink of winning a majority in the Electoral College while falling short of Al Gore's popular-vote total. As Senator Robert G. Torricelli, Democrat of New Jersey, put it, "Americans are about to engage in a great civics lesson."

Gore began the lesson today, when he appeared at a brief news conference that seemed intended, at least in part, to express his respect for constitutional rule and his willingness to abide by it. Democratic Congressional leaders did the same, brushing aside the notion that a president elected without a popular majority would lack legitimacy.

"The Constitution has laid out very clearly how a president is elected and selected," said Senator Tom Daschle of South Dakota, the Democratic leader.

"It seems to me that there should be no doubt about that. We respect the process. We respect the Constitution."

But as Daschle acknowledged, "There are many who will propose electoral reform and perhaps the abolition of the Electoral College." In fact, this would be the first election in a century that produced a split result between the popular vote and the Electoral College; three times in the 19th century, the candidate who won the popular vote did not win a majority in the Electoral College. The elections of 1960 and 1968 did not produce such a result, but their closeness spurred interest in changing the system.

The Electoral College is, essentially, 538 people who elect the president and vice president, based on each state's popular vote. Each state gets one electoral vote for every member it has in the House and Senate; the actual electors are chosen by parties and voters in the states. Most states have a winner-take-all system, so that the candidate who finishes first, even narrowly, gets all the state's electoral votes.

The system, which has changed through the years, reflected the framers' effort at compromise between directly electing presidents and leaving the choice up to Congress. Many see the system as a creaky anachronism, a last-minute deal that perversely endured and is ill-suited to modern politics.

"Every other office in the United States is elected on the basis of the person who gets the most votes," said Neal R. Peirce, co-author of *The Electoral College Primer 2000*. "But the Electoral College, for reasons no one can ever explain to you logically, values some votes over other votes. The result of this election, if it holds, would mean that a quarter-million-vote surplus for Mr. Gore nationally is worth less than a thousand or two thousand in Florida. Why?"

For all of that, nobody was predicting that abolishing the Electoral College would be easy. Daschle himself underscored the difficulties facing any would-be reformers, noting that he would worry about the effect of such a move on smaller states like his own. Defenders of the Electoral College contend that, like the Senate itself, it protects the franchise and identity of smaller states, a concern that was important to the framers.

They also say that it magnifies a majority, encouraging a consensus around a new president and the orderly transfer of power. But Professor Tribe said: "I've always had my doubts about that. People don't forget that the popular vote was close." This debate, of course, will not be confined to lofty constitutional concerns. Senator Richard J. Durbin, Democrat of Illinois, said a Republican-controlled Congress would be chilly to the idea of abolishing the Electoral College if, in fact, Mr. Bush wins the presidency as a result of the workings of the system. Mr. Durbin, who has pushed this cause since 1993, introduced legislation last week to amend the Constitution and create a system of direct election for presidents. He said he had no question about where the voters stand. "Everyone in the country thinks they're voting for president," he said. "And when you tell them they're not, they can't imagine why."

Still, advocates of scrapping the Electoral College have few illusions. In

1969, the House overwhelmingly approved a proposed constitutional amendment that would have abolished the Electoral College; President Nixon endorsed it and urged the Senate to adopt it. It was blocked and killed by senators from small states and the South.

Nov. 9, 2000, Robin Toner

OpEd

Electoral College, Safeguard of Federalism

With Al Gore leading in the popular vote, but the presidential election still up in the air, many constitutional scholars have called for abolishing the Electoral College.

This would not necessarily be a good thing. The Electoral College is one of the political safeguards of federalism: those structural features of our constitutional system — like the allocation of two senators to each state, whatever its size — that of their own force and without court intervention assure that the states count as distinct political entities, not merely administrative units of one central government.

In every presidential election, the candidates are forced to persuade the voters state by state. They must address the particular concerns of voters as citizens of those states. They must work through local organizations, which are almost always related to the same state parties that elect governors and state representatives. Presidential candidates court governors for their endorsements, appear at rallies with local political figures, learn the names of state party officials. This process, which we see played out on the nightly news as the candidates move across the nation, is not just an exercise. To connect with local politicians and local crowds, the candidates must be briefed on local personalities and local issues. Skillful politicians will remember these acquaintances, and this knowledge of local concerns will stick with them when they get to the White House.

Indeed many successful politicians not only know how to play this game; they actually like it. They like knowing that the speaker of the House in Tennessee knows where all the bodies are buried and where the levers of local power are. Thus are formed networks of concern and of mutual interest and understanding. Our national politics takes on a texture into which the threads of particular state concerns and personalities are tightly woven.

It has ever been thus. But it need not be. We could become a more centralized state, like France. A constitutional amendment to elect the president by the plurality of the popular vote would redirect the candidates' attention to national audiences. National issues would drive out any attention to local concerns or personalities. National television would play a larger role than it does now. And this would lead to a further Starbucks-ification of our political life, where every locality and region would slowly homogenize with every other into one undifferentiated mass. Economic interests — large business groups, unions and special interest groups whose focus was national, not local — would play a still larger role in presidential politics.

Some might favor such a change, finding it more in tune with what may seem modern realities, but you can't get something for nothing. Many, I suspect, would regret the loss of the distinct texture of our American polity.

Some critics of the electoral system have pushed for states to adopt the Maine and Nebraska system of allocating the state's electoral votes in part by district, and thus more nearly in proportion to the popular vote in that state, instead of adhering to the winner-take-all system. This might seem to offer a way to avoid the hard choice: no constitutional amendment is necessary, and the chance of a divergence between the electoral and popular vote would become vanishingly small. We would not have to pay the price for the federalistic effect of the Electoral College, as we may do this year.

But as a divergence becomes unlikely, the distinct federalistic effect would also vanish. After all, if we were guaranteed that the Electoral College — that is, the state-by-state system of electing the president — would never diverge from the popular vote, then it would be only the popular vote that counted.

If we want states to play a part in federal campaigns, we must be prepared occasionally to accept a divergence between the electoral and popular votes.

Nov. 9, 2000

By Charles Fried, a Law Professor at Harvard and former solicitor general

★ ★ ★

OpEd

THE ELECTORAL COLLEGE: UNFAIR FROM DAY ONE

As we await results from the Florida recount, two things should be clear. First, if George W. Bush, having apparently lost the popular vote, does indeed win at least 270 electoral votes when the Electoral College meets, he is the lawful winner, who played by the Constitution's rules and won.

Second, we must realize that the Electoral College is a hopelessly outdated system and that we must abolish it. Direct election would resonate far better with the American value of one person, one vote. Indeed, the college was designed at the founding of the country to help one group — white Southern males — and this year, it has apparently done just that.

In 1787, as the Constitution was being drafted in Philadelphia, James Wilson of Pennsylvania proposed direct election of the president. But James Madison of Virginia worried that such a system would hurt the South, which would have been outnumbered by the North in a direct election system. The creation of the Electoral College got around that: it was part of the deal that Southern states, in computing their share of electoral votes, could count slaves (albeit with a two-fifths discount), who of course were given none of the privileges of citizenship. Virginia emerged as the big winner, with more than a quarter of the electors needed to elect a president. A free state like Pennsylvania got fewer electoral votes even though it had approximately the same free population.

The Constitution's pro-Southern bias quickly became obvious. For 32 of the Constitution's first 36 years, a white slaveholding Virginian occupied the presidency. Thomas Jefferson, for example, won the election of 1800 against John Adams from Massachusetts in a race where the slavery skew of the Electoral College was the decisive margin of victory.

The system's gender bias was also obvious. In a direct presidential election, any state that chose to enfranchise its women would have automatically doubled its clout. Under the Electoral College, however, a state had no special incentive to expand suffrage — each got a fixed number of electoral votes, regardless of how many citizens were allowed to vote.

Now fast-forward to Election Night 2000. Al Gore appears to have received the most popular votes nationwide but may well lose the contest for electoral votes. Once again, the system has tilted toward white Southern males. Exit polls indicate that Mr. Bush won big among this group and that Mr. Gore won decisively among blacks and women.

The Electoral College began as an unfair system, and remains so. So why keep it? Advocates of the system sloganeer about "federalism," meaning that presidential candidates are forced to take into account individual state interests and regional variations in their national campaigns.

But in the current system, candidates don't appeal so much to state interests (what are those, anyway?) as to demographic groups (elderly voters, soccer moms) within states. And direct popular elections would still encourage candidates to take into account regional differences, like those between voters in the Midwest and the East. After all, one cannot win a national majority without getting lots of votes in lots of places.

Direct election could give state governments some incentives to increase voter turnout, because the more voters a state turned out, the bigger its role in national elections and the bigger its overall share in the national tally. Presidential candidates would begin to pay more attention to the needs of individual states that had higher turnouts.

The nation's founders sought to harness governmental competition and rivalry in healthy ways, using checks and balances within the federal government and preserving roles for state governments. Direct presidential elections would be true to their best concepts — democracy and healthy competition — rather than to their worst compromises.

Nov. 9, 2000

By Akhil Reed Amar, a law professor at Yale and author of *The Bill of Rights: Creation and Reconstruction*

day

3

FRIDAY,

NOVEMBER 10TH

★ ★ ★ ★ ★

BUSH LEAD COLLAPSES

The first unofficial tally of the machine recount in all 67 Florida counties reveals that George W. Bush's lead has fallen to only 327 votes. Republicans still demand that Gore concede, but the Democrats press hard for hand recounts in four counties — Broward, Miami-Dade, Palm Beach and Volusia — where problems with voting machines and alleged irregularities occurred on Election Day. Democrats also say they are considering a legal challenge to the "butterfly" ballot in Palm Beach County, where 30,000 votes were invalidated. Republicans threaten recounts in other states where the vote was very close. In Broward County, officials tell of the failure of voters to punch holes all the way through, thereby leaving tiny pieces of paper dangling from the ballot. And so the "chad" makes its first appearance in the election controversy.

AS BUSH LEAD SHRINKS TO 327 HE URGES GORE TO CONCEDE

AUSTIN —George W. Bush and his advisers said that they were moving forward with preparations for a new administration and beseeched Al Gore not to stand in their way, cautioning that legal challenges to the election could yield wrangling without end. Although they acknowledged that there were absentee ballots in Florida still to be tallied, they said that a nearly complete recount of the overwhelming majority of votes demonstrated that Bush had won both the state and the presidency, though barely.

"The vote here in Florida was very close, but when it was counted Governor Bush was the winner," James A. Baker III said at a news conference today. "For the good of the country and for the sake of our standing in the world, the campaigning should end and the business of an orderly transition should begin."

The latest results from Tuesday's election continued to show Gore with a lead in the nationwide popular vote, by a margin of 218,441 votes. But in Florida, whose 25 electoral votes hold the key to the outcome, Bush led by 327 votes, according to the Associated Press's latest unofficial tally of votes that were recounted by machines over the past few days.

> *"The more often ballots are recounted, especially by hand, the more likely it is that human errors... will be introduced."*
>
> *—James A. Baker III*

That total may change in the manual recounts that are to begin at 8 a.m. Saturday in Palm Beach and Volusia Counties, in response to requests from the Gore campaign. Palm Beach election officials will check ballots from three precincts, while those in Volusia will recount ballots from the entire county.

Officials in Broward County, which is heavily Democratic, were to manually recount ballots in three precincts, beginning on Monday [Nov. 13]. The vote in those precincts, county elections officials said, was overwhelmingly for Vice President Gore — 3,554, compared with 133 for Bush. But the county Democratic Party chairman, Mitch Caesar, said that as many as 6,686 ballots may have gone uncounted because of the shortcomings in the machine count.

According to several Republican officials, the Bush campaign was considering the possibility of seeking a legal injunction against manual recounts in several Florida counties, and Bush has given Baker permission to take that step. But campaign officials had not reached a decision late tonight.

In their comments today, Bush and his aides tailored their words and actions to underscore the assertion that Bush had, essentially, won the election by winning Florida. When Bush spoke briefly with reporters at the Governor's Mansion here this afternoon, the placement of his chair and the tableau of advisers around him evoked a meeting in the Oval Office.

"It's in our country's best interest that we plan in a responsible way for a possible administration," said Bush, making his first public comments in more than 48 hours. The strain of one of the strangest weeks in the history of American politics was obvious in his eyes, which looked tired, and his speech, which was halting and faint.

"I am mindful that there are still votes to be counted," he added, referring to the absentee ballots, which the Bush campaign believes will strongly favor the Texas governor. But, Bush said, "I think it's up to us to prepare the groundwork for an administration that will be ready to function on Day One." Sitting near him were Dick Cheney, his would-be vice president, and Andrew Card, the likely chief of staff in a Bush White House. Both men were scheduled to meet with Bush at his ranch near Waco this weekend.

As Bush took a tentative half-step toward the presidency, his advisers and the vice president's aides battled over the propriety of the manual recounts of votes in several Florida counties that were set to begin tomorrow. "The more often ballots are recounted, especially by hand, the more likely it is that human errors, like lost ballots and other risks, will be introduced," Baker said. "This frustrates the very reason why we have moved from hand counting to machine counting."

That specter hovered between the lines of comments made by Baker at a news conference in a room in the Senate Office Building in Tallahassee. Baker used phrases like "rule of law," "the good of the country" and "the sake of our standing in the world" to call on Gore and his advisers to accept defeat — providing that the uncounted absentee ballots did not cut in their favor — and move on.

"Let the country step back for a minute and pause and think about what's at stake here," said Baker, using a tone of moral suasion and even invoking Richard M. Nixon's actions in 1960 as a potential model for Gore. Nixon did not contest a narrow loss in that presidential election to John F. Kennedy. "The purpose of our national election is to establish a constitutional government, not unending legal wrangling," Baker said.

Less than two hours later, in the same room of the same Senate building, aides to Gore held their own news conference. They said they were adamant in their resolve to make sure that there were not flaws in the voting process that wound up shortchanging their candidate — and costing him the presidency.

"Other systems of government may work faster," said William M. Daley, the chairman of the Gore campaign. "Curtailing voters' rights may get a result that is faster. But no system of government is more just or more enduring than ours."

"I hope," Daley added, "that our friends in the Bush campaign will join us in our efforts to get the fairest and most accurate vote count here in Florida."

Late tonight, Kendall Coffey, a Florida lawyer working for the Gore campaign on election-law issues, sent a letter to Katherine Harris, the Florida secretary of state, urging her not to certify the results of the state presidential election until after the manual recount was completed.

The letter said that Harris's lawyer told the campaign the Elections Canvassing Commission planned to certify the results on Tuesday, a week after the election, regardless of the status of the recounts. Because some of the recounts may not be completed by Tuesday, Coffey argued that the results should not be certified.

Nov. 11, 2000, Frank Bruni

Democrats Seek Manual Recounts, Weigh Legal Battle

TALLAHASSEE — For all their threats of court action and dire warnings about illegal ballots, Democratic strategists said today that the last place they wanted the presidential election to wind up was before a judge. Before the disputed Florida election ever reaches the point of litigation, campaign officials said, they will try to win the vote outright for Al Gore.

Beginning on Saturday, Democratic officials will monitor the three counties that have agreed to a hand recount (Broward, Palm Beach and Volusia). Democrats have asked for a similar hand count in Miami-Dade County, where election officials will consider the request on Tuesday. Party officials also planned to observe the tabulation of absentee ballots from overseas, which are due by Friday.

Though they hoped the recounts would give Gore the lead, the lawyers acknowledged that both the hand count and the absentee ballots could end with Bush still ahead — particularly if ballots from military personnel favored Bush, as 54 percent did for Bob Dole in 1996.

If, near the end of next week, Gore was still not the winner, the Democrats would have to decide whether to go to court to challenge the ballot in Palm Beach County. They were laying the groundwork today to give Gore that option. "Right now, we're weighing our legal options, and no decision has been made about whether to go through the court system," said a lawyer working for the Democratic Party here. "But first, we need to know what the final count is. It might tell us one minor detail — did we win?"

In makeshift storefronts like this one in a shopping mall a few miles from the State Capitol, and in more formal offices across the state, Democratic lawyers from around the country have spent several days memorizing sections of Florida law governing the printing of ballots. The byzantine election law, the size of a small-city telephone book, would be the basis of any legal action that the party would take in its quest to gain the state's 25 electoral votes for Gore.

But filing a lawsuit 10 days to two weeks after the election could offend the public by prolonging the selection of a president at a time when many Americans might be tired of the process. Democrats, aware of the fatigue issue, hoped to generate sympathy for their cause by using some of the thousands of complaints from voters in Palm Beach County and elsewhere who believed they were the victims of ballot irregularities. Nearly 150 party volunteers have spent the last few days collecting these statements, and the best, and presumably most sympathetic, would become affidavits filed with any lawsuits.

"What we have to remember is that this is being done on behalf of people who lost their electoral voice in Palm Beach County because of an illegal ballot," said Jenny Backus, a spokeswoman for the Democratic National Committee. "This isn't about Al Gore or George Bush or Democrats or Republicans. It's about voters."

Democratic lawyers said they were researching legal precedents in Florida for challenging ballots and were also investigating possible civil rights violations in Tuesday's election. But the crux of their legal strategy was the physical layout of the printed ballot in Palm Beach, which they claimed was "clearly illegal" because it did not list the presidential candidates in linear order.

The lawyers were citing a section of Florida election law that described in detail how the names of presidential candidates must be arranged on paper ballots designed to be marked with an X. At the top of each ballot, the law says, there must be a heading saying "Electors for President and Vice President," and "thereunder" must be the list of candidates, beginning with the one who is the same party as the governor of Florida.

Democrats said that because Palm Beach County listed the candidates on two pages, instead of one, the ballot violated the provision that the candidates must be listed under the heading, in linear order. Many voters have said the arrangement caused them to unintentionally vote for Patrick J. Buchanan instead of Gore. Republicans cited a different provision that applied to ballots intended to be counted electronically, such as punch cards. That section says that such ballots "shall, as far as practicable, be in the order of arrangement provided for paper ballots." If the county believed such an arrangement was not practicable, Republicans say, they are allowed to change the order.

Democrats responded today that if 66 other counties had found a linear arrangement to be practicable, then Palm Beach could have done the same. The Democrats would have to convince a judge that the ballot was illegal and must provide the testimony of voters who said it caused them to vote twice. (The lawsuits would most likely be filed in southern Florida, where there is a greater likelihood of getting a Democratic judge than farther north.)

But the party lawyers said they had not decided what remedy to seek. There are really only two possibilities, the party lawyer said here today: a revote in Palm Beach County or a request that the 19,000 ballots thrown out because people mistakenly punched two names be apportioned according to the rest of the vote in the county, which favored Gore.

"This issue is totally up in the air," the lawyer said. "We really don't know which way we're going to go on it."

Reapportionment is a method sometimes used in civil rights cases elsewhere in the country but appears to have no precedent in Florida.

But the issue of a new vote has come up before in Florida. In 1974, several losing candidates in Pinellas County persuaded a state circuit judge to order a new vote because the ballot was long and confusing. But a state Court of Appeals overruled the judge, saying that "mere confusion does not amount to an impediment to the voters' free choice," if they have an opportunity to ask for help in the polling place. The ruling was later upheld by the Florida Supreme Court.

Two lawsuits have already been filed in state court in Palm Beach County over Tuesday's ballot. Although the suits were not filed at the behest of the

Gore campaign or the Democratic Party, William M. Daley, chairman of the Gore campaign, has indicated that the party would support such individual lawsuits. Daley also seemed to edge closer today to the idea of litigation by the Gore campaign or the Democratic Party. "Legal counsel have indicated that they thought it was not a legal ballot," he said, "and I assume that's an issue that will end up in dispute."

But before it reached that point, the party was hoping to avoid the appearance of being a litigious poor loser by simply winning the Florida election outright in the manual recount of ballots.

Nov. 11, 2000, David Firestone

Overvotes and Undervotes: The Palm Beach Ballot Flap Continues

WEST PALM BEACH — Bush campaign officials have tried to undercut criticisms of the fairness of the Palm Beach County ballot by saying there were plenty of safeguards and that the problems on Tuesday were not unusual. But interviews with voters and local officials today offered fresh evidence that an extraordinary number of Palm Beach County voters were confused by their ballots and unable to get help on Election Day.

Local politicians, administrators and voters suggested that the system put in place to help voters with questions on their ballots broke down on Tuesday. And one local official rejected as "absolutely false" Republican assertions that the number of voters who "double-voted" were roughly the same as in previous elections. Bob Weisman, the Palm Beach County chief administrator, said that the county had set up several telephone lines to help voters but some were unstaffed on Election Day. He said that the county set up 38 telephone lines to help voters and precinct workers calling in with questions, but hired only 34 people to operate them. It was possible, he said, that voters and precinct workers with questions might have had a difficult time getting through.

"There were telephone lines, but no one to answer them," said Weisman, a registered Republican. "The operators who were working were totally swamped."

At the same time, some precinct workers said that they were under strict instructions to turn away people asking for voting assistance — mainly out of fear that it would slow down the voting. Louise Austin, a precinct worker in Boynton Beach, said she and other workers at her precinct turned away voters who besieged them with questions.

"People were coming up to me," Austin said, "and I had to follow the directive — 'Don't help anyone. Don't talk to anyone.' "

Austin said that under directions given by the Palm Beach County supervisor of elections, precinct workers were supposed to provide assistance to voters only if there was a mechanical problem with the voting machine. Everyone else was supposed to be turned away.

A later directive by the supervisor of elections, Theresa LePore, a Democrat, telling precinct workers to help confused voters was prepared for all precincts on Election Day. But Austin said her precinct did not receive the memorandum until late in the afternoon. Austin also said she called county election offices several times for guidance but was unable to get through. "The lines were constantly busy," she said.

Weisman, the county administrator, said voters who needed help were supposed to receive it. "No one is supposed to be denied," he said.

Weisman said he that he had heard that at least one voter who had marked his ballot incorrectly had been refused a second ballot. Under state law, he said, voters who punch their ballot cards incorrectly are supposed to receive a second or third ballot so they can try again.

But that apparently did not happen in every case. Bernard Holtzer, who lives in The Fountains retirement community near West Palm Beach, said that when he unintentionally marked Patrick J. Buchanan's name on his ballot, he asked for another and was refused.

"I wanted to vote for Gore, and instead I pushed Buchanan," said Holtzer, a registered Republican who voted in the precinct near his home. "I told the clerk I made a boo-boo and that I wanted a new ballot. And she told me there was nothing she could do about it. So I ended up voting for Buchanan."

Republican officials have said that voters could have become familiar with the ballot — which listed the presidential candidates on facing pages instead of on one page, a design that some people believe prompted some voters to choose Buchanan instead of Gore — because voters received a sample in the mail. But Weisman said it may not have been seen by all the voters. He said that a sample ballot was mailed out, but that he never received one at his home.

"We don't know how many other people didn't receive the sample ballot," Weisman said.

Election officials also countered another major Republican contention: that the "butterfly" ballot that is believed to have caused so much confusion in Palm Beach County was used here in the presidential election in 1996. Bruce Rogow, a lawyer representing the Palm Beach County supervisor of election office, said the 2000 election was the first time that the butterfly ballot had been used in a contested race. A butterfly ballot was used in 1986 for constitutional amendment questions.

Also, while Republicans have said that Democrats should not complain about the ballot because they had previously approved it, Democratic officials said today that they never approved of the ballot layout used in Palm Beach County.

"Florida law leaves to each supervisor of elections, not the political parties, the official preparation of the ballot," said Bob Poe, the Florida Democratic Party chairman. "The ballot is illegal and confusing."

Officials with the Bush campaign contend that the total number of "overvotes" tossed out in Palm Beach County in the 1996 presidential election was 14,000.

But Carol A. Roberts, who sits on the local board that oversees elections, dismissed that figure as impossibly high. Roberts, a longtime elected Democratic official, said that the combined number of "overvotes" — ballots that voters punched twice — and "undervotes" — where they don't punch at all — together totaled about 14,000 in 1996.

The debate over the number of "overvotes" cuts to the heart of the Gore campaign's argument that ballot irregularities here may have reduced the number of votes that the vice president received. Gore campaign officials contend that the roughly 19,000 "overvotes" that were disregarded represented an extraordinarily high figure — and proof that voters found the ballot confusing. The Gore campaign also contends that the ballot is illegal.

On Tuesday, there were 19,000 "overvotes" and 11,000 "undervotes" in Palm Beach County.

Nov. 11, 2000, Dexter Filkins

Democrats Split over Court Fight

WASHINGTON — The Gore campaign's threat of a court fight over the presidential balloting in Florida set off a backstage debate in the Democratic Party today between party leaders who are rallying behind the vice president and others, including longtime Gore loyalists, who warn that such a fight could damage the party and the democratic process.

In a range of interviews, most Democrats said that, at least for now, they were fully supportive of Gore's decision to follow through with the recount of the vote in Florida, and some were passionately behind Gore. Yet a smaller number contended that if Bush was still ahead after the final count of absentee ballots late next week, Gore should back down and not prolong the battle. These Democrats said they feared that Gore's aggressive strategy could make them look like sore losers and hinder the party's drive to capture control of the House and Senate in the midterm elections.

Gore campaign officials, nervous that the misgivings of some Democrats could undermine their effort, urged Democrats to unite behind the vice president — and prevent open defections. They delivered talking points to Democratic state chairmen and to members of Congress. And they planned to dispatch party leaders — and probably Gore himself — to meet with Congressional Democrats, possibly as early as this weekend.

"Obviously," said Mark Fabiani, Gore's deputy campaign manager, "this is a situation where consensus is very important, and everyone needs to understand what's at stake here and what we're fighting for and how we're fighting for it."

The Congressional Democrat who has been most vociferous in raising questions about the Gore strategy is Senator Robert G. Torricelli of New Jersey, who heads the party's drive to help Democratic Senate contenders. Far beyond Washington, other Democrats have raised questions as well. Many leading Democrats were just as outspoken in their defense of the Gore campaign. They said they saw no need to avoid court.

"I don't understand why it's a controversy," said Representative Barney Frank of Massachusetts. "Inauguration Day is more than two months away. This doesn't interfere with anything."

Referring to suggestions that many voters in Palm Beach mistakenly voted for Patrick J. Buchanan when they intended to vote for Gore, Frank added, "Why would you not clean this up?"

He wondered sarcastically whether Bush wanted to "become president because of the involuntary existence of a group known as Jews for Buchanan."

The two Democratic leaders on Capitol Hill fell into step with the Gore campaign, playing down the possibility of a court challenge but leaving the door to one open.

"Obviously there are diverse opinions," said Senator Tom Daschle of South Dakota, the minority leader. "I would say the overwhelming consensus appears to be the vice president needs to exhaust the remedies available to him to hold open the possibility of a court settlement. That shouldn't be rejected outright before we know the facts. Most of us are interested in finality but not at the expense of fairness."

Representative Richard A. Gephardt, the House minority leader, who held a conference call on Thursday with House Democrats to assess the election results, said: "My sense is that people are patient. They think this is really close, and Florida is the obvious decider of this race."

Gephardt said he thought it would be a mistake to rule out going to court.

Nov. 11, 2000, Richard L. Berke and Alison Mitchell

African-Americans Seek Inquiry into Florida Vote

WEST PALM BEACH — African-American voters and community leaders here are calling not just for a recount, but also a re-vote, saying that irregularities at polling places and what they insisted was an illegal ballot layout in Palm Beach County thwarted the true intent of their vote.

African-American voters said many minority voters were denied the chance to vote because their names did not appear on voting lists, and because understaffed and overworked poll workers were unable to resolve discrepancies. Haitian-American voters said that some polling places in Miami did not have Creole interpreters and that some poll watchers were not allowed to help them.

These complaints may add to the stalemate in Palm Beach County arising from the ballot layout that Democrats said led to the invalidation of 19,000 ballots because of double-voting and to some 3,000 more being mistakenly cast.

The accusations have also prompted national black organizations to call for a federal investigation into election irregularities in Florida. Spurred by politicians, education campaigns and radio talk shows, a record number of African-American voters, overwhelmingly favoring Gore over Bush, went to the polls on Tuesday, surpassing their 1996 numbers by 60 percent.

"The bottom line is, the electoral process was the best, I thought, in terms of getting out the vote," said Evette Simmons, a Florida lawyer who is the president of the National Bar Association, the largest group representing black lawyers. "But the result is one of the worst because despite those who voted, we may not know which candidate truly represents the will of the people."

While not claiming foul play, the National Association for the Advancement of Colored People has said many blacks were not allowed to vote in the state. Lawyers from the N.A.A.C.P. will be in Miami on Saturday to speak with voters who say they had difficulty voting.

"We are trying to get sworn testimony to use to present to the Justice Department in support of a request for an investigation," said Thomasina Williams, the assistant general counsel for the Miami-Dade chapter of the N.A.A.C.P. "We need to get sworn, factual testimony so we can get an idea of what happened: are these isolated cases or sufficient in number or concentrated, to see if there is a systemic problem."

Part of the problem, some politicians said, was that election officials were not prepared to handle the large numbers of African-American voters who went to the polls, many for the first time. Representative Alcee L. Hastings, a Democrat from South Florida, said the turnout in some predominantly African-American precincts in Broward County was as high as 85 percent.

"I don't think they were staffed for the overall amount," Hastings said. "It's so easy to cry race and to demagogue the issue based on race. Here we have a pretty grave situation for our country, and it should not, in my judgment, be relegated to the continuing dispute that is going to go on for time immemorial regarding black and white folks in this country."

Attorney General Janet Reno said on Thursday that the Justice Department would carefully review any complaints from Florida or any other state that federal election laws had been violated. But Reno said that so far she had seen no reason to "jump in" to an issue that is largely regulated by state laws.

In various parts of the state, people who thought they had registered to vote when they obtained their driver's license were told that their names did not appear on the lists. Several African-American politicians said they knew of instances where blacks who were waiting in line to vote were turned away when the polls closed.

At Bethune-Cookman College, a historically black college in Daytona Beach, many students who said they had signed up in voter-registration drives on campus said they had been turned away from the polls because their names were not on the rolls. Some students, especially those who argued or cajoled, said they were able to vote by presenting a photo identification and signing an affidavit. But many more students said they had no idea what to do and just left the polling stations.

At least 40 written complaints have been collected so far by the local Democratic Party officials.

Ursula Harvey, 20, said she went to the same polling place near the college as she had two years ago but was told that her name was not on the list and that she would have to vote 120 miles away in her hometown. But Harvey said she was unable to make the trip.

"It's for the presidential election," Harvey said, holding a flier with a photograph from 1965 of black men being beaten by the police. "It's for our financial aid, it's for our Social Security, it's for our life."

The students who were unable to vote said they thought they could have given Gore the edge he needed to win the state.

David Byron, a spokesman for Volusia County, which includes Daytona Beach, said he was not familiar with the specific complaints raised by the students, but he insisted that anyone who registered to vote on time was allowed to cast a ballot.

"I feel confident saying we didn't turn away any registered voters," Byron said.

Phillip Brutus, a Haitian-American who was elected on Tuesday to the State Legislature, said that some polling places in Dade County closed early and that at others, people were turned away erroneously because they did not have their voter registration card.

"That's not right because you're supposed to be able to vote," Brutus said, "and they are supposed to have a system where you can look up a voter's name."

Nov. 11, 2000, David Gonzalez

day 4

SATURDAY,

NOVEMBER 11TH

★ ★ ★ ★ ★

BUSH GOES TO COURT

With a manual recount in several Florida counties set to begin, the Bush campaign files a lawsuit in United States District Court in Fort Lauderdale seeking an injunction to stop all manual recounts. Bush's team argues that with no clearly defined standard for judging a voter's intent, a recount would be subject to manipulation by partisan vote counters and that "tainted" recount results will undermine public confidence in the election process. The Gore campaign criticizes the move as a delaying tactic and reiterates its position that all votes, including those on ballots that counting machines were unable to read, should be counted. They also point out that Governor Bush signed a law in Texas authorizing hand recounts of ballots in disputed elections. Despite the suit, Palm Beach County conducts a manual recount of 1 percent of the county's vote to determine if there are enough irregularities to warrant a hand recount of the county's 462,657 votes. Election officials in the other counties in question declare their intent to conduct hand recounts unless prevented by a court order.

BUSH SUES IN FEDERAL COURT TO STOP RECOUNT

TALLAHASSEE — The disputed presidential election in Florida moved into the federal courts when George W. Bush's campaign filed suit to block the manual recount of ballots sought by Al Gore. The campaign cited the "potential for mischief" and said the process was inherently less fair and more subjective than counting by machine. The suit is to be heard by Judge Donald M. Middlebrooks, a Clinton appointee, on Monday morning [Nov. 13].

The announcement, by James A. Baker III, came a day after the Republicans criticized the Democrats for threatening to take the ballot issue to court, a step that the Republicans said would lead to endless wrangling in a number of states. But Baker contended this morning that the Democrats had effectively started the legal battle because their supporters — though not the Gore campaign itself — had already filed state lawsuits in Florida.

"The lawyers are running the show now."

—Senior Republican Official

At a news conference at the Capitol here, Baker said that the manual count requested in four Democratic counties by the Gore campaign would be far less accurate than the machine count that has already determined Bush to be ahead by 327 votes. "It is precisely for these reasons that over the years our democracy has moved increasingly from hand counting of votes to machine counting," Baker said. "Machines are neither Republicans nor Democrats, and therefore can be neither consciously nor unconsciously biased."

The Gore campaign has sought the manual recount because thousands of ballots were rejected by tabulating machines when voters failed to properly punch the holes in their punch-card ballots. Democratic officials say that a manual inspection of such ballots will reveal the intent of the voters in case a piece of the ballot is still clinging to the punched hole.

But Baker said that such a determination by county election workers would be so subjective as to be meaningless. "A manual recount permits the electoral boards in each county in Florida to determine the intent of the voter without setting forth any standards for deciding that intent," Baker said. "One electoral board may decide to count votes that are not fully punched; another may not. One electoral board may decide that a stray mark indicated an intent to vote for a particular candidate; another may not."

A senior Republican official with ties to the Bush campaign said that the campaign was prepared, if the injunction was denied, to appeal this to the United States Supreme Court. "They absolutely will appeal it all the way up, as high as they have to go. The lawyers are running the show now."

Democrats, delighted to have forced the Republicans to file a lawsuit first, immediately seized on the court filing to turn the tables on the Bush officials and accuse them of using delaying tactics. Speaking for the Gore campaign, Warren Christopher called on Bush to withdraw what he called the "surprising action" and allow a full count of the Florida votes. "If Governor Bush truly believes that he has won the election in Florida, he should not have any reason to doubt or to fear to have the machine count checked by a hand count," Christopher said in Washington. "This procedure is authorized under Florida law, under Texas law, and under the law of many other jurisdictions." He said it was a common procedure that is often used around the country when a machine fails to fully read a ballot, and noted that Bush recently signed a law in Texas authorizing hand counts in disputed ballot situations.

Gore's spokesman, Chris Lehane, quickly accused the Bush campaign of trying "to use every legal means available, including lawyers and court injunctions, to block the speedy and accurate count of Florida votes." He added, "We are confident that Americans will reject Bush's arrogant stance and will demand a full, fair and accurate counting of Florida's votes."

Officials in the Bush campaign said they decided to go to court even though they might be seen as the first ones to throw the fate of the presidential race into the courts. "The decision to do it was made on the basis that if you didn't, it would look like you weren't fighting hard enough," said one of these officials. "There's a very fine line here, and Gore is walking it as well."

Baker urged the Gore campaign to accept the results of the machine recount, along with the overseas absentee ballots that are due on Friday, whatever the result. He said the Bush campaign would drop its request for a federal injunction if the Gore campaign made such an agreement, and the Bush campaign would accept the results if they showed that Gore had won.

The decision to be the first campaign to seek court relief represents a calculated risk for the Republicans. But the risk to the campaign of a manual count was clearly seen as greater than the perception that both sides were reduced to legal squabbling. A hand count of ballots in counties where Gore did well has the effect of raising the turnout, because some ballots that were rejected by machine will most likely be added to the total vote. Statistically, a majority of those new votes will probably be for Gore.

The Republican lawsuit was filed this morning in United States District Court in Fort Lauderdale on behalf of Bush and Cheney as well as seven Floridians who say they voted for Bush and believed that the recounts would injure their voting rights. The suit says the First Amendment rights of the voters would be deprived through a manual count, and their equal-protection rights under the 14th Amendment would also be infringed, because different counties may use different methods for interpreting the ballots.

The suit says a temporary restraining order must stop the hand counts before they are finished, because once the "tainted results" are broadcast to the nation, an irreparable harm will occur to the presidential transition. The recounts might raise questions about the tallying process in other counties or states, interfering in the "powerful national interest in the finality of the selection of the president."

Manual recounts, however, are explicitly allowed under Florida law if any candidate requests them within 72 hours of the election, and though they are not common, election officials here said they had often been used in local races.

Baker said he regretted that the campaign felt it necessary to go to court, but it did so to bring finality to the election. He used the opportunity to chide Gore for his efforts at a further examination of the ballots, comparing him unfavorably with President Gerald R. Ford, who he said chose in 1976 to concede a close election to Jimmy Carter rather than prolong the count.

November 11, 2000, David Firestone and Michael Cooper

Why the Republicans Went to Federal Court

The Republican decision to sue in federal court appeared to be a strategic effort to take the politically volatile case out of Florida — and possibly the hands of local elected judges — as quickly as possible, experts on election law said yesterday.

Federal courts are generally more reluctant than state courts to overturn election results declared by state officials, the legal experts said. It was possible, they said, that the Republicans had concluded that federal judges might consider the repeated recounts in Florida as, in effect, another way of overturning the officially announced election results. But several experts said the Republicans also appeared to be gambling that federal courts, and ultimately the United States Supreme Court, might be more willing to consider an unusual claim that recounts should be halted for the stability of the national political system.

Some of the experts said a Republican effort to pre-empt the Gore forces from giving Florida judges control over the legal battle appeared to be as much a political calculation as a legal one. Several noted that the counties where the Gore campaign has focused many of its complaints were generally Democratic, raising the possibility that trial judges there could be under intense political pressure to favor the Gore camp. Federal judges are appointed for life, but trial judges in Florida are elected. E. Joshua Rosenkranz, president of the Brennan Center for Justice at the New York University School of Law, said that because Florida's State Supreme Court was controlled by justices appointed by Democratic governors, Bush strategists might have felt they had to try to get the controversy out of the Florida courts.

After a ruling by a federal trial-level judge in the case, an appeal would be to the United States Court of Appeals for the Eleventh Circuit in Atlanta, the same court that was drawn into the Elian Gonzalez battle. The next step would be to the United States Supreme Court.

Federal courts interpret state election laws as well as federal statutes, like the Voting Rights Act. But because they see issues like recount disputes as procedural, they have demanded a high standard of proof before second-guessing the actions of local election officials.

Several of the experts said that might have convinced Bush strategists that a federal court would be more willing to halt a recount that, the Bush lawyers would argue, appeared aimed at frustrating voters' true intentions. "Historically, voting has been a state law issue and the federal courts have only involved themselves when there is an allegation of a specific federal violation — like the protection against racial discrimination in voting or some gross violation" of voters' rights, said Professor Richard Briffault, an election law specialist at Columbia Law School. But state courts, he said, have typically been more open to technical challenges to voting routines and more willing to get into an analysis of whether voting procedures brought a victory to a candidate that had not been intended by voters.

On one level, some of the election experts said, there was justification for the filing of a federal case because there are already disputes in several areas of the state. It would be chaotic for trial courts in different counties to be dealing with questions pertaining to the presidential election, they said. A federal court, in contrast, could have full jurisdiction over the entire matter.

Nov. 11, 2000, William Glaberson

HAGGLING OVER CHADS IN PALM BEACH COUNTY

"Hanging chads means every recount is different."
– Doug Lewis, director of the Election Center

★ ★ ★

WEST PALM BEACH — The manual recount of 4,000 votes, or 1 percent of the total cast in Palm Beach County, was not expected to be completed until late tonight or early Sunday morning [Nov. 12]. If election supervisors find enough votes that machines failed to detect, the Palm Beach County canvassing board could decide to recount by hand all 462,657 ballots cast here. That would include all 10,361 ballots that were not counted because the voters did not punch any hole at all for presidential candidates.

The manual ballot recount was requested by the Florida Democratic Party, which chose three Palm Beach County precincts with an unusually high number of ballots that did not choose a president at all in Tuesday's election. Democrats were optimistic that some of the 501 nonvotes that were reviewed Saturday would be transformed into votes for Gore, who trails Bush in Florida by just 327 votes out of nearly 6 million votes cast after all 67 counties were counted again this week, according to a count by The Associated Press.

The painstaking process of counting votes by hand in a presidential election so close that every vote actually could count led to constant partisan challenges during the day over exactly what constituted a vote. Teams of Democrats, Republicans and election officials argued over whether the ballots were actually perforated or just dented, and then argued over exactly what the policy was and whether it had changed as the day had worn on.

Again and again, the counting stopped when the two sides accused each other of miscounting and misinterpreting the ballots. What should have been a simple question — whether or not a vote was cast when a hole was punched in a piece of paper — was complicated because the hole was not punched through cleanly and left a hanging or torn piece, known as a chad.

The chads could explain why after the machine recount earlier this week, Gore added roughly 600 votes in Palm Beach County. In fact, election experts say, each time the ballots are run through a machine, the tiny chad is more likely to fall off, and the vote will be recorded.

Twice, Bob Nichols, a spokesman for the election supervisor, tried to explain the rules of the manual recount, which were adopted in 1990. Democrats accused Republicans of discarding ballots that should not have been set aside. Republicans accused Democrats of including ballots that had dimples, not hanging chads. Mistrust seemed to grind the process even slower. "We can't keep stopping when you all raise your hands," said Charles Burton, a county judge who is the chairman of the Palm Beach County canvassing committee, according to a pool report by a reporter who was in the room. "This will never work."

At one point, an angry Republican said to a Democrat who challenged another vote, "Excuse me, just let them do their job." The Democrat shot back, "I don't know what you are talking about."

The Bush campaign quickly seized on the discord, saying it considered the hand count to be flawed, no matter what the results are. "The changing standard used to judge ballots, the inability of the officials in charge to explain their procedures and the secretive fashion in which decisions were made risk undermining people's confidence in the results," said Ari Fleischer, a spokesman for the Bush campaign.

Nov. 11, 2000, Don Van Natta Jr. and Rick Bragg

Hanging Chads May Hold Key to Election

The leadership of the free world may be decided by chads.

No, not election observers from the African country, but tiny bits of cellulose that, under the pressure of a citizen wielding his voting franchise and a metal stylus, are supposed to detach sharply from a punch-card ballot. Most do so, remaining as trash in the voting machine after the ballot is removed. The rectangular hole is interpreted as a vote by an electronic reader, while all unpunched holes are considered nonvotes.

The problem with chads is that they often do not fully detach — until the recount. Then they're called "hanging chads," and the computers can interpret them in various ways each time they are run through.

The issue is significant in Florida because thousands of ballots were read by voting machines as having no vote in the presidential column. Democrats hope that when the paper cards are reviewed one by one, many will be seen to have partly punched holes next to Gore's name. In Palm Beach County alone, as many 10,000 ballots were recorded as having no choice for president. The Bush campaign filed suit today to prevent the hand counts, arguing that they are inaccurate and inevitably subject to political influence.

Hanging chads, the principal shortcoming of the cheap and popular punch-card voting systems by which more than a third of all American votes are cast, have been a consistent but mostly local headache for election officers for decades. But this year, they could take on huge significance if Democrats win their demand for a recount of votes in four large counties that use the punch-card systems in Florida: the more the ballots are handled, the greater the chance that the hanging chads will close, open or detach.

"Hanging chads mean every recount is different," said Doug Lewis, executive director of the Election Center, a nonprofit organization in Houston that monitors voter registration and election issues. "You can change the way the chad closes or opens, even if you don't mean to do it."

They litter the floor when officials are counting ballots. "You go to the counting room, and there are hundreds of them," said Tony Sirvello, administrator of elections for the Harris County (Houston) clerk's office. So if it is a recount, every chad means a vote that might not have been recorded the first time. "What they represent is votes," said Sirvello of the confetti on the counting-room floor.

In counties with Democratic majorities, more of the chads represent previously uncounted Democratic votes. "The theory is that each time you run them through, the chad comes out," said Representative Peter Deutch, Democrat of Florida. "I think it will help the vice president," he said, referring to the recount.

Chads — the term dates to the late 1950's when punch cards were the standard way of reading data into a computer — may be unknown to the lay person, but they are so contentious that some election officials will not talk about them on the record.

Nov. 11, 2000, Ford Fessenden

Using the Votomatic Punch Card Machine

Votomatic punch card devices were used in many of the Florida counties where ballots were disputed.

1. The voter slides a punch card into the holder. The card is held in place by two pins.
2. Using a punch tool, the voter makes a hole in the ballot card corresponding to their choice.
3. As each page of the ballot book is turned, a new column of holes is revealed. The butterfly-design ballot that was used in Palm Beach County is shown below.

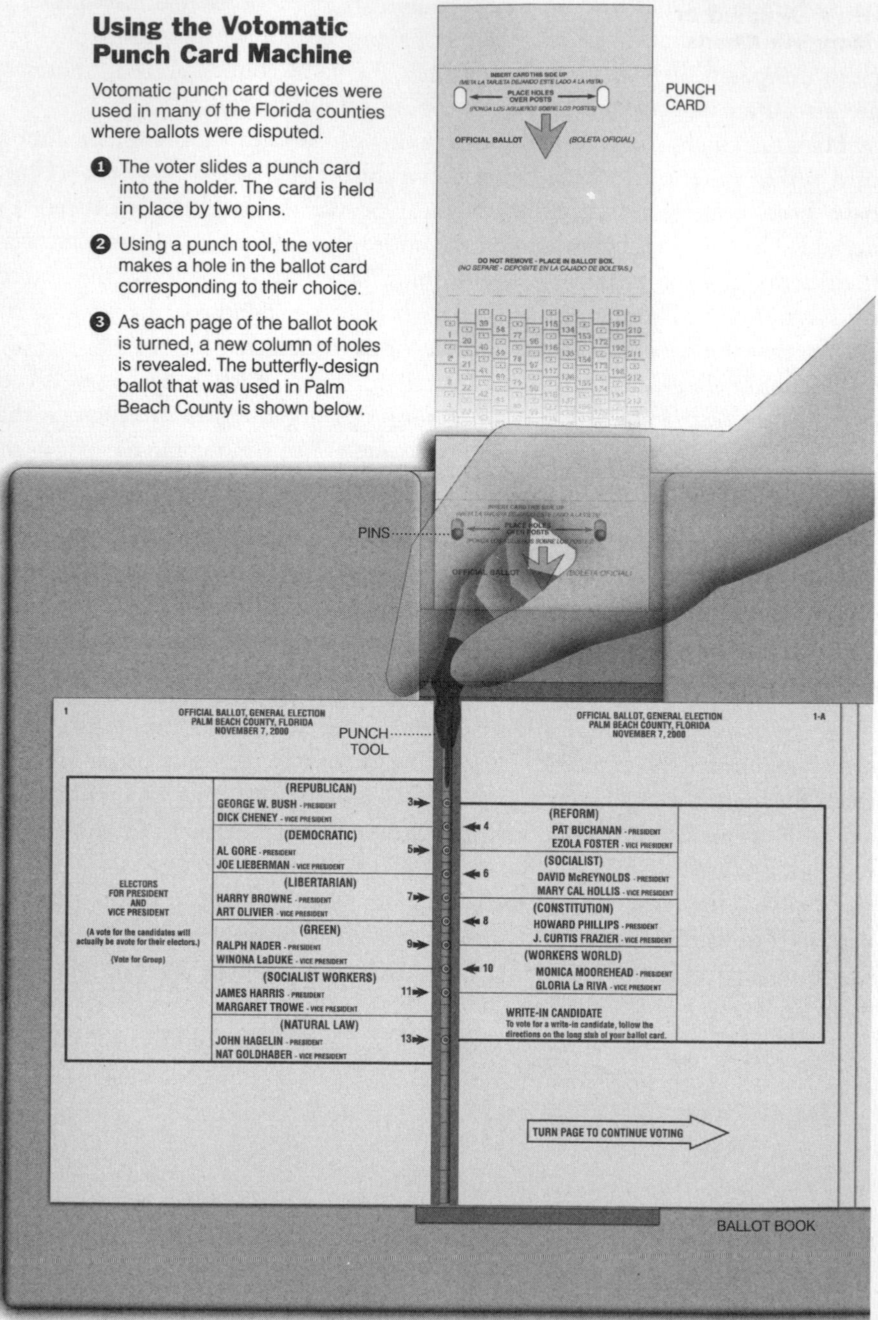

Sources: Election Resources Corporation; Election Systems and Software; Sequoia Pacific

Archie Tse/The New York Times

How Dimpled or Hanging Chads Could Be Created

There are at least two reasons dimpled or hanging chads could have been created in the punch-card voting machines used in Florida: aging parts and misalignments.

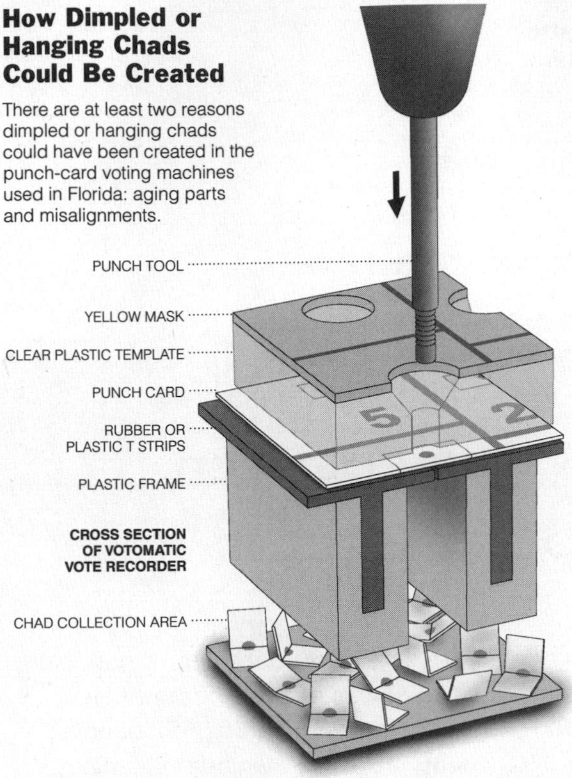

HOW IT SHOULD WORK

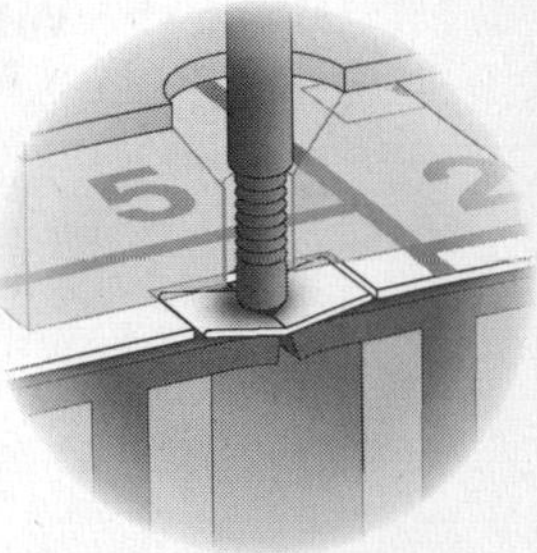

❶ The mask and template direct the point of the punch tool to the center of the chad and through two T strips.

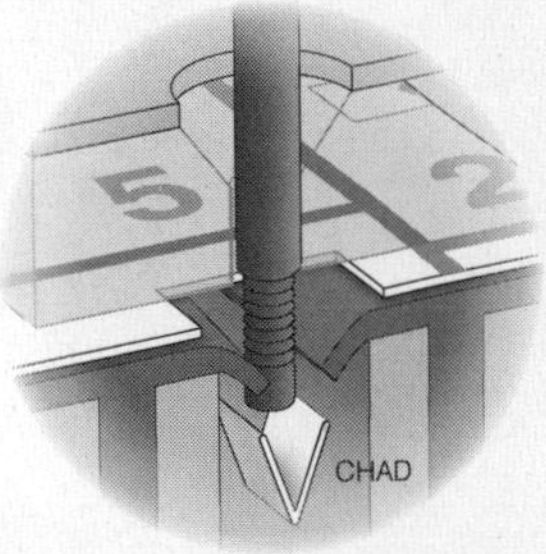

❷ The strips keep the chad from staying attached to the card. The chad falls into the collection area.

THE PROBLEMS

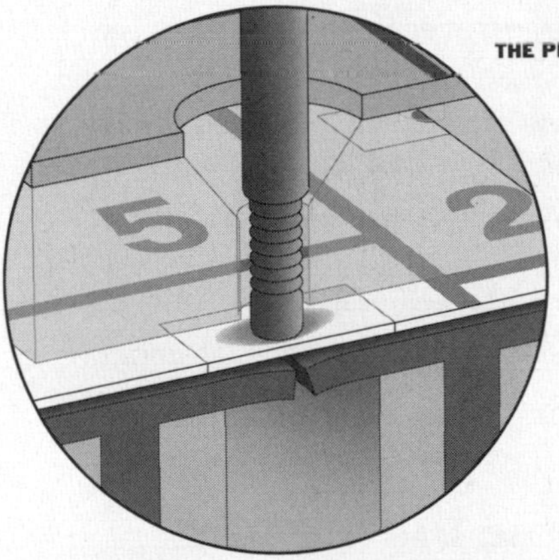

AGING PARTS *As the T strips age, they may become too stiff to allow the chad to pass through, creating a dimpled chad.*

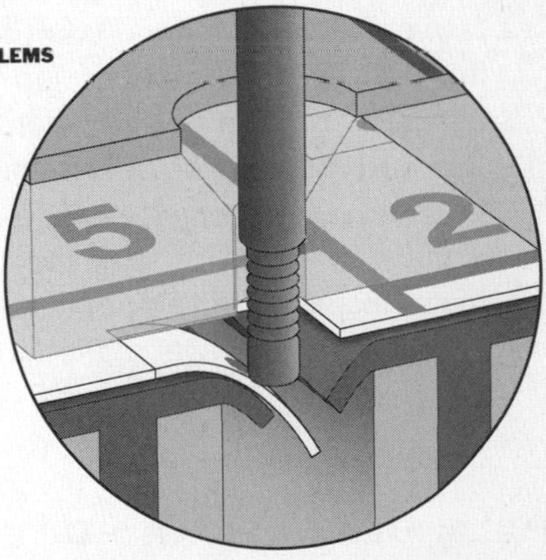

MISALIGNMENT *If anything is misaligned, the punch tool may only press on one side of the chad, creating a hanging chad.*

Sources: Florida Division of Elections; Election Resources Corporation; Election Systems and Software; Sequoia Pacific Archie Tse/The New York Times

day

5

SUNDAY,

NOVEMBER 12TH

★ ★ ★ ★ ★

AN UNPRECEDENTED RECOUNT BEGINS

After a twelve-hour recount of 1 percent of the county's ballots produces 55 new votes for Al Gore, the Palm Beach County election board calls for a hand recount of the county's 462,657 ballots. Soon the board can be seen examining those hanging rectangles most of the world will soon know as "chads." Later that morning lawyers arrive in federal court to argue over Bush's efforts to block any such recounts. Spokesmen for Bush and Gore again take to the airwaves in sharp disagreement over how to end the deadlock. In Broward County, however, the possibility of another enormous hand recount emerges, while a new controversy arises in Seminole County when it is revealed that a Republican election supervisor allowed Republican Party officials to add missing voter identification numbers to absentee ballot applications, a practice Democrats charge is illegal under Florida law.

PALM BEACH BOARD DOES THE UNTHINKABLE

WEST PALM BEACH — The presidency of the United States could be determined here by a margin of votes counted not by machines, but by people. Shortly after 2 a.m. this morning, the Palm Beach County Canvassing Board approved an unprecedented hand recount of all 462,657 presidential ballots, saying it was the only way to determine the true intent of all the voters. With recounts also set to begin Monday [Nov. 14] in Broward County (Fort Lauderdale) and a possible recount this week in Miami, it now appears that the nation's highest office could be determined by a hanging speck of paper from a single ballot.

And that prospect has the Republicans angry and frightened, saying that there are no uniform standards in Florida to govern hand recounts of the ballots conducted by local canvassing boards. They also say that the process is fraught with potential for human error and even mischief. "What's happening in Palm Beach is exactly why our nation switched from hand counting ballots to the more precise, less subjective counts done by precision machines," said Ari Fleischer, a spokesman for the Bush campaign. James A. Baker III said the machines remove political shenanigans from the process of counting ballots. "Machines are neither Republicans nor Democrats," Baker has said repeatedly this weekend. "And therefore can be neither consciously nor unconsciously biased."

"Do you brush these votes under the rug?"

—recount supporter Pat Jones, of Clayton, Ga.

But machines are not perfect. Three machine counts of all the votes in Palm Beach County have produced three different results. The second machine recount in Palm Beach County was conducted Saturday and early today. Although it was demanded by the Bush campaign, it actually cost Governor Bush three votes. Bush had 152,954 votes in Palm Beach County after the first mandatory recount, concluded last Wednesday. But the second mandatory recount, completed early today, gave Bush 152,951 votes.

Gore campaign lawyers and local Democrats acknowledged that the hand recount here was often frustrating, but they said that enduring the process was worth the effort to ensure that every last voter's voice was recorded. "It was the most open example of democracy in action that one could imagine," said Bruce Rogow, a lawyer who represents the county's elections supervisor, Theresa LePore, a Democrat, who is held responsible for the butterfly ballot design some voters called confusing.

The recount in Palm Beach had some Democrats celebrating as if they had won already, and others optimistic that a statewide recount is all but a sure thing for Gore.

The hand count was conducted in one precinct chosen by the county, in Palm Beach Gardens, and three precincts chosen by the Democratic Party — two in Boca Raton and one in Delray Beach. They were selected because party officials determined each one had high numbers of "undervotes," the ballots that the machines did not detect any vote for president. Democratic officials said they believed they could gain the most votes for Gore through the "undervotes."

The marathon hand recount of the four precincts, which represent about 1 percent of the county's total vote, was conducted by three members of the local canvassing board who tried to determine each voter's intent by carefully scrutinizing the tiny rectangles known as chads — one-eighth of an inch long — punched on the ballots.

They decided, one by one, whether a ballot was a valid vote based on whether they could see a "hanging chad," which is a hole punched partly through a ballot, or a "pregnant chad," which is only an indentation created when the voter failed to pierce the ballot. A "hanging" chad is a legal vote. A "pregnant" chad is not.

The board — made up of a county commissioner, Carol Roberts, a county judge, Charles E. Burton, and LePore, the election supervisor (all Democrats) — presided over a confusing process in which the rules for what constituted a vote shifted in the middle of the day. When the hand count began shortly before 2 p.m. Saturday, the elections officials used the "sunshine" rule, meaning they looked to see whether a sliver of light peeked through a ballot punch. If it did, the vote counted.

But midway through the first precinct, after Gore had quickly compiled a net gain of 11 votes, the Republicans objected, and the canvassing officials agreed that the standard was incorrect. Instead, elections officials followed a 1990 county rule that said sunlight could be used as a guide, but votes would be counted only if a chad was found to be hanging. If the box was merely indented, the vote would not count, assuming that the voter may have placed the tiny stylus in the position but then decided not to punch through. Democrats complained about the rule change, saying that if the rules had remained the same, Gore would have added even more votes.

The vote counting was a painstakingly slow process. Bracketed by Republican and Democratic observers and lawyers who watched every move, the elections officials here scrutinized every ballot, sometimes holding them up to the light to see if they could see through them — even if the tear in the ballot was not much bigger than a pinhole. They passed the ballots among them, holding them gingerly and squinting at them carefully. When the board rejected a ballot, Democrats almost always challenged the decision, but that could be explained by the fact that there were far more possible votes for Gore than Bush.

The canvassing board took careful note of the "double votes" when voters punched their ballots for two or more presidential candidates. The vast majority of double votes were for Gore and Patrick J. Buchanan, and many voters here complained that they were confused by the ballot design, and unintentionally voted for Buchanan.

After the recount, the tension continued. The canvassing board immediately met to decide how it would respond to the new totals. That meeting lasted nearly two hours, to just before 2 a.m. With more than a hundred bleary-eyed reporters and expectant voters looking on, Roberts asked for a vote on a countywide recount. Judge Burton, who was appointed by Gov. Jeb Bush, argued that it would be premature to call for a vote then, and asked for an advisory opinion from the Florida secretary of state. "I would like to be more fully informed before this board makes such a serious decision that affects the whole country," he said.

Mark Wallace, a lawyer for the Republican Party, asked the board to reject the countywide recount. "It was pandemonium today," Wallace said. "We vigorously lodge our protest and plead with you not to put the county through that."

But Roberts repeatedly insisted on a vote, arguing that all the voters' voices should be heard, and that a countywide recount would ensure that. The vote was 2 to 1 for a countywide recount, with Judge Burton the dissenting vote.

It was the only moral outcome, said Pat Jones, 53, who came here from Clayton, Ga., to support the recount. "Do you brush these votes under the rug?" she said.

Nov. 13, 2000, Don Van Natta Jr. and Rick Bragg

Broward County Might Do Its Own Hand Recount

"We're in every other country telling them to watch their ballot box and we can't even watch our own."

– Anonymous Broward County voter

★ ★ ★

FORT LAUDERDALE — A funny thing happened at the polls here and in many other sites in Broward County last week. After waiting in long lines caused by heavy turnout, 6,686 people stepped into the voting booths and then, if the results are to be believed, did not vote for president.

The Republicans say they believe the counting machines. The Democrats say a hand recount will prove that it is a matter of poorly set equipment or "hanging chads" that led to thousands of uncounted votes for president. The dispute might be resolved on Monday when county officials plan to inspect a sampling of ballots.

Broward is now poised for the same storm that has swamped its neighbor Palm Beach County, 20 miles to the north, which is undergoing a manual recount for a different reason. Its "butterfly" ballot was accused of misleading supporters of Vice President Al Gore into voting for Patrick J. Buchanan. Broward County did not use the butterfly ballots.

In Broward, Republicans contend that many voters routinely opt to pass on some races and that the unpunched ballots are a perennial phenomenon. Certainly, some counties in Florida this year reported similar numbers of ballots on which no choice for president was punched.

But a weekend tour of this county, famous for its spring-break events and docked cruise ships, turned up mostly people with strong political convictions, people who take sides. If anyone who actually voted decided to skip the race for president, no one was admitting it.

At a break in services at the 15th Street Church of Christ in Pompano Beach today, the pastor, the Rev. Matthew Moore, saw heads shaking no when he asked his flock if anyone had flipped past the first page of the ballot. "There was no apathy of voting in this county, let me tell you," Moore, a 75-year-old evangelist, said later. "The people went to the polls and they voted." Lenny DeGeorge, 45, who owns the L Coin Laundry a few miles west, said: "Everyone who comes in here is involved in issues. Very astute, sharp."

After a big voter turnout that topped 66 percent, many people here have not bothered to take down their campaign posters. "I think everybody had a personal interest in the presidential race, especially black folks," said the Rev. Aaron Wiggins, a Baptist pastor, except on Saturdays when he serves roadside ribs in Pompano Beach.

Broward hardly stood out in Election Day tumult. The county has swelled to an estimated 1.4 million people, causing some of its 609 precincts to burst at the seams. But it was the 6,686 ballots with seemingly no vote for president — out of 558,007 ballots cast — that caught the attention of local and state Democrats. "We don't believe that any people came to vote and didn't vote on the presidential race," said former Congressman Larry Smith, now a lobbyist and a Democratic activist. There certainly was not much else on the ballot to draw such a large turnout, Smith said. The United States Senate race was notable, but a local park referendum handily passed.

Nonsense, said the Republican county chairman, Ed Pozzuoli. "Look, we heard throughout the campaign a lot of people say George W. Bush doesn't thrill me because fill in the blank, Al Gore doesn't thrill because fill in the blank, and Ralph Nader isn't a serious candidate," Pozzuoli said. "So what's the best way for me to say I'm going to vote for 'none of the above?' Why is that so impossible?"

Down the boulevard at John's Barber Shop in Pompano Beach, John Moss, the owner, held up his shears for a moment to disagree. "Anybody who went to the polls and didn't vote for nobody has to be about the dumbest person in the world," Moss said. "That isn't what happened."

The Democrats are banking on that. Unless a court intercedes, the Broward canvassing board at 2 p.m. on Monday will manually recount the ballots cast in three precincts: one in the largely black neighborhood around the 15th Street Church of Christ, and two in the Wynmoor retirement complex. The three precincts combined had 85 ballots with no presidential choice punched, or 2 percent of the ballots cast, compared with the 1.1 percent average countywide. All three precincts are heavily Democratic, 91 percent on average. Democratic officials did not dispute the obvious: that any new votes found by scrutinizing the ballots would be for Gore.

It is not clear how this year's election compares with the last presidential race. County attorneys said that only Ms. Carroll, the election supervisor, had that information, and that she was on her way home from North Carolina after having left for a vacation last week. In any election, the attorneys said, disqualified ballots would include unpunched ballots, as well as those in which people voted for more than one candidate.

Nov. 13, 2000, Michael Moss and Dana Canedy

AWAITING COURT, BOTH SIDES SPIN HARD

TALLAHASSEE — The effect of the decision to do a hand recount in Palm Beach County remained unclear because, Democratic aides said, Katherine Harris would refuse to certify any vote tallies reached by manual recount and would accept only the mechanical recount automatically triggered by law last week because the election was so close. That would presumably help Bush. An official in Harris's office would say only that she would make a statement about certification on Monday, a day before the certified results are due in her office here.

Both sides are due in federal court in Miami tomorrow for a hearing before Judge Donald M. Middlebrooks on the Republicans' request for an injunction on the grounds that selective recounts in some counties would be unconstitutional under the 14th Amendment's guarantee of equal protection of the law.

Gore aides said that they would argue in federal court that the hand counts should proceed because they were allowed under Florida law and would be more accurate. They also said any disputes about the state law governing them should be heard in state and not federal court. Republicans vowed to press their claim that selective counts would be a violation of the constitutional guarantee to equal protection of the law, and refused to rule out seeking recounts in Republican-dominated Florida counties and in other states like Iowa, Wisconsin and Oregon where Gore's advantage is slim.

Bush's chief representative here, James A. Baker III, called the stalemate "a black mark on our democracy and our process." He said the Republicans would drop their request for an injunction to block the hand recounts if the Democrats would stop the recounts and agree to abide by last week's mandatory statewide automated recount, plus the overseas absentee ballots, which Republicans have said they expect to break in their favor.

"Whoever wins then, wins," Baker said Sunday on the NBC News program *Meet the Press*. "We will accept that result." Speaking on the CBS News program *Face the Nation*, he added that there were "no uniform standards, no objective standards, simply no standards to guide these elected officials" in the hand recounts, which he said would be subject to error or mischief.

The Bush camp seized on the tableau of the manual recount of sample precincts in Palm Beach, which stretched into the early morning hours Sunday and involved officials peering at paper punch cards to check for snagged perforations and then arguing about the results, as an example of the kind of chaos that could ensue. "No matter whether Governor Bush gains or loses votes, the confusion on display in Palm Beach County demonstrates that the results of this hand recount will be flawed," said a Bush spokesman, Ari Fleischer.

Warren Christopher, Gore's chief legal adviser in the recount, said the manual recounts were proper under Florida law. "This is a procedure that is not only common around the country, but it's a very open procedure," Christopher said on "Meet the Press." "They had the press in there, they had a pool of press persons sitting there, they had . . . observers from both parties." He added that he believed the issue could be resolved in "a matter of days — not weeks, not months." But Gore's campaign chairman, William M. Daley, declined to rule any options in or out, or to accept Baker's challenge. "The decision has not been made yet," Daley said of the question of whether Gore would seek to challenge disputed results in court.

In fact, one senior Republican official with ties to the Bush campaign and prominent Democratic friends said that both campaigns had come to see their struggle as an all-out war of good versus evil, right versus wrong and playing fair versus playing dirty, with no easy choices. "How could they be feeling anything but apprehensive and concerned?" the official asked of the Bush camp. "If they have options, then the other side has options. And when you think about what are their options, what are our options, your head just explodes."

Nov. 13, 2000, Todd S. Purdum

What Next? Republicans Corrected Thousands of Absentee Applications

WEST PALM BEACH — An election official in Seminole County allowed Republican Party workers to correct errors on thousands of applications for absentee ballots for Republicans, a Democratic lawyer said tonight.

The lawyer, Harry Jacobs, said the applications were missing required information and would otherwise have been invalid. But he said the election official allowed Republican campaign workers to set up shop in her office and work for several days to complete the forms.

The effect of the action by the election official, Sandra Goard, was to provide thousands of absentee ballots to Republican voters whose applications should have been rejected, the Democrats said.

And Democratic campaign officials asserted that the practice was a violation of Florida laws on the handling of absentee ballot applications. Republican officials tonight acknowledged making the changes to the applications but said Goard had broken no law in permitting it.

Bush easily carried Seminole, a suburban county north of Orlando, winning 75,677 votes compared with 59,174 for Gore. And his showing was boosted by an extraordinarily strong showing of absentee ballots; he had 4,800 more absentee ballot votes than Mr. Gore in the county. But there is no way of knowing whether the applications under scrutiny affected the final vote. Tonight, Mr. Jacobs, a member of the Democratic Executive Board, said he had filed a notice of intent to file a lawsuit against the election supervisor's office in Seminole County.

It is a common practice for the Republican and Democratic parties to send out nearly completed applications to potential absentee voters. They ask the voters to simply sign the requests for the absentee ballots and then forward the applications to the election supervisor's office. But the vendor hired by the Republican Party to prepare the applications for voters had inadvertently dropped off the voter identification numbers from thousands of applications. The voter identification number is required to obtain a ballot, according to Florida state law. And the Republican workers were allowed to fill it in.

"I don't think any partisan member — Republican or Democrat — should have been allowed to alter a request for an absentee ballot," Mr. Jacobs said tonight. Mr. Jacobs filed the notice of intent to sue on his own, but Democratic lawyers helping the recount effort have consulted with him.

James Stelling, vice chairman of the state Republican Party and chairman of the Seminole County Republican Party, said that Republican officials had spent as long as 10 days in the office.

Ms. Goard, the election supervisor, noticed that the numbers were missing from thousands of applications and informed an official of the Republican Party, Republican and Democratic lawyers in Seminole County said. "She refused to process them without the voter ID numbers, and she notified us and the party," said Mr. Stelling. "She agreed to allow us to send our own person there with our own laptop. All we used of her office was a chair."

Mr. Stelling said Michael Leech, a Republican Party employee, and Ryan Mitchell, a volunteer, were in the election supervisor's office adding the voter ID number to thousands of applications.

When asked if the Democrats were extended the same opportunity to review their voters applications for completeness, Bob Poe, the state Democratic Party chairman, snapped: "Hell no." Mr. Poe said he had complained about the practice to Ms. Goard last month, but she told him to "go fly a kite."

"She said she thought it was the appropriate thing to do," he said. "But I don't think it's fair and I don't think it's legal."

Nov. 13, 2000, Don Van Natta Jr. and Michael Moss

Some G.O.P. Leaders Question Bush's Campaign

WASHINGTON — As George W. Bush struggles to win a bare electoral margin, many prominent Republicans and party operatives are now questioning his strategy in the final days before the election. They say the campaign's top advisers were consumed with such confidence that they made crucial mistakes that probably cost Bush a comfortable victory.

The biggest complaint of many Republicans is that Bush strategists, savoring polls showing consistently that they were slightly ahead in the nationwide vote, were so certain they had locked up many battleground states that they sent the candidate on what some feared looked like a victory lap to states they had little chance of winning. That included trips to California and New Jersey in the last days of the campaign.

These Republicans said one result of the campaign's and the candidate's sense of confidence, even hubris, was that Bush took a Sunday off the trail just over a week before the election. And, they said, he did not stump as energetically as Al Gore. "Had Bush not taken that Sunday off, I don't think he'd be in this situation," said Roger Stone, a Republican strategist. "The guy thought he was coasting toward a big win."

Bill Dal Col, who ran the losing Senate campaign of Representative Rick A. Lazio in New York, said, "In the last four days in particular, Gore looked like he was running a 100-yard dash, and Bush looked like a guy who was finishing a 26-mile marathon."

Throughout the primaries and general election, the Bush campaign had been unusually confident, partly because Bush and his aides genuinely seemed to think they would win. But advisers also said they were trying to convey a sense of inevitability to Bush's candidacy. Since the election, the Bush team has done much the same thing, striking the posture of victory, which helps explain why Bush spoke last week about his planning for the transition and his aides leaked the names of potential top cabinet members.

By contrast, Gore, in part because his camp felt far less assured of a victory, concentrated far more effort in states like Florida, Wisconsin and Michigan. Even on Election Day — after 30 hours of barnstorming around the country — Gore did not sit still, calling radio stations in Western states. The Gore operation was also more aggressive in the final days in producing new commercials and emphasizing issue differences with Bush.

Even Bush operatives said, in retrospect, that they had underestimated the potency of the Democrats' get-out-the-vote operation. John Ellis, Bush's first cousin, said Bush and his aides were convinced that they would win a decisive, if not comfortable, margin and did not have to worry much about many states they ended up losing, including Pennsylvania, Wisconsin and Iowa. Ellis, who heads the election desk at the Fox News Channel, also said campaign officials thought they would pull ahead in Florida, where the results are, of course, in contention.

Ellis said Gov. Christine Todd Whitman of New Jersey led the campaign to believe it could even prevail there, a state most Republicans had written off months earlier. Others advising the campaign, he said, thought Bush could carry California. Gore won New Jersey with a resounding 56 percent of the vote, and California with 54 percent.

"There were people in the campaign who felt that with the Republican base so fired up and unified, and Governor Bush not threatening elements of the Democratic base, that the result would be even more decisive," said Ellis. "They thought they had a good shot at Pennsylvania. They thought they might eke out Michigan. They thought they'd win Wisconsin. They thought they'd win Iowa. They thought they had a shot at California."

No matter what the polls showed, from the start, Gore was known as a more relentless campaigner than Bush. It is easy after an election to second-guess decisions, especially after an outcome that could wind up being the tightest in history. Experts in both parties agree that during the campaign, the Gore camp made more stumbles and poor decisions than the Bush team. It could be that the Bush campaign was misguided by polls that did not reflect that the race was closer than either side had thought. And there is no way of knowing if a different game plan in those final days would have made a difference, or whether the much-publicized 11th-hour disclosure that Bush had been arrested for driving while intoxicated in 1976 could have had some small but telling effect.

Yet many Republican strategists agree that the campaign squandered its lead in the closing days. Scott Reed, who ran Bob Dole's campaign in 1996, said Gore was more aggressive in the end, seizing on a comment Bush made — inadvertently, his aides said — that Social Security was not a federal program. "The bottom line is Gore appeared to have a strategy to close the campaign," Reed said. "Gore closed very strong, picking up on the Bush mistakes of Social Security not being a government program. He used it in his free media and paid media to clobber us. Clearly Gore picked up a bunch of senior voters near the end."

Reed added: "These guys were spread way too thin, spending time on the West Coast, Oregon and Washington, when they never needed those states to win. It appeared they were just trying to run up the score."

Ari Fleischer, a spokesman for the Bush campaign, said Bush traveled to some states in the closing days as much to excite Republicans and help Congressional candidates as to help himself. "We made a decision at the end to do as much as possible to both win states where we might have a chance as well as to help maintain margins in Congress," Fleischer said. "Given the close margins, our efforts were successful." Asked if the campaign had regrets about the strategy, he added, "There will be plenty of time for Monday morning quarterbacking after this overtime period."

But Bush advisers were surprised by the tight race. Karl Rove, Bush's chief strategist, had told *The New York Times* two days before the election, "We're going to have a six- or seven-point victory and a substantial margin in the Electoral College of 320 votes or so."

In part of that interview that was not published, Rove, speaking by telephone from Miami, was enthusiastic about Florida. "We're here in Miami, man," he said. "It's going pretty wild!" Asked if Bush's campaigning in Florida so late suggested he was in trouble there, Rove replied: "Look, Florida's where you've got to come and campaign. We were likely to be in Florida under any scenario."

The Bush campaign was so confident, Dal Col said, that Bush mistakenly stumped in big states like California not so much so he could win those states but to assure that he would capture a clear majority in the popular vote. Now, it looks like Gore won the popular vote. "They probably thought they were in better shape than they were in those key states," said Dal Col, who was the campaign manager for Steve Forbes, who lost to Bush.

Mel Sembler, the Republicans national finance chairman who is a developer in Florida, said Bush operatives thought they were in a more comfortable position in his state. "We were maybe a little bit too confident down here," Sembler said. The reason Bush campaigned in California, he said, was to reward donors.

Ellis said campaign officials had been somewhat concerned that many of the polls did not adequately account for likely voters. Still, he said the sense was always that Bush would prevail. He said he did not expect the governor to engage in second-guessing. "George is not somebody who's going to have a big meeting and say, 'Why were we in Minnesota.' " Ellis said. "If you start opening up this stuff it doesn't do any good. The lessons are already learned."

Richard N. Bond, a former Republican national chairman, said he was puzzled at the time that Bush was not focusing more on certain battleground states but figured his advisers knew what they were doing. "I thought they were a tough, disciplined bunch and had a very good reason," Bond said.

Ronald Kaufman, a Republican committeeman from Massachusetts who is a political adviser to former President George Bush, said all the grousing is unfair. "I give these guys credit; they ran a brilliant race from beginning to end," Kaufman said. Of Gore, he added: "You can't ever forget that this guy is a sitting vice president in a great economy. I think Bush is going to be president. But I think it's going to get messy."

Nov. 13, 2000, Richard L. Berke

day

6

MONDAY,

NOVEMBER 13TH

★ ★ ★ ★ ★

HARRIS TAKES CHARGE

Amidst intense wrangling between Democrats and Republicans in and out of court over the legality of several manual recounts, Katherine Harris announces she will adhere to the deadline of 5 p.m. Tuesday [Nov. 14] for certifying the votes in the state's 67 counties. Democrats go to state court to gain an extension, arguing that Harris is arbitrarily holding to the deadline to prevent full manual recounts that might erase Bush's very thin lead. In federal court Bush receives a setback when the judge rejects his request for an injunction to stop the manual recounts. Uncertainty surrounds the future of recounts, however, as the election board in heavily Democratic Broward County votes down a proposal to conduct a county-wide manual recount. Palm Beach County election officials on the other hand begin to make plans for a manual recount of the county's nearly half million votes, and Volusia County officials say they are almost finished with a recount of 185,000 votes. With the Gore camp urging patience and Bush's people saying it's time to end the counting, a Times/CBS poll indicates that Americans are divided essentially along partisan lines in their assessment of the post-election struggle, but are not alarmed by the impasse.

Democrats Scramble over Tuesday Deadline

TALLAHASSEE — The disputed presidential election results were thrown into new uncertainty today when Florida's Republican secretary of state declared that she would enforce a Tuesday evening legal deadline for certifying the statewide vote, even as predominantly Democratic counties moved forward with hand recounts of ballots that might not be finished in time and both sides wrangled in court.

Katherine Harris met briefly with both camps this morning and then issued a two-page statement that she presented as a simple recitation of her duties under the law. But in the politically charged reality here, Harris's statement also amounted to a tactical line in the sand, one that the Texas governor's legal advisers hope could force the Democrats to finish whatever recounting they hope to do in less than 36 hours and freeze the official results in the Republicans' favor.

A running tally by The Associated Press of the recounts to date showed Bush with a lead of 388 votes out of some 6 million cast statewide.

> *"I would not want to win the presidency by a few votes cast in error or misinterpreted or not counted, and I don't think Governor Bush wants that either. While time is important, it is even more important that every vote is counted and counted accurately."*
>
> —*Al Gore*

Democrats argued that Florida law gave Harris flexibility to wait at least until Friday [Nov. 17], when the deadline expires for overseas absentee ballots to arrive in Florida. "Her plan, I'm afraid, has the look of an effort to produce a particular result in the election rather than to ensure that the voice of all the citizens of the state would be heard," Warren M. Christopher said this afternoon. "It also looks like a move in the direction of partisan politics and away from the nonpartisan administration of the election laws."

Jeb Bush recused himself last week from serving on the three-member state Election Canvassing Commission, which includes Harris and the state director of elections, Clay Roberts, a Republican appointee, and is responsible for certifying the final vote. But the governor's replacement, Robert Crawford, the Democratic agriculture commissioner, is a Bush ally who said today that he was required to enforce the deadline.

There was considerable confusion about just what would happen if a county's tallies were not finished by the Tuesday deadline. One section of the state's election law, governing the canvassing board, stipulates that all counties missing by the deadline "shall be ignored, and the results shown by the returns on file shall be certified." The following section of the statute, adopted subsequently, states that such returns "may be ignored" by the Department of State "and the results on file at that time may be certified."

Harris said the law gave her no discretion to extend the deadline, except possibly in the event of a natural disaster like Hurricane Andrew, when compliance would be impossible, though the law makes no such specific exception. Her statement said, "But a close election, regardless of the identity of the candidates, is not such a circumstance; the law provides for automatic recounts, protests, and manual recounts, and it plainly states when this process must end."

But this afternoon, lawyers for Palm Beach and Volusia Counties, Democratic strongholds where Gore is ahead in the vote, told Judge Terry P. Lewis of the state's Circuit Court that Harris was arbitrarily imposing a deadline even as the hand count went on, and Dexter Douglass, a lawyer for the Gore campaign, ridiculed Harris's reasoning.

"The issue is," said Douglass, "does Florida stand up for an honest vote, that people in other countries can look to and say that the United States has honest elections, or are there elections where some bureaucrat writes a letter and says, you lose, your vote doesn't count."

Under sharp questioning from Judge Lewis, lawyers for Harris acknowledged that the second section of the law did give the state some leeway in the timing of the certification. The judge expressed a good deal of skepticism that there was any point in certifying the results on Tuesday, while waiting until Friday to certify a winner.

Although Judge Lewis gave no indication of how he would rule, his questions made it clear that he saw no reason a county should not have enough time for a manual recount. "How could you conceivably do a manual recount in a large county without enough time?" he asked a Bush campaign lawyer. "It seems kind of futile to give someone an option for a manual recount, but no opportunity to do it."

For her part, Harris sent workers from her office to election supervisors' offices in each of the state's 67 counties, so they would be available to receive the latest returns by the Tuesday deadline. "They will remain in the offices of those supervisors of elections until 5 p.m. tomorrow in order to be available to officially receive the certified returns of that county until the last moment, thus providing the maximum possible time for recounting and certification," she said in her statement.

Harris also said she would ask county election officials to certify the results of the overseas absentee ballots by Saturday morning at the latest. "Therefore, I anticipate that the presidential election in Florida will be officially certified by Saturday afternoon, barring judicial intervention," she said.

Nearly a week after the election to choose the 43rd president, Gore made his first public comment about the Florida situation, addressing reporters outside the West Wing of the White House this afternoon. He said it was important to "spend the days necessary" to determine the winner in his bitterly close race against George W. Bush.

"I would not want to win the presidency by a few votes cast in error or misinterpreted or not counted, and I don't think Governor Bush wants that either," Gore said, adding: "While time is important, it is even more important that every vote is counted and counted accurately."

Bush remained in relative seclusion at his ranch near Waco and made no public appearances. But his camp has suggested that it would carry its fight to block the hand recounts all the way to the United States Supreme Court if necessary.

In the swirling atmosphere of recriminations, each side turned familiar arguments against the other. The Bush partisans accused the Gore camp of seeking loopholes in the Florida laws it had cited as controlling the situation in federal court just this morning. Top Gore advisers rebutted the Bush camp's repeated assertions that the vice president wants to keep counting until he likes the result by accusing the Bush forces of trying to cut off the count while Bush is ahead, in an effort to guarantee their desired outcome.

Nov. 14, 2000, Todd S. Purdum and David Firestone

FEDERAL JUDGE DEFERS TO STATE COURT

MIAMI — After hearing two hours of argument about the nexus between democracy and chads, a federal judge paused barely an instant today before handing Al Gore an important victory in the first courtroom battle of the post-election. The hearing before the judge, Donald M. Middlebrooks of Federal District Court here, gave life to the very circumstance that the campaigns had said they hoped to avoid: the transformation of presidential candidates into litigants and the relinquishment of this year's uncertain outcome to lawyers and judges.

Judge Middlebrooks denied Bush's request for an injunction that would have stopped the manual recounting of ballots in Florida counties. The judge rejected Bush's lawsuit largely on the ground that it was more appropriately considered by the state courts than the federal courts, which typically shy away from becoming involved in state and local elections. "These are serious arguments," Judge Middlebrooks wrote in his order. "The question becomes who should consider them." He added, "Intervention by a federal district court, particularly on a preliminary basis, is inappropriate." But he made it clear that he also was not persuaded on the merits.

Lawyers for Bush had argued that Florida's manual recount laws subject the tally to capriciousness by allowing some, but not all, counties to recount by hand and by allowing counties to set standards for what constitutes a legal vote. But Judge Middlebrooks wrote in his order that the recount procedures allowed by Florida law "appear to be neutral." He added, "The state election scheme is reasonable and nondiscriminatory on its face."

The state's manual recount provision, he found, "is intended to safeguard the integrity and reliability of the electoral process." Unless all counties use the same automatic tabulation system, he said, there will always be local discrepancies. And he addressed the Bush campaign's claim about the dilution of votes. "The provision strives to strengthen rather than dilute the right to vote," the judge wrote, "by securing, as near as humanly possible, an accurate and true reflection of the will of the electorate."

The judge issued his ruling immediately after a more than two-hour hearing and followed it with a 24-page written order. His decision allowed election officials in Palm Beach and Volusia Counties to continue with the hand recounts that were requested last week by the Democrats. The canvassing board in Miami-Dade County is to hold a hearing on Tuesday to decide whether to grant a recount request by that county's Democratic Party.

A total of 30 lawyers — seven for the plaintiffs and 23 for various defendants and intervening parties — squeezed around tables before the judge's bench today. They included Laurence H. Tribe, an expert in constitutional law at Harvard Law School, who represented Gore, and Alan M. Dershowitz, also a Harvard law professor, who represented a group of Palm Beach voters. In a race that was not particularly close, both men beat the lead defense lawyer, Bruce S. Rogow of Fort Lauderdale, Fla., to the television cameras outside the courthouse.

But the morning also included lighthearted exchanges, most having to do with lawyerly explanations of the idiosyncrasies of chads, the tiny flecks of punch-card ballots. When Rogow began, he said that his adversary, Theodore Olson, had "put the chad before the horse."

Gore's team used today's ruling to encourage the Bush campaign to drop its lawsuit. "We were very pleased naturally by this decision," said Warren Christopher, "and hope the Bush campaign will reconsider its efforts." But the Bush camp gave no quarter. In Austin, Tex., Bush's spokeswoman, Karen P. Hughes, said all America wants a fair and accurate count in Florida. But, she said, "we are increasingly convinced that a manual recount, which is now under way in selective, heavily Democratic, hand-selected counties, cannot produce that fair and accurate result."

Nov. 14, 2000, Kevin Sack

PALM BEACH COUNTY PREPARES TO RECOUNT 462,587 VOTES

WEST PALM BEACH — There were so many lawyers jammed into Courtroom 4C here today that they filled every seat in the jury box and the first three rows of the gallery. One lawyer even sat, cross-legged, on the carpeted floor. The 50 lawyers had come to Palm Beach County Circuit Court for a hearing in the six lawsuits filed by voters who have challenged the fairness of last Tuesday's election here, especially the county's controversial and allegedly confusing "butterfly" ballot.

But the hearing did not last long. The judge, Stephen A. Rapp, recused himself after a lawyer for several voters claimed that the judge made derogatory comments last week about the Democrats and Palm Beach County voters. In a signed affidavit, one lawyer said he overheard Judge Rapp saying, in a courthouse elevator on Election Day, that by voting he was doing his part to "make sure the Democrats are run out of the White House." He also purportedly made a negative comment about Hillary Rodham Clinton, the lawyer said. In another signed affidavit, a second lawyer said he heard Judge Rapp saying, from the bench, at 8:20 a.m. on Nov. 8 that any voter who mistakenly voted for the wrong presidential candidate was "stupid" and did not deserve the right to vote.

In announcing that he would recuse himself, Judge Rapp denied all the accusations. The cases were immediately assigned to another circuit judge, Catherine M. Brunson. The recusal amounted to another delay of lawsuits filed by voters who seek a re-vote in Palm Beach County.

Earlier today, Palm Beach County election officials said they would begin the immense task of a manual recount of the county's 462,587 votes at 7 a.m. on Tuesday.

Canvassing board members estimated that the recount could last until late Sunday, five days after Tuesday's 5 p.m. deadline set by Katherine Harris, for the certification of all 67 Florida counties' votes. Palm Beach officials today joined a lawsuit filed by Volusia County seeking to extend the Tuesday deadline.

The Palm Beach count will be conducted at the county's emergency operations center. "An appropriate place for another recount," Bush campaign spokesman Ari Fleischer said. Election officials here spent the day busily preparing for what they said would be six consecutive days of 14-hour shifts. Teams of workers will work seven-hour shifts each day.

At a late afternoon rally in downtown West Palm Beach that attracted whites, blacks, Hispanics and Jews, the Rev. Jesse Jackson drew cheers when he said democracy must be "transparent." Jackson said what was happening in Palm Beach County was not a constitutional crisis, but a simple matter of making sure that every vote counted. Earlier in the afternoon, some 2,000 people gathered in the city's downtown to prepare for the short march to a bayside amphitheater for the rally. They waved signs stenciled with references to chads, which have become part of the vernacular in Florida and around the country since the election.

"It's the illegal ballot, stupid," read one.

Nov. 14, 2000, Don Van Natta Jr. and Rick Bragg

After a Partial Recount, Broward County Drops the Whole Idea

After a full day of partisan bickering and hand counting of 4,000 ballots, Vice President Al Gore today picked up only four votes in the heavily Democratic Broward County, and officials declined to order a broader recount of all the county's ballots.

Democrats had hoped that today's recount would prompt a full examination of all ballots cast in the county last Tuesday, when Gore received 386,561 votes to 117,323 for Bush. But one of the Democrats on the canvassing board, Judge Robert Lee, sided with the lone Republican to vote against the broader count. The Democratic National Committee said tonight that it would go to court Tuesday to seek to overturn the board.

Judge Lee said he voted against a broad recount after reading an opinion by the state's director of elections, L. Clayton Roberts, that said a full-scale manual recount would be warranted only in the event that "the vote tabulation system fails to count properly marked" ballots. Suzanne Gunzburger, the other Democrat on the three-member canvassing board, voted for a broader recount saying, "I'm saddened that the people who really wanted to vote for president didn't have their votes counted."

The count of 4,000 ballots, about 1 percent of the county's total, began this afternoon after officials spent nearly an hour and a half debating the procedures they would use. The board debated at length when a partially punched ballot would be counted as an acceptable vote and when a baellot marking would be considered too ambiguous and therefore invalid. There was even debate over whether the doors to the meeting room had to be open to comply with Florida's Sunshine Law, which mandates public access to official governmental meetings. For about an hour, reporters were barred from the proceedings until several reporters called their lawyers on cellular phones. Soon after, the room where the recount was taking place was opened to the press but not to the public at large.

Broward's partial recount was ordered after officials in the largely Democratic county realized that more than 6,600 ballots registered no selection in the presidential race because punch holes were not pressed through fully.

Nov. 14, 2000, Dana Canedy

Volusia County's Recount Discovers 320 New Ballots

DeLAND, Fla. — Volusia County tonight neared the end of its hand count of 184,339 ballots cast in the presidential election last Tuesday, and gave new details about an initially unrecorded batch of 320 votes. Just before 5:30 p.m. today, teams of county workers, flanked by Democratic and Republican observers, finished their share of the work in the manual recount. But much of the more difficult task remained: the three-member county canvassing board, overseeing the tally, continued to inspect disputed ballots.

County officials said they did not know how many of these contested ballots remained, and declined to give an estimate. But board members said they expected to finish on Tuesday, in time to certify the vote and submit results to state election officials by the 5 p.m. deadline. Nevertheless county officials were hedging their bets. Lawyers from the county attorney's office were in a state court in Tallahassee, along with representatives of Palm Beach County, challenging a decision by Katherine Harris that the deadline could not be extended. Judge Terry Lewis said he expected to issue a ruling on Tuesday morning.

In partial figures released tonight, the recount had been completed in 140 of Volusia County's 172 precincts and, after resolution of ballot disputes, had brought Gore a net gain of 24 votes beyond his margin of last Tuesday, when he won the county with 97,063 votes, to 82,214 for Bush.

The recount results released tonight were significantly different from those of Sunday night, which showed Bush with a net gain of 33. Those results followed the discovery of the 320 ballots that had at first gone unreported. Those ballots, the first cast by voters at one precinct in DeBary, a town in the southwest corner of this central Florida county, were discovered during the manual recount.

Neither the initial machine count last Tuesday nor a state-mandated reinspection of that tally a day later detected the missing ballots because, county officials said today, the electronic voting machine inexplicably shut down sometime between 7 a.m. and 9 a.m. on Election Day. In effect, the machine forgot about the first 320 ballots.

When the problem was discovered, the precinct clerk, Rosemary Obenland, tried to alert county election officials but was apparently unable to get through on the telephone. The precinct clerk simply noted the problem on her ballot accounting form, county officials said. Normally, the officials said, members of the canvassing board would have inspected the accounting forms well before now, and discovered the unrecorded ballots then, had they not been busy doing the manual recount instead.

Having vigorously defended their machine tally until late Sunday night, county officials this morning acknowledged embarrassment but insisted that the missing votes would have been discovered before certification in any case. "We are out of sequence in the process," said a county spokesman, David Byron. "This would have been rectified, and it will be rectified before board certification."

Nov. 14, 2000, Somini Sengupta

Poll: Americans Are Divided but Calm

Americans are polarized along party lines over whether Gov. George W. Bush or Vice President Al Gore should rightfully claim the presidency, but they are not panicked over the uncertainty and expect the battling to continue for days if not for the next month, the latest *New York Times*/CBS News Poll shows.

The public is not gripped by the sense of urgency that has marked statements from some campaign officials, lawyers and academics — as well as news coverage — decrying the demise of the political system if the stalemate persists. Six out of 10 Americans say the lack of resolution is not a colossal problem for the country right now. And most voters say they are confident that their own votes were counted properly.

Strikingly, the sentiment of voters is as divided along partisan lines as it was in polls before the election, and on Election Day itself. People who voted for Bush say he is the deserving winner; those who backed Gore say their man is. On question after question, the gulf remained. Gore voters said, overwhelmingly, that they did not approve of how the Bush campaign has handled the unsettled election. Bush voters, by wide margins, said they did not approve of how the Gore campaign has handled things.

Asked whether the confusion and bewilderment created by the "butterfly" ballot in Palm Beach County — where the Gore camp contends the vice president won more votes than the number initially reported — should result in a new election for the county, most Gore voters said there should be a second election. But most of Bush's backers said there should not be another election.

The nationwide telephone poll was taken Friday through Sunday of 1,720 adults who had been first contacted before the election for polls for *The Times* and CBS News. The survey has a margin of sampling error of plus or minus three percentage points.

The patience among Americans seemed to play into the Gore campaign's strategy emphasizing that the nation should take the necessary time to determine which candidate actually prevailed in Florida — and in electoral votes nationwide. It was a message voiced again yesterday by Gore, who said at the White House, "While time is important, it is even more important that every vote is counted and counted accurately."

Despite the partisan divide, many Americans accuse both camps of playing politics with the impasse, and they blame the Gore side slightly more than the Bush side.

Americans, particularly Democrats, say Bush should refrain from his public moves to begin assembling a new administration, which his advisers say are partially designed to convey a sense of inevitability that he will be president.

But many Americans, especially Republicans, objected to the Democrats' challenge to the results in Florida. They say that the challenge was not motivated by a sense that the election was conducted unfairly but because Democrats did not like the outcome.

If one candidate wins the electoral vote and the other wins the popular vote, Americans said in the *Times*/CBS Poll that the winner of the popular vote should become president. Under the Constitution, of course, the popular vote is immaterial and the winner must prevail in the electoral vote. But that public sentiment is helping drive the public relations strategy of the Gore campaign. Gore is leading in the popular vote, at least for now, and his advisers say if he does not become president that would thwart the will of the people.

Still, a majority of Americans say that even if the loser of the popular vote becomes president, that should not hamper his ability to lead effectively.

The predicament over the presidency has revived a public debate over whether the Electoral College — created by the Founding Fathers in 1787 in part to protect states from encroaching federal power — is obsolete and should be replaced by the popular vote. Most Americans said they would like to see the Constitution amended to abolish the Electoral College. But the limited number of questions in the poll did not allow for a particularly full examination of the issue.

The public is monitoring the wrangling of the Gore and Bush camps with an intensity similar to how they observed the closing days of the election. Americans are somewhat interested, but hardly alarmed. A little more than half say they are paying very close attention, about the same number that were paying a lot of attention to the campaign itself in the closing days.

More than half of the people who did not vote last Tuesday now say that given the suspense — and the sense that people's votes did count — they wish they had voted.

Nov. 14, 2000, Richard L. Berke and Janet Elder

day

7

TUESDAY,

NOVEMBER 14TH

HARRIS UPS THE ANTE

Leon County Circuit Court Judge Terry P. Lewis issues a ruling regarding the requirement that vote totals for all 67 counties must be filed by 5 p.m. Tuesday. With Bush's lead at only 300 votes, Republicans are pleased by the ruling's assertion that Katherine Harris has the authority to insist that all counties file their totals by that deadline. Democrats take heart in his statement that Harris has the discretion to accept amended totals based on manual recounts after the deadline. They are also buoyed by the arrival of David Boies, whose legal reputation is formidable. Meanwhile, Palm Beach County prepares for a countywide hand recount of nearly half a million votes. In Broward County, officials vote to reconsider their earlier decision not to hold a countywide manual recount.

DEMOCRATS DISPUTE FRIDAY DEADLINE

TALLAHASSEE — The Florida secretary of state announced tonight that she would comply with a state judge's order to consider results of further recounts in the disputed presidential election, but she gave the two Democratic counties that are moving ahead with, or considering, a time-consuming hand recount a deadline of 2 p.m. Wednesday to explain their reasons in writing.

After eight days of deadlock, the decision by Katherine Harris propelled the situation to a critical turn. Allies of Al Gore forged ahead with the hand recounts and possible further court challenges, but aides to George W. Bush claimed to see the end in sight.

At about 7:40 p.m., Harris appeared on national television to announce that with all 67 counties reporting by the legal deadline of 5 p.m., Bush led by 300 votes, or 2,910,492 to Gore's 2,910,192 votes, pending the counting of an unknown number of overseas absentee ballots due by midnight Friday. Her action followed a midday ruling by a state judge who upheld today's deadline for all counties to certify their votes, but said that later returns could also be considered.

"When is it going to end; I ask you when is it going to end?"

—James A. Baker III

"Unless I determine in the exercise of my discretion that these facts and circumstances contained within these written statements justify an amendment to today's officials returns, the state elections canvassing commission, in a manner consistent with its usual and normal practice, will certify statewide results reported to this office today," Harris said. "Subsequently, the overseas ballots that are due by midnight Friday will also be certified and the final results of the election for president of the United States of America in the state of Florida will be announced," Harris said.

Both sides said the judge's ruling should soon settle the question of who will carry Florida's 25 electoral votes and win the White House.

Less than an hour after Harris's announcement, Gore's campaign chairman, William M. Daley, took to the airwaves to accuse Harris of trying to cut off the count in a way "not required by the court." He said it was "just another attempt to slow this down."

It was not clear just how much authority Harris has. While Harris said she was basing her position on the ruling today in the Leon County Circuit Court, Judge Terry P. Lewis said she had discretion on whether to include any recounts in the final tally. But the judge said the local election boards had the authority to decide whether a manual recount should be done. "There is nothing," Judge Lewis said, "to prevent the county canvassing boards from filing with the secretary of state further returns after completing a manual recount. It is then up to the secretary of state, as the chief election officer, to determine whether any such corrective or supplemental returns filed after 5 p.m. today are to be ignored."

In agreeing that the counties must file their returns by tonight, Judge Lewis said he gave "great deference" to Harris's interpretation of the election law. But he disagreed that she had no discretion to count votes that arrive after that time, and said the procedures outlined in the law for contesting votes had to allow for some flexibility. "Depending on when a request is made and then acted upon, it is easy to imagine a situation where a manual recount could be lawfully authorized, commence, but not completed within seven days of the election," he wrote.

Judge Lewis said that nothing in the law compelled Harris to accept late filed returns, but he said that by announcing "ahead of time that such returns will be ignored," unless "caused by some act of God, is not the exercise of discretion; it is the abdication of that discretion."

Before Harris appeared tonight, both the Gore campaign and lawyers for Bush claimed vindication in the split ruling of Judge Lewis that all 67 Florida counties must submit their certified vote totals this evening. But both sides were banking on opposite legal strategies, with the Bush camp, which has never trailed in any statewide tally, assuming that their ally, Harris, would find ample reason to dismiss any recounts, and Gore advisers concluding that Judge Lewis's ruling left them enough room to fight on.

Harris's announcement tonight effectively upped the ante. The Bush campaign's worst nightmare is for Gore to gain a lead in any count, and it had hoped to bar recounts outright — even going into federal court in a failed effort to win an injunction. Now, if Gore should gain an overall lead in any recount, which would occur in public and be reported instantly, Harris could have a hard time rejecting the results.

Once again, in a surreal atmosphere of dueling news conferences and conference calls, political jockeying and threats of further legal jousting, the increasingly embittered rival campaigns courted advantage in public opinion. Most of the drama was carried live on television, and as the 5 p.m. deadline approached, MSNBC carried a countdown clock as if awaiting a space launching.

"When is it going to end; I ask you, when is it going to end?" James A. Baker III demanded this morning as he offered to drop his objections to including any hand-counted ballots and accept however many could be submitted by this evening if the Gore campaign would drop its effort to prolong the count. Warren Christopher dismissed that, saying it was akin to "offering you sleeves from a vest." Christopher insisted: "I see a yearning in the country for the vote to be correctly counted, and I think we're going down that path."

In his remarks this morning, Baker flatly rejected any notion of accepting a statewide hand recount of ballots, a possibility that some Gore partisans have floated as a potential compromise. And the Bush camp filed notice of its intent to appeal a federal judge's denial on Monday of its request for an injunction to block hand recounts.

"It took 15 hours to count four precincts in Palm Beach County," Baker said. "There are 6,000 precincts in the state of Florida. It would take an inordinate amount of time to count 6,000 precincts manually. Furthermore, we have made very clear since we've been here, our problem with the fundamentally flawed process of manual counting here, how it promotes — how it could lead to human error or even mischief."

It was this language in particular that the Gore legal team seized on as helping its effort to have additional manual recounts added to the final tally. "Those counts must, under this ruling, be considered by the secretary of state," Christopher said. "And we certainly hope that she would conclude that lawfully counted votes would be included in any final tabulation." New Gore lawyer David Boies added: "This is an injunction issued by a Florida Circuit Court telling her that she can't just stand firm and say, 'I'm not going to think about this after 5 p.m.' If she violates that, she violates a court order."

One Republican official close to the Bush campaign said that the campaign believed the judge's ruling will cut in its favor, because there is certain to be so much confusion and inconsistent standards in manual recounts that Harris will have ample grounds not to accept many such votes and be able to be seen as acting appropriately.

"I believe we've won," this official said. "There will be disputes within the hand recount and any discretion she exercises will benefit Gore and Bush equally."

Barely five minutes before the 5 o'clock deadline, the Democratic stronghold of Volusia County became the only county to complete a manual recount, one that awarded Gore a net gain of 98 votes, which was reflected in the secretary of state's official figures.

But election officials in another Democratic stronghold, Miami-Dade County, first conducted a sample recount of 1 percent of the precincts, then decided that a full recount was not warranted. That decision could easily dim the prospects of an ultimate Gore victory in Florida.

And in yet another development in a day of uncertainty caused by conflicting legal opinions, Palm Beach officials finally agreed to begin a full recount on Wednesday.

The Democratic Party filed a motion in Broward County arguing that the county should be ordered to conduct a full hand count of its 588,000 ballots. The motion said the decision on Monday by the county canvassing board not to conduct such a recount was based on an erroneous opinion by Harris, who said a manual recount can only be conducted if the board finds a problem with the computer that counted the ballots.

The candidates themselves stayed out of sight all day, with Gore inside his official residence in Washington. As reporters and news crews huddled in the cold outside the gates, Mrs. Gore sent out doughnuts, cookies, hot chocolate and coffee. The vice president also set up a tent outside the gate. Bush remained in semi-seclusion at his ranch near Waco, Tex., talking to advisers by phone and conducting some state business. Senior Bush aides in Austin kept a deliberately low profile, letting all public statements come from the lawyers and officials here in an apparent effort to put some distance between Bush and the wrangling.

Nov. 15, 2000, Todd S. Purdum

Palm Beach Panel Votes to Recount

"What happens then? Do we go to jail? Because I'm willing to go to jail."
– County Commissioner Carol Roberts, asking about the consequences of conducting an "unauthorized" recount

★ ★ ★

WEST PALM BEACH — Palm Beach County election officials decided today to move forward with the mammoth task of manually recounting all 462,657 ballots cast here, a process that Democrats believe could provide them the best chance of putting Al Gore in the White House. Surrounded by chanting crowds as they met in an outdoor parking lot at the county's emergency operations center to accommodate the crowd, Palm Beach election officials also voted to submit the vote totals from last Sunday's machine recount to the secretary of state, Katherine Harris, by today's deadline of 5 p.m. But, more significantly, the officials on the county's canvassing board vowed to go ahead with the second countywide recount in the state, saying they would then do everything possible to persuade Harris to accept those hand-tallied results.

County Judge Charles E. Burton, the canvassing board chairman, admonished the crowd to stay quiet, threatening to resume the meeting inside, where there was little room for the hundreds of journalists and demonstrators. He said the crowd would be forced to watch it on a county-run television station. "This is not a political rally," Judge Burton said. Before and after the judge's warning, the crowd chanted: "We want a re-vote!" The Republicans in the crowd wore T-shirts that read, "I live in Palm Beach County and I voted right."

The Democrats said they believed they could gain the most in the recount from the county's 10,361 "undervotes," ballots on which the counting machines indicated no choice for the presidential race. A manual recount could determine either a partial hole punched for a candidate or an indentation. The partial hole could be counted as a vote, the indentation could not.

Elections officials here had intended to begin the full countywide recount this morning at 7. Moments before they were scheduled to begin counting this morning, the canvassing board postponed the count. They were concerned by an advisory opinion given by L. Clayton Roberts, the director of the Division of Elections, that the planned hand count was "not authorized" because there was nothing wrong with the county's ballot machines. That opinion was contradicted by Robert A. Butterworth, the state's attorney general and co-chairman of Gore's Florida campaign, who called the recount legal.

Because of the conflicting legal opinions, lawyers for the three-member canvassing board, all Democrats, sought guidance from the Florida Supreme Court. Meanwhile, Harris's 5 p.m. deadline to certify the county's election results loomed, causing officials here to worry that the county's vote count, submitted today, would not reflect all the votes cast in Palm Beach County until after a complete manual recount.

But to accomplish that task, the lawyers had to find a county judge willing to hear nine lawsuits filed by voters challenging the legality of the county's "butterfly ballot," which they say is confusing. It was a mission that proved to be especially frustrating as judge after judge refused to accept the case. As the afternoon wore on the matter eventually landed in the courtroom of Judge Jorge Labarga. He accepted the case and at 3:05 p.m., he issued a series of rulings: he permitted the canvassing board to conduct a countywide manual recount, if the board chose to do so. The judge said the county could try to submit the hand recount votes to Harris, the secretary of state. "If she decides to accept them, fine," the judge said. "If she doesn't, then you need to talk to her about it."

Perhaps most important, he dissolved a restraining order that had prohibited election officials from filing their returns by 5 p.m. The judge also denied a motion by the Bush campaign to move the cases to Tallahassee.

Nov. 15, 2000, Don Van Natta Jr.

Broward County Panel Reconsiders Manual Countywide Recount

FORT LAUDERDALE — The Broward County canvassing board voted to reconsider its decision against a complete, manual recount of its presidential ballots. The board, which had earlier rebuffed a Democratic request for a hand recount, voted 2 to 1 to revisit the issue, with a Democratic judge who cast the deciding vote on Monday against a fuller recount providing the margin of victory.

Robert Lee, a local judge who is chairman of the canvassing board, gave no reasons for his change of heart and briskly walked out of the side door at the county courthouse immediately after the meeting ended. The lone Republican on the canvassing board, Jane Carroll, voted against the motion to reconsider the hand count, saying that she wanted a conclusion to the election and that the more ballots are handled the less integrity the election has. Suzanne Gunzburger, the other Democrat on the board, voted in favor of reconsidering a countywide recount.

A manual recount of three sample precincts on Monday representing 1 percent of the countywide vote turned up only four additional votes for Vice President Al Gore. The canvassing board, with Judge Lee casting the deciding vote, concluded that same day that the change was not sufficient to justify a hand recount of all ballots. The board said then that it was relying on Harris's opinion, which said counties could not order hand recounts unless voting machines were found to be faulty.

Democrats in Broward County went to court this afternoon and won a judge's ruling that they did not have to abide by the 5 p.m. Tuesday deadline set by Katherine Harris. The judge, John A. Miller, did not set any time for the county to reach a decision.

The issue was further complicated this afternoon when Harris herself lifted the deadline for Broward, Palm Beach and Miami-Dade Counties, saying that they had until 2 p.m. Wednesday to offer justifications for a hand recount. Her ruling returns the issue to the canvassing board, and it was unclear tonight how they might respond or whether they would use Judge Miller's ruling to extend the new deadline past 2 p.m.

Nov. 15, 2000, Dana Canedy

Profile: DAVID BOIES
SLAYER OF MICROSOFT JOINS GORE TEAM

At his first public appearance today on behalf of the Gore campaign, David Boies, the latest big-name lawyer to join the vice president's legal team, discounted a comparison to his role as the victorious trial attorney retained by the government in the Microsoft antitrust case.

But in fact Boies is clearly hoping that the kind of crucial insight and strategic decision he made in the Microsoft case may yet work again in the legal battle for Florida's electoral votes.

Justice Department lawyers battling Microsoft were crestfallen by a 1998 federal appeals court decision that seemed to most experts an across-the-board victory for the company and a potentially fatal blow to the government's suit. But once Boies had had a chance to read the decision carefully during a plane ride to visit the government's legal team in California, he saw that it bore a silver lining: an outline of what antitrust approach would prevail at trial. "By the time I got to San Francisco, I was convinced it was a good thing for us," he later recalled. "It gave us a road map of what the court of appeals criteria would be."

On the basis of that court decision, Boies went on to tailor his case, and trounced Microsoft at trial. Now the 59-year-old Boies (pronounced boys) is hoping that the decision issued today by a Florida circuit court judge, Terry P. Lewis, has likewise provided a road map. While the decision upheld Secretary of State Harris's discretion to enforce a deadline of 5 p.m. today for all Florida counties to have their ballot tallies turned in, it also said the discretion could not be exercised arbitrarily. "The court on Page 6 of the opinion goes through and identifies the kinds of considerations that the secretary of state has to take into account," Boies said at a news conference in Tallahassee.

Perhaps no trial lawyer in the United States is better suited to pursue this case for the Gore campaign than Boies, who to great effect uses a photographic memory of minute details, a disarmingly persistent style of questioning and a flair for drama.

In addition to the Microsoft case, which is now on appeal, he has enjoyed a remarkable string of court triumphs. He successfully defended CBS in a $120 million libel suit brought by Gen. William C. Westmoreland, represented the Resolution Trust Corporation in its $1 billion settlement against Drexel Burnham Lambert and Michael Milken, represented Texaco in its landmark legal struggle with Pennzoil in the 1980's and was one of the lead lawyers for I.B.M. in its defense against government antitrust claims. More recently he has been representing Napster in a copyright lawsuit that may set important precedents for intellectual property on the Internet.

Boies does not wear his success on his sleeve. He prefers knit ties and inexpensive blue suits, and usually wears his Timex over his shirt sleeve so he can see the time without raising his cuff. An Illinois native and 1966 graduate of Yale Law School, Boies began his career at Cravath, Swaine & Moore in New York, where at 31 he became the youngest partner. He left in 1997 to start his own firm, Boies, Schiller & Flexner.

Nov. 15, 2000, Stephen Labaton

FLORIDA SECRETARY OF STATE'S STATEMENT

Following is an excerpt from the statement by Katherine Harris, as recorded by The New York Times:

"As of 5 p.m. today, the director of the division of elections reported receiving certified returns from all 67 counties as required by law. In the race for the president of the United States, these certified results from Florida's 67 counties for the top two candidates are as follows: Gov. George Bush, 2,910,492; Vice President Al Gore, 2,910,192.

The usual practice of the State Elections Canvassing Commission is to certify these returns as soon as the compilations are completed by the division staff. However, in three Florida counties — Palm Beach, Miami-Dade and Broward Counties — these counties may be contemplating amended returns based upon manual recounts not completed as of today's statutory deadline.

Within the past hour, the director of the division of elections faxed a memorandum to the supervisors of elections in these three Florida counties. In accordance with today's court ruling confirming my discretion in these matters, I'm requiring a written statement of the facts and circumstances that would cause these counties to believe that a change should be made before the final certification of the statewide vote. This written statement is due in our office by 2 p.m. tomorrow.

Unless I determine, in the exercise of my discretion, that these facts and circumstances contained within these written statements justify an amendment to today's official returns, the State Elections Canvassing Commission, in a manner consistent with its usual and normal practice, will certify statewide results reported to this office today. Subsequently, the overseas ballots that are due by midnight Friday will also be certified and the final results of the election for president of the United States of America in the State of Florida will be announced. We will continue to keep you informed of the relevant developments as they occur."

day

8

WEDNESDAY,
NOVEMBER 15TH

★ ★ ★ ★ ★

PARTISAN TENSIONS RISE

Election officials from Broward, Miami-Dade and Palm Beach Counties meet the 2 p.m. deadline set by Katherine Harris and submit written requests to include hand recounts in Florida's certified vote. Early in the evening Gore shocks the Bush camp by making a dramatic announcement, timed for the network news reports, asking for a statewide hand recount and pledging an end to all legal challenges. This move is quickly overshadowed by Harris's curt rejection of all hand recounts and Bush's televised response to Gore in which he rejects any idea of continuing recounts. While Gore's aides continue to say they want to avoid lawsuits, Harris's action makes a Palm Beach challenge more certain.

As the post-election debate grows more contentious and the final result more in doubt, the role of Congress and the place of the Electoral College begin to surface as legitimate concerns. In Washington the first murmurs are heard from Republican Congressional leaders about how they might play an important part in the future.

HARRIS STYMIES GORE'S RECOUNT STRATEGY

WASHINGTON — The Florida secretary of state tonight rejected efforts to recount votes in two large Democratic counties, ruling shortly before George W. Bush brushed aside a public proposal by Al Gore to break their deadlock over the results of the presidential race in Florida.

The unexpected move by Katherine Harris came on a night of long-distance, televised exchanges between the candidates themselves. Gore made the first move, proposing on national television that he and Bush should meet and agree to abide by the results of hand recounts in two heavily Democratic counties, plus the uncounted overseas ballots that are due by midnight Friday. Or, if Bush wanted, Gore said he would be willing to extend the recount to all of Florida's 67 counties. In return, he vowed not to pursue any further legal action to overturn the results, which his aides had been preparing in case Gore could not find enough votes in Florida to erase Bush's lead.

"This is a time to respect every voter and every vote."

—Al Gore

"We need a resolution that is fair and final," Gore said in a statement timed to break dramatically into the network evening news programs, after giving their producers enough notice to build up the expectations. "We need to move expeditiously to the most complete and accurate count that is possible."

Responding on television three hours later, from Austin, Tex., Bush said he would not go along with Gore's deal. "The outcome of this election will not be the result of deals or efforts to mold public opinion," he said in remarks that were broadcast live by the three major networks. "The outcome of this election will be determined by the votes and by the law."

Before Bush addressed Gore's offer, Harris, a Republican elected official, announced in Tallahassee, Fla., that it was "my duty under Florida law" to reject requests from several counties to update their totals. She also announced that she was certifying the results that were sent in by the county canvassing boards on Tuesday. "The reasons given in the requests are insufficient to warrant waiver of the unambiguous filing deadline imposed by the Florida Legislature," she said, gripping tightly a dark binder that held her statement and biting her lip several times while reading. She left all questions to her aides as she rushed from the room.

Harris had acknowledged that her decision was likely to set off a court battle over the manual recount, which had been requested by the Gore campaign, and Gore aides immediately announced that they would return to court on Thursday. She said that Florida's vote count would be official when overseas absentee ballots are rolled into the totals after midnight Friday. She has been castigated by Democrats as being a partisan who backed Bush for president.

The announcement by Harris seemed a clear tactical move to freeze the election results in Bush's favor, and she was under no legal compulsion to make it. In fact, the circuit court judge who ruled Tuesday to uphold the state's Tuesday deadline for counties to submit their vote tallies went out of his way to say that Harris should exercise discretion in considering whether to accept later returns. The language of his ruling was ambiguous about whether she needed to wait for those returns to be filed, which she chose not to do tonight. The ruling also said that the state did not need to certify the votes twice — once based on Tuesday night's results and once more based on the count of the overseas ballots. Harris seemed to depart from that guidance tonight. Harris emphasized that she was closeted with advisers to reach her decision. But the timing of her announcement prompted much debate.

Earlier in the day, Harris went to the Florida Supreme Court to seek more guidance on how she should proceed. And she appeared tonight after Gore spoke, but before Bush responded to the vice president's proposal. That gave Bush a basis for saying that he was merely following Florida law and procedures in rejecting Gore's overtures.

Nov. 16, 2000, Richard L. Berke

Gore Speech Stuns Bush Team

Gore's announcement tonight was the first time that he had publicly proposed a full statewide recount, which he said could end all the wrangling, which some officials on both sides said could easily spill into December. The statewide recount could carry more risk for him because Bush could potentially pick up extra votes in Republican strongholds. Nevertheless, Gore's recommendation was not markedly different from suggestions put forth by others close to Gore or in the Democratic Party — or all that different from his campaign's known public position on the recounts.

The vice president's aides said his offer was partly an attempt for him to seize the public opinion advantage in what has become a daily battle of legal skirmishing over the airwaves. Campaign officials said that while Gore had for days floated the proposal among his advisers, he told them of his decision to go on television tonight as a fait accompli. Officials said there was some resistance among Gore's aides, some of whom expressed fears privately that the vice president was foreclosing his legal and political options. "It set a good tone," said one official familiar with the discussions. "I thought he looked very presidential. It was probably the right thing to do. But I'm not sure it helps him in the strategic sense of winning."

Gore sought to project that he was above the legal brawls that have marked both campaigns and that he was calmly thinking about the nation and the Constitution. "The campaign is over," he said, "but a test of our democracy is now under way. It is a test we must pass. And it is a test we will pass with flying colors. All we need is a common agreement that what is at stake here is not who wins and who loses in a contest for the presidency, but how we honor our

Constitution and make sure that our democracy works as our founders intended it to work. This is a time to respect every voter and every vote."

Gore sought to put Bush in a box by saying that there should be nothing more definitive than the actual votes. And he took issue with the objections of the Bush camp that hand counts are open to mistakes. "Machines can sometimes misread or fail to detect the way ballots are cast," he said, "and when there are serious doubts, checking the machine count with a careful hand count is accepted far and wide as the best way to know the intentions of the voters."

Gore also called on his rival to join him for a face-to-face meeting before the outcome is known so he and Bush could reassure the public that the government was not in peril after the remarkable turn of events that left Americans not knowing who would be the 43rd president because Florida had not decided the winner of its 25 electoral votes. "Shortly after the results are known, we should both come together for another meeting, to reaffirm our national unity," Gore said at the vice presidential residence here. "If I turn out to be successful, I'll be ready to travel to Governor Bush's home. If I am not, I'll be ready to meet him wherever he wishes."

Nov. 16, 2000, Richard L. Berke

Bush Sticks to the Script

AUSTIN — Only an hour or so after Gore made his televised proposal, Bush hit the road tonight, making the 90-minute drive from his ranch near Waco to the Governor's Mansion here. The trip was entirely unplanned and wholly rushed. But the Texas governor and his aides, who clearly were caught by surprise, recognized that he, too, needed to get in front of the television cameras, camped nearly 100 miles away in Austin. As his aides quickly composed remarks rejecting Gore's suggestion of a statewide manual recount in Florida and a one-on-one meeting before the election results were known, Bush hurtled down the highway.

By the time he spoke, about three and a half hours after Gore had, those remarks had been put on a teleprompter, so Bush could look straight into the camera and appear appropriately presidential. There was tape on the floor of the Governor's Mansion to show him where to walk and stand, and an American flag was tucked neatly and perfectly into the backdrop.

He repeated his objection to manual vote counting in Florida, where he said there were no uniform standards for the process. "This means every vote in Florida would be evaluated differently, by different individuals using different judgment and perhaps different local standards," he said. "This would be neither fair nor accurate. It would be arbitrary and chaotic."

The Bush campaign's aggressive maneuvering illustrated that, beyond the legal skirmishing in Florida, the candidates and their allies were engaged in a furious public-relations war. Gore's strike was not foreseen, and Bush had to retaliate.

For four days, Bush had not once stepped into public view, while tonight was Gore's second turn before the television cameras since Bush last faced them. Republicans in Washington had begun to fret that Bush and his aides were not adequately joining the battle for public opinion. And Bush's decision over the last five days to remain in relative seclusion at his ranch, far from the press corps, meant that hours went by tonight before he could respond in his own voice to Gore.

But when he did, his words were carefully chosen and weighed. He talked repeatedly about principles and fairness and accuracy, and even threw in references to responsibility and dignity. He mentioned Gore only a few times, dwelling instead on larger points.

Bush, countering the vice president, vehemently rejected the accuracy of hand recounts. "I was encouraged tonight that Vice President Gore called for a conclusion to this process — we all agree," Bush said. "Unfortunately, what the vice president proposed is exactly what he has been proposing all along: continuing with selective hand recounts that are neither fair nor accurate."

And he implicitly cast what Gore was doing as an effort to manipulate Americans' thinking and what he was doing as a defense against that. "The outcome of this election," he said, "will not be the result of deals or efforts to mold public opinion. The outcome of this election will be determined by the votes and by the law." He said he would meet with Gore once a winner had been declared.

When he finished, he headed back to his ranch. That decision showed just how much he wanted to be there and how keenly he felt it was important to emerge tonight.

Nov. 16, 2000, Frank Bruni

Gore's Lawyers Put Palm Beach Ballot in Their Sights

WEST PALM BEACH — In the hours before Gore made tonight's statement, senior members of his legal team prepared for what they called "the nuclear button" option: contesting the election results in Palm Beach County. And tonight, despite Gore's pledge not to pursue legal action if Bush agrees not to interfere with the manual recounts in three Florida counties, preparations for a lawsuit contesting the Palm Beach County results continued. The lawyers said they were confident that they could successfully challenge the ballot's legality, but they emphasized that it was an option of "last resort."

The Gore team contends that the design of the ballot in Palm Beach County did not conform to state law and was so confusing that many voters who supported Gore mistakenly voted for Patrick J. Buchanan or invalidated their ballots by punching holes for both men.

Gore would prefer not to challenge the Palm Beach results, a senior adviser said. But that sentiment seemed to be changing late tonight, two aides said, after Harris's rejection of manual recounts.

Gore aides said that they were still optimistic that hand recounts in Palm Beach, Broward and Miami-Dade Counties would proceed and erase Bush's narrow lead in the fight for Florida's 25 electoral votes. Gore won Palm Beach County by nearly 117,000 votes. "It's Palm Beach, stupid," emerged as the Democrats' post-election mantra, a slogan that reflected the strong sentiment that a countywide manual recount here could deliver enough votes to secure a victory in Florida for Gore.

"The vice president has focused on the recounts only," said a senior Gore adviser. "But a lot of people are telling him that we would win a legal challenge in Palm Beach." In particular, lawyers said that Palm Beach County's hand recount of 1 percent of the ballots showed that a majority of the double votes were for Gore and Buchanan. Eighty ballots, out of 144, had votes for Gore and Buchanan, the canvassing board reported.

A computer analysis by *The New York Times* showed that Buchanan faired best in Palm Beach County precincts where Gore received a large percentage of the vote. For example, in Gore's best precincts where he received 87 percent of the vote, Buchanan also made his strongest showing with 1.3 percent. In Bush's best precincts, Buchanan received less than half of the votes that he received in Gore's best precincts.

In other Florida counties, Buchanan fared best in the precincts where Bush won the majority. In Broward County, a predominantly Democratic county just south of Palm Beach, Buchanan did best in Bush's best precincts, receiving nearly three times the vote — almost nine-tenths of a percent — than in Gore's best precincts, where he received under three-tenths of a percent.

Gore aides said the analysis, which has findings similar to their study, is further evidence that many of the 3,407 votes cast here for Buchanan and many of the 19,120 double votes were intended for Gore. Such an argument would be a cornerstone of a legal challenge in Palm Beach County that would attack the confusing nature of the ballot, they said.

Since the election, the Gore campaign has avoided filing any lawsuits, though they have joined several lawsuits filed by others. Instead, their strategy, as one lawyer said, is to continue to focus on a recount, seeking countywide hand counts in Volusia, Palm Beach, Broward and Miami-Dade Counties.

A Florida law states that a candidate has 10 days after a vote is certified to contest the election. Harris certified the election results on Tuesday night, meaning that candidates would have until Nov. 24, the day after Thanksgiving, to challenge any results, lawyers said today.

On Gore's legal team, the momentum for a challenge changes by the hour, but several aides said today that the resolve for such a move deepened on Tuesday after Harris certified the results before several hand recounts were completed. After Gore's statement tonight, a senior adviser said everything depends on the Bush team's response. "We bumped up against the secretary of state, who is acting more in her capacity as a Bush co-chair than in her capacity as the top election official," a Gore aide said. "If people feel they are not getting a fair shake in Florida, it increases the chances we will feel a need to pursue a challenge down the road."

Nov. 16, 2000, Don Van Natta Jr.

A Memo from the House Whip

WASHINGTON — While Bush remained in relative seclusion on his ranch and both candidates' legal teams prepared to square off in court, Republican lawmakers in Washington were busy preparing a contingency plan in the event that a recount delivers Florida's electoral votes to Al Gore. This week Representative Tom DeLay, the Republican leader who drove the House forward to impeachment, sent a staff memorandum to Congressional Republicans pointing out that the House and Senate can reject a state's electoral votes if they decide that the votes are tainted.

The memorandum, with the neutral title "Electoral College Process in the Congress," is one of several research efforts under way by senior Republicans as members of their party express fears that ballot recounts could deprive Bush of a victory in Florida, and as scholars disagree over what would happen if there is no one to represent a stalemated Florida when the Electoral College meets in December.

DeLay, a Texan who is the House majority whip, had his aides distribute the two-page e-mail memorandum in recent days. It sets out Congress's role in tallying and certifying electoral votes and the circumstances that could lead to the House itself choosing the president.

Representative Bill Thomas, the California Republican who is chairman of the House Administration Committee, has asked the nonpartisan Congressional Research Service to report to him on the constitutional and legal role of the House. And one senior House Republican lawyer said that he and other party lawyers were boning up on the arcana of Congress's role in the electoral process.

The research comes as partisan tensions are rising and are beginning to remind some lawmakers of the impeachment battle of two years ago, with the presidency at stake and fights brewing over due process and the rule of law. House Republicans from Florida and their Democratic compatriots had dueling news conferences today, and one of the Republicans, Representative Dave Weldon, called the recounting in his state "an outrage." Speaking in defense of Florida's secretary of state, Weldon said that Vice President Al Gore had "studied at the feet of Bill Clinton. And his classic technique with political opponents — we saw it in the Lewinsky affair — is character assassination."

Republicans described the research as precautionary and probably unnecessary, and Speaker J. Dennis Hastert said he and his senior lieutenants had not discussed the possibility of invalidating a state's electoral votes. A spokesman for DeLay, Jonathan Baron, said that DeLay was "confident" that Bush would win the election and that staff members had prepared the memorandum to answer questions from individual lawmakers. "Members of the leadership have responsibility to perform due diligence in these kinds of questions," Baron said. "The operating principle must be prepare for the worst and hope for the best."

Another Republican close to DeLay described the memorandum as similar to the "impeachment book" his office sent out in 1998 when DeLay began providing information about impeachment to Republicans and subsequently driving it through the House. "If there are feelings this is being stolen, there will probably be calls for action," the Republican said.

The memorandum does not mention Florida or any other state. It recommends no course of action, but explains a little-known section of law, enacted after the contested presidential election of 1876, which gives the House and Senate the ability to reject a state's electoral votes by a majority vote of both houses. It also spells out that under the 12th Amendment to the Constitution, the House chooses the president if no nominee has an electoral majority.

Democrats, too, are starting to study the law, the Constitution and its ambiguities. Experts disagree over whether the election would be thrown into the House if Florida was could not seat a delegation in the Electoral College by Dec. 18, and there are also questions of what would happen if majorities in the House and Senate used their power to object to and reject the electoral votes of some states.

Representative David E. Price, Democrat of North Carolina, has introduced a resolution to have the archivist of the United States provide the House with information about Electoral College preparations. And aides to the House minority leader, Representative Richard A. Gephardt of Missouri, said they had asked the parliamentarian to give them a copy of any research prepared for the Republicans.

No matter what happens in the presidential race, there are now calls from members of Congress from both parties to review everything from the elimination of the Electoral College to the role of the television networks in calling elections to whether the law allowing voter registration when getting a driver's license is causing fraud.

Nov. 16, 2000, Alison Mitchell

day

9

THURSDAY,

NOVEMBER 16TH

★ ★ ★ ★ ★

"There Is No Legal Impediment To The Recounts"

With the blessing of the Florida Supreme Court, recounts continue in Palm Beach and Broward Counties, while Miami-Dade moves closer to deciding whether or not to begin its own recount, even though Katherine Harris has refused to consider the results of any recounts and the Supreme Court did not say she had to. Democrats go to court to argue that Harris's decision, despite earlier orders from Judge Lewis, was arbitrary and unfair. In a new suit in a federal appeals court, Republicans contend that the recounts are unconstitutional because they treat some votes differently from others.

Florida Court Rules for Recounts and Bush Goes Federal Again

"It's a little surreal."

– Gov. Jeb Bush

★ ★ ★

TALLAHASSEE — The Florida Supreme Court ruled that at least two largely Democratic counties could continue recounting ballots by hand, but a welter of pending legal challenges left it unclear whether any such votes would officially count in determining the outcome of the presidential race.

The court's unanimous opinion, issued in one paragraph without comment, upheld lower court rulings allowing recounts and created some vulnerability for George W. Bush, who leads by a mere 300 votes in the state's official tally. It paved the way for Palm Beach County to join Broward County, where a recount was already under way, in manually recounting a total of some one million ballots. That could potentially give Al Gore an unofficial lead that would instantly become public knowledge, a psychological reversal that the Bush campaign had been trying to avoid.

But the question of whether any such recounts would be included in the state's official results, and thus in awarding Florida's 25 electoral votes, was not before the Supreme Court today. That issue was left for Judge Terry P. Lewis, who held on Tuesday that Katherine Harris could enforce the state's legal deadline of 5 p.m. that day for counties to submit certified vote tallies. Democrats contend that Harris abused her discretion by announcing on Wednesday that she would not consider any such late results, even before she received them. Judge Lewis said he would issue a decision at 10 a.m. Friday [Nov. 17].

Bush's representatives also said they were giving up any effort to contest the count in another close state, Iowa, a decision that suggested that they were putting all of their efforts into winning the battle here. To that end, lawyers for Bush filed papers with a federal appeals court in Atlanta arguing that recounts were unconstitutional because they would treat some votes different from others, and that they should stop at once.

Nine days into the post-electoral limbo, the latest legal twists seemed to buttress the words of Bush's brother Jeb, who began a routine cabinet meeting in the Capitol this morning by declaring, "It's a little surreal."

The Supreme Court's ruling today was the second defeat Harris has suffered there this week. On Wednesday, the court declined her emergency request to block further recounts. Tonight the Gore camp claimed vindication in the court's terse order that "there is no legal impediment to the recounts continuing." The Gore campaign chairman, William M. Daley, declared, "The Florida Supreme Court has spoken: the counts can continue, notwithstanding the secretary of state's deadline."

But James A. Baker III said the ruling "does nothing more than preserve the status quo," and declined to characterize it as a setback. He added: "Let's be real clear about the real meaning of this order. It was not a decision on the merits. It was an interim order."

The Supreme Court's ruling came on a request from officials in Palm Beach County, joined by those in Broward County, Harris and both campaigns, for a ruling on whether recounts were legal. Palm Beach County officials had repeatedly postponed a full-scale manual recount on the ground that conflicting advice from the Republican secretary of state and the Democratic state attorney general had left them confused about whether they could legally proceed.

All week, in frantic rounds of public appearances, television appeals and legal proceedings, both camps have raced to beat the state's legal deadline of Saturday [Nov. 18] for certifying results, including several thousand overseas absentee ballots due Friday night. Such ballots have historically broken in favor of Republicans.

All eyes are now on Judge Lewis, who held on Tuesday that Harris could enforce the state's legal deadline of 5 p.m. that day for counties to submit certified vote tallies. But he also ruled that she could not arbitrarily refuse to consider later returns.

Gore Challenges the Harris Decision

This morning, lawyers for Gore were back in Judge Lewis's courtroom, arguing that Harris had done just that on Wednesday night when, citing state election law precedents, she rejected the counties' explanations of why they needed more time, without waiting to review late tallies.

The Democratic lawyers contended that bad legal advice from Harris's office had kept the counties from completing their recounts in time in the first place. Her office instructed election officials that only machine malfunctions could justify a manual recount.

"We think that her failure to take the direction of the court should be corrected by the court in an order which would direct her to allow these recounts to continue, again, for a reasonable period of time, recognizing that a lot of delay has now taken place because of the various actions that are shown in here on the part of the secretary that resulted in the delay and confusion," said Dexter Douglass, a lawyer for the Gore campaign.

Lawyers for Harris and the Bush campaign responded that she had done just what the judge allowed her to do: consider the reasons each county was counting by hand, and then reject those reasons based on her own criteria.

"The secretary of state took those criteria and then applied them against the documents that she received from the canvassing boards," said Joseph P. Klock Jr., a lawyer for Harris, "and made a determination, your honor, based upon their explanation of their decision. She exercised her discretion reasonably in determining whether or not those explanations complied with acceptable standards in the exercise of her discretion."

Nov. 17, 2000, Todd S. Purdum

The Florida Supreme Court: A Democratic Oasis

TALLAHASSEE — In a state where the Legislature is controlled by Republicans, the top elections official is a Republican, and the governor is not only a Republican but also the younger brother of George W. Bush, the Florida Supreme Court is the one branch of government where Democrats still feel comfortable. The seven-member court is composed entirely of justices appointed in Democratic administrations, and it has often sided with Democratic constituencies, including trial lawyers, while striking down initiatives of Republican legislators and of Jeb Bush, the governor.

"The conservatives are in charge generally of the Legislature today, and many conservatives feel the court has been too liberal," said Jon L. Shebel, president of the Associated Industries of Florida, the state's largest business lobby group.

Speaking to reporters today, Governor Bush of Florida acknowledged that "there has been a little bit of tension" between himself and the justices. But he said he anticipated that "they will do the right thing" in handling the recount lawsuits. Lawyers for the Gore campaign have asked the justices to resolve all election litigation pending in state courts themselves. But senior Gore aides insist that the court's political makeup did not factor into that request.

Tensions between the state Supreme Court and Republican lawmakers rose so high earlier this year that legislators tried to pass measures that would have let Governor Bush add two new justices to the court, given the governor more power in picking justices and put a constitutional amendment before voters to sharply reduce the court's power in certain types of criminal cases. All those measures failed.

Republicans had been angered by several rulings, but the most significant was a decision in April striking down parts of a new law intended to hasten the pace of executions. The court held unanimously that the law, a priority of Bush, had unconstitutionally usurped the justices' authority. Republicans cited the ruling in accusing the court of favoring the rights of criminals and defendants over the rights of crime victims.

Five of the seven justices were appointed by Lawton Chiles, the three-time Democratic senator who served almost two full terms as governor before dying in late 1998. A sixth was named under an agreement Chiles reached with Bush, who was then governor-elect, shortly before Chiles's death. The seventh justice was appointed by Bob Graham, a Democrat who is now a United States senator.

In spite of the rancor with Republican lawmakers, the Florida Supreme Court is generally considered less partisan than some other state supreme courts, partly because of the way justices are selected. A commission selected by the governor and officials of the state bar names three candidates for each vacancy; the governor then picks one. Justices face retention elections in which they run unopposed.

Nov. 17, 2000, Richard A. Oppel Jr.

Palm Beach Starts Recount, Finally

WEST PALM BEACH — After getting permission from the Florida Supreme Court to proceed with a countywide hand recount of 462,657 ballots, election officials in Palm Beach County put more than 100 volunteers to work on the long-awaited, fiercely debated recount. After days of delays and uncertainty over whether elections officials here would be breaking the law if they went ahead with the recount, the court issued an interim order today that allows the county's canvassing board to conduct it.

The recount is expected to take six days, but if Katherine Harris has her way, the new tally will not matter. Harris said she will not recognize the recounted votes, and will close the election on Saturday after overseas absentee ballots are counted. But with a battery of lawyers arguing for their parties in federal and state courts, Palm Beach County decided to proceed with its recount.

For many Democrats, who believe a recount here will put Al Gore in the White House, it seemed like it would never happen. County Judge Charles E. Burton, the chairman of the canvassing board, said the county, which had been reluctant to proceed even after a Florida Supreme Court decision to allow the counties to proceed, now had specific permission from the court to go ahead. The county had filed its own suit with the court seeking guidance. "So, we intend on proceeding," Burton said.

But in a county in which the recount has amounted to arguments and not much else, a promised 6 p.m. start time came and went without a single vote being counted. And many people here thought it might be postponed again. This time, however, the recount finally began — at 7:16 p.m., with Republican and Democratic monitors watching over teams of two volunteers each as they began what was expected to be an arduous process. But it was still unclear late tonight whether so-called dimpled chads would be counted.

He made his announcement of the recount as stragglers from a Republican rally here earlier in the day heckled him. "Quite honestly, there's been a Florida statute that provides for a manual recount that has been on the books for I don't know how many years," said Burton, who had voted against the recount when it was first proposed after the election by Carol Roberts, a county commissioner and member of the canvassing board. "I never heard anyone complain about it before."

Just before the count began, the canvassing board released a statement that said the volunteers would follow the guidelines set down in the Broward County recount. The tiny pieces of paper that are punched through on a clean vote will be automatically counted if they remain attached to the ballot by one or two corners. If they remain attached by three corners, or are just dimpled, they will be set aside, and each ballot will be counted or discounted according to the volunteers' evaluation of the voters' intention.

Republicans were furious about the whole thing. Earlier in the day, about 400 Bush supporters rallied at the emergency center, where the recount would take place, in support of Harris. They waved signs that said "Go Kat Go" and "In Harris We Trust" and "Reject Rigged Returns."

With the radio voice of Rush Limbaugh urging them to fight against the Democrats from the open doors of parked cars, they marched in a blocked-off street and pulled on free T-shirts that trumpeted their support of Harris. The throng of Republicans chanted "Bringing America Together" as they marched, but had an embarrassing moment when white supremacists joined their march waving a Confederate battle flag. Republicans asked them to leave.

Nov. 17, 2000, Rick Bragg

Counting Chads

The Problems

Votes are initially counted by a machine which determines where light shines through the ballot card. If the holes are blocked by the punched-out paper, called the "chad," the machine will not count it. Many of those votes, however, will be included in the hand count.

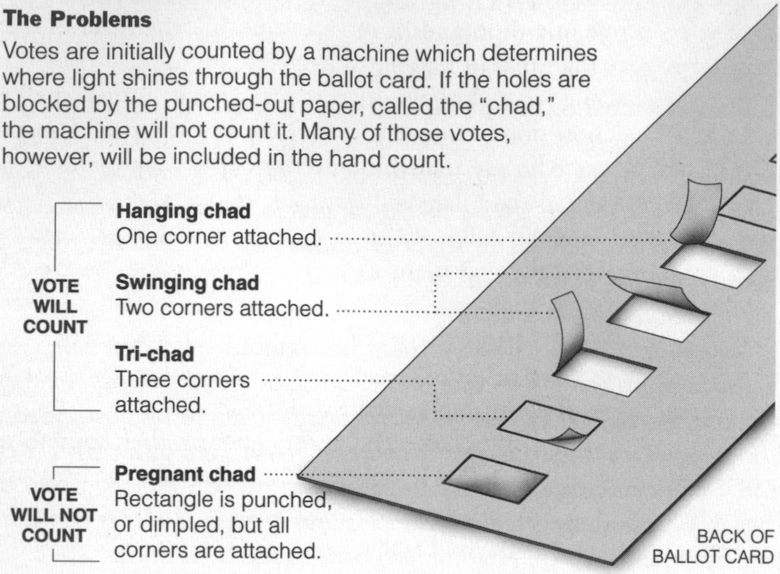

Palm Beach County Had Prior Complaints About Counts

WEST PALM BEACH — Nationwide, about 2 percent of ballots cast in presidential elections are not recorded because they are marked for two or more candidates or for none. But in the presidential election in Palm Beach County, 19,120 ballots, or about 4 percent of those cast, were thrown out because of double votes. On some 10,000 ballots, or about 2 percent, the machine count indicated no selection for president. It is with those ballots that Democrats believe they have the best chance to make up votes in the hand recount.

Palm Beach County has traditionally had a higher number of double-votes than other counties in Florida, but experts are split on the reason — the punch-card system or mistakes by voters. Palm Beach County uses Votomatic machines, which were developed in the 1960's, and I.B.M. punch-card technology. Punch ballots are used in 27 of Florida's 67 counties.

Lawyers for Al Gore have been researching the accuracy of the voting machines, an issue that came up this week when Florida's director of elections, Clay Roberts, ruled that hand recounts could be conducted only if voting equipment was proved to be faulty.

The state's attorney general, Robert A. Butterworth, a Democrat, disagreed with that opinion. And the Palm Beach County canvassing board asked the Florida Supreme Court for guidance; late this afternoon, the high court said the county could continue its hand recount.

A senior member of Gore's legal team, who asked not to be identified, said: "The worst machines in the state are in Palm Beach County. They are old and are the cause of numerous problems. We have a presidential election where the margin of votes is one one-thousandths of a percent, but the machines have a much greater chance than that of making a mistake."

For now, the challenge in eight lawsuits by county voters is over the legality of the design of the notorious "butterfly" ballot used in the presidential election. On Friday, voters who say that the butterfly ballot caused them to vote for the wrong presidential candidate will try to persuade Judge Jorge Baraga of Circuit Court to declare the ballot illegal and order a new vote. Lawyers for the voters say they will argue that many of the 3,407 votes cast for the Reform Party candidate, Patrick J. Buchanan, were intended for Gore, whose name was on the opposite half of the ballot's face. They say they are also prepared to argue that voters selected two or more presidential candidates on the 19,120 discarded ballots because of confusion over the ballot's design.

"If the will of the voters of Palm Beach County matters, then something has to be done about the ballot's legality," said Alan Dershowitz, the Harvard law professor who is helping lawyers for voters who filed the lawsuits here. "I don't think a reasonable person of good will would allow hundreds or perhaps a thousand ballots in which the people intended to vote for Al Gore to be discounted."

Lawyers plan to argue that voter confusion over the butterfly ballot was reported in precincts all over the county just moments after the polls opened at 7 a.m. on Nov. 7.

Nov. 17, 2000, Don Van Natta, Jr.

Still Another County with the Ballot Blues

JACKSONVILLE — Democrats in Duval County prepared meticulously for Election Day. They registered thousands of voters and ferried enough people to the polls in predominantly African-American precincts to give a solid boost to Al Gore in a county expected to swing reliably into George W. Bush's column.

But the results of Duval County's vote left Democrats here shaking their heads. More than 26,000 ballots were invalidated, the vast majority because they contained votes for more than one presidential candidate. Nearly 9,000 of the votes were thrown out in the predominantly African-American communities around Jacksonville, where Gore scored 10-to-1 ratios of victory, according to an analysis of the vote by *The New York Times*.

The percentage of invalidated votes here was far higher than that recorded in Palm Beach County, which has become the focus of national attention and where Democrats have argued that so many people were disenfranchised it may be necessary to let them vote again. Neither Democrats nor Republicans have demanded a hand recount or new election in Duval County.

Local election officials attributed the outcome to a ballot that had the name of presidential candidates on two pages, which they said many voters found confusing. Many voters, they said, voted once on each page. The election officials said they would not use such a ballot in the future.

Rodney G. Gregory, a lawyer for the Democrats in Duval County, said the party shared the blame for the confusion. Gregory said Democratic Party workers instructed voters, many persuaded to go to the polls for the first time, to cast ballots in every race and "be sure to punch a hole on every page."

"The get-out-the-vote folks messed it up," Gregory said ruefully.

If Gregory's assessment is correct, and thousands of Gore supporters were inadvertently misled into invalidating their ballots, this county alone would have been enough to give Gore the electoral votes of Florida, and thus the White House. The voters turned out by Democrats, Gregory said, took the instructions to vote in every race to mean: "I've got to vote for Gore. I've got to be sure Bush doesn't get elected. I've got to vote on every page."

The Duval County ballot listed Gore on the first page, along with Bush, Ralph Nader and two other candidates. Then on the second page were the names of five other presidential candidates. After voting for Gore, many Democratic voters turned the page and voted for one of the remaining names, Gregory said.

The double-marked ballots substantially affected Gore's showing, a *Times* analysis of voting data suggests. More than 20 percent of the votes cast in predominantly African-American precincts were tossed out, nearly triple the amount in majority white precincts. In two largely African-American precincts, nearly one-third of the ballots were invalidated.

Altogether, 21,942 ballots were rejected because the voter punched the hole beside the name of more than one candidate, and another 4,927 were invalidated because the voter punched no hole next to a presidential candidate, said the Duval County supervisor of elections.

The *Times* analysis shows that about 16,500 of the votes thrown out were cast in precincts with Democratic majorities that, when taken together, were comfortably carried by Gore. The remaining 10,000 invalid votes were cast mostly in precincts in which Republicans outnumber Democrats and that were, as a group, solidly behind Bush.

Although there is plenty of grousing about the ballot, the Democrats have not mounted a challenge to the vote here as they have in other parts of the state. For one thing, confusing though the ballot might have been, "there is nothing illegal about that ballot," said James Holland, a lawyer who worked as a poll watcher for the Democrats on voting day.

A spokesman for the Duval County elections office, however, said the 26,000 invalidated votes were four times the total recorded in 1996. Susan Tucker Johnson said the county had fit the presidential candidates on one page in 1996, but had gone to two pages this year because there were so many parties. In the final tally for Duval County, Bush received 152,114 votes, or 58 percent, and Gore 108,048, or 41 percent.

Nov. 17, 2000, Raymond Bonner with Josh Barbanel

day

10

FRIDAY,
NOVEMBER 17TH

★ ★ ★ ★ ★

FLORIDA HIGH COURT RESTARTS RECOUNTS

Judge Terry P. Lewis of the Florida Circuit Court rules that Katherine Harris may declare the winner of Florida's presidential election on Saturday, without including results of hand recounts. But this apparent victory for the Bush team is short-lived as the Florida Supreme Court promptly bars the state from certifying results until it issues its own ruling on the disputed vote. Later, the U.S. Court of Appeals denies a Bush campaign request to block hand recounts.

The Supreme Court ruling prompts officials in Miami-Dade County to join Palm Beach and Broward Counties in attempting a full manual recount. This brings the total number of ballots to be recounted in the strongly Democratic counties to 1.5 million. Republican lawyers and observers fiercely contest another circuit court judge's decision that ballots with pregnant or dimpled chads can be included in Palm Beach and Broward Counties at the discretion of the canvassing boards.

Meanwhile, the statewide count of absentee ballots grows increasingly chaotic. Not only have counties applied different standards in rejecting overseas ballots, but some officials are also confused by new guidelines from Katherine Harris that apparently contradict Florida state law. Democrats are also protesting thousands of votes for Bush in Seminole County, where absentee ballot applications were corrected by Republican campaign aides after being signed and submitted.

Bush Hammered in Several Courts

TALLAHASSEE — The Florida Supreme Court barred the state from certifying official results in the presidential election until the court rules on the disputed vote. It allowed a manual recount in three Democratic counties and the continued counting of overseas absentee ballots statewide, which more than doubled the 300-vote lead of George W. Bush.

Ten days after Election Day, the court's unanimous two-sentence ruling was the most dramatic legal development yet in the battle between Bush and Al Gore. It came on the eve of the deadline originally set by the state's top election official for announcing a final tally and set off a fierce race between both sides to accumulate as many votes as possible before Monday afternoon [Nov. 20], when the court is to hear the case.

> *"We're getting good at riding the roller coaster."*
>
> *—Aide to George W. Bush*

The absentee ballots from Floridians abroad, due by midnight Sunday, Nov. 18, have historically broken for Republicans, and returns trickling in from around the state appeared to raise Bush's slender lead. With 65 of 67 counties reporting, according to a running tally by The Associated Press, Bush led by 760 votes out of six million votes statewide.

But after the Supreme Court's ruling, officials in Miami-Dade County voted this evening to join Palm Beach and Broward Counties in a full manual recount of some 500,000 ballots there. That raises to 1.5 million the number of ballots to be recounted in South Florida Democratic strongholds that could help Gore.

Also this evening, the full United States Court of Appeals for the 11th Circuit, in Atlanta, denied a request by the Bush campaign to block any further hand recounts as unconstitutional. The federal appellate court declared that "states have the primary authority" over selecting their delegations to the Electoral College, and that "state procedures are not in any way inadequate to preserve for ultimate review in the United States Supreme Court any federal questions arising" from the case.

In all, it was a day of sharp swings in the campaigns' fortunes. It began with a state Circuit Court judge's ruling this morning that cleared the way for Secretary of State Katherine Harris to declare an official winner on Saturday as she had planned, without including any hand recounts of ballots. Judge Terry P. Lewis of Leon County Circuit Court rejected the Democrats' arguments, and ruled that "it appears that the secretary has exercised her reasoned judgment to determine what relevant factors and criteria should be considered, applied them to the facts and circumstances pertinent to the individual counties involved and made her decision."

The Bush team gave the strong impression they believed that ruling would make their candidate the winner of Florida's 25 electoral votes, and thus the White House. The Gore campaign promptly filed an appeal with the state Supreme Court, but did not expressly ask for an order to block Harris's planned certification. Democratic lawyers were later elated that the high court, the only branch of state government dominated by Democratic appointees, later did so on its own. In its ruling, the court said it acted "to maintain the status quo." But it was a very fluid status quo, because the court also expressly allowed counting of the absentee ballots and the hand recounts to continue.

Tonight, Bush's chief representative, former Secretary of State James A. Baker III — who this morning had also approvingly cited "the rule of law" and looked forward to the prompt "process of achieving a final result" — took to the microphones here in a more sober mood. He noted that the Florida Supreme Court had "issued an order that neither side requested" and took pains to note that neither the high court here nor the federal appeals court in Atlanta had yet issued a ruling on the merits of the cases before them. Baker also said he was encouraged that the appeals court had left open the door for a later review of the case.

Nov. 18, 2000, Todd S. Purdum

JUDGE OKS CHADS, DIMPLED OR OTHERWISE

FORT LAUDERDALE — A Broward County circuit court judge here said that elections officials recounting the county's presidential ballots need not reject ballots on which voters did not perforate the punch cards. Democrats said that bit of arcana meant that more ballots in the heavily Democratic county could be considered in the recount, possibly increasing the vote for Al Gore.

The Democrats had asked Judge John Miller to tell the canvassing board that its decision to consider only ballots on which chads — the bits of paper that are detached from a ballot when it is punched — were separated from the ballot by two or more corners could be too limited. The Democrats, over strenuous objections from Republicans, wanted the judge to order that indented ballots, also known as pregnant or dimpled chads, be counted as votes.

Instead, Judge Miller said he believed the board could use its own discretion, using prevailing guidelines, to determine the voters' intent. He noted that Judge Jorge Baraga of Circuit Court in West Palm Beach had ruled this week that the canvassing board in Palm Beach County could not reject ballots that were not fully perforated. "I'd like to presume the county canvassing board knows the law they are supposed to follow in counting the ballots by hand," Judge Miller said. "I'd like to think they know they are not supposed to limit it to one or two criteria."

Larry Davis, a lawyer for Suzanne Gunzburger, a Democratic member of the board, said board members would later vote on whether to adopt new standards and consider the nonperforated ballots, a couple of hundred of which he said had been put aside.

Scott McClellan, a Bush campaign spokesman, accused the Democrats of changing the rules in the middle of the game. "It sounds like the Democrats and Al Gore are looking for creative ways to continue counting until they come up with the result they are looking for," McClellan said.

While the lawyers were arguing in court, sheriff's deputies carried seven metal cases containing overseas ballots to the Emergency Operations Center, where the recount was being conducted. Immediately, Republicans began challenging the count. One lawyer for the Republicans complained that the signatures on the ballots were not being matched with registration cards in the room. But the canvassing board responded that the signatures were checked when the ballots first arrived in the mail.

A late-night count showed a gain for Gore of 48 votes, with about one-fifth of the county's 609 precincts counted. A tally of overseas ballots from the previous night gave Gore 53, Bush 37 and Ralph Nader 1. Two hundred forty ballots were rejected.

In the hearing on the lawsuit, Judge Leonard Stafford rejected the Republicans' requests for an emergency hearing this afternoon to present evidence. "Where's the emergency?" Judge Stafford asked.

Nov. 18, 2000, Dana Canedy and David Gonzalez

Furor over Absentee Ballots

TALLAHASSEE — The tally of overseas absentee ballots by county officials across Florida yielded rampant confusion, partisan wrangling over which votes to count and which to discard, and widespread uncertainty about the rules on what makes for a valid ballot.

Counties applied vastly different standards in deciding whether to throw out ballots. A few county officials openly defied the Florida secretary of state's instructions to accept otherwise-valid ballots from overseas that were postmarked after Election Day. Others freely admitted that they did not understand those instructions. And officials in several counties said they feared that the count was being botched, and that another round of delays and court challenges was likely.

"It seems like everybody's been changing the rules to suit their satisfaction," Fred Galey, the Brevard County supervisor of elections, said dryly. "This certainly has been educational." The overseas ballots, at least 2,000 of them, represent the last, precious trove of votes that both Republicans and Democrats agree should be counted in the disputed presidential race.

The Associated Press reported that with 65 of Florida's 67 counties reporting, Bush had picked up 1,057 votes, and Gore 597. With these results, Bush's overall lead grew to 760 votes.

In each county, canvassing boards pored over the overseas votes that were received after Election Day, with lawyers for the Republicans and Democrats watching their every move, sometimes raising objections to the boards' rulings as to whether a ballot should be counted or thrown out. In many counties, the process was overseen by a phalanx of reporters and television crews.

There was particular confusion over the rules for postmarks on the ballots, and many county officials complained of contradictory — and possibly incorrect — instructions from Secretary of State Katherine Harris, a Republican and a Bush ally whom Democrats have already accused of bias in her handling of the overall count.

Well into the evening — and hours after they had planned on doing the count — several of the state's large counties had not yet opened a single ballot because officials and lawyers from both parties were still debating the rules for gauging their validity. State law says that ballots from other countries must be postmarked. But Harris issued a statement earlier this week saying that they did not have to be postmarked by Election Day, as long as they were signed and dated by Election Day. In other words, a ballot that was filled out on Election Day but mailed the next day would still be valid.

Election officials in several counties, however, said that they had always understood that ballots postmarked after Election Day were invalid, and that they had rejected such ballots in previous elections. Democratic officials in several of those counties said Harris wanted the maximum number of overseas votes counted in the belief that they would benefit Bush. Harris's office did not return repeated calls seeking comment.

Canvassing boards in counties carried by Gore invalidated ballots at a far higher rate than those in counties carried by Bush, in part because Republican-dominated counties accepted ballots postmarked after the election or with no postmarks, while Democratic counties rejected them. Among counties with large numbers of overseas votes, for instance, Broward, Miami-Dade and Orange, which voted for Gore, threw out more than 80 percent of the ballots, while Escambia, Clay and Okaloosa, which went for Bush, threw out about 40 percent.

Here in Leon County, the three-member canvassing board, controlled by Democrats, rejected several ballots postmarked after the election, insisting that Harris had misinterpreted the law and that they would ignore her instructions.

"Hello, Katherine Harris, is anybody there?" said Bob Rackleff, a Democratic county commissioner and member of the board, rolling his eyes and miming holding a phone to his ear.

Time and again, the board's rejection of a ballot produced a polite but spirited debate with representatives of the Republican Party.

"There is no requirement for a postmark by Election Day, and we are registering our objections," said Jason Unger, a lawyer for the party, but he said it was not clear if the party would take the matter to court.

In Orange County, which includes Orlando, the canvassing board invalidated 117 out of the 147 overseas ballots on hand, more than two-thirds of them because of absent or improper postmarks. In many instances, the board there, like the one in Leon County, threw out ballots that were postmarked after Nov. 7 or had illegible postmarks — disregarding Harris's instruction that the date on the postmark did not matter. In several other cases, officials said, it appeared that people in the military had turned their ballots over to military post offices, which had failed to postmark them, and the ballots were rejected.

In Miami-Dade County, the canvassing board rejected 209 out of 312 votes, to almost no objection from either party. Once again, many of the votes were invalidated because they were postmarked after Election Day or had no postmark. Officials said they were aware of Harris's instructions, but disregarded them.

But in several other counties, officials took Harris's directives to mean that votes could be accepted with no postmark at all, and some said that they had been advised as much by her office over the phone. "We've never done it that way before, so we're a little confused about that, but that's what they've told us," said Stephanie Thomas, assistant supervisor of elections in Clay County.

In Escambia County, after much wavering, the canvassing board decided to accept 50 military ballots that had no postmarks — the opposite of the call made in Orange County. Two of the three Escambia board members at first said they were inclined to reject the votes, but Republican Party lawyers swayed the board with the argument that since people in the armed services can send their votes through military post offices without paying any postage, there is no stamp to cancel, hence, often no postmark.

When asked what guidance the secretary of state's office had provided about postmarks, Karen Butler, deputy administrator of elections in Pinellas County, said, "Not enough."

Nov. 18, 2000, Richard Pérez-Peña

Seminole County Absentee Dispute Goes to Court

MIAMI — When the chairman of Florida's Republican Party needed some advice two years ago on how far the party could go to help Republicans obtain absentee ballots, he turned to the secretary of state for some advice. Officials working for the Republican who occupied the office at the time, Sandra Mortham, ruled that voters or their immediate families had to complete applications for absentee ballots. The forms required several pieces of personal, identifying information.

But this week Katherine Harris moved to accept vote tallies from heavily Republican Seminole County, where local election officials acknowledge they allowed Republican campaign aides to correct errors in thousands of applications for absentee ballots after they had been signed and submitted.

A Democratic lawyer has gone to court to throw out those ballots. And Judge Debra Nelson of Circuit Court has scheduled a hearing on Saturday morning to consider the case.

Tom Slade, the former state Republican chairman who asked for the opinion from the secretary of state's office in 1998, now believes that the Democrats have a serious argument for throwing out the absentee votes involved. "I'm surprised the litigation hadn't already started," Slade said in an interview. "I'm not a lawyer, but it is absolutely an issue of controversy as to whether public documents can be altered on an after-the-fact basis." Harris, who took office three months after the ruling by her predecessor, Mortham, did not respond to requests for comment.

James Hattaway, an Orlando lawyer representing the supervisor of elections and canvassing board in Seminole County, predicted George W. Bush's 10,006 to 5,209 lead in absentee ballots over Al Gore would survive the court challenge. "The lawsuit is interesting, and you got to admire the folks' passion," Hattaway said. "But legally, they are inaccurate. The law they have cited cannot support their cause of action."

Hattaway said Florida's election statute did not say whether mistakes on absentee applications could be corrected. "This is a situation that does not deal with ballots," he said. "The allegation deals with absentee ballot requests, and as with so many things in this election, the statutes are silent on the issues the plaintiffs are trying to address."

A company hired by the Republican Party to prepare tens of thousands of applications for voters complicated the party's plans by omitting voter identification numbers from many of the forms it sent out. The incomplete documents poured into county offices. Some election supervisors said in interviews that they took it upon themselves to supply the voter identification numbers and send out the absentee ballots.

What happened in Seminole was that Sandra Goard, the elections supervisor, after rejecting the Republican ballot requests as invalid, allowed two of the party's workers to sit in her offices for as long as 10 days to write the voter identification numbers on the flawed cards.

Goard has also acknowledged that, in the weeks before the election, she let other incomplete ballot applications from individual voters pile up in her office because she was too busy to notify the people who had sent them that they had been rejected. Goard said that Florida law does not obligate her to assist voters in completing a flawed application.

After objecting to the application process this week, Harry Jacobs, a local Democratic lawyer, said in filing suit that he would seek to identify those votes cast through the modified ballot applications. But he said he did not believe they could be identified, and that he would likely seek to have every absentee vote in the county thrown out.

Nov. 18, 2000, Michael Moss

day

11

Saturday, November 18th

★ ★ ★ ★ ★

Bush Winning Overseas Count

As expected, initial results from the overseas ballot count favor Bush, more than tripling his lead in Florida. But even this count is immediately disputed as both sides argue over postmarks on discarded military ballots. Hand recounts continue in Broward and Palm Beach Counties, and Miami-Dade officials say they will begin their count — which may take two weeks — on Monday. Bush's lead in the overseas ballot count raises the bar for manual recounts, however, and initial results do not favor Gore as much as Democrats had hoped. Republicans continue to accuse Democratic vote-counters of deliberately mishandling ballots, and Democrats respond by charging Republicans with outrageous delaying tactics.

Meanwhile, Gore's legal team files a brief with the Florida Supreme Court, arguing in favor of manual recounts and accusing Katherine Harris of taking an unreasonable approach to the voting dispute. And in the Florida state capital, Republican lawmakers announce that if hand recounts lead to a Gore victory, they may invoke a never-used federal statute that they claim allows them to name their own pro-Bush slate of electors.

OVERSEAS BALLOTS BOOST BUSH LEAD TO 930

TALLAHASSEE — George W. Bush's lead more than tripled as all absentee ballots from overseas were opened and tallied. But his campaign was unable to claim the victory it had expected, as both sides awaited a hearing on Monday in the Florida Supreme Court.

Just as Republicans had predicted, Bush received an overwhelming share of the overseas ballots, which came in from military personnel and Floridians living abroad, leaving Al Gore with a far more difficult obstacle to hurdle.

Official but uncertified figures from all 67 counties released by the Florida elections division today showed that Bush had gained 1,380 votes, or 64 percent of the overseas ballots, while Gore gained 750 votes. That left Bush with an overall Florida lead of 930 votes. All counties were required to report their absentee totals by noon, and the two campaigns spent the morning trading accusations of misconduct and manipulation over several hundred overseas ballots that were discarded because of postmark disputes.

Nov. 19, 2000, David Firestone

RANCOR PREVAILS IN DEBATE OVER MILITARY VOTES

"We're distressed that it appears there's a statewide effort on behalf of Al Gore to discredit military votes."

– Mindy Tucker, Bush spokesperson

★ ★ ★

The two sides traded accusations of misconduct and manipulation today in the overnight counting of absentee ballots cast by Floridians abroad, a tally marred by confusion over rules and vastly differing standards from one county to the next.

The Bush campaign accused Democrats of conspiring to knock out as many ballots as possible from members of the military, who were expected to have voted mostly for Bush. The campaign issued a statement from retired Gen. H. Norman Schwarzkopf, who had campaigned for Bush, calling it "a very sad day in our country" when service members find that "because of some technicality out of their control they are denied the right to vote for the president of the United States, who will be their commander in chief."

Democrats countered that Republicans set out to keep military ballots in the count even when they should have been thrown out. "I think that they wanted to get every military vote they could counted, regardless of the law," said Bob Poe, chairman of the Florida Democratic Party. "They use the law when it suits their purposes, and ignore the law when it suits their purposes. There's an amazing, tremendous inconsistency on their part."

Democratic officials said that they were insisting on abiding by the rule that all ballots bear postmarks, and that the ballots most likely to lack postmarks were military ballots. But they denied that they were trying to systematically disenfranchise military voters. "I guess I wouldn't be surprised if there was another round of challenges in court because of this," said Jenny Backus, spokeswoman for the Florida Democratic Party.

In county after county, officials said that never before had anyone questioned the way they counted a handful of overseas ballots more than a week after the election, because never before had those votes mattered to the outcome. "Normally, we're the Maytag repairman around this time," said Fred Galey, supervisor of elections in Brevard County. "No one needs us or pays much attention to us."

But on Friday, county officials across the state gathered to count overseas ballots received after Election Day, with the eyes of the nation — and indeed much of the world — on them, and the presidency potentially in the balance. Both parties had observers in each county, inspecting ballots and raising objections to some, while defending the validity of others.

Those officials across the state complained of unclear instructions from Katherine Harris and her office, contributing to differing interpretations of the law. In particular, there was widespread disagreement over the rules on postmarks, which was also the subject of the partisan charges and countercharges.

In heavily Republican counties, county canvassing boards reviewing the ballots yesterday often decided to include military ballots that had no postmarks. In mostly Democratic counties, canvassing boards tended to throw out those ballots. Ballots could usually be identified as military or civilian by their envelopes, without being opened.

That discrepancy contributed to — but did not fully explain — a stark difference in the count: In counties carried by Bush, 29 percent of the overseas ballots were ruled invalid, but in counties carried by Gore, the figure was 60 percent. In Duval County, carried by Bush, the canvassing board rejected 64 of 542, or 12 percent. The second-largest number of ballots was in Broward County, a Gore stronghold, where the canvassing board threw out 304 of 396, or 77 percent.

In Escambia County, two of the three canvassing board members at first said they were inclined to invalidate 50 military ballots without postmarks, but were swayed by arguments from Republican lawyers present, and ultimately, the board voted to include them. John Gannon, a lawyer observing the counting there for the Democratic Party, protested, complaining that without postmarks, "We're going down the slippery slope of how the votes got into the supervisor's office in the first place."

In Orange County, the canvassing board rejected about 60 military ballots with missing postmarks or postmarks dated after the election, over the objections of Republicans. In Polk County, a Republican lawyer, John Stargel, said the party had directed people like him who were observing the counting to simply do whatever they could to make sure military ballots were included.

Florida law states that an overseas ballot must have a postmark, either from a foreign country's postal service or from a United States military post office. But the military often fails to postmark mail.

A federal law says that the military must mail service members' ballots from abroad "expeditiously and free of postage." Republicans contend that without any postage, there is often no postmark, so the intent of the federal law is that military ballots without postmarks must be considered valid.

The Bush campaign obtained and gave to reporters a copy of instructions the Democratic Party had sent to its observers and canvassing board members, reinforcing the need for a postmark and drawing particular attention to the possibility that they might be missing on military ballots. The Democrats, in turn, obtained and distributed the Republicans' instructions to their observers, reminding them of the federal law and instructing them in defending military ballots. Each party argued that the paperwork was evidence of malfeasance. In fact, each set of instructions simply offered a differing interpretation of the law.

Adding to the confusion, Harris instructed counties that ballots postmarked after Election Day but signed and dated on or before that day be counted. County officials said that was a reversal of past practice, in which ballots postmarked after the election were thrown out, and some complained that when they sought clarification, Harris's office gave them contradictory instructions. Harris's office refused to comment on the complaints.

Nov. 19, 2000, Richard Pérez-Peña

Gore Lawyers Blame Harris For...Well, Everything

"Taken as a whole, her approach has been Kafkaesque"
—from the Gore brief

★ ★ ★

TALLAHASSEE — Hand ballot recounts are an essential part of election law in Florida and other states, and the most accurate method of objectively determining voter intent. But they are complicated and take time — plenty of it.

That was the nub of Al Gore's legal argument in asking the Florida Supreme Court to force the state to include the results of hand ballot recounts in the final tally here — or at least block a final tally until the recounts now under way can be finished and reviewed. And in crisp language that blended citations of case law and statutes with the ringing tones of a political manifesto, Gore's lawyers insisted that most delays in the process so far had been caused by bad legal advice and meddling by Florida's chief election officer, Katherine Harris.

Noting that two courts, including the Supreme Court itself, had rejected Harris's efforts to cut off further recounts, the lawyers declared: "Taken as a whole, her approach has been Kafkaesque." Gore's lawyers contended that by not waiting to see what the recounts might produce, Harris was acting contrary "to a democratic system that rests on elections being determined by the will of the people, not the whim of state officials."

"Even if the secretary of state does have discretion to disregard authorized manual recounts in some circumstances," the 62-page brief concluded, "her pre-emptive declaration that she will, in no event, accept manual recounts in this election, was an abuse of that discretion."

In his own brief in the case, the state's Democratic attorney general, Robert A. Butterworth, argued that L. Clayton Roberts, the director of the state division of elections in Harris's office, also erred last week when he advised that counties could conduct hand recounts only if "the vote tabulation system fails to count" properly marked ballots because of problems like mechanical malfunctions or software glitches. Butterworth, the chairman of Gore's statewide campaign here, argued that the relevant law refers "not to an error in the vote tabulation system but to an error in the vote tabulation," and that under Roberts's interpretation, disputed votes "would be rejected even if a human review of the ballot revealed the voters' choice among candidates."

Today, Gore's brief also criticized Harris on this point. "To the extent that her rejection of these ballots rests on her opinion that such manual recounts are available only in cases of machine breakdown, that view is wholly unsupported by statute or case law," the lawyers argued. "This view articulated in the midst of litigation, in the heat of a political controversy, and contrary to the practice in this state for more than 150 years is not entitled to any deference."

Moreover, Gore's lawyers argued, Harris did not reject all manual recounts. She accepted them from Volusia County, which finished just five minutes before last Tuesday's 5 p.m. deadline for counties to submit their tallies. The recount produced a net gain of 98 votes for Gore.

His lawyers contended today that that deadline, one week after Election Day, is simply the deadline for counties "to submit their first returns as they exist." Nothing in Florida law, they argued, "imposes any deadline for the submission of corrected, amended or supplemental returns deemed necessary by the county canvassing board to ensure that the return submitted accurately and completely reflects the votes counted initially and in any recount."

Nov. 19, 2000, Todd S. Purdum

A Recount Moment: Eating the Chads

WEST PALM BEACH — Amid charges of chaos and chad eating, a recount in two crucial Florida counties has not, so far, produced the results that campaign workers for Al Gore had hoped.

In Palm Beach County, the vote recount crawled on with a gain of 12 votes for Bush. Gore had hoped to pick up a significant number of votes in this Democratic stronghold. In Broward County, where Gore has picked up 79 votes, the recount proceeded more or less smoothly, despite one Republican observer's charge of what people here are calling "chad eating." George S. Lemieux, vice chairman of the Broward County Republican Party, charged on Friday that a Republican observer saw a Democratic observer "putting chads in his mouth."

Republicans in Broward and Palm Beach Counties are pointing to the number of chads — the tiny scraps of paper from the holes in a punch-card ballot — left on the counting room floor as proof that the ballots are being roughly handled or perhaps even punched out on purpose. Lemieux said that he had heard rumors that Democrats were telling counters to conceal the chads, and that that was why the Democratic observer was eating them.

Republicans were counting the chads in Broward County. On Wednesday, they found 78 in the counting room; on Thursday they found 270; and on Friday, 142. "We walk around and we find them on the floor, tables and chairs," Lemieux said. That has Republicans charging that the handling of the ballots actually alters the way the ballots are counted.

The alleged chad eater had not been identified by the Republicans. It was just one more development in a process that has had people here, and around the world, shaking their heads at this history-making but sometimes comical process.

The process, which Republicans have described as chaos, is going painfully slow for the people watching it around the nation. Republicans say some volunteers are, either by accident or on purpose, dislodging the chads. Democrats this morning accused Republicans of trying to sabotage the election by challenging even clear votes for Gore.

But exactly what is going on inside the counting room — a hurricane bunker in the Palm Beach County Emergency Operations Center — depends on who is asked. Republicans describe a miserable, chaotic atmosphere. Democrats say all is going smoothly. Pool reports from reporters describe a scene somewhere in the middle, a tense atmosphere in which people occasionally disagree or snap at each other, but not chaos. Tonya Davis-Johnson, a vote counter from West Palm Beach who volunteered for the recount, told reporters that the process was not nearly so complicated or contentious as others have made it seem. County Judge Charles E. Burton, who presides over the canvassing board in Palm Beach County, said that counters are getting along and that altercations are infrequent and minor.

When this morning's recount began in Palm Beach, volunteers had 420,000 of the more than 462,000 votes to recount, in a process that was first intended to take six days, and now may take longer. In Broward County, elections officials said they could finish as early as Monday. When Miami-Dade, the largest county in the state, begins its recount on Monday of the county's almost 654,000 votes, it hopes to have 25 two-person teams of county employees in place to do the work. The officials speculated that the recount could take as long as two weeks, including weekends, with a one-day break for Thanksgiving.

But even before it started, the Miami-Dade recount is working through controversy. Republican Party officials have vigorously objected to a decision by elections officials to run the ballots through a counting machine on Sunday to cull voting cards on which no choice was made for president. Miguel A. DeGrandy, a lawyer for the Republican Party, said he was concerned that chads would fall off when the ballots are inserted. But elections officials denied the request, saying that, in any handling of the ballots, the chads could fall off. A lawyer for the Democrats, Stephen Zack, said the request was just another stalling tactic by Republicans. "It's time to find out what the people said," Zack said.

Nov. 19, 2000, Rick Bragg

An Ace in the Hole for Republicans

TALLAHASSEE — Republican state lawmakers here are homing in on an obscure, never-used federal statute that, they contend, could offer them a decisive hand in choosing Florida's precious 25 electors if the normal voting process somehow leaves the outcome unclear.

Ordinarily, presidential electors are chosen through the popular vote and are expected to cast their ballots for the winning candidate. But Republican leaders, who control both houses of the State Legislature, say they are examining a federal law that they believe gives them power to seat electors if the outcome of the popular vote in Florida is unclear. The development was first reported by The Pensacola News Journal and The Wall Street Journal.

"The specter is raised," said Tom Feeney, a state representative from Oviedo expected to be elected as speaker of the House. "If the courts don't allow the executive branch to do their duty, then at some point we would have to review our constitutional responsibilities. . . At this point we're watching and waiting."

Electors must be seated by Dec. 12. Republicans and Democrats interviewed today said they hoped the matter would be resolved long before then. But if that did not happen, Republican lawmakers said today that they could invoke the federal statute. They were far from certain exactly how to apply the law, and they said they were looking at retaining election law experts to help them wade through the statute.

Johnny Byrd, a Republican state representative from Plant City, added, "If the secretary of state is still under an injunction at noon on Tuesday, at that point it's just a question of when to pull the trigger." The trigger he is referring to is the Republicans' interpretation of Title 3, Section 2 of the United States Code. "Whenever any state has held an election for the purpose of choosing electors and has failed to make a choice on the day prescribed by law," the law reads, "the electors may be appointed on a subsequent day in such a manner as the Legislature of such state may direct."

The law has never been used, and by all accounts it is most likely to invite a bitter political tussle. "To end an election with the Legislature taking over for the will of the people, that would be politically very risky," Lois Frankel, a Democratic state representative from West Palm Beach, said today. Indeed, she added, she was doubtful of the prospect. "I can't even imagine why they would want to go there," Frankel said. "It almost leaves me speechless."

Nov. 19, 2000, Somini Sengupta and Dexter Filkins

day

12

SUNDAY,

NOVEMBER 19TH

★ ★ ★ ★ ★

THE COUNT DRAGS ON, THE LAWYERS FACE OFF

In anticipation of Monday's hearing before the Florida Supreme Court, both sides file legal briefs outlining their positions. All through the day the tedious hand recounts continue in Broward and Palm Beach Counties with little change in the vote tally evident. After the Democrats succeed in setting new standards for counting votes, Republicans express their outrage with a new ferocity. The issue of absentee ballots from overseas stays in the news as the Democrats try to quell a backlash against the invalidation of many military votes.

REPUBLICANS BLAST NEW RULES ABOUT DIMPLED CHADS

WEST PALM BEACH — Election workers in two Florida counties today resumed the laborious manual process that in recent days has been slowed by fatigue, partisan disputes and, in one county, another change in the definition of a vote.

The Republicans again harshly criticized the process as unfair, pointing particularly to the decision this morning by the Broward County Canvassing Board to adopt a broader standard when determining what constitutes a vote. The board, made up of two Democrats and a Republican, voted unanimously to consider dimpled or one-corner chads, the tiny pieces of paper that are normally dislodged from punch cards when a voter makes a choice, as possible votes for either Gore or Bush. Previously, the board had counted only chads with two or more corners punched through as votes.

The change came at the request of Democrats, who are clearly discouraged that the hand recounts in Broward and Palm Beach Counties have yet to produce the huge surge of additional votes for Gore that they had hoped to see by the time the Florida Supreme Court convened on Monday afternoon to consider whether the hand recounts should be included in the official count. With 428 of Broward County's 609 precincts manually counted by tonight, Gore had a net gain of 108 votes over the official tallies sent to the secretary of state on Tuesday. In Palm Beach County, workers have completed 31 of the 531 precincts and have come up with a net gain of 12 votes for Bush.

"It is wrong, it is flawed and it is a process that is simply and quite honestly not worthy of our democracy."

—Gov. Marc Racicot, Republican of Montana

Workers in Miami-Dade County have not begun to count the more than half-million votes there. With those votes outstanding and the counts in Broward and Palm Beach still incomplete, it remained unclear whether Gore would overcome the 930-vote lead Bush holds in the official count. The winner in Florida will receive the state's 25 decisive electoral votes.

Broward County's revised definition, adopted after recounting was completed in nearly half of the county's precincts, enraged Republicans, who accused the Democratic-controlled canvassing board of bowing to political pressure by maneuvering to achieve a result-oriented count.

The Gore campaign had hoped that the hand recount of the 587,928 ballots in Broward, a Democratic stronghold where Gore won 69 percent of the vote, would have netted the vice president more additional votes by now. This point was emphasized repeatedly today by Republicans, who compared the board's action to changing the rules in the third quarter of a football game. "They changed the rules so they could manufacture additional votes for Gore," said Gov. Marc Racicot, Republican of Montana, who held a news conference today in Austin, Tex. "It is wrong, it is flawed and it is a process that is simply and quite honestly not worthy of our democracy." Racicot added, "I've seen more stability, more predictability and more of a set of standards in place when you have a zoning hearing."

Edward J. Pozzuoli, the chairman of the Broward County Republican Party, said considering dimpled ballots "increases the subjectivity by tenfold" of workers. Racicot argued that eight of the nine members of South Florida's three canvassing boards are Democrats.

The Democrats countered by saying that the hand recount standard that was adopted today mirrors a Texas law that was signed by Bush. "We want a fair, accurate count," said Charles Lichtman, counsel for the Democratic Party.

In Palm Beach County, another Democratic stronghold just north of here where the Gore campaign hopes to pick up a large number of votes, Bush had a net gain of 12 votes but that total was after just 31 of 531 precincts were counted, officials said. "People may be surprised by the results here," Palm Beach County Judge Charles E. Burton, the chairman of the canvassing board, said in an interview today. "These allegations of widespread problems are wrong. The workers are doing the best they can, under extremely difficult circumstances."

As both sides escalated a war of words and exchanged new charges and countercharges, there were thousands of challenged ballots piling up in both Palm Beach and Broward Counties. Republican monitors in both counting rooms are meticulously collecting fallen chads in cellophane bags. "Evidence," one Republican lawyer called the chads.

Democrats say that Republicans are challenging one in five ballots in Palm Beach County as an attempt to delay the process. Officials in both Palm Beach and Broward Counties acknowledged that it would be extraordinarily difficult to meet their deadlines to complete the tedious task of hand-counting each ballot. Broward had set a goal of 5 p.m. Monday; Palm Beach County had hoped to finish before Thanksgiving Day.

In Miami-Dade, the canvassing board began preparing for its full recount on Monday by feeding all of the 653,963 ballots through machines to separate those that had no vote for president so that they could be made immediately available for the board's review. But Republicans cried foul, saying the machine would merely remove even more chads. Officials estimated that the hand recount in Miami might not be completed until early December.

The tedious process was cited by Republican officials, who continued to portray the hand recounts here and in Palm Beach County as a chaotic, unruly process that was vulnerable to evolving standards, workers' subjectivity, wear and tear of the ballots and even outright mischief. "There continues to be serious flaws in this process," said Scott McLellan, a spokesman for the Bush campaign. "The workers are tired, and this increases the risk of human error."

Jenny Backus, press secretary for the Democratic National Committee, said the Republicans' motives were clear. "This is about sowing the seeds of doubt in a process that federal law, state law and local law — and both Republicans and Democrats — have consistently supported," Backus said today.

Nov. 20, 2000, Don Van Natta Jr.

LEGAL BATTLE LINES ARE DRAWN

TALLAHASSEE — Lawyers for George W. Bush contended today that Florida law set a clear deadline of last Tuesday for counties to submit all vote tallies except those for overseas absentee ballots, and they asked the Florida Supreme

Court to let the state reject any manual recounts conducted after that date.

In a 56-page brief that focused narrowly on the specific language of Florida's election statutes, Bush's legal team argued that the State Legislature had fully understood that a manual recount could take longer than the seven-day deadline and had nonetheless come down squarely on the side of a clear cutoff, one week after Election Day, at 5 p.m.

"If a county board believes that a manual recount is important to ensure an accurate vote count in a closely contested election, it has a statutory duty to appoint enough counting teams to get the job done by the deadline," said the Republican brief, submitted for a hearing by the court on Monday. "If a board is unable or unwilling to do so, it should not exercise its unfettered discretion to embark on a manual recount."

Much of the Republican case, in fact, is built on a contention that the Florida Legislature knew exactly what it was doing in enacting election laws that at times appear to conflict with one another, like the provisions requiring a tight deadline and allowing a manual recount, which is time-consuming and complex. Comparing the legislature to the "framers of the Constitution," Bush's lawyers wrote, "Surely the legislature would not have enacted two conflicting provisions at the same time."

In their reply to the Bush brief a few hours later, lawyers for Al Gore said that an accurate determination of the voters' intent was more important than a "hypertechnical compliance" with a deadline in the law. They also went a step further, asking the high court for the first time to set a firm standard for how a punch-card ballot should be examined to determine a voter's intent, suggesting that all marks and indentations on a ballot should be broadly interpreted as a vote.

Such a ruling by the Supreme Court could bring some uniformity to the hand counts now going on in three Florida counties, which have used differing standards to determine a vote.

In her own brief filed separately with the court today, Katherine Harris struck a note of equanimity and tried to separate herself from the two partisan sides. Her lawyers even asked the court not to include her position on the Republican side, even though her arguments are very similar to those of Bush.

"The Democrats' perspective is that the election code has to be read as mandating that each voter's intent, irrespective of whether the voter has properly punched or marked his or her ballot, must take precedence over statutory deadlines, the constitutional construction of statutes, and the discretion and operative duties of executive officers," Harris wrote. "The Republicans, not to be outdone, are complaining about procedures for manual recounting and the sanctity of the machine tabulation."

"It is clear," Harris added, "that for the Democrats and the Republicans, the object is to win, and that is understandable. The stakes are very high."

Lawyers for Bush and Harris insisted that she had acted properly, and well within the discretion allowed by law, in rejecting explanations from the three counties saying they might need more time to conduct manual recounts. Only proof of fraud, substantial noncompliance with election procedures, or an act of God could justify missing the legal deadline, she said.

"Every voter is entitled to have his or her ballot treated in the same fashion, irrespective of where he or she lives," Harris's brief contended. "A decision to screen voters for voter error cannot be indulged in one county but not another." Bush's lawyers went even further, arguing that the Democrats were asking the high court to "rewrite the law" pertaining to elections.

"Simply put," Bush's brief said, "they ask this court to revise the statute's plain directive that late-filed returns 'may be ignored' to read instead that the secretary 'may not ignore' late-filed returns if the county board is conducting a manual recount." It said the Democrats were "not coy" about seeking to rewrite the law, although Democrats have said they were simply interpreting it properly.

The Republicans also made the argument — which has so far not been persuasive in the federal courts — that the United States Constitution forbids the manual counts in three Democratic counties. Because the hand counts are not being held in all counties, they said, the process violates the equal-protection clause of the 14th Amendment. Adding a federal argument to a state supreme court case is often a way to create a vehicle for appealing to the United States Supreme Court, which the Republicans have suggested they are prepared to do. But a top Gore legal adviser said today that he expected the issue to be settled by the Florida court.

Nov. 20, 2000, Todd S. Purdum and David Firestone

Military Ballots Merit a Review, Lieberman Says

TALLAHASSEE — Canvassing boards meeting Friday night and Saturday in all 67 Florida counties threw out 1,420 absentee ballots from overseas without opening the envelopes, or 39 percent of the total, according to an unofficial tally by The Associated Press. Reasons for the disqualifications included missing postmarks. Of those that were counted, 1,380 were for Bush and 750 were for Gore, widening Bush's overall lead in this state to 930 votes out of almost six million cast.

Senator Joseph I. Lieberman, the Democratic candidate for vice president, said today that Florida election officials should reconsider their rejection of military ballots from overseas, even if they might not comply with the law.

Lieberman's comments, a retreat from the position the Democrats had taken since Friday, came after they were stung by Republican charges that they had made a concerted effort to disenfranchise members of the military. While Republicans painted their opponents as being willing to use any means to manipulate vote totals in the extraordinary, tense and prolonged Florida count, Democrats complained that they were losing a nasty public relations battle for simply insisting on following the law as it has been applied in the past.

"My own point of view, if I was there, I would give the benefit of the doubt to ballots coming in from military personnel, generally," Lieberman said on NBC's *Meet the Press*. Of the local canvassing boards, he said, "If they have the capacity, I'd urge them to go back and take another look, because again, Al Gore and I don't want to ever be part of anything that would put an extra burden on the military personnel abroad."

A senior Republican official close to the Bush campaign said that the campaign was contemplating a federal court suit challenging the dismissal of the military ballots, but that a decision would not be made until lawyers for Bush see how they fare before the Florida State Supreme Court, which is considering the validity of manual recounts requested by Gore in some counties.

It is not clear whether Lieberman's statement will have any practical effect, except perhaps to shield the Democrats from criticism, since the votes have been counted and the tallies sent to the secretary of state's office. It would be up to election officials in each county to seek to alter that count, and it is not at all certain that they would want to. And local Democrats could still challenge any changes in court.

Lieberman tried to turn the softening of the Democrats' position to the campaign's advantage, arguing that in the same spirit that the overseas ballots should be counted, the manual recount the Gore camp has demanded in certain Florida counties should be included in the final tally. The principle to follow, he said, is that "every vote cast there must be counted."

County elections officials, Republican and Democrat alike, agree that overseas ballots have always been thrown out in large numbers for the same kinds of technical violations cited this weekend, though the voters who cast them were unaware of it because the process had never before been subjected to such scrutiny.

Democratic lawyers who watched the counting on Friday night of overseas votes, which normally favor Republicans, insisted that local canvassing boards stick to the detailed requirements of Florida law. In some counties, particularly those controlled by their party, the Democrats were successful in having a large proportion of the ballots — civilian as well as military — invalidated. Republican officials' lawyers argued that a federal law supersedes the Florida law, an argument whose merit is far from clear.

David C. Leahy, supervisor of elections for Miami-Dade County, said today that elections officials were being assailed for doing nothing more than abiding by the law, the same law they have abided by for years, without complaint. The Miami-Dade canvassing board, of which he is a member, threw out 209 of the 312 overseas ballots it reviewed Friday, and the most common reason was that the people who had sent them turned out not to be residents of that county. "The board had no discretion with any of those 209 kicked out," he said.

On Friday, Fred Galey, elections supervisor in Brevard County, said: "In the past, we have not counted ballots that didn't have a postmark. This is the first year anybody has told us something different."

Other military ballots throughout Florida were rejected because the voters were not recorded as having requested Florida absentee ballots. Federal law permits members of the military to use what is called a federal write-in ballot, but only if they requested, but did not receive, one of their home state's absentee ballots.

Nov. 20, 2000, Richard Pérez-Peña

Profile: KATHERINE HARRIS
WICKED WITCH OR QUEEN ESTHER?

TALLAHASSEE — They just can't stop talking about her. Her integrity, her ignorance. Her lashes, her lipstick.

She, of course, is Katherine Harris — Florida's secretary of state, co-chairwoman of George W. Bush's campaign here and scion of a citrus aristocracy who eight years ago was playing a Vanna White-like character in a Sarasota nightclub act. Since Election Day, she has emerged as more of a political lightning rod than anyone in recent years except perhaps Hillary Clinton.

She is reviled by some as Gov. Jeb Bush's ignorant puppet (actually, far more unflattering terms have been used) and heralded by others as an icon of grace and courage. She is the screen on which both sides, it seems, have projected their own fears. The Democrats' chief fear, of course, is that Harris, 43, a conservative Republican who had mused aloud about an ambassadorship in a Bush administration, will serve as the agent of Jeb Bush in locking up the election for his brother. The Republicans, fearing an army of shrill, litigious Democrats, see her as their defender, the voice of reason and arbiter of Florida law.

That is arguably more true for Florida Republicans than for anyone else. They regard Harris, a fourth-generation Floridian, as one of them, a bulwark against liberal outsiders. "I think it's highly chauvinist for some of these brutes to come down here and attack her this way," growled Tom Feeney, the Republican speaker-elect of the Florida House of Representatives.

To properly understand the yin and yang of Harris's iconic stature these days, consider this scene from West Palm Beach last night. Among the rabble of dueling protesters was one who hoisted an effigy-like inflatable doll. Its head was plastered with a photo of Harris. It was dressed in an Oz-like Wicked Witch costume. On her torso was pinned a maliciously insulting sign. All evening, every time the Harris-loathing protester got in view of the television news cameras, Republican supporters, carrying placards of their own, rushed over to try to keep him off the air.

Alan M. Dershowitz, the liberal Harvard law professor who was among the legions of lawyers who arrived here last week, has called Harris "a crook." A Gore campaign aide, Paul Begala, likened her to Cruella De Vil, the lithe and mean villain of *101 Dalmatians* fame. (He apologized a few days later, though it stuck in the national discourse.) *The Washington Post* yesterday devoted an entire, entirely snarky piece to her makeup. Those were surely falsies, the article concluded of her eyelashes — "cartoon lashes," the Post article declared.

From the other side has come equally hyperbolic kudos. Among the thousands of messages that poured into her e-mail inbox since Election Day was one that described her as the Queen Esther of Sunshine State politics. For the Old Testament-ignorant, Queen Esther is remembered for having used her influence with the King of Persia, Ahasuerus, to overturn an order to kill the Jews. (Harris did little to dispute the comparison.)

Her pedigree only helps detractors slam her as a rich dilettante. In the Florida caste system, Harris is a Brahmin of the highest order. Her grandfather, Ben Hill Griffin, was a citrus and cattle baron who served in the Florida Legislature in the 1950's. The University of Florida football stadium is named after him, thanks to a $20 million donation.

Harris attended the exclusive all-girls Agnes Scott College in Atlanta; one classmate remembered her as the picture of charming, polished Southern aristocracy. She was an agile tennis player. She studied in Switzerland. In 1992, she was hired to entertain at the Florida Studio Theater in Sarasota, leading the crowd in a chicken dance and distributing fast-food gift certificates.

Her conservative stripes are well established. During her stint in the State Senate, from 1994 to 1998, Harris garnered approval ratings of 100 percent from Florida Right to Life and 86 percent from the Christian Coalition.

Nov. 20, 2000, Somini Sengupta

day

13

MONDAY,

NOVEMBER 20TH

★ ★ ★ ★ ★

RECOUNT DEBATE REACHES FLORIDA SUPREME COURT

After hearing arguments about ongoing hand recounts, the Florida Supreme Court expresses skepticism about the arguments made by both sides. Republican lawyers are asked to justify their rejection of the time-consuming counts in certain large counties, while Democrats attempt to justify a course of action that jeopardizes Florida's representation in the Electoral College. Also today, a state judge in Seminole County agrees to hear a lawsuit over local absentee ballot applications, while another judge in Palm Beach County rules, with some regret, that the U.S. Constitution expressly forbids a revote in his county. Meanwhile, Democrats are fighting hard for looser recount standards as it is becoming apparent that the current standards will not produce enough votes for a Gore victory.

A SKEPTICAL FLORIDA SUPREME COURT ASKS TOUGH QUESTIONS

TALLAHASSEE — The Florida Supreme Court sharply challenged lawyers for Vice President Al Gore and George W. Bush on parallel tracks, asking the Republicans to justify a state deadline that ignored hand recounts in big, largely Democratic counties, and pressing the Democrats to explain how the court could set a new deadline without jeopardizing Florida's voice in the Electoral College.

In an extraordinary, nearly two-and-a-half-hour hearing carried live on television, justices of the state's highest court peppered lawyers for both sides with searching, skeptical questions. The justices homed in particularly on the Republicans' contention that state law allowed no leeway in the deadline for counties to submit their returns by one week after Election Day. They repeatedly asked whether that was enough time to conduct laborious hand counts in the populous counties where they are now under way.

But the court, the one branch of Florida government dominated by Democratic appointees, also expressed clear unease at the Democrats' suggestions that it, not the Legislature or the state's top election official, should set a new deadline or outline its own standards for how ballots should be recounted around the state. And the justices showed concern that prolonging the post-electoral wrangling without an official winner could short-circuit the eventual loser's right to contest the election, as provided by state law. The court recessed for the night without issuing a decision. It was unclear when one might come.

"Isn't there something unusual about changing the rules in the middle of the game?"

— Florida Supreme Court Justice Major B. Harding

The stakes in the court's elegant chamber could not have been higher, nothing less than the presidency itself. And the principal question of law was fairly narrow: whether Florida's secretary of state has the right to refuse results of manual recounts submitted after the normal legal deadline for counties to certify their vote tallies last Tuesday at 5 p.m. But there was nothing simple about what the justices themselves suggested they were being asked to do: revise and elaborate on the state's election laws under intense time pressure, with few settled facts and little in the way of a lower-court record to go on.

Paul Hancock, a lawyer for the state's Democratic attorney general, Robert A. Butterworth, was frank in urging the court to use "the full reach of its authority to establish procedures that ensure that this results in a process that, first of all, is fair, that is perceived as fair to the world and in fact is fair, that it counts the votes of all people who attempted to exercise that vote."

When one justice, Major B. Harding, asked Gore's chief litigator, David Boies, if the court had reliable information on how long such counts might take, Boies acknowledged that the record was limited, and said, "I believe there is going to have to be a lot of judgment applied by the court."

Joseph P. Klock Jr., a lawyer for the Republican secretary of state, Katherine Harris, said that under state law, such judgments were up to her and that she had properly exercised her discretion under state law in deciding not to accept late recounts.

Klock said the law was clear, that the secretary was required to collect certified results from all counties by one week after Election Day, and then reach a final tally including overseas absentee ballots three days later. But several justices also asked lawyers for the Republicans whether it was really fair to expect populous counties like Miami-Dade to conduct recounts in the same one-week time frame as smaller, rural counties.

"Don't we also end up discriminating between small counties and large counties?" Justice Harry Lee Anstead asked.

Klock said the Legislature had considered such realities. "It is part of the scheme," he said. "It has to be done in seven days." Klock urged the court to let the state certify final returns now, and said Gore would be free to challenge the results in court, a course the vice president's lawyers have so far resisted for fear of seeming to be sore losers.

"The problem with respect to the electoral votes in Florida only occurs if the status quo is maintained, if the votes cannot be certified, if the contest procedure cannot begin," Klock said.

A lawyer for Bush, Michael A. Carvin, argued that while Florida law allowed manual recounts if counties chose to conduct them, nothing in the law favored them, or gave counties extra time to complete them. He said the Democrats "want this court, on the basis of no evidence, to enter a judicial fiat that the only way to determine a voter's intent is through manual recounts."

Carvin added: "Anything which departs from the rules that were set before Nov. 7, before the election, by the Florida Legislature, would be gross abuse of discretion and impermissible. And that's why we have deadlines, and that's why we have uniform rules."

A few moments later, under pointed questioning from the court's newest member, Peggy A. Quince, Carvin did acknowledge that sometimes the only way to determine a voter's intention was to "look at the ballot," in an effort to determine whether the voter punched through the card enough to show what he or she intended to do. But Carvin quickly went on to insist that "this is a standardless and subjective inquiry which there are not Florida rules on, and that is why they are asking you for some guidance."

In fact, at least one county conducting recounts, Broward, voted on Sunday to broaden its standards for determining a vote, agreeing to consider dimpled or one-corner chads, the tiny pieces of paper normally dislodged from punch card-ballots, as valid votes. Previously, the board had been counting only chads with two or more corners punched through.

"Isn't there something unusual about changing the rules in the middle of the game?" Justice Harding asked a lawyer for the Broward County Canvassing Board, Andrew J. Meyers.

Meyers replied: "I think the important thing is that we do what's right at the end, and this has been an evolving area."

Nov. 21, 2000, Todd S. Purdum

Seminole County Absentee Case Goes to Court

A local judge agreed to hear a lawsuit seeking to throw out the 15,000 absentee ballots cast in heavily Republican Seminole County, Fla., where Sandra Goard, the county supervisor of elections, allowed Republican Party workers to correct Republican voters' incomplete absentee-ballot applications that had been rejected in the weeks before the election. George W. Bush garnered 10,006 absentee votes in Seminole County, just northeast of Orlando, compared with 5,209 for Al Gore.

A local lawyer, Harry Jacobs, a Democrat, filed suit maintaining that Goard broke a Florida law requiring that only the voter, members of the immediate family or a guardian provide all information for the ballot application. Judge Debra Nelson of Seminole County Circuit Court, who disclosed at a hearing that her campaign manager was a local Republican official, denied a motion to have Jacobs's suit dismissed, and gave him permission to begin gathering evidence.

Since it can no longer be determined which ballots went with which applications, Jacobs is asking that all the absentee ballots in the county be invalidated. "I'm very satisfied," Jacobs said after Judge Nelson's ruling, adding that he intended to begin questioning elections office employees and other prospective witnesses as early as today. Jim Hattaway, an Orlando lawyer representing Goard and the Seminole County Canvassing Board, said that he was "not surprised or disappointed" but that he expected to prevail once the merits were argued.

Nov. 21, 2000, Michael Moss

Judge Says He Can't Order Palm Beach Revote

WEST PALM BEACH — A state judge here concluded that he lacked the legal authority to order a second presidential election in Palm Beach County, even if he were to determine that the county's "butterfly" ballot design had confused enough voters to make a difference in the election.

The judge, Jorge LaBarga of Palm Beach County Circuit Court, rejected the revote remedy that had been sought by dozens of voters here, saying that the Constitution stated clearly that the presidential election must be held on the same day throughout the United States.

"Given the uniqueness of presidential elections and the undue advantage a revote or new election may afford one candidate over the other(s), it was the clear and unambiguous intention of the framers of the Constitution of the United States that presidential elections be held on a single day throughout the United States," Judge LaBarga wrote.

Palm Beach County voters who filed the lawsuit said they were extremely disappointed. Within an hour of the judge's order this morning, lawyers for the voters filed an appeal with a state appeals court.

The butterfly ballot in Palm Beach County was "illegal, unfair and misleading," Andre Fladell, the lead plaintiff, said at a news conference at his lawyer's office in Boca Raton. "We went to court to prove that. Today, the judge said even if we are right, there is nothing he could do. If the people are expected to adhere to the rule of law and be held responsible, then so, too, should the government be held responsible to the rule of law."

Never before in American history has a judge ordered a revote in a presidential election. "The plaintiffs in this action cite no case law authority in the history of our nation, nor can the court find any, where a revote or new election was permitted in a presidential race," Judge LaBarga said.

The judge's order also canceled an evidentiary hearing that was to determine whether the ballot's design had confused voters. "He cost me my right to vote," Fladell said of the judge, "and that upsets me."

Judge LaBarga, who emigrated from Cuba as a young boy, said at a hearing on Friday that he cherished the sanctity of the vote. He said if the Constitution required him to reject a county revote, it would represent "the hardest decision I would ever have to make."

In his order today, Judge LaBarga wrote, "Clearly, a great number of patriotic and deeply concerned citizens of Palm Beach County fear that they may have unwittingly cast their vote for someone other than their candidate."

"However," the judge wrote, "for over two centuries we have agreed to a Constitution and to live by the law. Indeed, it is because we are first and foremost a nation that respects our constitutional tradition that our country continues to go about its business, despite the very important issues raised by the election of Nov. 7, 2000. Consequently, this court must follow the mandates of the law."

Nov. 21, 2000, Don Van Natta Jr.

Parties Clash over Recount Standards

"They've gone from counting votes to looking for votes to now manufacturing votes."

— Rep. John Sweeney (R-N.Y.)

★ ★ ★

WEST PALM BEACH — Disappointed by the results so far of the hand recounts, Democrats have set aside hundreds of ballots with no holes punched for a presidential candidate in the hope that they can persuade the canvassing boards or the courts that an indentation next to Vice President Al Gore's name should be counted as a vote for him.

Democrats want the canvassing boards in Miami-Dade and Palm Beach Counties to use a broader standard to count the so-called dimpled ballots as votes for either Gore or Gov. George W. Bush. The Democrats have already succeeded in persuading the Broward canvassing board to consider approximately 1,200 such ballots.

Democrats said they hoped for a surge of votes in Miami-Dade, the state's most populous county, where the canvassing board this morning embarked on Florida's fourth countywide manual recount. With 67 of Miami-Dade's 614 precincts counted today, Gore had a net gain of 46 votes. With 535 of Broward County's 609 precincts manually counted tonight, Gore had a net gain of 117 votes since the recount began. Broward County's dimpled ballots have been set aside for review by canvassing board members, a process that is expected to begin on Tuesday.

But that task was complicated late today by the sudden resignation of the Broward elections supervisor, Jane Carroll, from the canvassing board. Carroll, 70, the lone Republican on the board, said a long week of 15-hour days had threatened her health, and she planned to go on a family vacation on Wednesday.

Broward County election officials had hoped to finish the recounting by 5 p.m., but said that the board now hoped to finish its hand recount on Tuesday and then move on to a recount of the 50,000 absentee ballots cast there. And Palm Beach officials acknowledged that they would be unable to complete the hand recount before Thanksgiving. The board said it would quit early on Wednesday for the holiday, and workers would not be asked to return until Sunday.

Over all, the partial results from the three counties seem unlikely at the current pace to overcome the 930-vote lead Bush has established in the official tally, deepening the Democrats' resolve to push hard for a broader standard in determining what constitutes a vote. Meanwhile, Republicans are continuing their attacks on the recounting process, using some of the harshest language yet to criticize what they consider shifting standards. "They've gone from counting votes to looking for votes to now manufacturing votes," Representative John E. Sweeney, Republican of New York, said today.

Chris Lehane, a spokesman for Gore, rejected those accusations, saying the Democrats were simply asking for a widely accepted standard that hand recounts should gauge the voter's intent on ballots, which includes the tabulation of those with dimpled chads. Lehane said the vice president's campaign felt certain that Gore would erase Bush's lead if the canvassing boards searched ballots for the voter's intent.

"As long as the manual recount is allowed to go forward," Lehane said, "we firmly believe that when all is said and done, the recount will show what we believe — and what the Bush campaign also knows to be true — that more people went to the polls to vote for Al Gore on Election Day in Florida than went to the polls to vote for George Bush."

In their case before the Florida Supreme Court, the Democrats have also asked the justices to set a standard for how punch cards should be examined, suggesting that all marks and indentations be broadly interpreted as votes.

Even before the counting began this morning, the Republicans sought a hearing in Circuit Court, where it had hoped to present evidence to support its contention that the recount should be stopped. In the meantime, Republicans asked the canvassing board for a set of guidelines to protect the integrity of the manual recount. Miguel A. DeGrandy, a lawyer for the Republican Party, requested that the board allow his team to view both sides of every ballot during the recounting and have every contested ballot marked and set aside for use as evidence in court proceedings.

The board turned down those proposals and the Democrats were quick to call them stalling tactics.

Nov. 21, 2000, Don Van Natta Jr.

REPUBLICANS SEE A "MESS," DEMOCRATS SEE "SMOOTH" PROCESS

TALLAHASSEE – The battle for Florida was distilled to its essence: a sharpening contest between dueling images of chaos and order. Across the state, through legal arguments, protests and news conferences, Republicans intensified their campaign to portray the hand count of ballots here as a confusing, corrupt circus that mocks democracy. Their word of the day was "mess." Likewise, the Democrats worked to portray the recount as a calm, careful, civic-minded endeavor that venerates democracy. Their chosen word was "smooth."

Each side has labored mightily to cement its preferred image of Florida's recount into the public's consciousness, and for good reason, strategists in both parties said. The image contest, they said, is now at the strategic heart of each side's legal and political objectives. It is the subtext that helps explain the confusing flurry of tactical maneuvers, the connective tissue that binds each side's legal and public relations postures.

Simply put, Republicans calculate that if the public views Florida as a state locked in bitter chaos, it will respond with mounting disgust and mistrust, which in turn will pressure the courts to call an end to the election while George W. Bush holds the lead. Democrats, meanwhile, are betting that if the public perceives the Florida recount as an open and orderly process, this will produce an atmosphere of patience and trust, which in turn will buy time to continue a hand count they believe will ultimately leave Al Gore the victor.

And so as the Republicans continue to roll reinforcements into Florida to protest ballot recounts, the Democrats are trying to hold their union partisans back to avoid the sort of ugly street clashes that might contribute to an ominous image of disarray. And while Democrats speak in soothing tones about allowing elections professionals and earnest volunteers to proceed in uninterrupted peace, Republicans continue dire warnings of mischief and cover-ups.

This message has been reinforced daily by recruits from Austin and Washington, where at last Tuesday's morning meeting of the House Republican caucus about a dozen Republicans complained that Bush and his advisers were losing the public relations war and that members of Congress were not being kept enough in the loop to be able to help. The result is that more members of Congress are starting to turn up as surrogates for Bush, repeating his position that the manual recounts are subjective, subject to shenanigans, simply a mess. Late last week, Congressional aides said, the Bush campaign began recruiting Hill staff members willing to take vacation time and go to Florida to monitor the recount.

Words such as "bullying" and "selective" and "vote theft" have been tossed around in recent days, and bags of chads have been brandished before television cameras as still more evidence of a sloppy process. Today, signaling its intention to continue on this course while the legal fight rages, the Bush campaign called for still more volunteers in an e-mail message sent out to various Republican groups.

"It's all delay, delay, delay."

—Gore campaign labor organizer, about Republican tactics

The Democrats have employed an entirely different set of catchwords, manners and tactics to reinforce the image of an orderly process. They praise the "ordinary citizens" who have shown up faithfully day after day to count ballots. They praise the professionalism of the canvassing boards. They use words like "sober" and "wise" to describe the members of the Florida Supreme Court, dominated by Democrats. Under no circumstance is Florida's recent history of vote fraud mentioned.

But perhaps even more telling, the Democrats have chosen to avoid where possible the sort of angry mass demonstrations that could contribute to a perception of street chaos. The Gore campaign, for example, could have easily tapped into its labor base to mobilize supporters on the streets. But, campaign officials say, a decision was made right after Nov. 7: union organizers would be mobilized to act as Democratic observers of the recount, but not to match the Republicans' street soldiers, who have been a noisy presence at rallies across the state.

And at the recount tables in South Florida, Democratic observers have repeatedly accused their Republican counterparts of raising objections to the tiniest details — a pencil mark here, an overfilled bubble there — as a way to manufacture the very chaos they are now condemning.

"It reinforces their own message that it's chaotic," complained one labor organizer on loan to the Gore campaign. "Secondly, it's a delay factor. It's all delay, delay, delay."

Nov. 21, 2000, David Barstow with Alison Mitchell

Florida Attorney General Orders Review of Military Votes

TALLAHASSEE — Retreating under fire from Republicans, Florida's attorney general, a top ally of Al Gore, said today that local officials should count absentee ballots from overseas military voters that were thrown out because they lacked postmarks.

But the statement by Robert A. Butterworth, Gore's state campaign chairman, may have less to do with votes than with cutting Democrats' losses in what they concede has been a losing public relations war. Today, Butterworth sent a letter to county elections officials around the state, urging them "to immediately revisit this issue and amend their reported vote totals, if appropriate."

Ari Fleischer, spokesman for the Bush campaign, dismissed Butterworth's letter as "a belated attempt at damage control after they've done the damage" to people in the armed services. "This has no legal impact, and it's really just a political press release," he said.

Nov. 21, 2000, Richard Pérez-Peña

★ ★ ★

OpEd

The Florida Court Should Boldly Take Charge

With its aggressive and broad-ranging questions, the Florida Supreme Court assumed its place in the eye of a political hurricane as tumultuous in its way as the other type that traditionally hits the state. The Supreme Court is now the only state institution able to quell the political paranoia of all but the fiercest partisans and bring this presidential election to a credible close. To do that, it must do more than address the immediate issue before it — whether hand-counted votes must be tallied — and take command of the entire dispute.

This is not a role judges usually relish; they prefer to answer each legal question one case at a time. But with the meeting of the Electoral College less than four weeks away, that slow pace will soon make the court irrelevant and create a vacuum for three less desirable competitors.

The court should set a timetable for the resolution of all election challenges before the Electoral College meets on Dec. 18. The timetable must have accelerated procedures for asserting claims and filing appeals. The court should also provide guidance on issues now before lower courts — whether a pregnant chad is a vote, which absentee ballots count, whether it was proper for Republican workers to complete absentee ballot applications, and what remedy, if any, there should be for juror confusion over the Palm Beach butterfly ballot. Because United States Supreme Court review of these issues is remote, the State Supreme Court's answers to them now will hasten the end of the story.

The alternatives are not attractive. The court might choose to defer to any decision that Katherine Harris, Florida's partisan secretary of state, makes, as long as she can offer a plausible reason for it. Or, if the legal cases drag on and Florida is unable to certify a winner, the state's Republican-controlled legislature may appoint the electors. They are likely to be the same ones that Ms. Harris was prepared to certify on Saturday, before the State Supreme Court stopped her. One Florida legislator, citing a federal statute, has already said he may push for this action in the legislature.

Or, if the state is unable to certify any electors, Al Gore will have a majority of the Electoral College vote but will be at least four votes shy of an absolute majority of all possible electors. Does that make him president-elect? The question would be resolved by a closely divided Congress.

These three paths to Inauguration Day would give us a president, but none would carry the kind of legitimacy that a decisive court decision can offer. Of course, if the court's s rulings enhance Mr. Gore's chance of victory, we can expect claims of bias, since six of its seven judges were appointed by Democratic governors. That charge will be hollow. One rarely gets to be a judge without a party affiliation. But unlike others competing to write the final chapter here, the judges have not been, and could not ethically be, politically active.

The court is removed from politics in other ways, too. It must apply rules and legal opinions written well before the current controversy. The court must adhere to accepted methods of interpreting and applying legal texts. And judges must defend their decision in a detailed opinion.

The Florida Supreme Court has an excellent reputation. That is no accident. Nor is it likely that the court will squander its reputation to satisfy the ambitions of either presidential candidate. Precisely because the court has this reservoir of trust, a form of capital no other player in this drama can claim, it also has the responsibility to prescribe and monitor the way to a satisfying conclusion.

Nov. 21, 2000

By Stephen Gillers, Vice Dean and Professor of Legal and Judicial Ethics at New York University School of Law

day

14

TUESDAY,

NOVEMBER 21ST

★ ★ ★ ★ ★

FLORIDA SUPREME COURT BACKS RECOUNTS—AGAIN

The Florida Supreme Court rules that the results of hand recounts must be included in Florida's final vote tally and sets a new deadline nearly a week away. The Gore team claims a victory, while the Bush campaign hints that it will fight the decision in the courts and in the Florida Legislature. The court's ruling offers no explicit guidelines for discerning voter intent, but Democrats believe that certain passages allow for the counting of "dimpled" chads, which may be the key to winning in the Florida recount.

FLORIDA COURT UNANIMOUSLY AFFIRMS GORE'S CASE

TALLAHASSEE — The Florida Supreme Court ruled unanimously tonight that the results of manual ballot recounts in three heavily Democratic counties must be included in the state's final tally, as long as they are submitted no later than Monday morning. But it set no firm standards for determining how to count partly punched ballots.

"Courts must not lose sight of the fundamental purpose of election laws: The laws are intended to facilitate and safeguard the right of each voter to express his or her will in the context of our representative democracy," the court held in a 42-page opinion that amounted to a substantial legal victory for Al

Gore. "Technical statutory requirements must not be exalted over the substance of this right."

With the presidency hanging in the balance, the court's spokesman, Craig Waters, appeared shortly before 10 p.m. tonight to announce that it had ruled. The court ruled that the state could not certify official results of the election until at least Sunday evening, or Monday morning if the secretary of state's office is not open Sunday, and it required the state election board to include in its final tally any manual counts submitted by that time.

The court said the secretary of state could reject a board's manual returns if they are so late that they blocked a candidate's ability to contest the election under state law, an action that can only take place after the votes are certified. The only other reason the returns can be rejected, the court said, was if waiting for them would preclude Florida voters from participating in the electoral process, by making the votes too late to be counted in the Electoral College, which meets on Dec. 18.

"We will now move forward with a full, fair and accurate count of the ballots in question."

— Al Gore

And the court ruled emphatically that rejecting the hand counts simply because election boards could not complete them in the seven-day deadline would punish the wrong group of people. "To allow the secretary to summarily disenfranchise innocent electors in an effort to punish dilatory board members, as she proposes in the present case, misses the constitutional mark," the opinion said. "The Constitution eschews punishment by proxy."

The court set no clear standards on the crucial question of how a ballot should be read to learn a voter's intent — declining to wade into an area now in great dispute in the three South Florida Democratic enclaves where hand recounts are proceeding.

But it cited with approval an Illinois Supreme Court case mentioned in the Democrats' legal papers that said indications of a voter's intent should be considered and not just those ballots that were completely punched:

"Voters should not be disfranchised where their intent may be ascertained with reasonable certainty, simply because the chad they punched did not completely dislodge from the ballot," the justices ruled. "Such a failure may be attributable to the fault of the election authorities, for failing to provide properly perforated paper, or it may be the result of a voter's disability or inadvertence. Whatever the reason, where the intention of the voter can be fairly and satisfactorily ascertained, that intention should be given effect."

Such guidance, although apparently not intended as a blanket rule for the state, could be interpreted in various ways by county election boards struggling to determine which ballots should be discarded and which should be counted.

The court ruled that society could not yet place "blind faith" in machines, and it rejected a legal opinion issued by the state election division last week that said hand recounts could only be justified by mechanical failure, not possible error by voters who may have failed to mark their ballots completely enough to be read by the machines.

"Florida law provides a human check on both the malfunction of tabulation equipment and error in failing to accurately count the ballots," the opinion said. "Thus we find the election division's opinion regarding the ability of county canvassing boards to authorize a manual recount is contrary to the plain language of the statute."

Although Gore's lawyers claimed victory, the court's ruling came as hand recounts in the three counties showed only small net gains for Gore that could cut Bush's lead of 930 votes out of 6 million cast statewide to just under 700 if they were included in the final tally. Several thousand other potential votes remained tied up in new rounds of recriminations over whether "dimpled," or partially punched, ballots should be counted.

Hours after the court ruling accepted most of his lawyers' arguments in favor of an expansive interpretation of Florida election law, Gore appeared at his residence in Washington to say, "We will move forward now with a full, fair and accurate count of the ballots in question." He again proposed that he and Bush meet to cool the oratory of their supporters. He vowed to reject any effort to persuade Electoral College members pledged to Bush to switch their votes, and said they should both proceed with planning the transition to a new administration.

Nov. 22, 2000, Todd S. Purdum and David Firestone

Bush Camp Angrily Vows to Fight Ruling

"I mean, it's pretty clear that the Legislature has a role in this, should it get to that."

– Gov. Jeb Bush

★ ★ ★

In a voice of moral outrage, the Bush campaign's representative in Florida, James A. Baker III, denounced the Florida Supreme Court's ruling as a gross usurping of its bounds and all but invited the state Legislature to step in and take action against the manual recounts in several Florida counties. The harsh, even bellicose remarks of Baker made clear that in his view, the court had done as much to unsettle as to settle things and that Bush and the Republicans were determined to seek some manner of recourse.

"Two weeks after the election, that court has changed the rules and has invented a new system for counting the election results," Baker said at a news conference in Tallahassee shortly before midnight. "So one should not now be surprised if the Florida Legislature seeks to affirm the original rules."

It was not clear whether he was signaling that the Bush campaign would appeal to the Legislature or simply predicting that state lawmakers would act. And Baker would not specify what actions in court the Bush campaign would take, although he said that there were a number of options it would carefully weigh.

But what was all too clear was the Bush campaign's decision to treat what had happened as a horrendous miscarriage of justice and that the campaign was determined to act accordingly.

"It is simply not fair, ladies and gentlemen, to change the rules, either in the middle of the game or after the game has been played," Baker said. "Therefore, we intend to examine and to consider whatever remedies we may have to correct this unjust result."

Other Republicans were considering potential remedies. Daniel Webster, a Republican state senator from Orlando and former speaker of the Florida House, said the court had totally disregarded the Legislature's authority to set policy. He said the Republican majority was considering a special session to take up the matter, or moving to the federal courts to demand that power be restored to the legislative branch.

"In order to assert ourselves, we have to take some decisive action before this date," he said, referring to the Sunday deadline that the court set for the state to accept the results of manual recounts. "We're talking about whether we let the Legislature write the laws of this state," he added. Referring to the justices, he said, "You might as well let them write the budget next year."

The idea that the Florida Legislature might get involved had been raised earlier in the day by Jeb Bush, the Florida governor. He said that if the election in Florida was not resolved promptly, it could wind up in the hands of the Legislature, which has a prerogative to choose the state's electors itself.

"I think it depends on the circumstances of this ruling and how all this plays out," Jeb Bush said. "They clearly have a responsibility under certain circumstances, or they have the right at least granted to them by the United States Constitution. I mean, it's pretty clear that the Legislature has a role in this, should it get to that. I hope it doesn't."

Nov. 22, 2000, Frank Bruni

DIMPLED VOTES ARE NEW HOPE FOR DEMOCRATS

WEST PALM BEACH — Senior Democratic strategists said tonight that the Florida Supreme Court's unanimous decision set a broad enough standard for hand recounts that they would be able to accumulate the indented ballots that

Gore needs to win the presidential election. Without those ballots, these strategists conceded, Gore was likely to fall short of the votes needed to defeat Bush.

By their count, Gore aides said, if indented ballots were included, they would erase the 930-vote official lead held by Bush and Gore would win Florida's decisive 25 electoral votes. Moments after receiving the ruling from Florida's highest court, members of the Gore team searched the text of the opinion for some direction about whether the three South Florida canvassing boards must count indented ballots as evidence of a voter's intent.

They were disappointed to learn that the court did not set its own standard on how to count ballots — something the Gore camp had sought today in a new filing with the court — and instead left it to the boards to establish their own standards.

But Gore aides were gratified to find that the court quoted from an Illinois Supreme Court opinion that "voters should not be disfranchised where their intent may be ascertained with reasonable certainty, simply because the chad they punched did not completely dislodge from the ballot."

A senior Gore strategist exulted in that citation, drawn from the Democrats' brief to the court. The court's opinion, this strategist said, had first seemed to be a "triple" for the Gore campaign. That citation, he said, turned it into a "home run." Gore strategists said tonight that the language would be introduced in a courtroom here on Wednesday morning when the Florida Democratic Party is to ask a judge to order the Palm Beach County Canvassing Board to apply their proposed more lenient standard of counting indented ballots as votes.

Dennis Newman, a lawyer for the Democrats, said that there were 703 dimpled ballots for Gore and 404 for Bush so far in Palm Beach County's recount. Democrats contend that the dimples indicate the voter's intended selection, but Republicans say the three canvassing boards are controlled by Democrats and have been using differing — and constantly changing — standards as to what constitutes a dimpled-ballot vote.

"At least one of the Democrat-controlled county election boards has already decided to use this new standard, and the others are considering it," said Bush spokesman James A. Baker III. "No hole in the ballot is necessary, not even one loose corner is necessary, not even seeing any light through the ballot is necessary. Even if a voter decided not to make a choice because he or she could not decide between two closely competitive candidates, the Democratic county election boards can divine a choice based on an apparent indentation."

He added: "All of this is unfair and unacceptable."

Before tonight's state Supreme Court ruling, a senior Democratic strategist was blunt about the Gore campaign's chances if the hand recounts were ordered to a halt. "If dimpled ballots don't count," the strategist said, "it's over."

Nov. 22, 2000, Don Van Natta, Jr.

Where the Three Counties Stand Now

BROWARD COUNTY — Ballots with clearly marked votes or chads that have at least two corners detached have already been counted in all precincts. The county's three-member canvassing board will review hundreds of ballots with just one corner of the chad detached or ballots on which the chad is merely depressed, or dimpled.

The board first said it would not consider votes with anything less than two corners of the chad detached but reversed the decision after being told that standard might not hold up. A judge has ruled that board members could consider a dimpled chad as a vote if that seemed to be the voter's intent.

PALM BEACH COUNTY — Teams of counters have tallied about 50 percent of the precincts. Disputed ballots are being set aside to be considered later by the canvassing board. When the recount process began, the board decided it would count any vote in which the corners of the chad were punched. The board then decided to use the "sunlight test," which would count a vote if light came through the indentation. Later, that method was found to be flawed and the board returned to disqualifying votes not punched through. A judge has said, however, that the board cannot automatically disqualify a ballot with only a dimpled chad.

MIAMI-DADE COUNTY — Before beginning their recount, elections officials had a computer sort out about 10,000 ballots on which there was no clear presidential selection, although most of those had been declared blank. The canvassing board is considering those ballots.

Counters are also poring over other ballots and passing on to the board any without at least two corners detached. The board said it would accept all ballots, including those with dimpled chads.

★★★

OpEd

Florida's Justices Went too Far

In a bold example of judicial activism, the Florida Supreme Court has ruled that the technical requirements of state election law are less important than vindicating the will of the voters. The court allowed manual recounts to continue in Democratic counties, and without saying so explicitly, it strongly hinted that dimpled ballots should be part of the count.

Although the Florida Supreme Court may have imagined that it could save the country from the worst partisan impulses, the justices have intervened in a political battle that neither state courts nor the United States Supreme Court can ultimately resolve. Republicans in Florida and throughout the United States would never accept a Gore victory won on the basis of a court decision. They would argue plausibly that activist Democratic judges changed the counting rules in the middle of the game, only after it was obvious that the Democratic candidate needed dimpled ballots to win. And rather than accept the Florida Supreme Court's ruling, Republicans are preparing to take their objections to the United States Supreme Court, the Florida legislature and ultimately the United States Congress, which has final responsibility under the Constitution for deciding electoral disputes.

If the state Supreme Court had shown more caution, it might have avoided a showdown with the executive and legislative branches in Florida that judges may well lose. Indeed, until the state Supreme Court's intervention, state and federal courts acted with admirable restraint.

When the Bush campaign asked federal judges to block the manual recount, the district and appellate courts declined to intervene, noting that federal courts should interfere in state elections only as a last resort. When Democrats asked a circuit court judge to order a new election in Palm Beach County because the butterfly ballot was confusing, that judge, too, stayed his hand. And when the Gore campaign sued Katherine Harris, Judge Terry P. Lewis of Leon County Circuit Court deferred to Ms. Harris's judgment, holding that she had exercised "reasoned judgment" in rejecting the results of manual recounts filed after Nov. 14.

The Florida Supreme Court reversed Judge Lewis's decision, and the part of its opinion that allowed manual recounts to proceed was plausible. Ms. Harris, the justices ruled, had misinterpreted Florida election law by holding that only a machine error could justify a manual recount, even though the law clearly anticipates manual recounts in cases where ballots have not been accurately counted. But in the rest of its ruling, the court vastly overplayed its hand. It hinted broadly that dimpled chads should be counted, quoting an Illinois Supreme Court opinion declaring that "voters should not be disfranchised where their intent may be ascertained with reasonable certainty." A circuit court judge in Palm Beach County invoked this reasoning yesterday, when he ordered the county canvassing board to abandon its previous standard and to count dimpled chads.

If Al Gore pulls ahead next week on the basis of dimpled ballots, the victory will be tainted because the Florida Supreme Court changed the rules. The justices might have avoided this conflict by making clear that the local canvassing boards should apply existing standards for manual recounts rather than altering the standards after the count has begun. Palm Beach, for example, had decided in 1990 that only partially punched chads should be counted and that dimpled chads should not.

So, Bush had a point when he criticized the Florida Supreme Court for pressuring lower courts to change the counting rules. But his solution, an appeal to the United States Supreme Court, is no better. Bush asked the nation's highest court to hold that the Florida recounts are so selective and unevenly carried out that they violate the Constitution. In this case, the justices in Washington have no business second-guessing a state court on the interpretation of state law.

Bush also charged that the Florida Supreme Court violated federal law, which allows the state legislature to direct the "manner" in which electors shall be appointed whenever a state fails to choose them on the day prescribed by law. But the federal law is unclear on this point. Another section of the same law suggests that state judges have the final word about electoral disputes that are resolved before Dec. 12 and that the legislature can only intervene thereafter.

Rather than repeating the Florida Supreme Court's error, the United States Supreme Court should resist the urge to intervene. As it is, neither the state nor federal courts may have the last word. If the dispute is not resolved by Dec. 12, Republicans can take their case directly to Florida's Republican legislature. The legislators might then decide that the Florida Supreme Court has usurped their authority and order the state canvassing board not to certify any dimpled chads.

Alternatively, the legislature could ignore the Florida Supreme Court's ruling and appoint a slate of Republican electors on its own. And if the dispute between the Florida Supreme Court and the state legislature continues in late December, Congress may have to make the final choice.

Whatever happens, the Florida Supreme Court's decision to change the counting rules has made the justices appear to be partisans rather than neutral arbiters. By trying to take charge of the electoral dispute, the justices may have imagined that they could resolve it. Instead, they may have succeeded only in making it worse. Let's hope the United States Supreme Court resists the temptation to lend a similar helping hand.

Nov. 23, 2000

By Jeffrey Rosen, associate professor of law at George Washington University and legal editor of ***The New Republic***

day

15

WEDNESDAY,

NOVEMBER 22ND

★ ★ ★ ★ ★

MIAMI-DADE GIVES UP, G.O.P. MAKES THREATS

Al Gore is dealt an enormous setback when Miami-Dade County abandons its manual recount after a boisterous and briefly violent Republican demonstration. Faced with the prospect of losing hundreds of potential votes, the Gore team seeks a court order to force the recount to continue. Palm Beach and Broward Counties are set to examine dimpled ballots, still without clear guidelines for determining voter intent. And as if the day does not bring enough tumult, George Bush's running mate, Dick Cheney, is hospitalized for what doctors later determine to be a mild heart attack. And while Bush and his staff deal with the issue of Cheney's health, his lawyers press on with multiple lawsuits and appeals in venues from a circuit court in Tallahassee to the United States Supreme Court. At the same time Republican lawmakers in Florida and Washington threaten to challenge Florida's electors if they are awarded to Gore.

MIAMI-DADE HALTS RECOUNT

TALLAHASSEE — The disputed presidential election was thrown into new turmoil today as Miami-Dade County, the largest Florida Democratic enclave still recounting votes by hand, abruptly decided to stop, and a state court judge in Palm Beach County gave ballot counters there wide discretion about which of hundreds of disputed votes should actually count.

Miami-Dade canvassing officials had started the morning by moving to recount manually only some 10,000 ballots that registered no vote for president on Nov. 7, but later reversed themselves and said that it would not be fair to count anything less than all the county's nearly 700,000 ballots. Since that could not be achieved by the Sunday deadline set by the Florida Supreme Court in its ruling Tuesday night, they said, none should be recounted at all. That knocked out 157 potential new votes for Gore that had already been counted, and perhaps hundreds of others in precincts yet to be reviewed. The decision was potentially devastating to Gore. That left the race once again frozen, with Bush holding a small but steady lead in uncertified returns and searching for a way to compel the State of Florida to certify those returns and Gore struggling to overtake him in the unofficial tally before that happens.

The Gore campaign sought an emergency court order to compel the recount to resume, contending that under state law, once local election officials find that such a recount is justified, it must be completed. But a state appeals court ruled against the Gore campaign, upholding the board's decision to end its manual recount. Jenny Backus, a spokeswoman for the Democratic National Committee, said the Gore camp planned to appeal to the Florida Supreme Court.

Gore's other main hope remained Palm Beach County, where about 2,000 dimpled punch-card ballots had been set aside in disputes, awaiting possible recounting. Late today, Judge Jorge Labarga of Palm Beach County Circuit Court, like the Florida Supreme Court before him, disappointed Democrats by declining to offer specific standards for how to evaluate such ballots.

Instead, he held that the Palm Beach election officers must closely examine all such ballots for signs of a voter's intent. If that intent cannot be determined, he said, the ballot must be rejected. "Each ballot must be considered in light of the totality of the circumstances," he ruled. "Where the intention of the voter can be fairly and satisfactorily ascertained, that intention should be given effect."

That echoed the language of the State Supreme Court's ruling, which did not set standards for counting such contested ballots but suggested that wide discretion was allowed. Without counting such disputed ballots, Gore has made virtually no gains in Palm Beach, with about a third of its precincts recounted.

In Broward County, the last of the three counties that started the day with recounts, election officials finished their count, except for roughly 2,000 disputed dimpled ballots, with Gore receiving a net gain of 137 votes. The officials planned to review the dimpled ballots Thursday.

Nov. 23, 2000, Todd S. Purdum

Chaotic Protest Influences Miami-Dade's Decision

MIAMI – The Miami-Dade County Canvassing Board's decision to shut down its hand recount of presidential election ballots followed a rapid campaign of public pressure that at least one of the board's three members says helped persuade him to vote to stop the counting.

Republican telephone banks had urged Republican voters in Miami to go to the Stephen P. Clark Government Center downtown to protest the recount. The city's most influential Spanish-language radio station, Radio Mambi, called on staunchly Republican Cuban-Americans to head downtown to demonstrate. Republican volunteers shouted into megaphones urging protest. A lawyer for the Republican Party helped stir ethnic passions by contending that the recount was biased against Hispanic voters.

The subsequent demonstrations turned violent after the canvassers had decided to close the recount to the public. Joe Geller, chairman of the Miami-Dade Democratic Party, was escorted to safety by the police after a crowd chased him down and accused him of stealing a ballot. Upstairs in the Clark center, several people were trampled, punched or kicked when protesters tried to rush the doors outside the office of the Miami-Dade supervisor of elections. Sheriff's deputies restored order.

When the ruckus was over, the protesters had what they had wanted: a unanimous vote by the board to call off the hand counting. One nonpartisan member of the board, David Leahy, the supervisor of elections, said after the vote that the protests were one factor that he had weighed in his decision. "This was perceived as not being an open and fair process," Leahy said. "That weighed heavy on our minds." After discussing the matter briefly with reporters, Leahy declined requests for interviews, as did the two other board members, one of them nonpartisan, the other a Democrat. But quite apart from any campaign of pressure, the board did say that the court-mandated deadline had been a factor that militated against even a limited recount.

Whatever the case, Democrats accused Bush supporters of gathering a crowd and riling it up in hopes of forcing the board to back down. "One hour they're telling us they're going to get it done," Luis Rosero, a Democratic aide, said of the canvassers, and "the next minute there were two riot situations and a crowd massing out in front. This was deliberate." Rosero said he had been punched and kicked by Republican supporters outside Leahy's office.

Republican supporters scoffed at the accusation that they had engaged in a scheme of intimidation, saying the protest had been nothing more than a spontaneous manifestation of people's anger. "It's the same type of democracy in action when Jesse Jackson parachutes in and starts a protest in the black community," said Miguel De Grandy, a lawyer for the Republican Party. "People have a right to express their opinions." Yet some Bush supporters did acknowledge that they had helped inspire the crowd in hopes that the recount would end, though saying they had certainly meant no one any harm.

Whatever problems the canvassing board encountered, Republicans said, it brought on itself. "Sure they were under pressure," said Paul Crespo, a Bush campaign worker. "They had taken so many illegal decisions that they were on the verge of provoking serious unrest."

Nov. 24, 2000, Dexter Filkins and Dana Canedy

Cheney in Hospital with Mild Heart Attack

WASHINGTON — Dick Cheney, the Republican vice-presidential nominee, suffered a mild heart attack early this morning, raising anew questions about his health and adding even more uncertainty to an already tense and confused election. Doctors at George Washington University Hospital here said Cheney, 59, experienced chest pains at his home in McLean, Va., around 3 a.m. Accompanied by his wife, Lynne, and Secret Service agents, he went to the hospital's emergency room, where he was first treated with nitroglycerine and blood thinner.

Doctors found that one of Cheney's coronary arteries was about "90 to 95 percent blocked," and tests later determined that he had what they eventually termed a "very mild heart attack." It was Cheney's fourth heart attack in 22 years, but his first since 1988, when he had quadruple bypass surgery. Cheney's physicians said he was never in any serious danger and could be released in 48 to 72 hours. They said there was no reason he could not resume his normal duties, though they told him that losing some weight would be prudent.

Cheney himself said he hoped to be out of the hospital in a couple of days. "I feel good and everything's looking good," Cheney said in a telephone interview on CNN's "Larry King Live." "I should be out of here in a day or two."

The declaration that Cheney had suffered a mild heart attack came during a day of confusion. Bush first described Cheney's hospitalization as a precautionary measure. His aides said he did not know of the diagnosis when he spoke in the morning. By the afternoon, doctors knew Cheney had suffered a heart attack, but neglected to mention that fact. They later apologized.

Hospital officials said the Bush campaign had no influence on the drafting of the statement issued at the first press conference. Dr. John F. Williams, the hospital's vice president for health affairs, said the statement was written in consultation with Cheney's family, who wanted to protect some aspects of his privacy.

Part of the reason for the confusion, the doctors said, is the changing definition of what constitutes a heart attack. With the continued development in diagnostic techniques through the analysis of cardiac enzymes, doctors can now determine much smaller levels of damage to heart muscles, the technical definition of a heart attack.

Cheney's health has been an issue since Bush named him to the ticket in July. Cheney suffered his first heart attack in 1978 at the age of 37 during his campaign for Congress from Wyoming. In 1984, he had a second heart attack, then had another one in 1988. In addition to his quadruple bypass operation, Cheney has stopped smoking and his doctors said he is taking medication to lower his cholesterol. But doctors declined to specify what that medication is.

If a vice-presidential candidate is removed from the ticket after the election but before the Electoral College meets on Dec. 18, the presidential candidate can choose a new running mate. The party has to ratify the choice. If the vice president-elect dies or is removed after the Electoral College meets, the 25th Amendment of the Constitution sets out the procedure for picking a replacement. The president-elect must nominate a new vice president, who must be confirmed by the House and the Senate.

Nov. 23, 2000, Steven A. Holmes

G.O.P. Launches Multiple Legal Attacks

"This appeal will not be hard in the least to defeat because the federal questions are frivolous."

– Laurence H. Tribe, Harvard University

★ ★ ★

TALLAHASSEE — A day after the Florida Supreme Court handed Gore a major victory by unanimously ruling that the recounts could continue and must be included in the state's final tally in an effort to "safeguard the right of each voter to express his or her will," Bush sharply denounced the finding as unfair and improper. "Make no mistake," he said in Austin, Tex. "The court rewrote the laws. It changed the rules and it did so after the election was over." He added, referring to his running mate, Dick Cheney: "I believe Secretary Cheney and I won the vote in Florida. And I believe some are determined to keep counting in an effort to change the legitimate result."

Even as the recount disputes dragged on, leaders of the Republican-controlled State Legislature here raised the specter of appointing the state's Electoral College delegation themselves if a clear election result could not be agreed on by early next month. Additionally, lawyers for Bush asked the United States Supreme Court to overturn the Florida Supreme Court's ruling that manual vote recounts must be included in the state's final tally.

In yet a further legal wrinkle, lawyers for Bush filed suit in State Circuit Court here in Tallahassee seeking to force 13 counties to count hundreds of previously disqualified overseas ballots, most of which came from members of the military and which were rejected because they lacked proper postmarks.

And even as they appealed to the United States Supreme Court, Bush's lawyers renewed a similar appeal pending in the United States Court of Appeals for the 11th Circuit, in Atlanta, which agreed to accept new briefs on Monday. Bush's lawyers have argued in federal court that selective counts in some Democratic counties were an unconstitutional violation of the 14th Amendment's equal-protection right because they treated some voters differently from others.

Laurence H. Tribe, a constitutional scholar at Harvard University who is leading Gore's legal team in the federal courts, said that he had expected the Bush appeal to the Supreme Court but that it would fail. "This appeal will not be hard in the least to defend, because the federal questions are frivolous," Tribe said. "There is no plausible basis for arguing that there is a federal constitutional flaw in the carefully reasoned way in which the Florida court deliberated."

A principal objection raised by Bush's lawyers to the Florida Supreme Court ruling was the imposition of new deadlines on the acceptance of manually counted returns, replacing the standard statutory deadline of one week after Election Day for counties to submit returns.

Tribe, though, said there was nothing unusual about high courts at the state or national level establishing arbitrary deadlines when issues had to be resolved expeditiously. He expressed dismay that the Republicans were attacking the legitimacy of the judiciary branch.

"These rather intemperate attacks by Governor Bush in denouncing the Florida Supreme Court were made in a completely unreasoned way," he said. "It suggests a circling of the wagons around the target of the rule of law as it now stands, and I connect that with riotous and violent mob behavior."

Nov. 23, 2000, Todd S. Purdum

Bush Files Suit to Restore Rejected Military Ballots

TALLAHASSEE – George W. Bush sued election officials in 13 Florida counties today for rejecting the absentee ballots of members of the military serving abroad, capitalizing on an issue that has been a public relations boon to the Republicans and that could determine the fate of hundreds of votes for the presidency.

Republicans have said that on Friday night, when the count of overseas absentee ballots took place, Democrats made a systematic effort to disqualify as many military votes as possible, a charge repeated by Bush's lawsuit, filed in state circuit court here. Overseas votes generally heavily favor the Republican candidate, and Bush took 62 percent of those that were allowed.

It is not clear how many votes could be reinstated on the grounds Bush's suit cites, though it could be hundreds, and the suit does not offer a number.

Bush's suit identifies 13 counties where, it contends, the largest number of military ballots were invalidated, and they do not include the Democratic strongholds of Broward, Palm Beach and Miami-Dade Counties. The 13 counties, according to The Associated Press, rejected 646 ballots.

Democrats have conceded that they sought to knock out as many ballots as they could, but they maintained that it was strictly on legal grounds, and without concern for whether the ballots were military or civilian. County election officials across the state, in both parties, said that the rules the Democrats cited in trying to disqualify ballots were the same ones the county canvassing boards had long used. But Democrats, unable to find an effective public response to the accusation that they were trying to disenfranchise men and women in uniform, have been forced into retreat.

Today, in Austin, Tex., Bush said that Gore "should join me in calling upon all appropriate authorities in Florida to make sure that overseas military ballots that were signed and received on time count in this election." He did not mention the suit, which had not yet been filed.

Republican officials close to Bush said that they viewed the issue as a clear winner for them, both in the struggle for public opinion, and in collecting more votes in a race where Bush leads by fewer than 1,000 out of 6 million cast. "We're going to get those military ballots in, one way or the other," one Republican official said.

Jenny Backus, a spokeswoman for the Gore campaign, dismissed the lawsuit as a public relations move. "We think that every legally cast military ballot should be counted," Backus said. "But we have respected the decisions of the locally elected canvassing boards to interpret the law and put it into practice."

Democrats contended that fewer than half of the rejected ballots were military, while Republicans said that more than half were. Most counties did not keep track. The reason Democrats cited most often in trying to disqualify ballots was that they had no postmarks, as required by Florida law. Bush's suit seeks to reinstate not only those ballots, but those thrown out because they were not dated, or because the signatures on the ballots did not closely match those on the absentee ballot requests, or because the county had no record of such requests. Interviews with officials in several counties indicate that perhaps fewer than 100 ballots were thrown out solely for lack of a postmark. Many others were thrown out for reasons that would be hard to dispute — for instance, that the voter had already voted, or was not registered to vote in that county.

Nov. 23, 2000, Richard Pérez-Peña

Florida Legislators Consider Options to Aid Bush

TALLAHASSEE – Openly contemptuous of the Florida Supreme Court, senior Republican legislators, led by men with strong political ties to the state's governor, Jeb Bush, searched with a partisan intensity today for a legislative stroke that would deliver Florida and the White House to Bush.

There was serious discussion about convening a special session of the Legislature, perhaps as early as next week, to supersede the state's vote if Vice President Al Gore comes out ahead in recounts ordered by the Supreme Court, and picking electors supportive of George W. Bush. There was also talk of challenging the Supreme Court's approval of the recounts, either in federal court or through legislation stating, in effect, that Florida's secretary of state, Katherine Harris, a Republican, had correctly interpreted the Legislature's intent when she disallowed the manual recounts in Democratic strongholds in South Florida. But they made no final decision.

"Unlike the Supreme Court, which was appointed by Democrats, the Florida Legislature has been elected by the people of Florida, and we will not allow the people's voice to be silenced," Representative Mike Fasano, the Republican majority leader in the Florida House of Representatives, said in a statement.

Lawyers for Gore said today that they would immediately challenge any such legislative maneuvers, most likely in federal court. Laurence H. Tribe, who is leading Gore's legal team in the federal courts, put his position this way: "The U.S. Constitution makes quite clear that the State Legislature is to determine the manner of choosing the electors, but that doesn't mean a Legislature can just toss aside the result of an election. An attempt by the State Legislature to act like a court, whether clothed in the garb of legislation or not, would be rejected by federal and state courts at this point. The very essence of judicial power is to interpret the laws to make them consistent with one another, and ultimately consistent with state constitutional principles."

And yet among Republican legislators here there were bitter outbursts about what they commonly described as a Democratic plot to "steal" Florida. Huddling with lawyers and aides, these same legislators sifted though obscure provisions of state and federal election laws today, exploring each and every clause, phrase, word and comma for a path to preserve what they asserted was a narrow but nonetheless unambiguous victory for Bush. One particular concern was finding a way that would save George W. Bush while sparing Jeb Bush from playing a direct role, like signing legislation that would lead to his brother's election, which could taint his own political future. Throughout the Capitol, there was an almost warlike air of defiance among Republicans. Clearly, their efforts were fueled by the Bush campaign's midnight call to arms by James A. Baker III.

Just as clearly, the legislators were fully aware of the mounting fury expressed through hundreds of phone calls from Republican loyalists across the country. But they were also driven by a sense of urgency brought about by a recognition that time is drawing short to move the machinery of legislation for George W. Bush. Under normal rules it would take at least five or six days to pass legislation, although a two-thirds majority vote could waive those parliamentary rules and accelerate the process.

Motivation also sprang from their deep antipathy toward the Florida Supreme Court, all of whose justices were appointed by Democratic governors. "What we have here is a court who has arbitrarily picked a new date and circumvented state law," State Senator Daniel Webster, a senior Republican, said today, "and actually stomped on our constitutional rights as a legislature."

The Republicans showed only the faintest concern that their efforts might somehow be thwarted by Democratic legislators, who are a 77-to-43 minority in the House and 25-to-15 minority in the Senate. Even leading Democrats agreed that they could do little more than slow the Republicans through a guerrilla campaign of procedural harassment.

Nov. 23, 2000, David Barstow and Somini Sengupta

Congressional Republicans Threaten to Challenge Electors

WASHINGTON — The Florida Supreme Court ruling in favor of hand recounts in three heavily Democratic counties provoked bitter denunciations by Republicans in Congress today, with the House majority leader calling for the Florida Legislature to step in. One House Republican threatened to challenge Florida's electoral votes in the House in January.

The escalating partisanship, which lawmakers called disturbingly reminiscent of the impeachment case two years ago, left members of both parties warning that without some letup in the battle, the contested presidential election could become the first business facing the 107th Congress.

"Those who attempt to prevail upon the Florida Legislature to nullify the court's decision risk provoking partisan skirmishing in Congress," said Senator Patrick J. Leahy, Democrat of Vermont. He said the House and Senate's insertion into the election would leave the next president "severely damaged throughout his term." He added, "I would not want to see that happen to either Al Gore or George Bush."

With Bush himself setting a tough tone, Congressional Republicans, in a flood of statements from the leadership on down, accused the Florida court of partisanship, "usurpation" and abuse of power, and some lawmakers said the ruling had to be overturned. Representative Dick Armey of Texas, the majority leader, said a "partisan court made a partisan decision." With some Florida Republicans suggesting that they could call a special session of the Florida Legislature to award the state's 25 electoral votes to Bush, Armey said the state's Legislature had a "duty to step in and restore honesty and the rule of law."

Senator Trent Lott of Mississippi, the majority leader, called the court decision a "chilling reminder of the need for vigilance to ensure that the actions of unelected judges do not usurp the right of the people to govern themselves in a democracy." Lott added, in a statement released by his office, "This cannot stand."

Nov. 23, 2000, Alison Mitchell

day

16

THANKSGIVING DAY,

NOVEMBER 23RD

★ ★ ★ ★ ★

GORE PLANS TO CONTEST ELECTION

After Gore's bid to force a recount in Miami-Dade County is unanimously rejected by the Florida Supreme Court, his campaign announces plans to formally contest the election results there and in other counties, although some Democrats question the wisdom of this new step. The Gore team also files a brief with the U.S. Supreme Court, asking for a rejection of two Bush appeals and arguing that the dispute over election results in Florida does not involve federal issues. Meanwhile, tensions rise in Broward County as a recount of dimpled ballots begins.

GORE LOSES MIAMI-DADE SUIT BUT PLANS FOR LEGAL CHALLENGE

TALLAHASSEE — A unanimous Florida Supreme Court refused today to compel Miami-Dade County to resume its manual recount of nearly 700,000 paper ballots. The ruling was a serious setback to Al Gore, whose aides promptly announced that on Monday [Nov. 27] he would formally contest the certified results of the Florida election.

Today's one-paragraph ruling effectively cut him off from a potentially rich source of Democratic votes in South Florida. That painful political fact forced him to prepare to take a step he has thus far resisted for fear that the American public, restless for a result 16 days after the presidential election, would begin to view him as ungracious. His prospects now rest more than ever with the trickle of votes in Broward and Palm Beach Counties.

Before the Miami-Dade recount was abruptly halted, Gore had a net gain of 157 votes there. By contesting the results in Miami-Dade, Gore hopes at least to recover the 157 votes, and, more ambitiously, to gain many more through a complete recount that could be conducted under the supervision of a state judge who would preside over his contest action. Thus far, aides said, Gore has plans to contest only the Miami-Dade results, but, they added, he may ultimately contest the results in other counties, too.

"I think the American people want to see a full, fair and accurate count of the vote, and they want to see the election certified for the candidate who got the most votes," said Doug Hattaway, a spokesman for Gore.

But David Boies acknowledged the public relations troubles implicit in challenging certified election results through a contest action, a seldom-used provision of elections law. By filing a formal contest, the Gore campaign will ask a state court judge in Tallahassee to invalidate the results of canvassing officials and supervise a recount of the ballots cast in Miami-Dade County. It will, as Boies said, "take some explaining." Aides to Bush declined to comment on today's court ruling.

Still, today's developments raised a whole series of complicated legal and political questions about a field of battle that now has many fronts, from Florida's capital to the nation's capital, from state courtrooms facing various lawsuits to the United States Supreme Court, where Bush filed an appeal to stop all hand recounts in Florida. Today, Gore's lawyers filed their response with the court. They called Bush's request a "bald attempt" to interfere in the Florida balloting.

Chief among the new questions is the length of time it will take for the courts to resolve any contest actions, and whether this new round of litigation will provoke the Republican-dominated Florida Legislature to intervene. But Gore's aides, while expressing regret and disappointment for any delay caused by the contest action, sought to present it as an entirely legitimate course that even Republican lawyers had referred to approvingly during arguments to the Florida Supreme Court. Gore's aides also noted that the Florida Supreme Court itself suggested on Tuesday that contest actions were an appropriate remedy.

Gore's lawyers said a contest action could be resolved before the 12th. But it seems likely, given the political fury on both sides, that his lawsuit will set off a whole new series of appeals.

"The court has indicated that the right stage to take it into account is at the contest stage," Boies said, referring to the Gore campaign's growing list of complaints about the county canvassing boards in Broward, Palm Beach and Miami-Dade Counties.

Nov. 24, 2000, David Barstow and Michael Cooper

Gore Asks U.S. Supreme Court to Reject Bush's Appeal

WASHINGTON – The Gore campaign told the United States Supreme Court that the appeals filed on Wednesday on behalf of George W. Bush were "a bald attempt to federalize a state law dispute" over how Florida election officials should determine the will of the state's electorate.

The Supreme Court's intervention in the ballot-counting dispute would "disserve the national interest" by further prolonging the dispute and driving it in "untoward and unprecedented directions," the Gore legal team said in a 31-page brief urging rejection of the Bush appeals.

The Gore brief, signed by Prof. Laurence H. Tribe as lead counsel and other lawyers who have become familiar during the past two weeks of high-stakes legal wrangling, portrayed the Bush effort in a manner intended to play on the justices' concerns about maintaining a distinct boundary between state and federal authority.

The brief said the two Bush appeals, one from Tuesday's ruling by the Florida Supreme Court that refused to stop the manual recounts and the other from a federal appeals court's refusal to intervene in the matter, presented "only questions of Florida law."

The federal constitutional issues raised by the Bush lawyers were "insubstantial," the Gore brief said, "and do not come close to meeting the high threshold that would require this court to interfere with a state's process for appointing its electors for president of the United States."

Far from violating the Constitution in any way, the brief said, the Florida Supreme Court's decision was a "routine interpretation" of state law. Governor Bush and the others joining his appeal should not be able to "transform their disappointment with the Florida Supreme Court's authoritative interpretation of Florida law into a 'constitutional' claim," the brief added.

Responding to the assertion in one of the Bush appeals that the Supreme Court's guidance was needed now to provide "finality and legitimacy" to the presidential election, the Gore brief said that, to the contrary, the court's intervention "would only diminish the legitimacy of the outcome of the election."

The brief hit hard at the federalism theme, based on the Gore lawyers' strategic calculation that the justices most likely to be sympathetic to the Bush appeals were the same conservative justices most wary of expanding federal authority over the states.

"The very suggestion that federal courts might reach into state governmental machinery to tell the states how to make and interpret their own laws would fly in the face of basic principles of federalism," the brief said, emphasizing the point by quoting from Justice Antonin Scalia's majority opinion in a 1997 case, *Printz v. United States*, which declared part of the Brady gun control law unconstitutional as a violation of states' rights.

In the briefs they filed on Wednesday, the Bush lawyers described the scene in Florida as a "circus" rapidly descending into chaos. The Gore brief described the state's provisions for manual recounts as "utterly unexceptional" and little different from those existing in Texas and 19 other states.

Assertions in the Bush briefs of widespread mishandling of ballots were "false and have not been tested in court through cross-examination, verification, or judicial fact finding," the Gore brief said.

Since the United States Supreme Court has jurisdiction only over questions of federal law and the United States Constitution, the Bush team faces the challenge of persuading the justices that substantial federal issues exist in the dispute over the timetable and method of certifying the election results in Florida.

The Bush brief is arguing that by conducting manual recounts in only certain counties, Florida is violating the equal-protection rights of the voters in other counties. The Gore brief was particularly pointed in responding to that argument.

"Governor Bush made the conscious, political choice not to request manual recounts in any county," the brief said, "a choice that manifestly does not create a constitutional violation conveniently inuring to his benefit." The brief also said that "where there was a request for a manual recount, it was granted," adding, "Where there was no request, it was not. Nothing could be more reasonable, or less discriminatory."

The law provided adequate guidance to county election officials, the Gore brief said, adding that any objection to the counting of a particular ballot and "any question about the meaning of the standard can ultimately be resolved before the State Supreme Court."

Nov. 24, 2000, Linda Greenhouse

Tempers Flare over Broward Recount

FORT LAUDERDALE – If Vice President Al Gore is to win the presidency, the winning votes must now come in stacks of already disputed ballots in two counties. And if today's recount in Broward County was any indication, a contentious, bitter process could get only more tense.

As Palm Beach County's elections canvassing board took the day off for Thanksgiving, and with Miami-Dade County no longer in the equation, Gore's hopes settled on Broward County, where election officials began to hand-count 1,800 ballots with dimpled chads or other unclear signs of the voters' intent.

Gore, who went into today's recount trailing Bush by the official tally of 930 votes in the race for Florida's all-deciding 25 electoral votes, has managed to pick up only 88 net votes so far from the disputed ballots now under review. In all, Gore has gained 225 votes in the Broward County recount.

The three members of the Broward County Canvassing Board scrutinized 327 ballots over six hours today, finding 136 votes for Gore and 48 for Bush. If this pace continues, Gore will pick up about half the number of votes he needs to overcome Bush's lead.

With such an outcome at stake, the atmosphere at times turned ugly. The members of the canvassing board, made up of two Democrats and one Republican, had to try to gauge — sometimes from unclear marks on the ballot — each voter's intent, as observers from the two campaigns looked on inside a wood-paneled courtroom in the Broward County Courthouse.

The candidates' lawyers were under orders from the board not to challenge its decisions ballot by ballot. But William Scherer, a lawyer for Bush's campaign, became so agitated by the board's decisions on dimpled ballots that he ignored the directive and was almost removed from the counting room.

From the beginning of the recount process, the dimpled ballots have been an object of scorn by Republicans, who have made fun of them in news conferences, on roadside signs and on T-shirts.

It was only natural that Republicans continued to criticize the dimpled ballots as the count of the disputed ballots began. Elections officials here, finished with the count of most of the 588,000 ballots from 609 precincts, moved from the Emergency Operations Center in nearby Plantation to the courthouse here to consider the disputed ballots.

Democrats said the board members were doing what the Florida Supreme Court had told them to do — trying to gauge each voter's intent to their best of their ability. And if a dimpled chad seemed to be a clear sign of a vote, it was being counted. "The canvassing board is taking each ballot one by one," said Charles Lichtman, a lawyer for Gore. "We think the process is moving smoothly."

Ballot by ballot, the three board members worked through envelopes of disputed ballots, holding the ballots up to the light. On the majority of ballots, the three came to an agreement within about a minute. But now and then they disagreed — and not always along party lines.

Scherer, who had begun the morning saying he was optimistic that Gore would not pick up many votes at all, later said the only reason the vice president had been able to garner 88 votes today was because the board did not use the same standards for dimpled chads throughout the day. "They have been consistently wrong," Scherer said.

Nov. 24, 2000, Lynette Holloway and Rick Bragg

Poor Handwriting and Mix-Ups Disqualified Absentee Votes

MIAMI – Absentee ballots cast by thousands of Floridians were tossed out because election officials rejected the signatures or found other flaws in their submissions. In a previously undisclosed aspect of the closest election in a century, it appears that many of these people are legitimate voters whose bad handwriting doomed their chances of participating.

These absentee ballots were thrown out without warning or appeal even as officials in three Florida counties prepared to undertake tedious recounts that involved minute examination of paper punch-card ballots in search of indentations or other signs of voter intent. But when it came to scrutinizing absentee ballots, the judges were amateur graphologists.

In another strange twist in this strange election, some of the troubles over absentee ballots were caused by the parties themselves. County election offices throughout Florida were deluged by absentee ballots this year because both parties waged huge campaigns to get out the vote.

Not only did these efforts overwhelm election officials, they sometimes misled voters into thinking they qualified as absentee voters when the voters did not meet the strict requirements of Florida law. In many pitches mailed to voters, the parties seemed to be encouraging healthy people to vote absentee from their homes. Florida law prohibits such voting.

Much of the country is making it easier to vote from home. A survey last year found that 10 states had passed laws making it easier to vote absentee, while Oregon moved exclusively to mail-in ballots. But Florida, stung by absentee ballot fraud in earlier elections, has moved in the other direction. New rules make it tougher to vote by mail. A change that tripped up some voters: witnesses must also include their addresses.

Florida law is strict about who can vote absentee. Voters must swear that they need help getting to the polls or that they will be away from their precinct on Election Day. Violators can face penalties.

In their mailings, both parties encouraged people who could have gone to the polls to vote by absentee ballots. "We had language in ours saying, You don't have to skip lunch at work; take just 5 minutes to vote; you don't have to cut out early from work or skip the gym," a Democratic Party strategist conceded.

Bob Poe, the Democratic Party's chairman in Florida, said he thinks both parties may have gone too far. "I don't think we were quite as broad as they [Republicans] were in terms of encouraging people to violate what the intent was of the law, but I think you're going to see a further tightening down of the absentee ballot issue."

Nov. 24, 2000, Michael Moss and Dexter Filkins

Democrats Fight on, but Some Lose Heart

WASHINGTON – As Vice President Al Gore confronts a ticking clock and mounting political and mathematical obstacles, officials in his campaign and in the Democratic Party say they are increasingly doubtful that he will come up with the votes necessary in Florida to overcome Gov. George W. Bush's slim advantage and become president.

Yet, if anything, some Gore campaign officials insisted that they would not back down, because of their unyielding view that more voters had intended to back the vice president. They repeated their rallying cry: that Gore won the national popular vote and that he believes he has the moral authority to keep his candidacy alive.

In plowing forward, the Gore campaign would be at odds with many influential Democrats — some of whom expressed optimism only a day or two ago — who are now weighing whether it would be worth the political risk for Gore to pursue other legal options should he not have enough votes by 5 p.m. Sunday, the deadline ordered by the Florida Supreme Court for the inclusion of hand-counted ballots in the overall vote tally. "People are assessing whether or not there is the political will," a top Gore official said.

While Gore supporters scrambled to plot a new game plan, officials at the Bush headquarters in Austin, Tex., were cautiously optimistic. Barring a dramatic, unexpected legal development, which in this unfolding event would not be unprecedented, one Bush official said he could not see a path for Gore to reach the White House. "They can't get there," the official said. "If at 5 o'clock Sunday we're ahead and we get certified, it's over." Saying Democrats would not want Gore to prolong the standoff, he added, "The pressure on this guy is going to be great."

Despite such confidence by Bush aides and concerns among some Democrats, a top Gore strategist insisted that he had spoken with Gore and that there was no backing down.

"The Gore team has to stay strong," the strategist said. "We're going to have to tell our fellow Democrats to suck it up. We have to ask our friends and allies to hang tough for us. This is not a hollow quest here. We know it's tougher to try to win it a second time, but we can."

Yet many officials in the campaign and in the Democratic Party said today that given the latest turns, a victory by the vice president would be quite difficult to assemble. In fact, Gore officials acknowledged that they were planning to contest the results in Miami-Dade County only because they were increasingly doubtful that they would have sufficient votes to overcome Governor Bush's slight lead by Sunday.

Nov. 24, 2000, Richard L. Berke

day

17

FRIDAY,

NOVEMBER 24TH

★ ★ ★ ★ ★

THE U.S. SUPREME COURT PLUNGES IN

Despite all the predictions to the contrary from virtually every constitutional law expert, the U.S. Supreme Court agrees to hear Bush's appeal from the Florida ruling that permitted hand recounts and extended Florida's certification deadline. Neither side, however, is assuming anything definitive will result from the court's hearing. So while the Republican offensive continues in the Florida Legislature, where party leaders clarify plans to intervene in the election, Gore's team is preparing to contest election results in Miami-Dade, Palm Beach and other counties. Gore's moves grow more desperate, perhaps because halfway through the Broward County recount, which may hold Gore's only hope of overtaking Bush's lead, Gore's gains continue at only a modest pace. In addition, Katherine Harris says she will officially certify the election on Sunday, two days from now.

HIGHEST COURT, SURPRISINGLY, AGREES TO HEAR BUSH'S APPEAL

WASHINGTON — The Supreme Court today unexpectedly placed itself in the middle of Florida's presidential vote-counting imbroglio, ordering arguments next Friday in Bush's appeal from the Florida Supreme Court's ruling that permitted manual recounts to continue beyond the state's deadline for certifying election returns.

By agreeing to hear the Republican nominee's appeal, the justices plunged into a turbulent situation that seems to change by the hour and put themselves, at least theoretically, in a position to decide the outcome of the presidential election. If the court rules that the manual recounting should not have gone forward, there is little prospect that Al Gore could be declared the winner of Florida's decisive 25 electoral votes. If the justices uphold the Florida Supreme Court's ruling, however, the Florida situation could remain up in the air. New legal challenges to aspects of the recount have been pressed by each side in the three days since the state court ruled, and others are likely as the election calendar moves forward. If Gore fails to overtake Bush by the current vote-counting deadline of Sunday afternoon, he will face considerable pressure to concede the election in any event. Friday's arguments may also come after Florida has certified a winner.

The court's midafternoon announcement that it would hear the appeal in Bush v. Palm Beach County Canvassing Board, No. 00-836, left much unexplained, as the court's orders in granting or denying cases almost always do. It takes the votes of four of the nine justices to agree to hear a case. But there was no indication today of whether the decision in this instance was by consensus or by a divided vote and, if so, which justices wanted to hear the case.

The court's interest in the case appears quite specific. The justices turned down Bush's broad constitutional attack on the manual recounts as violating the constitutional guarantees of equal protection, due process and freedom of political association. Rather, the court agreed to decide two more tightly focused questions presented in the Bush petition and added a question of its own. All three related to the intersection between the Florida Supreme Court's action on Tuesday and the prerogatives that a state legislature enjoys under federal law and the United States Constitution to determine how a state's presidential electors are to be appointed.

Bush's legal team is arguing that by letting the recounts continue past the seven-day deadline invoked by Florida's top election official on the basis of a provision in the state code, the Florida Supreme Court in effect rewrote the state law and disregarded federal law in the process.

The federal law that evidently most interests the court is Title 3, Section 5 of the United States Code, governing presidential elections generally and the resolution of disputes over electors specifically. Section 5 provides that in resolving a dispute, a state's laws enacted "prior to" Election Day "shall be conclusive, and shall govern in the counting of the electoral votes." In other words, electors chosen according to a state law in place at the time of the election are not subject to later challenge for having been improperly chosen.

The Bush team's basic argument, as expressed in the Supreme Court appeal filed on Wednesday, is that the Florida Supreme Court established new rules when it interpreted the state's election law to require that late-filed returns be counted rather than "ignored," as one section of the state law specified. The State Supreme Court set Nov. 26 as the date for certification, rather than Nov. 14 as specified by state law.

The federal law "serves obvious and important public policy interests by prohibiting precisely what is happening in Florida today," the Bush appeal told the justices, "where the candidate who did not receive the most votes and his supporters are attempting to overturn the results of the presidential election by changing the rules after the election has been held." Under this argument, any Gore electors chosen under the revised deadline would be subject to challenge as improperly appointed.

The Gore team, in responding to this argument in a brief filed on Thursday, said there was "literally nothing" to it because the Florida court's decision "amounts to an ordinary act of statutory interpretation of a law enacted prior to the election, not to a new 'enactment.' " In other words, the Gore brief said, by reading the state election law to provide the flexibility necessary to determine the will of the voters, the state court was interpreting the law as it had always been, not writing a new law.

The Bush campaign's line of argument is not without risk. Over the last few days, the focus of the Bush arguments had appeared to shift from judicial challenge to possible legislative action to overturn the state court's ruling and declare Bush the winner in Florida. Any newly enacted state law designed to accomplish that would be subject to the same attack under Title 3, Section 5.

To the question about the federal law presented by the Bush appeal, known as a petition for a writ of certiorari, the justices today added a question of their own: "What would be the consequences" of finding that the State Supreme Court's decision did not comply with Title 3, Section 5? In other words, if the Bush argument is correct that the state court lacked authority to permit the recounts to go forward, what should the remedy be at this point?

The court also agreed to decide a second question presented by the Bush appeal: whether the state court's ruling was inconsistent with a clause in the federal Constitution, in Article II, Section 1, providing that electors shall be chosen by each state "in such manner as the legislature thereof may direct." By taking up the question, the justices appear to be injecting themselves into the kind of struggle between two branches of state government that the court's institutional instincts ordinarily tell it to avoid at all costs.

However, the justices may have been persuaded that whatever is the correct answer to these questions involving the interplay between federal law and a state high court's decision-making, they alone could provide an authoritative answer.

The court set its accelerated argument schedule with an eye to the Dec. 12 deadline for formally appointing the electors, who will vote, in state capitals across the country, on Dec. 18. Each side was directed to file a brief by 4 on Tuesday afternoon, to be followed on Thursday afternoon by reply briefs. The argument will take place at 10 on Friday morning and will last 90 minutes.

While granting this case, the court turned down the Bush team's second Supreme Court petition, an appeal from the refusal of the federal appeals court in Atlanta to stop the manual recounts. That case, *Siegel v. LePore*, raised the same constitutional issues that the justices refused to address in the case they accepted.

The federal case remains alive in the United States Court of Appeals for the 11th Circuit, and the Supreme Court's order denied the appeal "without prejudice," meaning that it can be revived following a definitive ruling from the appeals court.

Nov. 25, 2000, Linda Greenhouse

Gore Set to Fight on Many Fronts

WEST PALM BEACH — Al Gore plans to contest the election results in Palm Beach County on the grounds that dimpled ballots are not being counted as votes and that voter confusion over the "butterfly" ballot cost him thousands of votes here, senior Democratic lawyers and strategists said today.

Another basis for that challenge is 10,000 sworn affidavits signed by residents ranging in age from 18 to 98. Many of these voters said they were confused by the butterfly ballot's design or were denied assistance or given wrong instructions by harried and often rude poll workers, according to a summary of 300 affidavits and copies of dozens of sworn statements provided today to *The New York Times* by a senior Democratic official.

Among the statements were hundreds from voters who complained that they struggled to get their paper ballots to fit properly into the county's punch-card voting machines. When Charles A. Bleich told a poll worker that his ballot did not align in the machine, he said the worker told him: "Thirty-eight states do it this way. Just vote."

On a six-page affidavit, Ilyne Cooper of Delray Beach wrote: "The ballot was an obstacle course. Everything should have lined up, but it didn't. The names, arrows and punch holes were not properly aligned. The ballot started with numbers '3' and '5.' What is that all about?"

Cooper added: "I hope I voted for Gore, but because of the misleading nature of the ballot, I cannot be sure I did."

The affidavits put names, ages, backgrounds and circumstances to the long-standing claims by the Democrats that nearly 30,000 voters here could not, for many reasons, register their choice for the nation's highest office. Democrats also contend that they help explain how 19,120 of the county's residents voted for at least two presidential candidates and 3,407 residents of this Democratic stronghold cast ballots for the Reform Party candidate, Patrick J. Buchanan.

Those issues have faded from public attention as the focus of public attention on the disputed Florida vote has fallen on the manual recount in Palm Beach and two other South Florida counties.

Today the Palm Beach County Canvassing Board resumed its manual recount, beginning the arduous task of scrutinizing at least 6,000 contested ballots and trying to determine whether the slightest indentation amounts to a vote.

Besides contesting the election here by challenging the legality of the butterfly ballot, senior lawyers and strategists for the Gore campaign said they would also challenge today's decision by the Palm Beach County Canvassing Board to toss out ballots that had only a single indentation in the column for the presidential candidates. Lawyers said a challenge of the board's standards on dimpled ballots is a stronger case to make than one of the legality of the butterfly ballot.

Despite urging by Democratic lawyers this morning, the board decided to count ballots that had a pattern of dimples, a standard that Democrats said was too strict and defied the spirit of an order by a circuit judge.

By tonight, Gore had gained a slight edge over Bush in Palm Beach County's manual recount, Democrats involved in the recound said. By the end of the night, Gore had gained 32 votes from the official number, those Democrats said.

With several Gore aides acknowledging that it appears increasingly unlikely that Gore will be able to use hand recounts here and in Broward County to erase Bush's 930-vote lead in Florida, senior lawyers have turned their attention to the arguments they will make for a planned challenge of the election results. The lawyers said the Gore campaign plans to contest the results almost immediately after Katherine Harris certifies the election result on Sunday, as is expected.

Nov. 25, 2000, Don Van Natta Jr.

Democrats Prepare Broad Attack on Harris's Certification

TALLAHASSEE — Under the Florida court's ruling, Katherine Harris, the secretary of state, may open her office on Sunday and certify the Florida vote. Harris's spokesman said today that she would do so, regardless of the outcome.

With no judicial chance of stopping the certification, the Democrats today began preparing the public for the legal contests to the certification that would be filed on Monday morning if Bush has declared himself the president-elect by then.

Employing Gore's running mate, Senator Joseph I. Lieberman, six other members of Congress, and its Florida legal team, the Gore campaign mounted an aggressive public relations effort today to accuse Republicans of physically intimidating the board, which they suggested violated voting-rights laws.

The Bush campaign denied any effort at organized intimidation. "Where was Joe Lieberman when Jesse Jackson organized Democratic protests in Palm Beach County to protest on behalf of Al Gore?" asked Ari Fleischer, a Bush spokesman. "Why didn't he publicly disclaim those protests? Today's remarks are the latest example of Al Gore saying one thing while doing another."

The contentions of intimidation are the foundation of Gore's challenge to the Miami-Dade County count, which is to be filed on Monday in State Circuit Court. Gore's lawyers hope to overturn the results in that county by demonstrating that civil-rights violations prevented a fair tabulation of the results.

But the lawyers said today that Miami-Dade would not be their only formal contest to the election next week. David Boies, Gore's lead lawyer here, said that the campaign would also file suit in Nassau County, a Republican enclave in Florida's northeast corner, which voted today to use the election-night tabulation of its vote instead of the required machine recount a few days later. The decision cost Gore 52 votes.

The Nassau election board went back to its election-night numbers after Shirley King, the county director of elections and a Republican, told the board that the first count was more accurate than the recount, which showed 218 votes fewer than the election-night tabulation — 124 fewer votes for Bush, and 73 fewer for Gore.

Judge Robert Williams of Nassau County Court, a member of the board, said that King acted on advice from Harris, who was also co-chairwoman of the Bush campaign in Florida, who advised King she could certify either count.

Boies said that the decision to discard the recounted tally violated state election law, which requires a recount if less than a half-percent difference in votes exists between candidates. "There is absolutely no precedent or justification for doing that," he said. "That machine recount was certified to the secretary of state by Nassau County itself, unanimously. Now, they see that Governor Bush needs a few extra votes, so what they do is go back and decertify what they already certified, and attempt to certify the election-night returns that have already been superseded. If I can't win that argument, I'm going to give up the practice of law."

Nov. 25, 2000, David Firestone and David Barstow

Florida Legislature Plans to Back Bush Suit

TALLAHASSEE — Florida's Republican-led Legislature announced plans today to join George W. Bush's Supreme Court challenge to hand recounts. Tom Feeney, the speaker of the Florida House of Representatives, said the Legislature believed that the Florida Supreme Court overstepped its bounds and changed the state's election laws on Tuesday when it unanimously ruled to require the inclusion of manual recounts in the state's final tabulation of votes.

To protect its right to set state laws, Feeney said, the Legislature planned to intervene in Bush's appeal of that ruling, which the United States Supreme Court agreed to consider. In announcing the Legislature's plans today, Feeney effectively outlined a two-track strategy that looks first to the Supreme Court to preserve Bush's narrow vote margin in Florida, but also holds open the option of calling a special legislative session to name electors who support Bush.

Feeney, adding that he was also speaking for John McKay, president of the State Senate, accused the state's high court of "rewriting laws" and of usurping executive powers held by Harris as the secretary of state.

Forming a committee called the Joint Legislative Oversight Committee on Electoral Certification, Fairness and Accuracy, the two Statehouse leaders signalled that they may call a special session to name electors who support Bush in the Electoral College. The committee, which could begin work as soon as

Tuesday, will be charged with "investigating and ensuring Florida voters will be included in the final nationwide election results," Feeney said.

The committee will consist of eight Republicans and six Democrats drawn from both chambers, and headed by two Republicans, Senator Lisa Carlton and Representative Johnnie Byrd. It is to investigate "voting irregularities" that Republicans have complained about. According to a statement by Feeney and McKay, irregularities included "failure to count overseas ballots; inconsistent standards used by counties; and changes in standards and manual recount procedures adopted after the election."

Nov. 25, 2000, David Firestone and David Barstow

MODEST GAINS FOR GORE IN BROWARD AS REPUBLICANS JEER

FORT LAUDERDALE — Heckled by hundreds of Republican demonstrators outside the Broward County Courthouse, election officials today reached the halfway point in their manual count of about 1,800 disputed ballots. With 1,206 ballots counted by this evening, Gore picked up 144 more votes, giving him a net gain of about 369 ballots in the county since the recount began. The county may prove to be Gore's only hope of overtaking the 930-vote lead Bush has in the official tally, since the vice president's gains in Palm Beach County have been modest.

The atmosphere inside the sixth-floor courtroom where the board of canvassers worked was less contentious today than yesterday, but the battle continued on a psychological front. The Republicans brought in well-known politicians, including Bob Dole, the former presidential candidate and senator from Kansas, and Gov. John Engler of Michigan, to sit at the table with the Democratic board members. Broward County Chief Judge Dale Ross also paid a visit to observe the proceedings. "It doesn't hurt to have them there," said William Scherer, the lawyer for the Bush campaign who was almost thrown out of the proceeding on the first day. "We put people with credibility at the table to put pressure on them to do the right thing."

The three-member canvassing board worked slowly in the morning. The lone Republican, Judge Robert Rosenberg of County Court, seemed to take the most time inspecting the ballots, objecting to counting punch-card ballots with indentations rather than perforations. The intense scrutiny frustrated Democratic lawyers. The two Democratic members of the three-person board, Judge Robert W. Lee of County Court, the board chairman, and Suzanne N. Gunzburger, chairwoman of the county commission, reviewed the ballots more quickly.

About 150 protesters — some carrying "Sore-Loserman" signs that resembled the Gore-Lieberman presidential campaign posters — gathered outside the courthouse to protest what they called unfair standards. The demonstrators, many of whom said they had come from around the country to serve as recount observers, stood about 80 feet from a couple of dozen Democratic demonstrators who arrived after hearing about the gathering.

Some of the Republicans jeered and scuffled with Democratic politicians who were on hand to observe the proceeding. Representative Peter Deutsch, Democrat of Florida, was surrounded by so many protesters at one point that sheriff's deputies had to escort him away. Deutsch said the demonstrators were being paid by the Republicans. While the demonstrators denied that, many said their hotel rooms and some meals were being paid for by the Republican Party.

Mitch Ceasar, the Broward County Democratic chairman, said that on Thursday someone threw a brick with a note attached through the window of the Democratic Party's offices at a strip mall in Plantation. "We will not tolerate any illegal government," Ceasar said the note read. "The bottom line," he said, "is it's a continuation of the present mob mentality."

Nov. 25, 2000, Lynette Holloway

★ ★ ★

OpEd

The Right Moment for the Supreme Court

Justice Robert Jackson once famously wrote of the United States Supreme Court that "we are not final because we are infallible, but we are infallible only because we are final." In this presidential election, the court's finality is a much-needed virtue. Indeed, both Al Gore and George W. Bush, not to mention the nation, have welcomed the court's announcement that it would review the Florida Supreme Court's decision to require that mandatory recounts be included in the state's certification tally.

If the court rules in favor of Bush, then manual recounts will be excluded from the final tally, the state's electoral votes will go to Bush and the election will be over. If the court rules in favor of Gore, the partisan fighting might continue or the court could make clear that the Florida judiciary is to have the last word on the election, which would bring it to a more timely end. Whatever the case, at this point, the United States Supreme Court may be the only institution left that enjoys the legitimacy to bring the partisan struggle over the presidential election to a final, if not infallible, conclusion.

Of course, there have been many arguments against Supreme Court review, from both the left and the right. Many liberal legal scholars, for example, argued that the United States Supreme Court and the federal courts should not get involved in the electoral dispute. They feared that the Supreme Court would only become embroiled in partisan politics, to the detriment of its role as a protector of individual rights.

Conservatives have generally criticized the court's expansion of its powers at the expense of the political process; they have made these arguments with particular force, for example, when court rulings had the effect of expanding privacy and abortion rights. And in recent years the court itself, as its membership has become more conservative, has frequently stood against federal intervention in state matters — a stance that may seem, on a superficial reading, to be in conflict with its acceptance of this case.

It is true that the specific case brought by Governor Bush and his backers is not the kind that usually calls for federal judicial review. The question that the justices agreed to hear — whether, by ordering manual recounts to be included in Florida's certification, the state Supreme Court has usurped the role of its legislature in setting electoral procedures — seems to turn fundamentally on the meaning of state law.

The case involves no conflicts among the lower federal courts about the interpretation of national law. No lasting change in constitutional doctrine, in the powers of the national government or in individual rights will result from the United States Supreme Court's decision in this case. Nevertheless, the nation now needs the Supreme Court's intervention. Mr. Bush's lawsuit does raise federal issues: federal law requires that Florida's legislature, not its judiciary, establish the rules for selecting presidential electors. While a state's separation of powers would normally be finally determined by a state supreme court, in this one instance the framers and Congress have federalized how a state government is to work.

Here, the court would not truly be deciding a question of constitutional substance on par with the scope of abortion. Instead, it would only be clarifying the rules of the game for selecting the two federal officials elected by a whole nation. It is difficult to conceive of a constitutional question that is more about pure process.

But the case does have a larger meaning — and an important one. By reviewing it, the Supreme Court could finally bring an end to the destructive partisan struggle over the presidential election, and would do it in a way whose legitimacy could be accepted by the nation.

Only the United States Supreme Court, which regularly receives broad approval in public opinion polls for its neutrality and fairness, enjoys the political legitimacy to end this rapidly escalating fight over electoral rules. While the justices themselves obtain their appointments through a political process, the court today is neither solidly conservative nor solidly liberal; it is currently closely divided, with several justices who have proven unpredictable on questions about issues like abortion and free speech.

If the justices could unite behind a set of rules to govern the selection of our next president, the nation would be more likely to accept its judgment, without further political fighting, than any other.

Nov. 25, 2000

By John Yoo, Law Professor at the University of California, Berkeley; served as general counsel for the Senate Judiciary Committee from 1995 to 1996.

day

18

SATURDAY,

NOVEMBER 25TH

★ ★ ★ ★ ★

CHECKING FOR DIMPLES AS DEADLINE NEARS

With the 5 p.m. Sunday deadline for certifying the state's vote looming, recounts in several Florida counties give Gore an additional 466 votes, cutting Bush's lead in half. Gore officials concede, however, that he will probably not pull ahead in the recounts by the Sunday deadline. Their hope lies in several lawsuits aimed at forcing a recount in Miami-Dade County and the inclusion of so-called dimpled ballots in recounts elsewhere. For their part, Republicans sue to have military absentee ballots that lack postmarks counted. Another ray of hope appears for Gore as new details come to light in Seminole County in the case involving G.O.P. officials adding voter registration numbers to thousands of Republican absentee ballot applications. Both sides begin preparations for arguments before the United States Supreme Court.

RECOUNTS GIVE GORE 466 MORE VOTES AS LITIGATION EXPANDS

TALLAHASSEE — With only hours to go before a winner is declared in Florida's presidential balloting, weary election officials in Broward County finished their manual recount of ballots late tonight, cutting George W. Bush's lead over Al Gore in half. At the same time, their counterparts in Palm Beach County prepared to spend the night checking frantically for dimples, hanging chads and daylight in hundreds of punch cards before the deadline of 5 p.m. Sunday. That time was set by the Florida Supreme Court on Tuesday for all counties to report their final results to Katherine Harris, Florida's secretary of state, who plans to go before the cameras shortly afterward to announce a winner.

The counting left Gore hundreds of votes behind Bush, and Gore's aides said they did not expect him to take the lead. Bush retained an official lead of 930 votes, but Gore had a net gain of 466 votes statewide in an unofficial tally of hand-counted ballots. If the votes hand-counted in Miami-Dade County last week were included in these figures, Gore would have 157 more votes, but the county election board stopped its manual recount on Wednesday, and those votes are not included in the unofficial hand-count tallies.

"We'll stay all night if we have to."

—Judge Charles E. Burton, chairman of the Palm Beach County Canvassing Board

The Broward elections board finished counting 2,422 votes at eight minutes before midnight, giving Gore a net gain of 567 votes. Wiping their eyes in exhaustion, the three members of the elections board stood up in satisfaction when the counting was done and shook hands with the partisan observers who had monitored their every move. A cheer went up in the courtroom in which the ballots were counted.

But the counting there broke out in acrimony this morning when the canvassing board began considering a stack of about 500 dimpled absentee ballots, where holes had not been punched all the way through. Lawyers for the Republican Party argued vehemently that such ballots should not be considered because absentee voters could see whether they had fully punched the hole. A Broward County spokesman said all of the dimpled absentee ballots had already been hand-counted in the presence of Republican and Democratic observers, but he acknowledged that they had not been mentioned when the county first released the number of disputed ballots it would count.

In Palm Beach County, the canvassing board said that Bush had gained 10 votes by late afternoon, but Democrats said that when later counts were included, Gore was ahead by 78 votes. Gore's poor showing in the Palm Beach County hand count was largely because of a tougher standard employed by county officials in judging whether dimpled ballots should be counted, a standard that Democrats pledged to challenge in court next week.

The manual count moved much more slowly in Palm Beach. Denise Cote, a spokeswoman for the county, said election officials there counted 2,000 ballots on Friday and 900 Saturday, but had roughly 7,000 left to finish by Sunday night. Judge Charles E. Burton, chairman of the Palm Beach County canvassing board, said that if the county did not finish, it would send whatever results it had completed to Tallahassee by the deadline. (The state elections division said it had not decided whether to accept partial results.) But Judge Burton was optimistic that the board would complete its task. "We'll stay all night if we have to," he said.

But even as the hand-counted ballots piled up in Palm Beach and Broward Counties, it became increasingly clear as the tumultuous week ended that the certified results Katherine Harris planned to announce on Sunday would immediately be swept away in a tide of litigation to be filed by both sides. No matter which candidate is able to declare himself the president-elect on Sunday night, lawyers for Gore plan to be in court first thing Monday morning to formally contest the election in three counties. "I think that both sides probably will want to be sure that the results in the counties they're contesting are heard in front of a court, regardless of how the overall statewide votes are," said David Boies. "I don't think either side will withdraw their contests just because on Sunday at 5 p.m. one side or the other is a few votes ahead."

The contests grew in importance for Gore as Democratic officials acknowledged he would probably not prevail in the hand counts. Assuming he mounts a legal contest, aides said the vice president would probably address the nation next week to explain his decision to press on. Aides worry that he has not stated his case plainly enough to voters and that his previous public comments have been more a call for patience than an explanation of his position. Without a clear explanation why he has refused to concede, the aides said, Gore knows his support could weaken.

An Expanding Universe of Litigation

Lawyers for both sides began work this weekend on briefs requested by the United States Supreme Court, which agreed on Friday to hear Bush's appeal from the Florida Supreme Court's ruling allowing manual recounts to continue beyond the state's deadline for certifying returns. The initial briefs have to be filed by 4 p.m. Tuesday, and the justices will hear oral arguments at 10 a.m. on Friday.

If the court rules in Bush's favor, saying that Harris was within her rights to cut off the hand counts after seven days, that could undermine the challenges Gore is mounting in the three counties, and would probably overturn a victory by Gore if he should be declared a winner by Harris on Sunday. A ruling for Gore would mean the election would probably be determined by the outcome of the challenges, which are likely to wind up back in the Florida Supreme Court.

The expanding universe of litigation made it clear that the real deadline in the case is Dec. 12, the date by which the states must select their Electoral College delegates. The Sunday deadline will be useful psychologically to the declared winner, who may in the public mind be harder to dislodge after a certification from Harris and the state's Election Canvassing Commission. But with so many hearings and briefs planned for the coming week, the joy of declared victory may be short-lived if the winner must struggle to avoid being unseated.

Florida, indeed, offers ample precedent for successful election challenges that topple victors. Most recently, in 1997, an appeals court unseated Xavier Suarez, who had been elected mayor of Miami, after his challenger, Joe Carollo, contested the election on the basis of fraudulent absentee ballots.

In the Bush-Gore case, the Gore camp will not be alleging fraud but rather errors and legal violations in counting ballots. In Miami-Dade County, the Democrats plan to sue because the elections board there voted to stop their manual recount of ballots, a direct result, according to the Gore campaign, of a heated demonstration by Republican partisans in the elections office. In Nassau County, the campaign will contest the decision to toss out a recounted tally where Gore picked up 52 votes. And in Palm Beach County, the challenge will center on the decision by the elections board not to count many dimpled ballots as votes.

The Democrats have seized in particular on the demonstration that they say caused the Miami-Dade board to stop its hand counts, charging that it was an orchestrated effort by Republicans to disrupt the count. Many of the demonstrators in Broward County said they were former recount observers who were being put up in local hotels and given meals by the Republican Party.

In this race, of course, it will not be possible for a state court to unseat a president-elect directly, so the object of Gore's contest will be the electors that the State Legislature must select by Dec. 12. The Legislature is dominated by Republicans, many of whom have said they are so angry at Gore's legal challenges that they would vote to choose electors pledged to Bush even if Gore should be certified as the winner on Sunday.

But after the United States Supreme Court agreed to hear the case, the leaders of the Florida House and Senate chose a somewhat less confrontational tack, announcing plans to join Bush's side before the Supreme Court. The Legislature's strategy will stay in the courts only for a short time, though. Johnnie B. Byrd Jr., a senior House Republican and co-chairman of the Legislature's select committee on the election, vowed in an interview today that even if contest actions are still unresolved by the Dec. 12 deadline for naming electors, the Republican-dominated Legislature will go ahead and pick a slate of 25 electors loyal to Bush. "It's been fun, but we're ready for a little finality," he said.

Nov. 26, 2000, David Firestone

NEW DETAILS IN ABSENTEE BALLOT CASE

In Seminole County, where the Republican elections chief allowed Republican Party workers to correct thousands of flawed absentee ballot applications, new details of the incident have emerged. Sandra Goard, the supervisor of elections, had described the area the party workers used as a warehouse. But in depositions Wednesday she said a Republican worker, Michael Leach, had brought his own laptop computer with which to add the missing voter identification numbers. He was later joined by a second man she could not identify. She said the room he had used served as her telephone bank and contained 18 terminals linked to a mainframe computer that stored all of her voter elections records. She said that the terminals had password protections, but that both men worked there unsupervised.

George W. Bush gained more than 10,000 absentee votes in heavily Republican Seminole County, compared with about 5,200 for Vice President Al Gore, and a lawsuit filed by Democrats is seeking to have all the absentee votes thrown out. Gore could win Florida, and thus the presidential race, if the lawsuit is successful. Lawyers for the elections supervisor and the state Republican Party, which also was sued, have said they did nothing wrong. They also stress that only absentee applications, and not ballots, were involved.

In yet another twist, the circuit judge set to hear the case on Wednesday, Debra Nelson, had her own absentee ballot mix-up during a September primary. Her campaign manager, Robert Lewis, a deputy chief clerk for the Seminole County courts, said Friday that Nelson's campaign had also left off the voter identification numbers on 60,000 absentee ballot forms that were mailed to potential supporters.

In this case, the 5,000 forms that voters returned were mailed directly to Nelson's campaign, where a volunteer spent two weeks adding the numbers, Lewis said. Noting that state law requires voters to supply those numbers, Lewis said of his decision to fix the forms after voters signed them: "It does sound like a technicality, but whether it's a fatal error or not, you could argue it both ways." Nelson could not be reached for comment.

Nov. 26, 2000, Michael Cooper

G.O.P. Sues over Rejected Military Absentee Ballots

TALLAHASSEE — After bludgeoning Democrats in the court of public opinion for a week with accusations that they had tried to disqualify overseas military ballots, Republicans abruptly withdrew one suit over the ballots from a court of law today before filing four new ones. Lawyers for George W. Bush began filing suits in five counties late today to force them to review military absentee ballots before Sunday's deadline for certification of a winner. As Al Gore ate into the extremely narrow Bush lead in other recounts, lawyers filed suits with court clerks in Hillsborough, Okaloosa, Pasco and Polk Counties. A Bush spokeswoman said a suit in Orange County would be filed early Sunday.

Just hours before a judge in Leon County was expected to rule in their suit to reinstate absentee military ballots in more than a dozen Florida counties, lawyers for Bush said, in effect, that they had already won their point: some counties were counting military ballots that had been disqualified. George Meros, a lawyer for Bush, said that he deemed that suit successful because the pressure it brought to bear on some of the canvassing boards caused them to reconsider the absentee ballots and count more for Bush. "Several of these boards were already doing what we requested," Meros said. "We did not want the suit to delay or hamper their counting of the ballots." An unofficial tally by The Associated Press indicates that the recounted military ballots netted Bush 45 more votes.

But lawyers for some of the canvassing boards named in the suit in Leon County said that they believed Bush's lawyers dropped the suit because they feared they would lose. "They saw the writing on the wall," said Wayne Malaney, a lawyer representing the supervisor of elections in Collier County. "Rather than putting themselves in the position of having to appeal a decision they didn't like, they punted." Indeed, in a hearing on Friday, Judge L. Ralph Smith of the Leon County Circuit Court said Bush's lawyers had failed to present any evidence that the local elections officials were violating the law when they rejected ballots for such reasons as lack of proper postmarks, dates and signatures.

But in court papers filed today, Bush's lawyers continued to exert pressure on those boards that have not decided to re-examine their absentee ballots. The lawyers threatened to file suits in other courts "against those defendant canvassing boards that continue to unfairly deny men and women in the armed forces their right to participate in the election of the next president of the United States and commander in chief." Ronald Labasky, an attorney who represented two elections supervisors in the Leon County case, said that any new lawsuits filed by the Bush camp may be an effort to find a more sympathetic judge.

The hearing on Friday underscored just how tangled the Florida election law governing absentee ballots is. One state law says that only ballots with a valid postmark should be counted, while another code states that ballots can be counted as long as they have either a postmark or are signed and dated before the date of the election. (One of Bush's lawyers, Fred H. Bartlit, suggested that some ballots should be counted even if they bore neither a postmark or a date, because many absentee ballots have no space where a date is requested.)

And the suit threatened to open a legal hornet's nest that neither Bush's lawyers nor the county canvassing boards they were suing appeared prepared for: Judge Smith noted repeatedly that one Florida law requires that all absentee ballots be received by 7 p.m. on the day of the election, while an administrative rule allows absentee ballots to be counted as long as they are received within 10 days of the election.

In this election, all of the counties in Florida followed the 10-day rule. But Judge Smith noted that state laws usually take precedence over administrative rules. Bush's lawyers noted that the rule was adopted to settle a federal lawsuit against Florida's elections laws, and said that it should be considered to have the force of federal law behind it.

Nov. 26, 2000, Michael Cooper

day

19

SUNDAY,

NOVEMBER 26TH

★ ★ ★ ★ ★

HARRIS DECLARES BUSH THE WINNER

Nearly two and a half weeks after Election Day, George W. Bush declares himself the next president in a subdued televised address. His statement follows an announcement by Katherine Harris that she has certified the vote tallies for the state's 67 counties, awarding Bush the state's 25 electoral votes. His final margin is 537 votes; Harris refuses to include results of a hand recount in Palm Beach County because the canvassing board there narrowly fails to complete the count by the 5 p.m. deadline. Democrats denounce the certification as premature and arbitrary, and vow to fight in state court to have the recount tallies included and to have thousands of dimpled ballots counted and included in the final totals. Gore himself is silent, but his running mate, Joe Lieberman, makes it clear that the vice president will not concede

BUSH WINS AGAIN BUT GORE WON'T CONCEDE

TALLAHASSEE – The State of Florida tonight declared George W. Bush the winner of its presidential election by 537 votes out of nearly 6 million cast. He promptly declared that meant he had won the White House and vowed to "undertake the responsibility of preparing to serve as America's next president." But Al Gore did not concede, and his campaign vowed to contest the election in state court in extraordinary legal proceedings not seen by any living American.

Moments before 7:30 p.m., Katherine Harris appeared in the Capitol here with the two other members of the state's elections canvassing commission to certify the official returns. "I hereby declare Gov. George W. Bush the winner of Florida's 25 electoral votes," she said as cheers went up from Bush supporters gathered outside. The 25 votes would give Bush the presidency.

Moments after Harris's announcement, Gore's vice-presidential running mate, Senator Joseph I. Lieberman, appeared on television from Washington to denounce "what by any reasonable standard is an incomplete and inaccurate count." He said Florida officials had left the Gore campaign "no choice but to contest their actions," and Gore asked for television time from the networks to address the nation at noon on Monday.

> *"At some point, the law must prevail and the lawyers must go home. We have reached that point."*
>
> *—James A. Baker III*

Tonight's announcement in Florida was a powerful turning point for both candidates, one that Gore had desperately sought to avoid. In all the counts and recounts in Florida since Nov. 7, there was never a moment when Gore held a statewide lead.

A frantic round of manual ballot recounts ordered by the Florida Supreme Court last week, and due this evening, nearly halved Bush's previous official, uncertified lead of 930 votes. But in a move that drew a sharp challenge from the Gore campaign, Harris refused to include the results of a nearly complete recount of votes in Palm Beach County that would have given Gore a net gain of an additional 192 votes. Harris cited a provision of state election law that could be read as requiring that counties "manually recount all ballots," in case of dispute. But lawyers for Gore dismissed that notion and noted that the returns already on file included the results of sample manual recounts in at least three South Florida counties, conducted earlier in an effort to determine whether full hand counts were justified.

About four and a half hours before the 5 p.m. deadline set by the State Supreme Court last week for finishing the recounts, election officials in Palm Beach County appealed to the secretary of state for more time, until 9 a.m. on Monday. Harris rejected the request, and at about 4:30 this afternoon, with 584 of 637 precincts counted in Palm Beach County, county officials stopped counting with about 1,000 votes to go, and they prepared to submit the results on hand. They faxed their tallies to Harris at 4:54 p.m., according to a stamp on the papers, then resumed counting in hopes that a final, amended count might somehow be accepted. "We're going to do the best we can," said

Judge Charles E. Burton, chairman of the county canvassing board. The board finished its count shortly before 7 p.m.

In Broward County, the manual recount ended just minutes before midnight on Saturday, producing a net gain of 567 votes for Gore, cutting Bush's previous lead in half and bringing the vice president within striking distance of overtaking him, depending on the Palm Beach count. A partial recount in Miami-Dade County last week had produced an additional 157 votes for Gore. But officials there abruptly stopped their recount last week, saying they could not finish a full recount by today's deadline, and those votes were not included in the new totals issued tonight. But they will be at the center of the Gore campaign's legal challenges under Florida law, which allows a loser to file a formal contest of election results once they are certified.

James A. Baker III held a news conference tonight to declare: "At some point — at some point — there must be closure. At some point, the law must prevail and the lawyers must go home. We have reached that point."

Lieberman cast the dispute in stark moral terms. "What is at issue here is nothing less than every American's simple, sacred right to vote," Lieberman said. "How can we teach our children that every vote counts if we are not willing to make a good-faith effort to count every vote?"

Nov. 27, 2000, Todd S. Purdum

Bush Quietly Claims Victory

"This has been a hard-fought election, a healthy contest for American democracy. But now that the votes are counted, it is time for the votes to count."

– George W. Bush

★ ★ ★

AUSTIN – After 19 days of waiting and worrying and watching his fortunes rise and fall, George W. Bush stepped out for the first time as the president-elect, talking about the important business to be done and imploring Al Gore not to stall him. On a victory night of sorts for the Bush campaign that did not have the full flavor of one, Bush did not emerge from the Governor's Mansion here until nearly 80 minutes after the certification. With all the uncertainty that remained, the Bush campaign had not manufactured a festive, traditional party. There was no surging music, no downpour of confetti. Bush made his remarks not on a brightly festooned stage but in a second-floor area inside the Capitol, and his audience was a relatively small group of reporters and television producers.

What Bush delivered in a relatively unemotional voice over the course of about seven minutes at the State Capitol here was nothing like a conventional victory speech. But he left no doubt that, with the certification of a vote total in Florida tonight that labeled him the winner of that state, he now saw himself and his running mate, Dick Cheney, as the victors in the presidential election, and they would begin acting that way. He said that Cheney would guide the transition, and Bush even announced that the chief of staff in a Bush White House would be Andrew Card, who was deputy chief of staff and then transportation secretary during the presidential administration of Bush's father.

"The election was close, but tonight, after a count, a recount and yet another manual recount, Secretary Cheney and I are honored and humbled to have won the state of Florida, which gives us the needed electoral votes to win the election," Bush said. "We will therefore undertake the responsibility of preparing to serve as America's next president and vice president," Bush added. He made no mention of the fact that later this week, the United States Supreme Court is scheduled to hear an appeal filed by his lawyers.

In what might, in any other presidential election, have been the kind of remarks that a winner delivered the morning after an enormous victory jubilee, Bush even ticked off issues that he wanted a Bush presidency to address. These included improving education and providing elderly Americans with prescription drug coverage, and Bush was careful to stress that the issues also mattered deeply to Democrats.

He called on Gore not to persist with promised legal challenges of the Florida results, deliberately choosing conciliatory over provocative language in a manner that reflected the politically charged circumstances. "This has been a hard-fought election, a healthy contest for American democracy," Bush said. "But now that the votes are counted, it is time for the votes to count. The vice president's lawyers have indicated he will challenge the certified election results. I respectfully ask him to reconsider."

Bush called for partisan healing tonight, his words underscoring the extraordinary outcome of the president election and willing an end to a narrative that is not yet truly over. "I will listen and I will respect the different points of view," Bush said, referring to Republicans and Democrats. "And most of all, I will work to unite our great land."

Later, he added: "All of us in this election fought for our views. Now we must live up to our principles. We must show our commitment to the common good, which is bigger than any person or any party. We cannot change yesterday, but we share a responsibility for tomorrow. Time runs short and we have a lot of work to do."

Even before Bush spoke tonight, his aides and supporters had begun an effort, also clear in his comments, to create a public climate in which Gore would feel pressured to concede. "Now the Gore campaign lawyers want to shift from recounts to contesting the election outcome," said James A. Baker III at a news conference there. "And they propose to do this notwithstanding the fact that America has never had a presidential election decided by an election contest in court."

Nov. 27, 2000, Frank Bruni

A New York Times Interview with Al Gore

Following are excerpts from a *New York Times* interview yesterday with Al Gore in Washington conducted several hours before the Florida votes were certified.

Q: Your lawyers said a few days ago that regardless of what the count turns out to be a couple of hours from now that you would contest certain places. Why are you pressing on longer than usual?

GORE: I think that it is important for the integrity of our democracy to make sure that every vote is counted. Especially in a close election because the foundation of our constitutional self-government is the consent of the governed. … [I]t is a relatively simple principle that lies at the heart of our democracy that every vote that is legally cast must be fairly and accurately counted in accordance with the law. That is a … a principle that must be upheld in order to make certain that the will of the American people is not only expressed but heard and abided by.

Q: Do you think that the presidency, with perhaps half the voters in the country thinking not only that their guy didn't win but a fair number of them thinking he was robbed in some fashion, is it going to be worth less than it would have been?

GORE: If … a full and accurate count of the votes results in my election, I will go to extraordinary lengths to build bridges to Republicans and independents and others. I will select an administration that is not purely partisan in cast. I will reach out regularly and often to the bipartisan leadership of the Congress and to political and civic leaders from across the spectrum throughout the country. There is ample precedent in American history for the winners of close elections to unite the country. This controversy in the year 2000, as difficult as it might seem to us, is nothing compared to the election of 1800, where Thomas Jefferson finally prevailed after 36 ballots in the Congress, if my history serves me correctly. … Jefferson's healing speech in March of 1801 is one of the most notable in the history of the presidency: "We are all Republicans. We are all Federalists." So the resiliency of our democracy is often underestimated, but it is always proven out in the end.

Q: You were talking about the value of the presidency after a close and bitter election. Suppose Governor Bush prevails? You were talking about reaching out. Do you have a sense of what you might do to help heal those wounds then?

GORE: Yes. I have previously said in a speech to the nation that if at the end of this process — when every vote is fairly and accurately counted — if Governor Bush is successful, I will spare no efforts to help him unify the country behind his leadership, and I would expect him to do the same if I am successful. It was for that purpose, it was in anticipation of that challenge, that I have suggested publicly and privately that he and I meet to try and improve the tone during this period of time, so that it won't be a cold start at the end of the vote-counting process. But I will respect his decision not to go along with that offer, and I don't want to criticize him for not accepting it, nor do I want to belabor the point by renewing it again. But I just want to make the point that I am trying to proceed in a way that honors my highest obligation in this matter, which is to the Constitution. ... Secondarily, I have an obligation to the 50 million–plus voters who supported the agenda that I laid out during the campaign. … I feel an obligation to them, very keenly, but it is secondary to the obligation that I have to the country as a whole and to the Constitution.

Q: It seemed 10 days or so ago that Republican officeholders were more intense in their insistence that Governor Bush had been elected and you ought to drop out than the reverse. Do you think that is the case, and if so, what's your sense of why it happened?

GORE: I have, publicly and privately, urged my supporters to show restraint in word and deed, not only in my speeches but also in numerous conference calls and private conversations. I have urged no one associated with my cause to ever charge that the other side is trying to steal the election or take the result away in an unethical way. I think such language is damaging to our republic, especially in a time of enhanced vulnerability and civic tension. In response, to those who have proposed matching demonstration for demonstration for demonstration, and crowd for crowd, I have counseled patience and forbearance. As Joe Lieberman said in his statement on Friday afternoon, the time for electioneering is now past. This is a time for counting the votes and preparing for the healing of our divisions in the aftermath of the final judgment of the voters. So, the fact that our side has not taken some steps that you have seen on the other side should not be taken as evidence of any diminished passion or strength of feeling on the part of those who supported the agenda that Joe and I have put forward . . .

Q: Republicans were very critical of the Florida Supreme Court even before it acted, saying it's seven Democratic appointees, it's partisan, nobody can trust it. A piece of this issue is now going before the Supreme Court, which has two Democratic appointees, and seven people chosen by Republicans. Should that give anyone pause?

GORE: No, it should not. And whatever their verdict, you will never hear me criticize their political provenance. I will accept whatever judgment they make on the issues with quiet respect and complete deference and acceptance.

Q: To the extent that you can advise your supporters, you don't want to hear them saying "It's a Republican Supreme Court"?

GORE: Correct, and I will call on all of my supporters to do the same. I think that respect for the rulings of our independent judiciary is an essential building block of the American republic. Our freedom depends ultimately on the way in which we live and breathe our commitment to the integrity of our democracy. And since Marbury v. Madison we have accepted the role of the courts in interpreting the meaning of the laws. And it has been a bulwark of the stability of America's democratic self-government.

Gore's Lawyers Outline Strategy for Contesting Vote

TALLAHASSEE – Even before the secretary of state certified George W. Bush as the winner of the Florida election, lawyers for Al Gore were finishing the drafts of what could be the most significant lawsuit of all the legal battles fought so far — maybe more important than the issues to be heard by the United States Supreme Court on Friday.

David Boies, Gore's chief trial lawyer in Florida, said his team planned to file a formal contest in the Leon County Courthouse here on Monday morning in an effort to demonstrate an incorrect outcome occurred in three counties: Miami-Dade, where officials first agreed to do a manual recount but then abandoned it abruptly on Wednesday; Palm Beach, whose manual recount was rejected today because results were incomplete; and Nassau, where officials recently threw out the results of a mechanical recount and relied instead on the initial count from Election Day. Though the grounds will be different for each county, he said, they will all be based on the concept that the state elections board certified the wrong total.

Gore's lawyers say this lawsuit will have a more direct impact on the election than the Supreme Court hearing — an assessment the Bush team reluctantly shares. Even if the high court rules against Gore and says the secretary of state was within her rights when she set Nov. 14 as the deadline for reporting results of manual recounts, that will not necessarily have any impact on the contests, they say. That is because Florida's laws on contests give judges wide discretion in considering proof that the wrong person was elected. In addition to things like bribery and fraud, the law allows the judge to accept "any other cause or allegation" that proves the outcome was wrong.

Gore's lawyers said they planned to concentrate on that phrase, and noted that a manual recount, whether or not the Supreme Court requires it be included in the state certification, can still be presented as valid evidence before a judge that the election should be overturned. "The hand counts will still be valid evidence in the contest action, no matter what the Supreme Court rules," said Ronald A. Klain, a senior legal adviser to Gore. "In fact, it could be very powerful evidence as to who got the most votes. The Supreme Court is looking at far more limited issues."

If anything, the lawyers noted, Secretary of State Katherine Harris's refusal tonight to consider the incomplete results of the Palm Beach County manual recount only adds to their case. "To reject a certified total by a county canvassing board — that's pretty strong evidence right there," Klain said.

Boies noted that the high court refused to consider the issue of whether the hand counts were legal, accepting the Florida Supreme Court's decision that they were. He suggested that the high court's opinion would now be almost a moot point, because it is dealing with issues related to the certification of the election nearly a week after the certification has taken place.

The Florida law is so broad that it allows a judge to perform a manual recount of a county's votes itself, or appoint someone else to do it. That is precisely what Gore's lawyers will ask a judge to do in the case of Miami-Dade County, where election officials stopped counting last week, unable to meet the deadline. Boies said he wants the court to appoint a special master to count disputed votes in Miami-Dade. The Miami-Dade contest, he said, will have two grounds: the 388 votes (which would add 157 to Gore's total) that were manually counted and then discarded when the board stopped counting; and the 10,000 or so ballots showing no vote for president that were never examined by the board. Democrats have charged that a demonstration by Republicans intimidated the board, although Republicans deny that.

The Palm Beach contest will also have two parts: the rejection of the manually counted ballots by Harris, and the standard used by the county board in judging dimpled ballots, which the Democrats have said discarded too many valid votes.

In Nassau County, the Democrats will ask that a judge look into the election board's decision to discard the machine recount that was required by law, and to revert to the election-night total. That decision, which county officials say was approved by Harris, removed 52 votes from Gore's column.

All three challenges will be presented to a circuit judge in Leon County, which has jurisdiction in statewide election challenges. Republicans say they will file no contests of their own, but will defend any of the contests filed by Gore.

Nov. 27, 2000, David Firestone

HOW HARRIS REJECTED PALM BEACH RECOUNT

WEST PALM BEACH – The idea of a hand recount in Florida was born here, with claims by mostly elderly voters that their ballots in the presidential election had been miscast and discounted. But tonight, the results of Palm Beach County's historic hand recount were not counted in Florida's official final tally.

It was a bitter end to an exhausting, frustrating marathon of tedious work that many people had branded as a partisan attempt to hunt for enough votes to steal an election. "A slap in the face to all the people who worked so hard in there," County Judge Charles E. Burton, the canvassing board chairman, said of Harris's decision.

Nineteen days after the Nov. 7 election, the county canvassing board frantically rushed to meet a court-ordered 5 p.m. deadline to recount the nearly half-million ballots, failed to do so, and sent by fax machine an incomplete tally to the secretary of state, just 800 to 1,000 ballots short of a complete hand recount. When it was clear in the early afternoon that the board could not meet that deadline, Burton faxed a hurried letter to Harris, pleading for a few hours more to allow the board to complete the job it began 10 days ago.

"We have been working diligently, including the last 24-hour period, to complete this critical portion of the hand count," Burton wrote. "Your consideration of our request to extend the deadline for final submission of this hand count until Monday, November 27 at 9 a.m., would be greatly appreciated, as we know you are interested in counting all votes as accurately as possible."

"I would not expect a positive response," Burton said after sending his letter.

Harris sent a reply by fax denying his appeal, then, several hours later, she refused to accept the incomplete total, leaving the canvassing board in this Democratic stronghold angry and frustrated. Burton called Harris's refusal to extend the deadline "bogus," saying that "a couple of hours should not make any difference," considering what was at stake and the ordeal of 20-hour days that counters had endured.

Thirty minutes after the deadline passed, and with no assurance that Harris would even accept the county's completed recount, Burton, County Commissioner Carol Roberts and LePore sat back down and began counting again. It was the 34th straight hour of work for the three canvassing board members. "We all want to finish the job we began," Judge Burton said. "We're going to send a report to the secretary of state, and it will be up to her whether she accepts it."

After the county's recount had tabulated 462,657 ballots by 5:30 p.m., Al Gore had gained a net of 192 votes in Palm Beach County, according to *The New York Times*'s count. Results from the final tally submitted to the canvassing board just after 7 p.m were not available. But even those additional votes would have failed to erase Bush's narrow lead in the battle for Florida's decisive 25 electoral votes. According to The Associated Press tonight, Bush led in Florida by 537 votes.

Lawyers for the Democrats said they had counted a total of 4,468 ballots with dimples, many of which had not been counted as votes by the board. Out of those, they said, Gore would have had 846 more votes than Bush, enough to swing the election. The Gore campaign said tonight that it would contest the election results in Palm Beach County on the ground that the canvassing board did not use the correct standard to count dimpled ballots. By counting some ballots with dimples and hanging chads, and some on which the voters had written their preference instead of punching it, the canvassing board had found an additional 758 ballots.

Members of the canvassing board said tonight that the experience taught them that hand recounts are more accurate than machine recounts, even as Republican lawyers and politicians continued to argue that human beings are more prone to mistake and mischief.

Nov. 27, 2000, Don Van Natta Jr. And Rick Bragg

Furor Erupts Over 218 Votes in Nassau County

FERNANDINA BEACH — It appears that one of two strange things happened here in Nassau County. Maybe 218 votes were skipped in one count, though no one involved can offer any evidence for that. Or maybe 218 phantom voters were created in another count, but there is no evidence of that, either.

In the long list of oddities that have marred the presidential balloting in Florida, tiny Nassau County, in the far northeastern corner of the state, has come up with something different. And the way county officials chose to resolve the issue, producing a net gain of 51 votes for George W. Bush, has led to charges of secretive, partisan manipulation of the totals, and yet another in the procession of lawsuits over this election.

Because the election-night tally of Florida's nearly six million votes was so close, state law mandated that county officials run the ballots through their counting machines again a few days later. That state count showed 4,000 more votes than the first one. Election officials say such an increase is standard fare, mostly because partially detached chads on punch-card ballots fall off the second time through, allowing the machines to see votes they had previously missed.

But in Nassau County, which Bush carried by more than 2 to 1, the second tabulation of more than 23,000 votes produced 218 fewer than the first count, narrowing the governor's lead over Gore by 51 votes. Like their counterparts in every other county, members of Nassau's canvassing board certified the recount figures and submitted them to the state.

On Friday, however, the canvassing board voted to rescind that certification, and certified the election-night count, adding 51 votes to Bush's lead at a time when recounts in two other counties — Broward and Palm Beach — were shrinking his lead statewide. Katherine Harris's office accepted that decision. Democrats cried foul, calling the reversal illegal, and today, David Boies, a lawyer for the Gore campaign, referring to "the inexplicable actions in Nassau County," said the vice president would oppose the county's reversal in a planned lawsuit contesting the election results.

Shirley N. King, the county supervisor of elections for 20 years, said that in reverting to the original count, she just wanted to ensure that 218 people were not disenfranchised. Democrats protest that the decision was made with little public notice, the day after Thanksgiving, and with many Democrats out of town, including a canvassing board member who, in his absence, was replaced by a Republican.

When Florida's 67 counties did the required machine recount, 44 of them came up with more votes than the first time, and 12 got the same totals. Ten counties besides Nassau reported lower figures, but in most cases, the decline was one, two or three votes.

Nassau's total changed about 1 percent from one count to the next, compared with an average, for all counties, of 0.07 percent. Only one other county, Gadsden County, whose vote increased, had a larger percentage change.

In Nassau, each voter filled out not one punch card but three, an unusual feature that may have added to the confusion. King said that in doing the recount, she decided that, to save time, her clerks would separate the red cards bearing the presidential votes from the others, and run only the red ones through the machines. "I think we goofed and we did not pull all of the red cards," she said.

But some Democrats say it is just as likely that a batch of ballots was accidentally counted twice the first time, or that the machines miscounted. "It could have been anything," said Linda Spencer, co-chairwoman of the county Democratic Party.

Nov. 27, 2000, Richard Pérez-Peña

Tracking Bush's Lead

Date	What Happened	Bush Lead
Nov. 9	Florida law calls for an automatic recount because of the narrow margin of Bush's lead. The Gore campaign requests manual recounts in four counties: Broward, Miami-Dade, Palm Beach and Volusia.	1,784
Nov. 11	Automatic recounts are completed in most counties.	327
Nov. 12	Palm Beach and Volusia begin manual recounts.	
Nov. 14	Harris certifies the votes. Volusia County is the only county to submit manual recount results.	300
Nov. 15	Broward County begins a manual recount.	
Nov. 18	Overseas absentee ballots are counted.	930
Nov. 20	Miami-Dade begins a manual recount that is later suspended.	
Nov. 21	The Florida Supreme Court rules that manual recounts must be included. Bush appeals the next day.	652
Nov. 26	Harris certifies Broward County's full manual recount but does not include a partial recount submitted by Palm Beach County. Harris declares Bush the winner of Florida's electoral votes.	537

day

20

MONDAY,

NOVEMBER 27TH

★ ★ ★ ★ ★

GORE CONTESTS THE ELECTION

Gore appeals to the American people to be patient while his campaign fights to have every vote counted. Central to this effort is a suit filed in state court seeking to have all the votes in Nassau, Miami-Dade and Palm Beach Counties counted in Tallahassee by a court-appointed "special master." Bush, despite being denied federal office space and funds by the Clinton administration, begins his transition. Republicans in the Florida Legislature move to call a special session intended to pass legislation awarding the state's 25 Electoral College votes to Bush. Bush's brother Jeb, Florida's governor, reportedly agrees to sign the act into law.

FLORIDA JUDGE ASKED TO DECLARE GORE THE WINNER

"The ballots are the witnesses that will speak volumes."

– Senior Gore adviser

★ ★ ★

TALLAHASSEE – Al Gore placed his last hope of gaining the presidency in a lawsuit filed today that contests the results of the presidential election in Florida, asking a circuit court judge to declare him the winner and award him the state's 25 electoral votes. But at a hastily called court hearing this afternoon before Judge N. Sanders Sauls of Leon County Circuit Court, it became clear that the sheer magnitude of the trial, which will include witnesses, exhibits, at least eight plaintiffs and defendants and the possibility of yet another recount, may burst a looming deadline of Dec. 12. That is the day the state's electors are to be sent to the Electoral College.

In the lawsuit, Gore's lawyers said the vote totals certified on Sunday night by the Florida secretary of state were wrong, contending that thousands of votes in three counties were uncounted. Had all the votes been counted in Nassau, Miami-Dade and Palm Beach Counties, the lawsuit said, Gore, and not George W. Bush, would have won.

In today's hearing, Gore's lawyers asked that thousands of ballots from Miami-Dade and Palm Beach be sent to Tallahassee to be examined by the judge or by a special master that he would appoint. The lawyers want the court to count the nearly 10,000 ballots that the Miami-Dade election board stopped counting when it aborted a manual recount last week, as well as 4,000 ballots that were set aside in Palm Beach because election officials conducting a manual recount there could not agree on their meaning.

Most of the arguments made in the lawsuit have become familiar over the last three weeks, particularly the recitation of the reasons the disputed ballots should have been counted by hand. But the movement of the legal battle into the contest phase — which can take place only after the election is certified and a winner declared — raised some new issues.

For one thing, the county election boards on which the Gore team had been relying to conduct hand counts now become the Democrats' adversaries because they must be named as defendants in a contest suit. The Democrats accuse the counties of "illegally and improperly" discarding thousands of legal votes, and in the case of Nassau County, of counting illegal votes. They asked Judge Sauls to transfer the ballots out of the counties' custody and into the hands of the courts.

Gore also asked the court to appoint an outside party, known as a special master, to count the ballots, which could take days or weeks, depending on the size of the staff the special master is allowed to hire. The lawsuit asks that the special master be allowed to examine the ballots under the most liberal possible standard of interpretation, which would allow dimpled ballots to be counted as votes.

The man being asked to overturn the certification is a former federal bankruptcy judge who was appointed to the bench in 1989 by Gov. Bob Martinez, a Republican. Judge Sauls, 59, was assigned to the case randomly by computer when it was filed.

Ronald A. Labasky, a Tallahassee lawyer who serves as general counsel to the State Association of Supervisors of Elections, said Judge Sauls was considered to be among the more conservative of the four civil judges on the county court, and was known as a fairly strict interpreter of the statutes. He is probably not the judge the Gore team would have picked if it had had a choice, Labasky said.

Because the hearing took place at 4 p.m., only a few hours after the lawsuit was filed, just after noon, Bush's lawyers had no time to respond formally, and the judge granted them until Wednesday to do so. But their opposition to the core demands of the contest quickly became evident at the hearing. Barry Richard, the lead trial lawyer for Bush, objected strenuously when Gore lawyers asked to have the ballots moved to Tallahassee. "What this motion is leading to is not about the preservation of these ballots," Richard said. "What it's leading to is the plaintiff's next motion, which is asking the court to appoint a special master to begin doing what the election board has already done: count these ballots. And there is no authority in any law or the rules to appoint such special masters."

No matter what the judge decides regarding the counting of the disputed ballots, the losing side will quickly appeal, and the case will inevitably wind up in the Florida Supreme Court and possibly the United States Supreme Court. It seems unlikely that all such appeals and the full trial could take place before Dec. 12, but Democrats vowed to try.

Because of the extremely limited time available before the Electoral College convenes, no other legal avenue would be open to Gore, his lawyers said. They also said they would consider themselves fortunate if the contest lawsuit, with all of its inevitable appeals, is finished before Dec. 12 and are giving no thought to any other legal recourse. To move their suit along rapidly, the Democrats said they would try to keep their witness list to a minimum, possibly placing their whole case on the counting of the disputed 14,000 ballots rather than having extended testimony by elections officials from the various counties. "The ballots are the witnesses that will speak volumes," said one senior Gore adviser.

Under Florida law, cited in the Gore team's brief, one of the grounds for a successful contest of the election is "receipt of a number of illegal votes or rejection of a number of legal votes sufficient to change or place in doubt the result of the election." The Democrats are claiming that both took place. In Nassau County, the elections board decided not to certify the votes tabulated in the required mechanical recount, reverting to the election-night tally and subtracting a net of 52 votes from Gore's column, which the Democrats say was illegal.

In Palm Beach and Miami-Dade Counties, the Democrats say that 14,000 votes for president were not counted, but the Republicans strongly dispute that. The 10,000 ballots in Miami-Dade were run through a machine tabulator but were not recorded as votes because holes in the ballot card were not fully punched. Most were never manually examined. In Palm Beach, the 4,000 disputed ballots were run through the machine and manually examined, but in neither case was a vote determined.

The Democrats say a special master, if ordered to count dimples as votes the way Broward County did in its manual recount, would find a net gain of 800 votes for Gore in Palm Beach County, and 600 in Miami-Dade. Bush, according to the state elections board, won the election by 537 votes.

Gore's contest lawsuit was the most significant election-related legal action taking place in Tallahassee today, but it was not the only one. Elsewhere around town:

— A lawsuit filed by supporters of Gore, alleging that the so-called butterfly ballot in Palm Beach County was so confusing that it disenfranchised thousands of voters, was appealed to the Florida Supreme Court. In an order late in the day, the court asked that legal briefs be filed by 5 p.m. on Tuesday but did not say whether it would accept the case.

— A Leon County judge will hear a lawsuit by a Democrat who says that about 15,000 absentee ballots in Seminole County should be voided because officials improperly let Republicans correct registration information on ballot applications. The Gore campaign decided not to include Seminole in its contest lawsuit.

Nov. 28, 2000, David Firestone

Bush Plans Transition as Gore Asks for Patience

"Ignoring votes means ignoring democracy itself."

– Al Gore

★ ★ ★

WASHINGTON — As Bush moved with determination to prepare his transition to the White House, Gore pleaded tonight for public patience while he contests Florida's decision to award its decisive 25 electoral votes to Bush.

In a brief address from the vice presidential residence just before 9 p.m., Gore said that he was challenging the vote count in Florida to ensure that every American had the chance to register a choice in one of the closest presidential races in American history. Gore asserted that he was not engaged in a struggle for power, but rather in an effort to preserve "democracy itself." "Whatever the outcome, let the people have their say, and let us listen," Gore said, standing before ranks of draped American flags. "Ignoring votes means ignoring democracy itself, and if we ignore the votes of thousands in Florida in this election, how can you or any American have confidence that your vote will not be ignored in a future election?" Gore continued. "That is all we have asked since election day, a complete count of all the votes cast in Florida. Not recount after recount, as some have charged, but a single full and accurate count. We haven't had that yet."

Gore said a fair count of the Florida vote would provide him with more than enough votes to defeat Bush and pleaded with the public to await a more complete tally. Aware of polls showing that the public is growing weary of the long postelection limbo, Gore tonight blamed "lawsuit after lawsuit" filed by Republicans and what he called "organized intimidation" of local canvassing officials for the delay in reaching a full count.

Undeterred by Gore's words or his legal actions in Florida, Bush pressed forward with his transition planning, meeting in Austin, Tex., with his designated White House chief of staff, Andrew H. Card Jr., a former secretary of transportation under President George Bush. Dick Cheney announced that he was opening a full-scale transition operation in rented office space in Washington, using money from private donations.

Cheney sharply criticized Gore and the White House for refusing to authorize public money and government office space for the Bush transition. He said the administration had a duty to honor the results of the Florida election as certified by Katherine Harris.

Cheney said Gore's obstinacy was getting in the way of a peaceful transfer of power. "We find ourselves in a unique and totally unprecedented position," said Cheney, a former secretary of defense and White House chief of staff. "Never before in American history has a presidential candidate gone to court to try to change the outcome of an already-certified presidential election. But whatever the vice president's decision, it does not change our obligation to prepare to govern the nation."

As Democrats emphasized the need to let the legal process play out in Florida, Republicans sought to create a sense of inevitability about the Bush ascension. Gov. Jeb Bush signed the document that certified his brother as the winner of the Florida vote. Senator Trent Lott, Republican of Mississippi, the Senate majority leader, instructed committee chairmen to prepare for hearings the first week in January on Bush's prospective cabinet nominees. Calling Bush the president-elect, Lott said the hearings should immediately follow the swearing-in of senators on Jan. 3. "Given the protracted contest to determine the presidential victor," Lott said in a statement, "it is critical that we move expeditiously and be prepared to confirm the new cabinet on Jan. 20 after the president has been sworn in to office."

Democratic Congressional leaders, in a carefully orchestrated display of support for Gore, flew in a chartered jet to Tallahassee, Fla., where they took part in a televised conference call with Gore and Senator Joseph I. Lieberman, his running mate. Gore told Senator Tom Daschle of South Dakota and Representative Richard A. Gephardt of Missouri, the Senate and House Democratic leaders, that thousands of votes cast in Florida did not register in machine counts and have never been tallied by hand. "If every vote is counted, there are easily more than enough to change the outcome and decide the election in our favor," Gore said. "It's about the principle. But there are more than enough votes to change the outcome, and that's an important factor as well." He said that he had petitioned the Florida courts to review the state's voting and "do the right thing."

Nov. 28, 2000, John M. Broder

Clinton Administration Denies Bush Team Money and Office for Transition

WASHINGTON – The Clinton administration and George W. Bush's transition team engaged in their first scuffles today, with administration aides declaring that they would not release $5.3 million in federal transition funds or turn over a transition office "until a final winner" emerges in the presidential race.

Within hours Dick Cheney responded by saying that he was "disappointed" in the decision and that the Bush organization would open its own, privately financed transition office, to house a sort of unsanctioned government-in-waiting just blocks from the White House.

President Clinton, speaking at the beginning of a cabinet meeting this afternoon, said he had not been involved in the decision, made by the General Services Administration, to deny the Bush team access to federal money and the government's official transition office. Were it up to him, the president said, he would offer transition assistance to both Bush and Al Gore.

Government officials said tonight that the Justice Department was examining whether the relevant law, the Presidential Transition Act of 1963, could be interpreted to fit the president's wish. That raised the specter, however, of dueling transition offices, each simultaneously deciding on a cabinet and a White House staff, receiving intelligence briefings and drafting a first-year budget.

While Clinton affected an air of detachment from the bitter struggle for Florida's votes, he clearly sided with Gore's arguments about the road to deciding on a president-elect. "We'll just watch it play itself out," he said. "In all this interplay, it's easy to lose what is really important, which is the integrity of the voter — every single vote."

In denying the Bush camp both funds and office space, the General Services Administration cited the Presidential Transition Act, which provides for such federal assistance to an incoming president but also stipulates that there must be a clear winner of the election before any taxpayer money can be so spent.

It is clear that in addition to the mandates of the transition law, some old grudges are playing out. Clinton's aides bitterly maintain that the administration of Bush's father did little to help the incoming Clinton team at the end of 1992, after a hard-fought campaign. They arrived, they say, to a White House lacking even basic office supplies.

Nov. 28, 2000, David E. Sanger and Marc Lacey

"[Jeb]'s saying, 'If my brother gets evicted by the Florida Supreme Court, boys, go ahead and we'll get him elected another way.'"

—Lois Frankel, leader of Florida's House Democrats

Jeb Bush Reportedly Ready to Sign Bill Giving Republicans Victory

TALLAHASSEE – The president of Florida's Senate said today that Jeb Bush had indicated his willingness to sign special legislation intended to award Florida's 25 Electoral College votes to his brother George W. Bush even as the election results were being contested.

Though George W. Bush has been certified the winner of the Florida vote, talk of a special legislative session continued unabated here today as local Republicans fretted about the possibility that the justices on the Florida Supreme Court, all appointed by Democrats, might uphold the challenge by Al Gore, ultimately awarding him the state's electoral votes. The driving force behind the calls for a special session is the Republican desire to use the Legislature to trump the state's Supreme Court, should the need arise.

Hours after Gore, the Democratic nominee, filed papers here formally contesting Florida's election results, John McKay, the Republican who is the Senate president, told reporters about a conversation he had had with Jeb Bush last week in which they discussed whether Bush should sign the bill.

But Katie Baur, a spokeswoman for Jeb Bush, said the governor had not yet made a decision. "I don't think he's made up his mind," Baur said, noting that the Legislature had not even said whether it would convene a special session to write such legislation. "It's too early to speculate."

The governor's reported willingness to sign such a bill is significant because it gives the Legislature's leaders more time as they weigh the political risks of calling a special session, and as they join with George W. Bush in asking the United States Supreme Court to overturn the results of Florida's manual recounts. Today, lawyers for the Legislature filed a friend-of-the-court brief at the Supreme Court that argued the Legislature's right to appoint electors when the results of an election are in dispute.

On a political level, the comments McKay attributed to Jeb Bush would further indicate an increasingly bold effort by the governor to deliver Florida to his brother. After initially taking a low-key, hands-off approach to the dispute about Florida's election results, Bush has gradually emerged from near-seclusion as a significant player in the unfolding struggle for power. Last week, in a conversation with Tom Feeney, the speaker of the House, Bush said Republican legislators would need to demonstrate political courage in calling a special session. Such a session, he predicted, would exact "a certain price" on the Legislature.

Bush has also moved quickly to notify the federal government that Florida's 25 electors have been won by his brother. On Sunday night, barely an hour after the state canvassing commission declared George W. Bush the winner in Florida, Jeb Bush's two most senior lawyers — who had taken leave in recent weeks to work on the Bush recount campaign — delivered the certified election results to the governor's mansion.

Bush then signed a "certificate of ascertainment," a vital ministerial document by which the state formally delivers its electors to the federal government, in this case the Federal Register of the Archivist of the United States.

Bush could have waited until Dec. 12 to send the document about Florida's results. Only two other states have delivered certificates. Just today, the archivist received papers from Idaho, conferring four electoral votes, and Louisiana, conferring nine. Should Gore succeed in contesting the results, Florida could send an updated certificate. "It wouldn't be out of the question to initially certify and to amend that certification subsequently," a Gore spokesman said said.

Representative Lois Frankel, leader of Florida's House Democrats, said today that Jeb Bush had acted like an "overanxious brother" in sending the certificate to Washington, even as Gore contested the final results. In so doing, Frankel said, Bush had raised the possibility that Florida would send dueling slates of electors to the Electoral College. She said, "He's saying, 'If my brother gets evicted by the Florida Supreme Court, boys, go ahead and we'll get him elected another way.'"

Meanwhile, as a necessary step toward calling a special session, a new select committee from the state Senate and House is to meet on Tuesday to discuss the Florida election. The session is to include testimony from a team of legal experts retained by Feeney and McKay, both of whom are also listed on the slate of official Bush electors submitted by Jeb Bush.

The team spelled out the Legislature's legal position today in a friend-of-the-court brief submitted to the United States Supreme Court. The brief argues that the Florida Supreme Court overstepped its authority last week when it ruled that the manual recounts could continue. Citing the federal code governing the appointment of electors, the brief contends that if the normal process breaks down — and if there is no clear agreement on which candidate's electors should represent the state — the Legislature is responsible for assuring that the state's voters are not shut out of the Electoral College tabulations. "The Legislature itself, and not the courts, is the arbiter of when a failure to make such a choice has occurred," according to the brief. "If the courts must step in," it continued, "the Supreme Court of Florida cannot have the last word on what is, after all, a question of federal law."

Democrats in the Legislature have complained bitterly about the hiring of the legal team. By all accounts, the Democrats have been excluded from telephone calls and meetings with the lawyers and the Republican leaders. Today, in a letter to Feeney, Frankel objected to using state funds to pay the lawyers and she warned that a special session would "place a dark partisan stain on our Legislature." She added, "The State Legislature should not become an arm of any one presidential campaign."

The complaints have had no apparent impact on the disciplined and determined group of Republicans, who control the House by a 77-to-43 margin and the Senate 25 to 15. Feeney has said that he feels no obligation under House rules to include Democrats in his discussions with the legal team.

Nov.28, 2000, David Barstow and Somini Sengupta

day

21

TUESDAY, NOVEMBER 28TH

★ ★ ★ ★ ★

TIME IS OF THE ESSENCE

With only two weeks remaining until the December 12th deadline for naming the state's slate of electors, Republican leaders in the Florida Legislature take their first serious steps in calling a special session to award the 25 electors to George Bush, thereby making him president. Democrats criticize the initiative as a partisan maneuver to thwart the will of the state's courts, which are considering a Gore request to manually recount 14,000 undervotes in three counties. In a setback for the Democrats, a state judge rejects Gore's request for a quick recount. He does, however, order the 14,000 ballots in question transported to Tallahassee just in case a recount is deemed necessary.

FLORIDA LAWMAKERS MOVE TO ASSURE BUSH VICTORY

TALLAHASSEE — Three lawyers hired by the Republican leaders of the Florida Legislature told a select committee today that the Republican-dominated body was duty-bound under the United States Constitution to promptly call a special session to name Florida's 25 electors. Several Democratic and Republican legislators agreed that today's carefully orchestrated testimony set in motion a process that virtually assures that the Legislature will meet in a special session to name its electors for George W. Bush. The Republicans hope to use the Legislature to take the decision out of the hands of Florida's courts, where Al Gore's lawyers are challenging the decision by the state canvassing commission that Bush won the state and thus its 25 electoral votes.

Each of the lawyers argued today that such a step, unprecedented in Florida's modern political history, was required to guarantee that Florida's six million voters were represented on Dec. 18, when the Electoral College meets to select the next president. What is more, they said, the Legislature, not the Florida Supreme Court, has exclusive authority to appoint Florida's electors when the outcome of an election is in doubt because of legal challenges, including the briefs filed today by the Bush and Gore campaigns with the United States Supreme Court.

But if the Legislature proceeds to choose its own slate of electors and if the courts ultimately rule that Gore won the state, Congress would be faced with having to choose between two slates of electors.

"If they do what they're talking about, it will be an assault on the rule of law."

—Dan Gelber, Democratic House member

The Democratic and Republican legislators said the testimony would almost certainly prompt the select committee to formally recommend a special session, perhaps as early as Wednesday. This in turn would clear the way for Tom Feeney, the Republican House speaker, and John McKay, the Republican Senate president, to sign a joint proclamation calling for the session. Two senior Republican legislators said that such a gathering was likely to begin next week. "I think the only thing to do is a special session," said Johnnie B. Byrd Jr., a Republican House member who is co-chairman of the committee. "It's the only way to take all doubt out."

But Democrats charged today that the only doubt plaguing Republicans was over Bush's ability to hold on to his 537-vote victory in the Florida election. With Gore contesting the final results in three counties, and with more than a dozen other lawsuits attacking the outcome of the vote, these Democrats said that Bush was turning to the Florida Legislature as an "insurance policy" to guarantee him the White House.

If so, Bush is on highly favorable political terrain. His younger brother, Jeb Bush, the Florida governor, is closely allied with Feeney and McKay. The three men have held discussions recently about a special session, and Republicans hold a 77-to-43 margin in the House and 25-to-15 margin in the Senate. "I certainly hope we are not here simply because the Bush campaign needs a backup plan in the event our courts indeed require every vote in Florida to be counted," Tom Rossin, leader of the Senate Democrats, said at the outset of today's three-hour meeting.

The Legislature's Republican leaders are acutely aware of how their involvement in the election is likely to be perceived across the nation. John Yoo, a law professor at the University of California at Berkeley, and the other Republican legal experts who testified today presented themselves as dispassionate authorities on the Constitution who were dispensing legal advice without regard to either Bush or Gore.

But their conservative credentials — and the fact that they were handpicked by legislative leaders loyal to the Bush family — had Democrats openly seething about a "scripted" hearing with a pre-ordained outcome. "If they do what they're talking about, it will be an assault on the rule of law," said Dan Gelber, a Democratic House member from Miami Beach, referring to the special session. Lois Frankel, the Democratic minority leader in the House, accused the Republicans of plotting to "steal this thing" from Gore.

And yet the Republican members took great pains today to show themselves as eager, open-minded students who simply wished to be schooled on what they often referred to as their "rights and responsibilities." Not one repeated the harsh Republican allegations of recent days, allegations that have Gore secretly mapping a path to victory by disenfranchising the nation's fourth largest state. Byrd, for one, spoke regretfully about "partisan barriers," and the committee's co-chairwoman, Republican Senator Lisa Carlton, spoke soothingly about embarking on a cautious, methodical "bipartisan process." One after another, the members waived their three-minute opening statements, saying they mainly just wanted to listen and learn from the assembled constitutional experts. "We have to be careful how this looks to the public," one Republican panel member said, insisting on anonymity while acknowledging the political risks inherent in going forward with a special session.

But their effort to appear evenhanded was undercut by the today's lineup of speakers. The only constitutional experts who spoke today were men who have strong credentials among conservative legal theorists. The first speaker, Yoo, clerked for Justice Clarence Thomas of the United States Supreme Court. Another speaker, Roger J. Magnuson, is a Minneapolis lawyer who has written extensively against gay rights.

Democrats Say They Were Duped

The absence of lawyers with a different point of view infuriated Democrats, who were clearly unprepared to match the Republican experts even though they had been allowed to present one expert of their own. On this point, the Democrats insisted that they had been duped into believing that the session would focus on an entirely different subject: allegations of voting irregularities across Florida.

As evidence of Republican trickery they pointed to the committee's unexplained name change. When formed last week, it was the Legislative Oversight Committee on Electoral Certification, Accuracy and Fairness, and its stated charge was to investigate voting irregularities among other things. But today, on the meeting agenda, the committee was renamed the "Select Joint Committee on the Manner of the Appointment of Presidential Electors." The agenda made no mention of voting irregularities. Instead, the chosen topic was constitutional law, for which the committee's Republicans were well prepared with their experts. The Democrats, meanwhile, had hired a lawyer to talk about voting irregularities. The lawyer, Bob Kerrigan of Pensacola, admitted right off the bat that he was no expert in constitutional law and that he was reduced to complaining about out-of-state "hired guns" lecturing the Florida Legislature as advocates for the Bush campaign.

Democrats, including Rossin, the party's leader in the Senate, repeatedly questioned the need for a special session now that Florida's results have been certified. "I'm still pretty confused," Rossin said. "The only scenario which calls for the Florida Legislature to insert itself in the electoral process is if there is no valid election or no currently certified winner. We have both of those."

In response, the Republicans' legal experts cited the United States Constitution, which grants state legislatures the power to appoint electors. Florida, like every other state, has decreed that its electors are to be chosen on the basis of the popular election. But the Electoral Count Act of 1887 says that the Legislature must step in and appoint electors if the results are in doubt, either because of an unresolved contest or because the results were produced by counting procedures that were altered after Election Day.

But Bruce Ackerman, a professor of constitutional law at Yale University, said today that this interpretation of the Electoral Count Act was flawed. "I'm just stunned at their dramatic incompetence," he said of the Republican legal advisers. (See OpEd article below.)

Nov. 29, 2000, David Barstow

State Judge Refuses to Count Ballots, Sets Hearing Four Days from Now

TALLAHASSEE — A circuit judge this evening denied a plea from Gore's lawyers to accelerate his lawsuit that seeks to overturn Bush's victory in Florida, refusing to recount thousands of disputed ballots at least until he holds a hearing on Saturday. Though the judge, N. Sanders Sauls, agreed to Gore's request that nearly 14,000 such ballots be sent up from South Florida, the judge's decision to call a hearing on whether to count them was a blow to efforts by Gore's lawyers to establish an accelerated timetable for contesting the election.

The lawyers are aware that they must wage a full-blown trial and several rounds of appeals in the two weeks before Florida sends its electors to the Electoral College, and they demanded that Judge Sauls set an extraordinarily fast schedule for the case. Under their proposal, officials would have begun counting 14,000 ballots from Miami-Dade and Palm Beach Counties on Wednesday morning, continuing through the weekend for seven days, with a ruling from Judge Sauls next Wednesday and any appeals to the Florida Supreme Court over the next few days.

Bush's lawyers, on the other hand, proposed a more leisurely schedule, one that would have ended the trial stage on Dec. 11, the day before the designation of electors, leaving no time for any appeals.

"They have proposed two weeks of additional court proceedings and additional hearings, right up to the Dec. 12 deadline for seating electors," Gore said in Washington today. "And under their plan, none of the thousands of votes that remain to be counted would be counted at all. I believe this is a time to count every vote and not to run out the clock. This is not a time for delay, obstruction and procedural roadblocks."

Judge Sauls, wielding folksy aphorisms to fend off the enormous pressure of the elite legal teams arrayed before him, tried to steer a middle course. He called for a hearing on Saturday to determine whether to count the ballots — three days after the Gore team wanted the counting to begin — and said the hearing would also take up the issue of what standards should be used to count the ballots and whether marks like dimples should be considered votes.

To prevent logistical delays, the judge ordered the two counties to send their ballots via police car to Leon County Circuit Court here by Friday afternoon, though he said the order did not necessarily suggest that he intended to tabulate votes. "This doesn't mean in any way, shape or fashion that we're going to be counting the ballots on Saturday, unless there is a basis that dictates they should be counted," he said. "But at least if we have them, we should be able to move."

The judge's actions were not good enough for either side, and particularly for Gore's lawyers. David Boies, Gore's chief trial lawyer, told the judge that if he insisted on a Saturday hearing, the Democrats would immediately appeal that scheduling decision to the Florida Supreme Court. "We can't afford to wait till Saturday to answer these questions," Boies said, his usual placid, smiling demeanor showing cracks of impatience. "Waiting until Saturday is tantamount to denying the relief we seek."

Barry Richard, Bush's lead lawyer here, said far more time was needed to debate the question of whether the ballots should even be examined. "My client is entitled to a hearing before Boies's client gets relief, but every time Your Honor gives him another thing, he's back on his feet asking for one more thing you've already denied him twice," Richard said, visibly angry. "He's asking this court to give him everything he's requested, which is to begin another ballot recount before he has provided one iota of evidence or permitted my client to have one hour of hearing on whether or not he's entitled to a recount."

Judge Sauls, joking that he was trying to be "unfair to everybody equally," said the timetable Boies was proposing would strip Bush of his basic due-process rights to respond appropriately to legal motions.

After the hearing, Boies tried to put the best face on the rulings, celebrating the decision to transport the ballots but conceding that the new schedule put his team "on a very tight leash." If the counting eventually begins, he said, it would probably have to go on 24 hours a day. Boies expressed skepticism that it could be finished in time. "Obviously the court is moving faster than the defendant would like but slower than we would like," he said. "It's going to be a very close call." Boies added, "Justice delayed here really is justice denied."

Bush's lawyers made it clear that they would not only fight any motion to count ballots, but also the Gore team's insistence that the ballots be counted using the most liberal standard, in which every dimple on a ballot is considered a vote.

Judge Sauls acknowledged that the decision on whether to count dimples would be a crucial question in the lawsuit. "We can't have people jumping on the horse and riding off in all directions just counting," he said, referring to the need for a single standard for all ballot counters. "They can count till everyone's slap-happy, but if they're not on the same page we won't know what's being accomplished."

Nov. 29, 2000, David Firestone

Another Absentee Ballot Controversy

A second heavily Republican county in Florida allowed party officials to fix hundreds of flawed absentee ballot applications that had been submitted by voters but rejected by the elections office, officials said yesterday. The Martin County supervisor of elections, a Republican, let Republican Party workers take away the ballot requests on a daily basis, add missing voter identification numbers and resubmit them, a deputy elections supervisor said. At the same time, the elections office allowed other incomplete applications submitted by voters, some of them Democrats and independents, to stack up without being corrected, the official said. George W. Bush edged Al Gore with 56 percent of the vote to 44 percent in Martin County, while the absentee votes broke nearly 2 to 1 for Bush — 6,294 to 3,479.

A similar situation in Seminole County has resulted in a lawsuit filed by a Democratic lawyer who says state law requires that only voters, or close family members or guardians, may submit personal identifying information, including voter registration numbers. The law is intended to prevent absentee voter fraud.

As Democrats did before the election, the Republicans mailed out tens of thousands of absentee ballot forms to registered supporters. As a convenience, both parties preprinted the forms with all required information except the last four digits of a voter's Social Security number. But a mistake by the company used by the Republicans to mail out the forms left off the voter identification numbers on many of the forms, said Jamie Wilson, Florida's Republican Party chief. In Martin, the voters' birth dates were printed by mistake.

Emma Smith, a deputy election supervisor in Martin County, said her office began noticing that many of the Republican forms coming into the office lacked the required numbers, and that they were not processed. She said she and her colleagues first tried to contact the voters who had sent the incomplete forms, "but as it got down to crunch, we were no longer able to do that — we were really swamped."

Rather, she said, as many as 500 forms were turned over to Republican Party workers to fix. Smith said the decision was made by the election supervisor, Peggy Robbins. She said Robbins, a Republican, was out of the office this week and could not be reached. "I think she called someone at the state to discuss it first, but I'm not sure," Smith said, referring to the state elections office.

"We're very upset about this," said Jeffrey Schooley, the Martin County Democratic chairman. "This is more than they did in Seminole. From what I understand, the Republican Party was allowed to take these request forms out of the supervisors office, which kept no track of how many went out or went back in."

Charles Kane, the Republican state committeeman for Martin County, said the forms were brought to Republican headquarters in Stuart, Fla., where workers tried to phone voters to notify them that their applications were flawed. "People weren't home," Kane said. "We ran out of time. So I called the state party in Tallahassee and asked them if I could use the numbers from our computer program. They said fine."

Nov. 29, 2000, Michael Moss

Error-Prone Voting Machines Lowered the Minority Vote — and Gore's Chances

When Florida's votes were counted on Election Day, George W. Bush had a tiny but possibly decisive edge: the majority of the state's black voters, Al Gore's most reliable voters, stalwart supporters, cast their ballots on punch cards that are more prone to voter error and miscounts.

Across the state, nearly 4 percent of the type of punch-card ballots most widely used in Florida were thrown out because the machines read them as blank or invalid. By contrast, the more modern, optical scanning systems rejected far fewer votes — only about 1.4 percent of those cast. A *New York Times* analysis shows that 64 percent of the state's black voters live in counties that used the punch cards while 56 percent of whites did so. While black voters made up 16 percent of the vote on Election Day, that small difference, the analysis suggests, could have had a decisive effect on an election decided by only a few hundred votes out of nearly six million. Exit polls show that blacks voted overwhelmingly for Gore.

Al Gore raised the issue of the disproportionate effect of the punch-card ballot yesterday as he defended the Democrats' demands for recounts in three counties that used them. "The old and cheap, outdated machinery is usually found in areas with populations that are of lower income, minorities, seniors on fixed incomes," Gore said.

When optical ballot scanners are used, voters mark their choice with a pencil next to the name of their candidate. This appears to make them less susceptible to voter error. The large number of ballots in Broward, Palm Beach and Miami-Dade Counties in which the paper punch-card machines detected no choice for president has stirred controversy. Democrats say many of these ballots were failed attempts to cast votes; Republicans say these voters had no preference for either candidate or failed to register their choice correctly.

A survey of several large Florida counties turned up an anomaly: Floridians whose ballots were read by the machines as not registering a choice for president were much more likely to have voted with computer punch cards.

In Orange County, the largest to use the optical equipment, only 1 in 300 ballots was blank in the presidential race. In Manatee and Brevard Counties, the rate approached 1 in 800. Bush easily carried Manatee and Brevard Counties while Gore prevailed in Orange. The punch-card-voting counties, by contrast, had sharply higher numbers of people tallied as having no vote for president. In Miami-Dade, the Florida county with the most votes cast, the machines read 1 in 60 ballots as having no vote for president. In Hillsborough, near Tampa, it was 1 in 67. And in Pinellas County, it was 1 of 96. Gore won Miami-Dade and Pinellas while Bush carried Hillsborough.

The *Times* analysis showed that registered Democrats in Florida were only slightly more likely to vote in counties that use punch-card machines than Republicans. But 63 percent of Gore's votes were counted on the type of punch-card machines at issue in Palm Beach County, compared with 55 percent of Bush's. Statewide, the pattern was reversed on the optical scan systems. Forty percent of the Bush votes were tallied on these systems, compared with 33 percent for Gore.

The impact of these differences on the outcome will never be known but their potential magnitude is evident in Miami-Dade County, where predominantly black precincts saw their votes thrown out at twice the rate as Hispanic precincts and nearly four times the rate of white precincts. In all, 1 out of 11 ballots in predominantly black precincts were rejected, a total of 9,904. Had all people cast ballots that could be counted along the same lines as their neighbors, Gore would have gained nearly 7,000 votes.

Across the country, the punch-card systems have resulted in significantly higher numbers of uncounted ballots. In 467 counties that used punch cards with pre-punched cards in the 1996 presidential election, according to a *New York Times* analysis, 661,000 of the 25 million ballots were not counted, or 2.6 percent of the total. In 729 counties that used optical scanning technology, 1.9 percent of the ballots cast had no votes for president counted, according to the Times analysis of data provided by Election Data Services, a nonpartisan consulting firm in Washington.

But in areas where the voting technology prevents voting for more than one person in a race — on lever machines, for instance — the percentage of voters who cast no presidential vote was low this year. In Connecticut, only one half of 1 percent of those who went to the polls failed to cast a presidential vote.

Nov. 29, 2000, Josh Barbanel and Ford Fessenden

Counting the Blanks

An analysis by The New York Times of vote data compiled from Florida county election supervisors shows that counties using Votomatic punch card ballots had an undervote rate five times as large as those using optical scan ballots.

Counties that used optical scan ballots

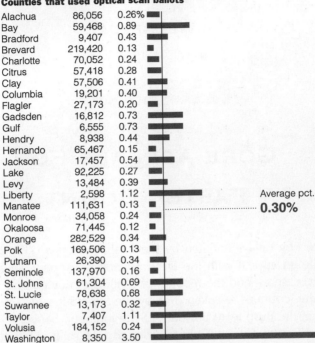

	TOTAL VOTES	PCT. OF VOTES WHICH HAD NO SELECTION FOR PRESIDENT (UNDERVOTES)
Alachua	86,056	0.26%
Bay	59,468	0.89
Bradford	9,407	0.43
Brevard	219,420	0.13
Charlotte	70,052	0.24
Citrus	57,418	0.28
Clay	57,506	0.41
Columbia	19,201	0.40
Flagler	27,173	0.20
Gadsden	16,812	0.73
Gulf	6,555	0.73
Hendry	8,938	0.44
Hernando	65,467	0.15
Jackson	17,457	0.54
Lake	92,225	0.27
Levy	13,484	0.39
Liberty	2,598	1.12
Manatee	111,631	0.13
Monroe	34,058	0.24
Okaloosa	71,445	0.12
Orange	282,529	0.34
Polk	169,506	0.13
Putnam	26,390	0.34
Seminole	137,970	0.16
St. Johns	61,304	0.69
St. Lucie	78,638	0.68
Suwannee	13,173	0.32
Taylor	7,407	1.11
Volusia	184,152	0.24
Washington	8,350	3.50

Average pct. **0.30%**

Counties that used Datavote (punch card) ballots

	TOTAL VOTES	PCT.
Baker	8,294	1.13%
Hardee	6,641	1.28
Nassau	25,162	0.77

Average pct. **0.93%**

Counties that used Votomatic (punch card) ballots

	TOTAL VOTES	PCT.
Broward	588,007	1.14%
Collier	95,326	2.18
Duval	291,545	1.70
Highlands	36,158	1.35
Hillsborough	369,467	1.50
Indian River	51,559	2.05
Lee	188,944	1.09
Marion	106,001	2.31
Miami-Dade	654,044	1.64
Osceola	57,341	1.12
Palm Beach	462,888	2.29
Pasco	146,648	1.21
Pinellas	406,956	1.04
Sarasota	164,180	1.10
Sumter	23,023	2.58

Average pct. **1.53%**

Undervote data were not available in 19 counties.

The New York Times

day

22

WEDNESDAY,

NOVEMBER 29TH

★ ★ ★ ★ ★

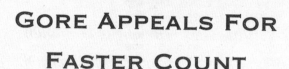

GORE APPEALS FOR FASTER COUNT

Frustrated by delays initiated by the Bush legal team, lawyers for Gore file an appeal with the District Court of Appeal, seeking to have the case — and the recount of 14,000 undercounted ballots from three counties — taken over by the State Supreme Court. In response, the Bush team persuades State Judge N. Sanders Sauls of the Leon County Circuit Court to order all 1.16 million ballots from the three counties transferred to Tallahassee. Democrats say that the move is merely another tactic designed to slow down the process. Meanwhile, Governor Jeb Bush openly throws his support behind an initiative to call a special session of the Republican-dominated Florida Legislature to select 25 electors for the Electoral College.

GORE LOSING TIME AS BUSH LAWYERS STALL

TALLAHASSEE — Lawyers for Gore said today that their only chance for victory in his contest of the Florida election would be shattered if they have to wait until Saturday to begin counting disputed ballots, and they began an appeal to the Florida Supreme Court to do the counting itself, immediately. The appeal was filed with the District Court of Appeal late this afternoon and will be submitted to the state's highest court early Thursday, Gore's lawyers said.

It essentially asks the Supreme Court to take over Gore's contest lawsuit from the deliberate-moving trial court, to count the ballots itself, and eventually to declare Gore the winner if he wins the recount.

But lawyers for Bush said they had no intention of allowing any hand counting to begin without a vigorous legal fight. To that end, they persuaded Judge N. Sanders Sauls of Leon County Circuit Court to order 1.1 million ballots — every vote cast in Miami-Dade and Palm Beach Counties — brought up from South Florida and placed in the court's custody. That represents 83 times the number of disputed ballots that the judge had agreed on Tuesday to transport to Tallahassee at the Gore team's request. And it could take weeks, if not months, to count them all, the point that Barry Richard, Bush's chief trial lawyer here, said he was trying to make in requesting that the ballots be transported here. "We did it to make a point," Richard said in an interview. "If you recount any ballots, you have to recount all of them. Now we don't think any ballots should be counted, because the manual recount of ballots is finished. But in the event the court determines that some ballots should be counted, we wanted them here so they could all be counted."

"It's a stunt. They're trying to bog down the case, the system, the clerk's office and everywhere else they can."

—Kendall Coffey, a Gore election lawyer

Aware that they could not stop the transporting of all the ballots, Gore's lawyers barely objected to the move, asking only that the disputed ballots that might contain hidden Gore votes be separated from the mass. "I know when it's futile," said David Boies, Gore's chief trial lawyer, to Judge Sauls.

Nonetheless, Gore's lawyers were furious at the move, aware that it represents yet another enormous barrier to their hopes for an immediate count of the 14,000 disputed ballots in the two counties and a quick decision from the judge that Gore really won the election. Even if the Florida Supreme Court should swiftly agree to their request and order the counting to begin by Friday, that would still put them three days behind their original timetable. And facing a Dec. 12 deadline for the state to name electors for the Electoral College, Gore has no days to spare.

"It's a stunt," said Kendall Coffey, one of Gore's election lawyers, as he stormed out of Judge Sauls's courtroom today, referring to the request for all the ballots. "They're trying to bog down the case, the system, the clerk's office and everywhere else they can."

The decision by Gore's lawyers to appeal the case shows how perilous their situation is. By appealing, the lawyers were forced to put on paper their fear that their case could be over if they cannot begin counting ballots until Saturday. The decision to wait until a Saturday hearing "is effectively a final order denying all relief sought by plaintiffs because the action now pending below must be completed before Dec. 12, 2000, in order to offer any relief," said the notice filed with the Court of Appeal. It adds, "The court must allow sufficient time to complete an accurate and fair count of the contested ballots, which is essential for the proper resolution of the contest action."

But the decision to bring up all the ballots means that they will not be assembled in Tallahassee until late Friday, a day later than planned. And even then, the hurdles are enormous. There will have to be another hearing before the Florida Supreme Court, and Gore's lawyers will have to refute three arguments to be raised by the Bush team: There should be no more counting at all; if there is any counting, it will have to include all 1.16 million ballots; and if there is any counting of disputed ballots, dimples cannot be counted as votes.

If these issues are heard before Judge Sauls, there will have to be briefs, witnesses and evidence on each point, which could take days. If the Supreme Court agrees to short-circuit the process, there will still have to be lengthy briefs filed, and the court may need to wait several days before finding time for yet another momentous hearing in its schedule.

The request for all 1.1 million ballots was a dramatic example of the many ways in which the Bush legal team can use the built-in safeguards and procedural cul-de-sacs of the law to its advantage in the contest phase of the election. The nation's legal system was built for fairness, not speed, and its infrastructure is simply not designed for the warp drive requested by Gore. "It's easier to cause delay than it is to move a case," said W. Dexter Douglass, a prominent trial lawyer working for Gore, on Tuesday. "We all know that from many years of experience."

Judge Sauls all but acknowledged as much when he denied the Gore team's initial request to begin counting without so much as a hearing. "I have just about stripped the defendants down to the bares of due process," Judge Sauls told Gore's lawyers on Tuesday, explaining why he could not agree to begin counting ballots without hearing arguments on both sides, and giving the defendants a chance to write and submit legal briefs. "I can't just absolutely dispense with due process as far as they're concerned."

The decision to try to move the case to the Supreme Court represents an effort to sidestep all the maneuvering, but Gore's lawyers acknowledge that they do not know if the high court will be as amenable to their arguments as it was earlier this month, when it allowed the hand counts to continue.

Even the decision to move all the ballots to Tallahassee came after an hour-long hearing that dealt largely with the logistical minutiae of how they should be transported. Using a speakerphone, lawyers for the two counties said they would send the ballots up in truck convoys escorted by the police. Palm Beach County plans to get its 462,000 ballots on the road by Thursday morning in a rented truck, while Miami-Dade County's 654,000 ballots will leave late Thursday or early Friday for the eight-hour drive.

Nov. 30, 2000, David Firestone

Jeb Bush Backs Plan for Legislature to Bypass Courts

"The Constitution provides that the Legislature be delegated this authority not the state, not anybody else but the Legislature. I think people understand that."

— Jeb Bush

★ ★ ★

TALLAHASSEE — Gov. Jeb Bush of Florida said today that it would be an "act of courage" for his state's Legislature to convene a special session to name Florida's 25 electors if Gore persisted in contesting the the state's presidential balloting. Bush also said, for the first time, that if such legislation was passed in a special session he would be willing to sign it and deliver the White House to his brother, George W. Bush. "I don't think I get points by not signing," Bush told reporters after a meeting with his cabinet this morning.

Bush's comments were perhaps his most openly partisan since the close results of Election Day made his state a battleground for the presidency. Bush said he would prefer that the courts rendered the issue moot by denying Gore's legal challenges. But, he said, legislative selection of electors would guarantee the state's representation in the Electoral College, which will decide on Dec. 18 whether the vice president or the Texas governor will be president.

Bush's views mirrored those of several lawyers hired by the Legislature's powerful Republican leaders to advise the members of the House and the Senate. On Tuesday, and again today, those lawyers told a select committee of lawmakers that the Legislature had an unambiguous obligation under the United States Constitution to step in and select electors when legal challenges threatened to leave the winner in doubt as the Electoral College prepared to meet. "This is so clear about who has the responsibility to do this in an environment where there is a contest," Bush said. "The Constitution provides that the Legislature be delegated this authority not the state, not anybody else but the Legislature. I think people understand that."

Republicans hold a 77-to-43 advantage in the Florida House and a 25-to-15 advantage in the Senate, and the leaders of both bodies have made it clear that any electors they choose will be for George W. Bush.

Bush, however, may yet avoid having to sign legislation from a special session. Increasingly, senior Republican legislators are talking about naming electors by resolution, which does not require the governor's signature.

At the same time, Democrats are continuing to portray the select committee's work as a partisan charade that had little to do with enfranchising Florida's six million voters and everything to do with providing Bush with an insurance policy should Gore begin to prevail in his legal challenges. At today's committee hearing, Democratic lawmakers presented two constitutional scholars who contended that a special session was not only premature and illegal, but also a threat to the stability of the nation's political system. "We are dealing here with the kind of precedent we are setting for the election of future presidents," said Bruce Ackerman, a constitutional scholar at Yale University. "If the Florida Legislature proceeds to intervene at this late stage in violation of federal law, it will be setting a precedent for future state Legislatures to intervene in every close election. This is a recipe for continuing instability in the process of presidential selection."

While the Democratic committee members are fully aware that they lack the votes to block a special session, they managed to outmaneuver the Republicans on at least one public relations front today. Earlier this week, the Republican leaders of the committee announced that they had set aside two hours today for members of the public to comment on the possibility of a special session. Fearing that the public comment session would be dominated by Republican partisans, organizers in the Democratic Party quickly rounded up dozens of people from Palm Beach, Duval and Miami-Dade Counties who were eager to share Election Day horror stories with the Legislature. Many flew here on Tuesday night on a jet chartered by the Democratic Party, which also paid for their rooms at the local Days Inn, and then bused them to the Capitol complex at 7:15 this morning so that they would be the first in line at the sign-up desk for public remarks.

The strategy was a smashing success for Democrats. The group made up 68 of the first 72 people who signed up to speak. As a result, anyone watching the proceedings on C-Span or news broadcasts was treated to a parade of voters who, one after another, implored the committee members not to intervene in the election. One man, a Baptist preacher from Belle Glade, drew loud applause when he likened the Republican leaders of the Legislature to bank robbers. An irate young mother said, "Knowing what I know about what you are thinking of doing, I wish the next election were tomorrow." She drew applause, too, as did 69-year-old Sylvia Shapiro of West Palm Beach, who told the panel, "I don't need somebody else to vote for me."

When Senator Lisa Carlton, one of the Republican leaders of the committee, tried to interrupt or limit some comments, she met with stubborn defiance. One 19-year-old woman said, "I drove seven and a half hours by myself, and I'm not going to be stopped." By the time the two hours allotted for public remarks had ended with the 62nd speaker, not a single Bush supporter had spoken. This left Alec Yasinsac, No. 64 on the list and an ardent Republican, fuming. "It was an organized effort to prevent opposing views," Yasinsac said.

Nov. 30, 2000, David Barstow and Somini Sengupta

day

23

THURSDAY,

NOVEMBER 30TH

★ ★ ★ ★ ★

G.O.P. CHALLENGES GORE, MOVES ON SPECIAL SESSION

In Washington both sides file their briefs with the U.S. Supreme Court with little fanfare. In Florida, however, the Republicans move aggressively to bring victory to George W. Bush. In court his lawyers go on the offensive, challenging the very essence of Gore's suit to force a manual recount of selected ballots and making demands clearly designed to keep the recounts from being completed by December 12th, the date on which the state must choose its 25 electors. Meanwhile, the Republican-led select committee of the Florida Legislature moves forward with a formal call for a special session that will name those electors for Bush. Some informed observers warn of the possible constitutional crisis such action could cause, while Democrats predict mass protests.

REPUBLICANS ATTACK GORE'S SUIT AND RESUME STALLING TACTICS

TALLAHASSEE — George W. Bush's lawyers unleashed a far-reaching defense against Al Gore's contesting of the Florida presidential vote, citing more than a dozen reasons why the lawsuit should be dismissed. They also announced plans to subpoena nearly 1.17 million ballots from three Florida counties, on top of the 1.16 million that began arriving by truck in the state capital this afternoon.

Responding formally for the first time to the lawsuit Gore filed Monday contesting Bush's victory in Florida, the Bush legal team filed a brief arguing that Gore had no ability to contest the results because he was never really a candidate in the election. Technically, only the electors supporting presidential candidates are on the ballot, the brief said, and only they can file contests. It also said the vice president had failed to prove that the outcome of the election would be different if 14,000 disputed ballots were recounted. And it argued that manually recounting only part of the ballots was illegal. The Republicans plan to call 95 witnesses at the trial, said lawyers who have seen their plans.

> *"A victory for petitioners in circuit court (or on later appeal from a circuit court decision) will be meaningless if it comes too late for counting the unlawfully rejected ballots before the Dec. 12 deadline."*
>
> *—from text of Gore's legal brief given to Florida Supreme Court*

The sweeping nature of the Bush defense, which raises several major issues that have never come up in the last weeks of legal struggle, means that Gore's lawyers may have to spend hours fighting off motions and arguments in a circuit court hearing to begin on Saturday, rather than focusing on the issue they care about most: forcing the immediate counting of 14,000 disputed ballots in Miami-Dade and Palm Beach Counties.

Republicans said they wanted hundreds of thousands more ballots brought to Tallahassee. In a letter to Judge Sauls, Jason Unger, one of Bush's lawyers, said his team was issuing subpoenas to the election boards in Broward, Volusia and Pinellas Counties, demanding that all of their 1.17 million ballots be sent to the courthouse by 5 p.m. Saturday. The reason was explained in the brief: Some of the ballots from those counties, particularly Broward, have indented chads that were counted as votes. These were illegal, the brief says, and must be excluded.

Judge Sauls expressed some skepticism about allowing the ballots to be transported, noting that the three new counties were not contested in Gore's lawsuit and thus might not be required to comply with the subpoenas. But he agreed to put the matter off until the Republicans raise it formally in open court.

Democratic lawyers dismissed all the new issues raised, including the demand for new ballots, as nothing more than a bid for time designed to drag out the lawsuit past Dec. 12, when the State Legislature will have named

Florida's presidential electors. "This is clearly just a formula for delay," said Ron Klain, Gore's senior legal adviser. "They will obviously throw any procedural or technical roadblock they can at the heart of the contest, which is the counting of ballots. Whether they are proposing 95 witnesses, or trying to argue that Al Gore wasn't a candidate in the election, it's just one thing after another."

The Gore team filed a lengthy appeal this morning with the Florida Supreme Court, asking its seven justices to begin counting the 14,000 ballots. The Democrats are hoping that a quick high court ruling will allow them to avoid the entangling arguments raised by the Bush team, eliminating the need to try to persuade Sauls to count the ballots that they believe contain enough votes for Gore to change the outcome of the election.

In their appeal, the lawyers said that even if they fended off the various issues raised by the Bush team in circuit court, their victory would be meaningless if it did not come in time. "Since the presidency is the office, and there are federal and constitutional deadlines at stake, any delays in the counting process may mean denial of meaningful relief in this action," they argued in their brief. "A victory for petitioners in circuit court (or on later appeal from a circuit court decision) will be meaningless if it comes too late for counting the unlawfully rejected ballots before the Dec. 12 deadline."

Bush's lawyers denied that they were trying to run down the clock, saying they were simply raising important legal issues necessary for their defense. "I don't think it's appropriate for a lawyer to delay legal proceedings, unless the lawyer has a basis that the law considers proper for the delay," said Barry Richard, Bush's chief trial lawyer here. "As a general rule, I don't practice dilatory law, and my client has not asked me to. We are proceeding to successfully try this case as rapidly and decisively as we can." If the Democrats are running out of time, Richard said, it is their own fault because they spent so long asking for manual recounts in several counties before filing the contest. He also said a legal contest to an election was never supposed to include manual recounts of ballots.

That was among several issues the Republicans cited as grounds for Judge Sauls to end the contest lawsuit. The lawyers also argued that:

—Gore's lawsuit was filed past the legal deadline.

—It failed to name Bush's Republican electors as a party to the suit.

—Manually counting ballots from only two counties violated the equal protection clause of the United States Constitution.

—The contest suit was prohibited by the "doctrine of laches," an old legal term meaning the failure to seize one's rights promptly. (This claim seemed to particularly stun Gore's lawyers, who noted that they have often been in court when the doors opened to file their many lawsuits.)

Dec. 1, 2000, David Firestone

TV Follows Truck Carrying Ballots

Tired of lawyers and politicians, maybe even the candidates themselves, television cameras and the eyes of ordinary citizens focused yesterday on a yellow rental truck. The truck was like those used by ordinary do-it-yourself movers, but it was no ordinary truck. No, as it journeyed north and west through Florida — a trek recorded on one cable news channel with an animated highway map — it carried a cargo that may help determine who moves into the White House.

The trip to Tallahassee was necessitated by a request from Gore, who wants more ballots included in the vote count in hopes of wiping out Bush's lead in Florida. Accompanied by police vehicles, the truck carried more than 462,000 paper ballots from West Palm Beach to the state capital, Tallahassee, some 450 miles away, where Democrats hope the ballots' punchholes, dimples and chads will be scrutinized.

Every mile was tracked by journalists in cars and helicopters. People waved from overpasses as the truck driven by Tony Enos, the voting-systems coordinator for Palm Beach County, made its way up the Florida Turnpike. "The whole world is watching!" the police officer driving the lead car marveled at one point. Not quite. But CNN certainly followed the truck's progress carefully, showing a helicopter shot of the vehicle moving along the highway every few minutes. So did Florida television journalists.

The truck and its escort made up the most closely watched highway procession since 1994, when a white Bronco driven by a former professional football player made for high live television drama.

In the age of 24-hour news channels, that analogy was lost on no one, including The Associated Press, which went so far as to interview O. J. Simpson. (He thought his televised highway cruise was more suspenseful than this one.)

As for the ballots being transported, they were just the first ordered up by Judge N. Sanders Sauls of Leon County Circuit Court. Two more trucks with some 654,000 Miami-Dade County ballots are to travel the 520 miles from Miami to Tallahassee today.

Dec. 1, 2000, David Stout

Lawmakers Move Closer to Special Session

"Somebody has to step in and make this final. Somebody has to have a solution. The people of the United States of America, the people of Florida, are yearning for someone to bring finality to this."

– Republican Rep. Johnnie B. Byrd Jr.

★ ★ ★

TALLAHASSEE — Taking its first formal step to intervene in the outcome of the presidential election, a select committee of Florida's Republican-dominated Legislature recommended today that a special session be held "as soon as practicable" to name Florida's 25 electors.

Based on the recommendation, the speaker of the Florida House of Representatives and the president of the Florida Senate were expected to summon lawmakers to the Capitol for a special session starting as early as Tuesday. It was unclear how long the session would last, but Republican legislators said today that they were determined to ratify George W. Bush's slate before Dec. 12, the deadline for naming electors to the Electoral College. "He who hesitates is lost," Representative Johnnie B. Byrd Jr., co-chairman of the select committee, said shortly before the party-line vote to recommend a special session.

With the United States Supreme Court set to hear arguments on Friday morning about the legality of Florida's manual recount, Al Gore's legal team filed papers today that asked the justices to block the Florida Legislature from directly appointing electors.

"Any state legislative attempt simply to appoint electors after the fact would appear to be federally pre-empted," the Gore brief argued.

Joe Lieberman, underscored the same point in an interview today. He contended that Republicans were trying "an end-run around the established political process" by seeking victory through the Legislature not the ballot box. "For the Legislature to bypass the established judicial process and appoint a slate of electors through a partisan political process is unjustified, unwarranted and unwise," Lieberman said. "It sets a dangerous precedent for legislatures in the future to try to pick electors when they don't like the candidate who won the most votes."

But Bush brushed aside suggestions that the Legislature's involvement had an appearance of partisan strong-arm tactics. "Here's my view," Bush said today, after meeting at his Texas ranch with retired Gen. Colin L. Powell. "I've won three counts, and I think it's time to get some finality to the process. I felt like we won on election night. Then there was a recount in all Florida counties. Then there was a selected recount in additional Florida counties, and each time Dick Cheney and I ended up on top."

The select committee, made up of eight Republicans and six Democrats, voted along party lines after two hours of impassioned debate this morning. Each side warned that history would judge the other harshly, and each side contended that it was acting in defense of Florida's voters without regard to the presidential ambitions of either Gore or Bush. Although members strained to maintain a polite tone, there was no disguising the partisan fury that has infused both sides.

"What the hell is going on?" Tom Rossin, the leading Democrat in the state Senate, asked the committee this morning. "Is this America? Is this democracy? Is this the legacy we want for our children?" Another Democratic senator, Betty S. Holzendorf of Jacksonville, said she was so disgusted by the whole affair that she planned to skip the special session. "I'm going on vacation," she said.

For their part, Republicans accused Democrats of ignoring their oath of office, of shirking their constitutional obligations and of putting Gore's interests ahead of an entire state's. The Democrats, they asserted, were aiding Gore in an effort to tie up Florida's election results in court challenges so that he would win by default with a majority of the remaining electoral votes.

> *"For the Legislature to bypass the established judicial process and appoint a slate of electors through a partisan political process is unjustified, unwarranted and unwise. It sets a dangerous precedent for legislatures in the future to try to pick electors when they don't like the candidate who won the most votes."*
>
> *—Joe Lieberman*

Fully aware of polls showing the political risks of intervening, Republican members said they regretted calling for a special session. But they said they had felt compelled to act because of uncertainty, which they blamed entirely on recent election rulings by the Florida Supreme Court and on Gore's decision to contest the results. Those actions, they said, had placed the outcome of Florida's election in doubt and thus posed a "significant risk" that Florida's six million voters would not be represented in the Electoral College.

If the Legislature chooses its own slate of electors, an action unprecedented in this state, and if the courts ultimately rule that Gore won the state, Congress would be faced with having to choose between two slates of electors.

Democrats accused Republicans of manufacturing a constitutional crisis to justify what the House minority leader, Lois Frankel, called an "unprecedented, dangerous power grab." Frankel and other Democrats said today that Republican lawmakers had been led astray by "right-wing scholars" who testified that the Legislature had an obligation under the United States Constitution to appoint electors if final results were not declared both in a timely fashion and in accordance with rules in place before the election.

The Republican legal experts said that both problems existed with this election. First, they said there was no guarantee that Gore's legal challenges could be resolved by Dec. 12, and second, they maintained that the Florida Supreme Court improperly rewrote election law after the fact when it extended the time limit for completing manual recounts. These arguments form the basis of the motion that was approved today, and they are likely to shape Republican arguments in any special session to come.

Democrats acknowledged today that they did not have the numbers to stop the Republicans in the Legislature from naming a slate of electors if they so chose. Republicans hold a 77-to-43 majority in the House and a 25-to-15 majority in the Senate. But few Democrats were prepared to join Holzendorf in sitting out any special session, and most said they would use every possible House and Senate rule to delay any legislation. "We will be voices of reason, and we will fight this," Frankel said.

Democrats were also preparing to turn any special session into a vehicle for portraying Republicans as elitists who casually trample the popular vote. Just as Bush and his allies dispatched Republican workers to lead demonstrations against manual recounts in South Florida, Democrats and their labor supporters were talking today about organizing demonstrations during a special session. "If this committee votes for a special session," Rossin said, "there will not be hundreds, but thousands, of people outside these walls."

Dec. 1, 2000, David Barstow

★★★

OpEd

Florida Legislature Plays a Dangerous Game

While the Supreme Court may ultimately determine the fate of this election, Florida's Legislature is determining the destiny of future presidential contests. The constitutional issues raised by the Legislature's impending action to name a slate of presidential electors for Gov. George W. Bush are far more important than whether Bush or Gore gets to the White House. If the Legislature is allowed to name electors on its own authority, it will establish a devastating precedent.

In the next close presidential election, what is to prevent party leaders in a swing state from deciding the election once the Florida strategy has been legitimized? The dominant party in such a state could simply string out a final tally until the end and then rush into special legislative session to vote in a partisan slate of electors at the finish line. If one state legislature succumbs to this temptation, another legislature — controlled by the opposing party — may well follow suit, creating a partisan battle far worse than what we have already witnessed in Florida.

The Florida Legislature may believe it has the power to name the state's electors. But it is absurd to believe that the United States Constitution would allow one state legislature to usurp a national election. An examination of two provisions in Article II of the Constitution shows why.

One provision grants state legislatures power over the manner in which electors are chosen. A second grants Congress power to set the day on which these electors are selected. The first provision appears to give the Florida Legislature the right to name its own slate. Many legislatures exercised this power during the early decades of the Republic. And as far as the Constitution is concerned, there would be no legal obstacle if Florida's Legislature decided that in future elections it would deprive its citizens of the direct right to vote on Presidential electors.

But the Florida Legislature is perfectly happy to have its citizens vote for President. It simply wants to pre-empt the Florida Supreme Court's effort to figure out who won the election last month. And in trying to act retroactively, the Legislature violates the second constitutional provision, which grants Congress power to set a uniform national day for choosing electors.

Acting under this power in 1845, Congress established a level playing field among the states by requiring them to hold elections on the same day — which is why we all go to the polls on the first Tuesday after the first Monday in November. Before 1845, states competed with one another for influence by setting their election dates as late as possible, thereby swinging close elections by voting last. But since then, nobody has tried the trick that Florida's Legislature is now attempting — intervening to swing the election to its favored candidate.

This effort is illegal under the statute established by Congress in 1845. Congress has allowed one narrow exception to its insistence on a uniform election day: It allows a state legislature to step in only when the state has failed to make a choice of its electors.

That is not the case in Florida. The state made a choice when Gov. Jeb Bush signed a formal notification that the state's 25 votes go to a slate of Republican electors. Since Florida has not failed to choose, its legislature cannot, under federal law, intervene further.

Even if the Florida courts ultimately find that Gore wins the state's electoral votes, Florida will not have "failed to choose." They will simply have determined that the voters chose him rather than Bush.

Florida's legislative leaders may want to end the election chaos by fiat. But the vote that occurred on Nov. 7 was properly cast by Floridians on the same day their fellow Americans cast their ballots. If Florida's Legislature is allowed to overrule that vote, other states may ponder the same power play four years from now.

Dec. 12, 2000

By Bruce Ackerman, Professor at Yale Law School.

day

24

FRIDAY,

DECEMBER 1ST

★ ★ ★ ★ ★

HISTORIC MOMENT AT THE SUPREME COURT

For the first time in American history, the Supreme Court of the United States hears a case involving a disputed presidential election. While thousands march and jeer outside, a small band of elite observers watches as the finest legal minds in the country argue their cases before the nine justices. For 90 minutes the observers sit stone silent as the justices ask tough, sometimes biting questions while occasionally making acerbic comments. From their questions it is clear that Justices Stephen Breyer and Ruth Bader Ginsburg, both Clinton appointees, have a different agenda from that of Chief Justice William Rehnquist and Justice Antonin Scalia, appointees of Nixon and Reagan, respectively. So, as has often happened in the past, Justices Sandra Day O'Connor and Anthony M. Kennedy, both Reagan appointees, seem to hold the key to any final decision by the court. While commentators focus closely on the questions these two justices ask, when the hearing is over no one will venture a guess as to what they — or the entire court for that matter — will decide. Much seems to depend on Article II of the U.S. Constitution as well as a 113-year-old federal law passed to avoid any upheaval caused by problems in the Electoral College procedures.

Meanwhile, in Florida, the Gore camp suffers two defeats in state courts that may prove much more important than anything the Supreme Court decides.

Sharp Questioning Reveals A Deeply Divided Court

"If it were purely a matter of state law, I suppose we normally would leave it alone, where the state supreme court found it. And so you probably have to persuade us there is some issue of federal law here. Otherwise, why are we acting?"

– Justice Sandra Day O'Connor

★ ★ ★

WASHINGTON — Appearing as divided as the rest of the country over Florida's disputed presidential votes, the United States Supreme Court grilled the lawyers for both sides today in an intense argument session that ended in uncertainty over how — or whether — the justices would decide George W. Bush's appeal of the Florida Supreme Court's extension of the state's vote-counting deadline.

Comments and questions by several justices raised the prospect that the court could conclude it lacked jurisdiction to decide the case. "Is there any respect in which this really makes a difference?" Justice Stephen G. Breyer wanted to know, noting that in the week since the Supreme Court had agreed to hear the appeal, Bush, who objected to the extended vote-counting, had been certified nonetheless as the winner of Florida's 25 electoral votes.

At the same time, it was evident that the court's more conservative justices were troubled by the nature of the state court's decision, which added 12 days to the certification deadline in Florida election law. "What we are talking about is having laws of sufficient specificity and stability that people can rely on them in advance and not have them changed after the fact," Justice Anthony M. Kennedy said sternly to Paul F. Hancock, a deputy state attorney general who was arguing in defense of the ruling. Justice Sandra Day O'Connor, echoing the same theme, said: "Certainly the date changed. And it just does look like a very dramatic change made by the Florida court."

But it was far from inevitable that the justices' discomfort with the state court's ruling would translate into a decision to overturn it. "I do not know of any case where we have impugned a state supreme court the way you are doing in this case," Justice Ruth Bader Ginsburg said to Theodore B. Olson, Bush's lawyer. Justice Ginsburg added, "In case after case, we have said we owe the highest respect to what the state supreme court says is the state's law."

While offered by one of the court's more liberal members, this appeal to federalism could exert a decided pull on some of the court's conservatives. Further complicating the picture, Justices O'Connor and Kennedy, who usually provide fourth and fifth votes for the court's conservative wing, were among the most openly dubious today about whether Governor Bush's appeal presented a case that the court could or should decide. "If it were purely a matter of state law," Justice O'Connor told Olson, "I suppose we normally would leave it alone, where the state supreme court found it." She added: "And so you probably have to persuade us there is some issue of federal law here. Otherwise, why are we acting?"

The tides of the argument shifted throughout the 90-minute session to a degree that left many in the courtroom audience almost disoriented. The court's jurisdictional challenges to Olson, who argued first, were so tough that it appeared by the end of his 35 minutes that lawyers for the Democratic side were about to coast to an easy victory.

But Chief Justice Rehnquist and Justice Scalia, who had been quite subdued during the first half of the argument, came alive during the second half, hurling so many questions at Laurence H. Tribe, the lawyer for Al Gore, that a case that had looked almost impregnable suddenly appeared vulnerable.

The tone inside the courtroom was sober and businesslike, leavened occasionally by a bit of welcome humor. Not only were the justices deeply engaged by the case, but their evident familiarity with its factual and legal setting was notable. The case raised issues of federal and state election law that the court has hardly ever had occasion to consider, and the final briefs came in less than 24 hours before the argument.

While adhering to its no-television rule, the court did acknowledge the intense public interest in the case by releasing an audiotape as soon as the argument ended. But while the justices were certainly aware that their voices were about to be broadcast to a national audience likely to hang on their every word, there was nothing in their demeanor that was different from any other argument. Only Justice Clarence Thomas, as is his custom, did not ask a question.

Olson, arguing for Bush that the state court overstepped its authority, pursued two lines of attack against the Nov. 21 ruling. One was based on a federal law, Section 5 of Title 3 of the United States Code, that protects a state's electors against challenges in Congress if disputes over the choice of the electors have been resolved according to state law in effect before Election Day.

But the Florida Supreme Court "overturned and materially rewrote portions of the carefully formulated set of laws enacted by Florida's Legislature," Olson said. By doing so, the court invited the "controversy, conflict and chaos" that Congress meant to avoid when it enacted Section 5 in 1887, in response to the electoral deadlock in the Hayes-Tilden presidential election of 1876.

Several justices wondered aloud whether, even if Olson's view of the case was correct, there was anything for them to do about it. "Isn't Section 5 sort of a safe-harbor provision for states?" Justice O'Connor asked. "And do you think it gives some independent right of a candidate to overturn a Florida decision based on that section?"

Justice David H. Souter noted that Section 5 was part of a broader statute that set out the procedures for handling Electoral College disputes on the floor of Congress. "It looks to me as though at this stage of the game, the statute has committed the determination of the issues that you raise and the consequences to follow from them to the Congress," Justice Souter told Olson.

"Why should the federal judiciary be interfering in what seems to be a very carefully thought-out scheme for determining what happens if you are right?"

Olson replied: "Because I submit that that writes Section 5 essentially out of existence," by permitting the Legislature's choices to be upset by another branch of state government, the state judiciary, without any further review.

Justice Souter said, "That seems to be precisely the resort that Congress has provided."

If Olson's statutory argument did not appear to have much traction, his second argument did — somewhat surprisingly, and to a degree that did not become clear until the justices confronted Tribe with it later.

Olson argued that under Article II of the United States Constitution, which gives states the power to appoint electors "in such manner as the legislature thereof may direct," a state court has no ability to revise the way a state has exercised its constitutional authority. For this proposition, he cited sentences in a Supreme Court decision from 1892, McPherson v. Blacker, in which the court had upheld the Michigan Legislature's right to divide the state into two districts for the purpose of separate slates of presidential electors from each.

Pressed by Chief Justice Rehnquist and Justice Scalia in questioning Tribe, the McPherson case suddenly took on an outsized importance. The two justices said that in their view, the Florida Supreme Court had relied on the Florida Constitution when it extended the certification deadline, thus trampling on the Legislature's rights under Article II in a way that the McPherson decision made impermissible.

Tribe objected that while the Florida court had cited the state Constitution to show the importance Florida attached to giving full effect to the right to vote, the decision itself was an ordinary exercise in statutory interpretation. He was supported in this analysis by Justice Souter and Justice John Paul Stevens. But the back-and-forth about the basis for the Florida Supreme Court's decision consumed a sizable portion of Tribe's 35 minutes.

In any event, Tribe said, the Florida Legislature had given the state courts the authority to interpret election law for all elections except their own. "They cut out judicial review for the election of their own members," he said.

Tribe said that under the Supreme Court's precedents, "the Constitution takes the state government and its arrangements as it finds it." Except for the constitutional amendment process under Article V, when a legislature acts outside its usual role in ratifying a proposed amendment, "it's therefore assumed that the legislature is surrounded with both executive and judicial authority." He said a state legislature's decision to "completely exclude the judiciary from any possible role" might itself be unconstitutional.

Moments later, the argument session ended, but there appeared to be widespread agreement in the crowd that slowly and — after 90 minutes of silence — talkatively made its way out of the courtroom that the justices' work had just begun.

Dec. 2, 2000, Linda Greenhouse

OUTSIDE, A LOUD JURY OF JEERS

Outside the Supreme Court, the atmosphere was more carnival-like than hostile. Thousands of supporters of Bush and Gore chanted and marched for hours, kept apart by police officers who separated them neatly down the middle of the sidewalk below the court steps like guests at a wedding — friends of Bush on the left, friends of Gore on the right.

There was Doug Graham, who dressed as a ballot box that read, "Get the Al Out." He expressed bewilderment over confused Palm Beach County voters, saying, "You don't have to be Hercules or Einstein to punch that vote out." Paces away, Clarence Hardy, a man who breeds thoroughbred horses in New Jersey and fights for black farmers, said he hoped the justices inside would bring justice back to America. He held a blindfolded black doll aloft. Using an expression that must be familiar to thoroughbred breeders, at least, Hardy said that Bush "has been behaving like a big horse walking on a bunch of roaches."

In a tit-for-tat street cantata, one chant was snuffed out by the next: "G-W-B. How many votes did you steal from me?" "Show Gore the Door." Not even Bush's running mate, Dick Cheney, was spared: "Cheney needs a heart. Bush needs a brain."

Just after 10 a.m., the Rev. Jesse Jackson showed up, linking arms with Patricia Ireland, the head of the National Organization for Women, and Representative John Lewis, the civil rights leader from Georgia. The Rev. Al Sharpton was there. They led a contingent of several hundred down the street. Some of the demonstrators were first-timers. Others mobilized en masse when called. A few drove from places south and north of here, either to lend support or go back home with a story to tell the grandchildren.

Marching outside was simple. Securing one of the 300 coveted seats inside the Supreme Court chamber took fortitude and patience, not to mention sterling connections. Most of the tickets, 100 or so, were reserved for members of the Supreme Court Bar, an exclusive club of constitutional lawyers. A few of them camped out overnight for tickets, in the drizzle and cold. Ordinary citizens started lining up even earlier, and there was a flurry of $1,000 offers for their spots.

There were V.I.P. tickets, as well. All four of Gore's children attended. One row alone included a panoply of politicians, advisers and Washington glitterati. Byron White, the only living retired justice, turned up too.

The demonstrators started to leave soon after the hearing was over, although a few stayed late. Although the day was trouble-free, few who turned out said they anticipated a smooth four years ahead, regardless of who is president.

Dec. 2, 2000, Lizette Alvarez

Excerpts from the Supreme Court Hearing

Questions to Theodore Olson

JUSTICE GINSBURG — Mr. Olson, would you agree that when we read a state court decision, we should read it in the light most favorable to the integrity of the State Supreme Court; that if there are two possible readings, one that would impute to that court injudicial behavior, lack of integrity, indeed, dishonesty, and the other that would read the opinion to say we think this court is attempting to construe the state law.

It may have been wrong. We might have interpreted it differently. But we are not the arbiters; they are.

MR. OLSON — I would like to answer that in two ways. In the first place, I don't mean to suggest, and I hope my words didn't, that there was a lack of integrity or any dishonesty by the Florida Supreme Court. We're saying that it was acting far outside the scope of its authority in connection with an exercise of power that is vested by the Constitution of the United States ——

JUSTICE GINSBURG — But if it tells us, "We see these two provisions in conflict," they need to be reconciled.

MR. OLSON — Under almost any other circumstances, yes, Justice Ginsburg. But in this context, we're talking about a federal right, a federal constitutional right, and the rights of individual citizens under the Constitution. And so, therefore, this court has a great responsibility to look —

JUSTICE O'CONNOR — Mr. Olson, I'd like to get focused a little more on this same area. If it were purely a matter of state law, I suppose we normally would leave it alone, where the State Supreme Court found it. And so you probably have to persuade us there is some issue of federal law here. Otherwise, why are we acting? . . . And are you relying, in that regard, on Title II? I mean, would you like to —

MR. OLSON — Article.

JUSTICE O'CONNOR — Article II. Would you like to characterize the federal issue that you think governs this?

MR. OLSON — Well, we are very definitely relying on Article II of the Constitution. The framers of the Constitution debated long and hard; it was one of the longest debates that took place during the formation of the Constitution. Where should this power be lodged — in the federal legislature, in the state legislature, at the ballot booth, or what? The one thing that was discussed and rejected by virtually everyone is that the power to select the manner in which electors would be appointed would be in that state judiciary. That was rejected. The notion that it would be vested in the state judiciary was something that was rejected. And what the framers decided to do is to vest it in the state legislature and did it invested that authority under Article II, not just in the state, but in the legislatures.

Excerpts from the Supreme Court Hearing

Questions to Laurence Tribe

JUSTICE SCALIA — Professor Tribe, can I ask you why you think the Florida Legislature delegated to the Florida Supreme Court the authority to interpose the Florida Constitution? I mean, maybe your experience with the legislative branch is different from mine, but in my experience, they are resigned to the intervention of the courts but have certainly never invited it.

MR. TRIBE — Well, I'd have to say my experience parallels that.

JUSTICE SCALIA — What makes you think the Florida Legislature affirmatively invited the Florida Supreme Court?

MR. TRIBE — The odd thing is that the system in Florida involves their own repromulgation of the Constitution. And their scheme with respect to the resolution of disputes over elections draws a sharp distinction between elections to their own House and Senate, which they won't trust the courts with as far as they can throw them, those are to be resolved exclusively in the House and Senate, and all others are to be resolved in the courts under a standard that they, understandably ——

JUSTICE SCALIA — They are resigned to. But they need not be resigned to the Florida Supreme Court interposing itself with respect to federal elections. They need not be because the Florida Constitution cannot affect it. And I just find it implausible that they really invited the Florida Supreme Court to interpose the Florida Constitution between what they enacted by statute and the ultimate result of the election.

MR. TRIBE — I suppose if they were at all far-sighted, if they looked at their own work and saw how self-contradictory it was, they might say, "We would want someone with the authority to reconcile these provisions to do so in the light not only of the literal language but of the fact that they're dealing with something very important, the franchise; that disenfranchising people, which is what this is all about, disenfranchising people isn't very nice, and it even violates the federal as well as the state constitution."

Article II and Section 5: The Heart of the Matter?

Lawyers for Bush and Al Gore take diametrically opposed positions on issues great and small, as the briefs filed demonstrate. Their differences range from how to characterize the Florida Supreme Court's decision to how to interpret the confusing language of a 113-year-old federal election law that most of the lawyers in the case will concede in their candid moments that they had never heard of until a few weeks ago to what should be the remedy if the justices decide to overturn the Florida Supreme Court's ruling.

Whether the newly prominent statute, Section 5 of Title 3 of the United States Code, is crucial to the outcome of this case depends largely on whether the justices conclude that anything has happened in Florida so far to make the provision relevant to this phase of the dispute and therefore ripe for review.

Title 3 is the compilation of federal laws dealing with the presidency. Chapter 1 of that title covers "presidential elections and vacancies." And Section 5 of Chapter 1, the provision arguably at issue in this case, is titled "determination of controversy as to appointment of electors."

Section 5 is one long, difficult 133-word sentence, constructed as an "if . . . then" proposition. If a state takes certain steps in appointing its presidential electors, then the choice of those electors "shall be conclusive, and shall govern in the counting of the electoral votes." Exactly what the "if" clause means, and what conclusions the Supreme Court should draw from whatever it decides, is very much in dispute.

What follows are the central decision points for the court and the contrasting arguments that the two sides make on each point.

The Florida Court

In the appeal, the Bush legal team argues that the Nov. 21 decision of the Florida Supreme Court, extending from Nov. 14 to Nov. 26 the statutory deadline for the official vote count, "cannot be reconciled with state statutes enacted before the election was held."

Because in the Bush view of the case, decisive legal consequences flow from that description of the state court's action, the justices must either accept or reject that premise at the threshold of the case: was the state court decision such a departure from normal judicial behavior that it brought about what can properly be called a "change" in the law, as the Bush side maintains, or did it simply interpret conflicting provisions to give effect to the underlying purpose of the statute as a whole, as the Gore side insists?

In the 20-page reply briefs they filed today, the two sides continue to press their competing views. The Florida Supreme Court, the Bush brief asserts, "decided to create, out of whole cloth, a new deadline for a selective, standardless, changing and unequal manual recount process for this particular election," an action the brief says was "completely untethered to any legislative judgment."

The new Gore brief, calling the state court decision "as routine as petitioner's request for federal court intervention is remarkable," offers this competing image of what that decision accomplished:

"Allowing the legislature's manual recount provisions to be given effect is not like changing the rules after the game has been played. It is instead like using a more powerful photo-finish camera — indeed, one already mandated by the legislature — to determine the winner of the race more accurately."

The Meaning of Section 5

Whether all of this matters depends in large measure on the Supreme Court's first interpretation of Section 5, which Congress passed in 1887 to avoid a repetition of the Hayes-Tilden electoral debacle of 1876 in which competing slates of electors vied on the floor of Congress.

The law says that if a state has provided "by laws enacted prior to" Election Day, a method of settling "any controversy or contest" concerning the appointment of electors, the determination made according to those laws shall not be subject to challenge in Congress.

The Bush position is that because the Florida Supreme Court "changed" substantive state election law after Election Day, there is no "prior" law in place and the condition of Section 5 is therefore not satisfied.

The Gore position is not only that the Florida Supreme Court decision did not change the law by interpreting it, but also that this entire argument represents a misunderstanding of Section 5. In particular, the Gore reply brief maintains that what has to have remained unchanged since before Election Day under Section 5 is not state election law as a whole, but rather a state's dispute-resolution process for dealing with electoral problems.

Because that process "did not change in any way" as the result of the State Supreme Court's ruling, the brief says, there is no Section 5 question that the justices even need to address at this point; Florida's Legislature long ago gave the state courts the authority to interpret the election code, which is all that happened here.

If a dispute later emerges over the legitimacy of the electors who cast Florida's votes in the Electoral College, the Gore legal team says, there will be time then to resolve the question of whether that slate is entitled to the "safe harbor" offered to electors whose choice meets the Section 5 condition.

Consequences of Section 5

In accepting the Bush appeal, the justices asked both sides to address the question: "What would be the consequences of this court's finding that the decision of the Supreme Court of Florida does not comply with Section 5?"

The Bush brief argues that in that event, the state's court's judgment should be vacated. "Such a result would permit Florida's executive official to perform their duties under the law as it existed on Nov. 7, 2000," the brief says.

Further, the Bush team maintains that such a reversion to the original vote-counting deadline would mean that the essential claims of Vice President Gore's new state-court lawsuit contesting the certification "will be rendered invalid." That is because there would be no basis for asserting that any post-Nov. 14 recounts should either have continued or been included in the official total.

The Gore brief says there would be no basis for overturning the decision, even if the justices found a Section 5 problem with the state court's ruling. That is because the only purpose of Section 5 was to offer states a "safe harbor" against challenges to their electors. If the condition of Section 5 is not met, the result is to simply to remove the benefit of the safe harbor, according the Gore lawyers, whose reply brief today tells the justices: "This court lacks the power to reverse a state's decision to forgo a benefit the federal government need not have offered in the first place."

As for the Bush assertion that the Gore post-certification contest would be doomed, the Gore reply brief today described the argument as a "breathtaking" and invalid request to have the Supreme Court "declare the game over."

Article II of The Constitution

Additional disputes revolve around a clause in the United States Constitution, contained in Section 1 of Article II, providing that "each state shall appoint, in such manner as the legislature thereof may direct," a slate of electors.

Under the Bush view, this provision is a delegation to the legislature that carves the state judiciary and the executive branch out of a role in interpreting or enforcing state laws having to do with the presidential election. Under the Gore view, nothing in Article II should be read to strip state courts of the ordinary review power that the framers intended them to have.

Nov. 30, 2000, Linda Greenhouse

Two Laws at Issue in Dispute before Supreme Court

Following are the laws at issue in the battle over the vote recount:

Title 3, U.S. Code, Chapter 1, Section 5:

If any state shall have provided, by laws enacted prior to the day fixed for the appointment of the electors, for its final determination of any controversy or contest concerning the appointment of all or any of the electors of such state, by judicial or other methods or procedures, and such determination shall have been made at least six days before the time fixed for the meeting of the electors, such determination made pursuant to such law so existing on said day, and made at least six days prior to said time of meeting of the electors, shall be conclusive, and shall govern in counting of the electoral votes as provided in the Constitution, and as hereinafter regulated, so far as the ascertainment of the electors appointed by such state is concerned.

Article II, Section 1, Clause 2 of Constitution:

Each State shall appoint, in such manner as the legislature thereof may direct, a number of Electors, equal to the whole number of Senators and Representatives to which the State may be entitled in the Congress; but no Senator or Representative, or person holding an office of trust or profit under the United States shall be appointed an elector.

TWO SETBACKS FOR GORE IN FLORIDA COURTS

TALLAHASSEE — The Florida Supreme Court rejected an appeal today by Al Gore that it begin the immediate manual recount of 14,000 disputed ballots from South Florida, forcing Gore's contest of the presidential election into a lower-court trial that begins Saturday morning. An hour later, the state's highest court dealt another blow to supporters of Gore in Palm Beach County, refusing to order a new election, which many voters said was necessary because of the confusing nature of the "butterfly" ballot.

The day in Tallahassee was not a complete loss for the Gore camp. Judge Sauls, who is presiding over the contest lawsuit, announced what could be a relatively brisk pace for Saturday's trial, expressing the hope that it could be completed in one 12-hour session. If the judge should agree on Saturday to Gore's demand that the ballots be counted, the Democratic team would not be much further behind schedule than if the Supreme Court had agreed to the appeal.

Lawyers for Bush have vowed to use every argument at their disposal to make certain that no ballots are counted, and that the contest lawsuit is dismissed. But they backed away today from some earlier plans that could have delayed the trial, including a demand that three Florida counties send 1.17 million ballots to Tallahassee, in addition to the 1.16 million ballots from Palm Beach and Miami-Dade Counties that finished arriving here today. Instead, the Bush lawyers agreed to the proposal by Judge Sauls that the ballots in Volusia, Broward and Pinellas Counties simply be impounded as possible evidence where they are, and not be transported.

Bush's lawyers also said they would not insist that the opening of the trial deal with a series of new issues they raised in a brief on Thursday night, agreeing to postpone them until later on Saturday. Those issues include whether Gore is really entitled to bring a contest lawsuit — technically, only the electors for a candidate are on a presidential ballot — and whether any presidential election can truly be contested under Florida law. The Bush team also agreed to call no more than 20 witnesses, not the 93 named in a witness list submitted Thursday night. Gore's lawyers plan to call two witnesses.

The willingness of the Bush team to pare down its demands may have come from the realization that Judge Sauls was not going to allow any obvious delays. The judge said he understood why Gore needed to accelerate the process; if the trial, the vote-counting and any subsequent appeals extend beyond Dec. 12, the Florida Legislature will send Bush's electors to the Electoral College and the contest lawsuit will likely become moot.

At a preliminary hearing this afternoon, Judge Sauls made it clear he would take a no-nonsense approach to the trial. Lawyers for the various parties to the suit would not be allowed to repeat arguments already made, he said, an important consideration because there are multiple defendants in the suit: Bush; Katherine Harris, the Florida secretary of state; and the election boards of three counties. He also refused to allow a lawyer for John Thrasher, the former speaker of the Florida House and an elector for Bush, to make a lengthy argument on Saturday that Gore was unable to bring a contest lawsuit because technically only electors are allowed to do so.

The judge disappointed the Gore team when he said he intended to hear arguments on whether to count the ballots — an issue the Democratic lawyers would prefer not to debate. The Republicans said they would argue that ballots could not be counted because there was no proof that the county canvassing boards had erred in their counts. Still, the debate on evidence is apparently to begin early in the day, giving the Democrats a quick chance to make their case on their most important issue.

If the judge agrees that the disputed ballots should be manually counted, Gore's lawyers have proposed several methods to handle the task. They include having the court clerk do the counting; asking other circuit court judges to count; or hiring a special master to supervise the counting at the court's behest.

In general, Gore's lawyers used the judge's call for a brisk schedule to put the best face on the loss suffered by their Supreme Court appeal, a unanimous dismissal by the seven justices which represented a significant setback to their timetable. When Gore's lawyers filed the appeal earlier this week, they said their case would be lost if they had to wait until Saturday to begin an argument over counting ballots. Today, they said there was still room for victory. "We're disappointed in the Supreme Court's decision, but we said from the beginning it was a very unusual request to ask them to take it up before the trial court had an opportunity to review the matter," said Boies. "On the other hand, we're encouraged that the trial court is moving very fast, much faster than in the past."

The Supreme Court gave no reason for its decision to dismiss the appeal, but Gore's lawyers acknowledged that it had been a long shot, particularly since they never even had a written order from Judge Sauls on which to base their appeal.

Benjamin L. Ginsberg, general counsel to Bush, said the Democrats were deservedly repudiated twice today. "The Gore campaign tactic ever since Nov. 8 has been to try to change the rules," he said. "They asked for an emergency recount, something heretofore unknown, and the Florida Supreme Court spanked them. Then they came up with a theory on the Palm Beach butterfly ballot that runs contrary to every other bit of Florida law, and fortunately that was bounced today, too."

The Gore campaign was not directly involved in the Palm Beach butterfly lawsuit, though it never discouraged supporters from filing it. In its unanimous decision on that case today, the court said the only remedies for a defective ballot were a revote or statistically reallocating the vote totals. Because of the drastic nature of those remedies, the court said, a defective ballot must be "in substantial noncompliance" with election laws. "In the present case, even accepting appellants' allegations, we conclude as a matter of law that the Palm Beach County ballot does not constitute substantial noncompliance with the statutory requirements mandating the voiding of the election," the opinion said.

Dec. 2, 2000, David Firestone

Profile: LAURENCE H. TRIBE
FOR DEMOCRATS, A LEGAL SCHOLAR

In his first appearance before the Supreme Court, in 1980, Laurence H. Tribe argued that the First Amendment required that trials be open to the public and the press. His father had died 10 days earlier, and Professor Tribe had inquired if the argument could be postponed — and was informed, politely but firmly, by the clerk's office that a delay was not possible.

He went on to win the case, *Richmond Newspapers v. Virginia*, on a 7-to-1 vote, producing a landmark ruling in which the court set broad and firm guidelines ensuring that trial proceedings must be open.

On Friday, Professor Tribe will argue his 30th case before the Supreme Court, which presents its own problem of timing. It will be the first time an argument before the court has forced him to cancel his classes at Harvard Law School, where he is the Ralph S. Tyler professor of constitutional law.

The rushed schedule also means his well-honed method of preparing for a Supreme Court appearance has been altered. He said in a recent conversation that he has always tried to remain somewhat isolated before a Supreme Court argument, reaching out to colleagues at the law school and elsewhere by telephone to test points.

Because of the unexpected (by him and most constitutional scholars) decision of the court to quickly accept the Florida case, he has not been able to deal with his colleagues on the Gore team at arm's length, as he and they have had to work together on the briefs.

But for the oral argument, Mr. Tribe said, he has prepared in his customary solitary fashion, practicing alone, ostensibly in his suite at the Watergate Hotel, but really in his mind. He does not, and never has, used a moot court session, as do most lawyers, in which a panel of lawyers acts as the court, tossing out questions as the justices will on Friday.

Between his first Supreme Court case 20 years ago and the one this week, Professor Tribe has become perhaps the most well-known constitutional scholar in the nation, writing several books, notably, *American Constitutional Law,* which he regularly revises. The book has been cited thousands of times in court rulings and is considered the closest thing to a definitive treatise on the Constitution.

He also earned the dislike of many conservatives for his role in the tumultuous Senate hearings in 1987 in which Robert H. Bork's nomination for the Supreme Court was rejected. In 1990, a conservative law journal, *Benchmark*, devoted an issue to attacking Professor Tribe as an ambitious and unscrupulous scholar, which was widely seen as an effort to vilify him to discourage any Democratic president from considering him for the Supreme Court.

Because of his intellect and friendship with Democratic lawmakers, he had naturally been thought of as a possible Supreme Court nominee. For a long time, he labored under the image of someone angling for the Supreme Court.

For his part, Professor Tribe insisted that such a view had never been accurate, that he decided early on that he would not tailor any opinion or action to maintain his viability for the court.

"The prudent course in terms of preserving options would have been to remain quiet and modulate my views dramatically," he said. "I decided quite long ago, the hell with that." Moreover, he said that it would be foolish for people to organize their lives around a single goal.

In any event, time and politics have combined to make a Tribe nomination remote. Once regularly described by acquaintances as brilliant but almost unbearably self-confident, Professor Tribe said he understood why people thought that of him. "I feel I'm quite different now," he said, describing himself as more mellow.

And Professor Tribe, who was the prototype of the by-now-familiar phenomenon of a law professor as a television commentator, used to list media appearances on his resumé. He no longer does that.

Laurence Henry Tribe was born on Oct. 10, 1941, in Shanghai, where his Russian Jewish parents had fled. At age 6, he moved with his family to San Francisco, where he grew up. He became a top undergraduate scholar in mathematics at Harvard. He said he changed to law to have a more tangible influence on the world.

In his cases before the Supreme Court, he has recorded 19 victories, 2 of them on the pleadings, that is, without having to argue the case. He has argued on behalf of gay rights and in support of busing to achieve school integration.

He once argued in Congressional testimony that flag burning could be outlawed through legislation, a position he now says he regrets. He is known among advocates for his intellectual nimbleness before the justices, who seem to take special satisfaction in engaging him.

Dec. 1, 2000, Neil A. Lewis

Profile: THEODORE B. OLSON
TRUSTED LITIGATOR FOR REPUBLICANS

WASHINGTON — When he argues George W. Bush's case before the Supreme Court on Friday, Theodore B. Olson will be performing the latest assignment in the informal role he has come to play in Washington, that of the most trusted appellate litigator of the Republican establishment.

While Olson will be arguing on behalf of a man he contends is a president-to-be, Governor Bush is not his first presidential client.

He represented President Ronald Reagan in the investigation by an independent counsel into the Iran-contra affair, the secret White House effort to sell arms to Iran and use profits to finance the contra rebels in Nicaragua.

Olson's journey to prominence in the capital began when he was a protégé of William French Smith, Reagan's first attorney general. Olson had worked with Smith at the Los Angeles law firm of Gibson, Dunn & Crutcher. When Smith came to Washington, he brought along to the Justice Department two of his favorite young assistants, Olson and Kenneth W. Starr. Olson has remained strong friends with Starr, until recently the Whitewater prosecutor.

Olson found himself installed as head of the Office of Legal Counsel in the Reagan Justice Department, the office that researched the constitutional implications of the administration's policies and legal actions. Heading the office was the closest thing inside an administration to being its resident constitutional law professor.

When he left the administration and returned to Gibson, Dunn, he developed an appellate practice that was modeled on the Office of Legal Counsel that has since flourished.

While he is not as well known nationally as Prof. Laurence H. Tribe, his adversary on Friday, Olson is wildly popular among conservative law school students who know him from his years of helping lead the Federalist Society, a Washington-based network of conservative law students and lawyers. In that world, an opportunity to be hired by Olson is valued almost as highly as a clerkship with one of the conservative justices.

He and his wife, Barbara, are a major power couple among Washington's conservative set. Mrs. Olson is a former federal prosecutor who worked for House Republicans in their investigation of the Clintons. She was a regular legal commentator on television in the Clinton impeachment, and wrote *Hell to Pay: The Unfolding Story of Hillary Rodham Clinton* (Regnery 2000), a book harshly critical of Mrs. Clinton.

In the 13 cases he has argued before the Supreme Court, Olson won 8 and lost 4; one was re-argued by another lawyer.

"What I love about this kind of work is the rigor of standing up there and trying to advance your case while answering questions from all sides," he said in an interview about his practice.

He is noted among fellow lawyers for his intellectual suppleness and gentle manner before the justices. In one of his most difficult cases, he failed in 1996 to persuade the justices to uphold the right of the Virginia Military Institute, a state-financed college, to exclude women. He has also fought the University of Texas before a federal appeals court in a successful effort to eliminate affirmative action in its law school admissions. The Supreme Court declined to review the ruling.

Theodore Bevry Olson was born in Chicago on Sept. 11, 1940. He graduated from the University of the Pacific and Boalt Hall, the law school at the University of California.

In preparing for arguments, Olson said he had a fairly set regime in which he held three moot court sessions, practices in which a handful of fellow lawyers act like the justices and pepper him with questions.

Before he became an experienced practitioner before the court, he was a party in a major Supreme Court case, *Morrison v. Olson*. Olson had unsuccessfully challenged the constitutionality of the law that allowed for the appointment of independent prosecutors to investigate high-level administration officials.

He was being investigated for giving possibly misleading comments to a Congressional committee when he was a Justice Department official about an environmental program. He lost the 1988 case, but after the court upheld the statute, the independent counsel, Alexia Morrison, announced that she had concluded there had not been any intent on Olson's part to mislead Congress and the case against him was dropped.

Olson has told friends that the 29 months in which he was under investigation was an awful period that has given him sympathy for people confronted with the force of the federal government.

Dec. 1, 2000, Neil A. Lewis

day 25

SATURDAY,
DECEMBER 2ND

★ ★ ★ ★ ★

"EVERY DAY, EVERY HOUR MATTERS"

In state court in Tallahassee, lawyers for Gore try to convince Judge N. Sanders Sauls of the need to conduct a hand recount of 14,000 disputed ballots, and to do so as quickly as possible. As evidence they cite the difficulties voters faced with punch-card ballots — difficulties that resulted in dimpled or partially punched chads. Bush lawyers counter that the Gore case should be dismissed since it fails to make a clear case for overturning the election results. Moreover, they argue, the case exaggerates the difficulties associated with punch-card ballots. To the Gore team's frustration, after 12 grueling hours the case is continued to Sunday. That night they probably see televised pictures of Bush meeting with Congressional leaders and acting presidential.

GORE'S TRIAL IN FLORIDA BOGS DOWN

TALLAHASSEE — The trial that may finally determine the outcome of the presidential election opened today. Lawyers for Gore, who filed the lawsuit to contest Bush's certified victory in Florida, pleaded with Judge N. Sanders Sauls of Leon County Circuit Court to begin a manual count of thousands of ballots that they believe contain enough votes to make Gore the winner. And because they want any such counting to include slightly indented ballots, they spent hours presenting testimony on how easy it is to partly punch a hole. "There is sufficient evidence that those votes could change or at least place in doubt the results of the election," David Boies said in his opening statement. "Those votes have got to be included in the vote tally."

But in a tense courtroom packed with lawyers, reporters and spectators, Bush's legal team told Judge Sauls that there was not nearly enough evidence to justify a new count, which the lawyers said was not permitted under state law. Barry Richard, Bush's chief trial lawyer, accused Gore of demanding "three free shots at the basket" to produce the results he wanted. "I suggest to the court that that's certainly not what the Legislature intended and in fact it is contrary to the longstanding and clear established law of the State of Florida, which Mr. Boies has meticulously avoided discussing."

Judge Sauls, along with the Democrats, had hoped to finish the trial today after a marathon 12-hour session. But only a few minutes after the opening statements, the trial quickly bogged down in often bitterly sarcastic argument between the two sides over the intricacies of punch-card voting — from what kind of rubber is used in the machines to the sharpness of the knives that are used to score punch-card holes.

The first of Gore's two witnesses, an elections administration consultant, spent more than three hours testifying, as lawyers for the two sides used him to score their own points on the reliability and accuracy of punch-card voting machines. At one point, one of Gore's lawyers walked through the courtroom with a ballot machine full of chads that had been punched from many ballots, as the consultant testified that the buildup of chads might have prevented votes from being read by a punch-card scanner.

Near the end of the day, there was even a sharp dispute between the sides over the qualifications of an expert on rubber and plastics, who spent nearly an hour discussing the deterioration process of rubber. (The issue plays a role in determining why some voters were not able to fully punch their ballots.) Judge Sauls — fairly tolerant with most of the lawyers during the day — got so angry with Stephen Zack, a lawyer for Gore who was interrogating the expert, that he ordered to him to sit down, although he later relented.

By 6:15 p.m., the clearly weary judge said his court employees were getting hungry and wanted to go home, so he ordered the second day of testimony. The cumulative hours of sparring thus added up to a serious setback for Gore's team, who had hoped the judge would issue an order today to begin counting ballots.

As the day ended, Benjamin L. Ginsberg, Bush's legal counsel, emerged from court looking quite pleased at the day's developments. "We look forward to another day tomorrow to correct some of the myths that have been out there for the last three weeks," he said. Ginsberg added that a two-day hearing to determine the next president was not too much to ask.

Boies said his side would grudgingly continue another day. "Every day, every hour matters," he said. "We would have liked to have had it over in a day, but I don't think the difference between tonight and tomorrow will be crucial."

The judge, who will be the sole arbiter of these issues at this stage of the trial, showed no early indication of his willingness to consider beginning a manual count. He listened intently to the opening arguments, leaning back in his large leather chair, occasionally taking notes. As the testimony delved into mechanical details, and the lawyers urgently objected to each other, the judge showed signs of weariness, and occasionally interrupted witnesses to cut repetition. Lawyers from all sides — and there appeared to be at least 40 of them in the room — alternated between whispered discussions of strategy and close scrutiny of the judge's facial expressions, searching for an opening.

If Judge Sauls finds there is enough evidence that Gore won the election, he is empowered by Florida law to order that Gore's electors be sent to the Electoral College, although that might conflict with the State Legislature's intention to name Bush's electors. Whatever decision Judge Sauls reaches will undoubtedly be appealed to the Florida Supreme Court and possibly to the United States Supreme Court, but Democrats say a final decision needs to be made by Dec. 12, the federal deadline for states to name electors.

The Democrats, fearful of missing the deadline, were pleased that the judge moved directly to testimony, and they began laying out their case that voters might have tried to cast a vote on a punch card without pushing the stylus all the way through it. If there is to be a manual count of ballots, the Gore team wants the judge to agree that indentations on a ballot card should be read the same way as a fully punched hole.

To that end, the Democrats called as their first witness Kimball Brace, president of Election Data Services of Fairfax, Va., who advises local governments on election administration. Brace testified that older and poorly maintained machines with worn-out rubber backing could sometimes prevent a voter from registering a vote with a fully punched hole, particularly if they have not been cleaned of old chads, which he said was the case in Palm Beach.

Bush's lawyers challenged Brace's expertise, suggesting that he was a partisan witness for having consulted with Democratic candidates in the past and that he lacked the mechanical engineering experience to judge the deterioration of voting machines. But despite the gaps in his knowledge, Brace was able to testify that manual recounts were often much more accurate than machine counts, the point the Gore forces wanted to make. "When you have a close election, a manual hand count is the only way of knowing exactly how many votes were cast for each candidate," Brace said. "In a very close election, that is the key."

Brace said many of the voting machines used in the Florida election had not been cleaned of chads for several years, which he said can make it difficult to force a stylus into the hole. This led to a debate over whether voting machines should be shaken to distribute the chads, and as lawyers in front of the judge shook a voting machine in demonstration, Judge Sauls shook his head in exasperation, as if he could not believe the contest had come to this.

Gore's second witness, Prof. Nicholas Hengartner, a Yale statistician, had a somewhat easier time. His job was to testify that the percentage of non-recorded votes for president was five times as high in counties with punch-card voting machines as in those with optical readers. He said a manual recount allowed about a quarter of those nonvotes to be identified as votes in Broward and Miami-Dade Counties, but only about 8 percent in Palm Beach County because it used a stricter standard in judging indented ballots.

Beck, on cross-examination of Dr. Hengartner, found some inconsistencies between his testimony and a written statement he had filed earlier. But the lawyer did not really shake Dr. Hengartner's testimony, suggesting only that voters who approached a punch-card voting machine tended to walk away without voting more often than those who used optical ballots. Dr. Hengartner said there was no evidence to back such a theory.

Because of all the cross-examination, Gore's case took seven hours, much more time than the Democrats intended to use. By the time Bush's lawyers began their case, with a 20-person witness list, members of the Gore legal team were despairing of being able to finish before Sunday night.

Bush's lawyers opened their case with a brief warning from Richard that they believed the case should be dismissed because the Gore team did not make a clear case for overturning the election. They set out to prove that by calling as their first witness County Judge Charles E. Burton, who testified about the lengthy deliberation the Palm Beach board went through in trying to determine the intent of the voter. Though the board usually decided not to count dimples as votes, Judge Burton said the board nonetheless went to great lengths to examine the ballots, supporting the Republican contention that it did not abuse its discretion in a way that would justify a judicial recount.

Under questioning by Boies, Judge Burton said that despite such effort, there were still 3,300 ballots set aside on which the board could not determine a vote — the very ballots that the Democrats want Judge Sauls to count.

The other witness for Bush, Richard Grossman, who teaches rubber and plastics technology at the University of Wisconsin at Milwaukee, testified that if the rubber used in the voting machines was properly mixed, it should remain stable for many years, presumably not affecting voting.

Gore has poured all his resources and hopes into this trial, which under Florida law represents his last recourse in trying to overturn the victory awarded last week to Bush by 537 votes. But his lawyers have acknowledged that such a contest is a steep uphill path that has not been taken in modern times to overturn anything larger than a local Florida race. State law gives a challenger broad latitude in trying to prove his case, but the legal presumption is always on the side of the declared victor, and the evidence of an incorrect outcome has to be beyond question.

Gore's team has based its case on a provision in the law that overturns the election if the challenger can prove "a number of illegal votes or rejection of a number of legal votes sufficient to change or place in doubt the result of the election." Two counties — Miami-Dade and Palm Beach — rejected a number of legal votes, Democratic lawyers say, while Nassau County allowed a number of illegal votes.

Dec. 3, 2000, David Firestone

A Ponderous Day at Trial

TALLAHASSEE — Today's first bad omen for Al Gore came at precisely 9:19 a.m. by the courtroom clock. This, of course, was the moment that Judge N. Sanders Sauls of Leon County Circuit Court ambled into his courtroom and plopped into his padded chair, already 19 precious minutes behind schedule.

The second bad omen came some 40 minutes later when Judge Sauls, ever the polite Southern gentleman, allowed a lawyer, one who did not even represent any of the principal players, to start a rambling discourse on the metaphorical links between manual recounts and George Orwell's *Animal Farm*.

It was that kind of day for Gore, whose twin foes are now George W. Bush and the calendar.

At this point, Gore's entire legal strategy is aimed at the single, paramount goal of getting the ballot counting resumed lickety-split. Without that, his lawyers concede, he has little hope of overtaking Bush's 537-vote lead in Florida's certified election results. But if Gore's legal team wants the courts to fly at warp speed, today it found the pace more akin to a Sunday stroll.

Today, at yet another crucial turning point in the battle for Florida, the simple act of introducing all 16 lawyers took three minutes plus. On a day when Judge Sauls hoped to resolve the simple question of whether contested ballots should be counted at all, the normally routine business of having a witness qualified as an expert dragged on for nearly 20 minutes.

Judge Sauls had said he hoped to finish today's minitrial in 12 hours. By late morning, as the lawyers struggled to get past the day's first witness, even he was expressing doubts about that goal. And just before 6:30 p.m., after the second Bush witness had finished testifying, Judge Sauls called a recess and scheduled the trial to resume on Sunday at 9 a.m.

"If we're going to have an hour and a half a witness, we're not going to finish," he had said earlier in the day, prompting a Gore lawyer to jump up and accuse a Bush lawyer of objecting too much, which prompted the Bush lawyer to accuse the Gore lawyer of asking too many objectionable questions.

"I hope we're going to proceed a little bit faster," Judge Sauls said wistfully when he adjourned for lunch at 1:30 p.m., having heard from only one witness.

Dec. 3, 2000, David Barstow and Somini Segupta

Judge Sauls Weighs Competing Legal Standards

The Tallahassee trial that could determine who won the presidency began with the lawyers outlining sharply different versions of the legal question before the court. How the court answers that question could determine whether Al Gore gets to count new votes or whether the lawyers for George W. Bush succeed in stopping new counts.

But before the judge addressed that question, the case gave the Gore team a symbolic victory of sorts: for the first time in what now seems a long legal battle, the focus was shifted in a pivotal case from lofty legal points to details on how votes were cast and counted in Florida. Still, through testimony about voting machines and statistics on voting patterns, the question hanging over the trial all day was that first one of the morning: what legal standard was Judge N. Sanders Sauls of Leon County Circuit Court to use in evaluating the evidence brought to court by the Democrats?

To David Boies the answer was clear: the judge should engage in what lawyers call "de novo" review, a brand-new consideration of whether legal votes were rejected or whether illegal votes were accepted. Such a review would be a matter of the judge making his own determination of whether ballots should or should not be accepted. "Our purpose today is to get to the evidence," Boies said, barely concealing the Gore team's need to get the case moving and to try to crash through any legal barriers erected by the Republican lawyers.

But the Republican lawyers came to court yesterday with their legal barriers already in place. They quickly told the judge that it was not up to him to engage in his own fresh review of the ballots. Instead, they argued, the only job of the court was to evaluate whether the county canvassing boards did their job without abusing their discretion in counting the ballots. That "abuse of discretion" standard is nearly the opposite of a new review of the facts by the court. The Republican lawyers said that the only legal standard the judge could use was to evaluate whether the county boards had used their powers reasonably, and that any results those boards certified to the secretary of state must be given "a presumption of correctness," as the Bush campaign's lawyer, Barry Richard, put it.

That presumption, of course, would be invaluable to the Bush legal effort because the Bush camp has the powerful advantage of the current winning total. From that posture, the Republicans win the case simply by not losing. If the tally stands as certified by Katherine Harris, they have won not only their case but also, quite possibly, the presidency. Richard said it was not the court's job to simply begin the counting all over again. If it were, he said, there would be no need for the canvassing boards in the first place. "We might as well take all of the ballots on election night and ship them to Tallahassee," he said.

As the day unfolded, each side tried to use the new focus to its own advantage. The Gore lawyers emphasized the possibilities for error by voters. The vice president's adversaries worked to portray his claims as absurd. The Gore evidence was a "voodoo presentation," said Joseph P. Klock Jr., the lawyer for Harris.

The judge will have to measure the testimony by the legal standard the two sides battled over. That dispute was a classic legal argument in which each side seems to be deeply concerned about legal principles, in this case about the proper role of the courts in reviewing the discretion of county canvassing boards. But, as in so many such arguments in the legal battle for the White

House, behind an intellectual dispute lay a deeply practical consequence.

If Judge Sauls is persuaded by the Democrats' argument, he would be free to simply make his own decision about what voters intended. And that could add votes to the Gore tally.

But if the judge is persuaded by the Republican assertion, his task would be much more constrained. He would only have the power to add to the canvassing boards' counts — if he decided that the boards abused their discretion.

Judge Sauls would have to decide, as Richard suggested, that the boards acted "in a fashion which no reasonable person could have."

David Boies did not dwell on this legal difference between the two sides, perhaps because it benefited him to simply go to the bottom line. "We believe those votes should be counted," he said several times.

Dec. 3, 2000, William Glaberson

day

26

SUNDAY, DECEMBER 3RD

A 14-HOUR DAY IN COURT

Judge Sauls had originally predicted the trial could be completed in a day, but it takes until nearly 11 p.m. Sunday, on the second day of the case, before the arguments and testimony are finished. Both sides say they are confident of victory, and the Gore lawyers, in particular, think they score big with what they call their "Perry Mason" moment, a surprise piece of evidence that undermines a key Bush witness on voting machines. But the Bush side also wins on several points, calling a statistician to cast doubt on the Gore team's interpretation of voting patterns among counties that use different voting machines. But time is clearly running out on Gore, so Cheney again calls on him to concede, suggesting that his failure to do so will affect the way history will judge him. Gore vows to press ahead.

IN LEON COUNTY, LAWYERS WRAP UP ARGUMENTS OVER THE VOTE

TALLAHASSEE —Veering between dramatic legal flourishes and dry statistical analysis, teams of Republican and Democratic lawyers completed their arguments in Al Gore's contest of the Florida presidential election. In their closing statements, both sides reminded the trial judge that his decision, which he promised by Monday morning, could determine who becomes the next president.

The two sides, along with lawyers for several county elections boards, voters and other parties involved in Gore's contest of Bush's certified victory, finished their closing arguments at 10:45 p.m., nearly 14 hours after they began the second day of the case. When they finished, the case was placed in the hands of N. Sanders Sauls of Leon County Circuit Court, whose close monitoring of the case and occasional sharp questioning gave no indication of his ultimate ruling. "I suppose at this time, counsel, I must tell you it was a case well tried and argued," said Sauls at the conclusion of the trial, his voice breaking after the long day.

In their arguments, the two sides differed as always over whether the judge should order a count of 14,000 disputed ballots from South Florida, which Gore's team believes contain hidden votes that will give him the election. Barry Richard, Bush's lead lawyer, said there was nothing in Florida law that permitted such a count, while David Boies, the chief lawyer for Gore, said a recent Florida Supreme Court ruling in the case supported the ability to count.

"It was a case well tried and argued."

—Judge N. Sanders Sauls, Leon County Circuit Court

Both sides left the courtroom predicting victory, although the Republican side was less cautious in doing so than the Democrats. Benjamin L. Ginsberg, Bush's general counsel, said his side's chances were "beautiful." Boies said he believed his team had put on a "strong case." On the other hand, the Democratic lawyers embraced afterward; the Republicans did not.

During the day's arguments, lawyers for Gore triumphantly used a surprise piece of evidence to get a Republican witness — a designer of the disputed punch-card machines — to admit that the devices used in Miami-Dade County and elsewhere can malfunction and fail to properly record a vote. That is precisely the point that Gore's legal team has been making in an effort to get Sauls to count the ballots.

But lawyers for Bush scored several major points as well, using a statistician and a voter to assert that there could be many reasons other than punch-card problems for a large number of unreadable ballots. The Republicans, who do not want Sauls to count the ballots locked up in the Leon County courthouse, said some voters may change their minds after placing a stylus next to a candidate's name, with one possible result being an indentation, while others may vote improperly because of ballot design.

But the various victories and losses in the testimony may not mean as much as the time spent in the testifying. With each hour that ticked by, Gore was pushed further from his goal of an immediate count of the ballots. His most realistic hope of gaining the presidency lies in overtaking Bush in a hand count, having the judge declare him the winner in Florida and then prevailing in the inevitable appeals. And all of that needs to happen by Dec. 12, when the State Legislature is scheduled to send Bush's electors to the Electoral College.

The Gore team's hope of finishing the trial on Saturday was dashed by nine hours of minute testimony on voting machines and their rubber backing, and today's proceedings moved only marginally faster. Just after a brief lunch recess, W. Dexter Douglass, one of Gore's lawyers, pleaded with Sauls to make a decision on whether to count the ballots, which he repeated with fervor later in the day. "If the court would rule we can count, we'd like the court to consider that as soon as possible," Douglass said. "I don't know how else to put this, but if we go another day or two, our remedy—" The judge interrupted. "It's not going to go another day or two," he said. But he refused the request for an immediate ruling, saying the Democrats needed to establish a legal foundation for doing so.

Voting Machines and Chads

The most surprising moment of the day occurred near the end of testimony by John Ahmann, a former mechanical engineer for I.B.M., who in the 1960's helped design the punch-card system still in use around the country and in several disputed Florida counties. Ahmann was presented by Bush's lawyers to testify that partly punched ballots were not likely to have been produced by failures in the machines, and he spent more than an hour defending the machines. "I seriously doubt that a voter would be unable to push a chad through on a normal voting device," Ahmann said.

But during cross-examination by Stephen Zack, a lawyer for Gore, an assistant ran up to Zack and handed him a copy of a patent that Ahmann had sought on a new design for his voting machine. In the patent application, which Zack read aloud, Ahmann said the old design — still in use in Miami-Dade County — could contribute to unreadable votes by leaving chads hanging on the ballot. It said the machine could become so clogged with chads that voters would not be able to punch all the way through, which "can cause serious errors to occur." This appeared to contradict an earlier statement he had made, that the machines did not need to be cleaned regularly because it was almost impossible for enough chads to build up to affect a voter's ability to punch.

Ahmann acknowledged that he had made the statement in his application and had also tried to get Miami-Dade to buy a new stylus he had designed that was supposed to make it less likely for a voter to fail to punch a card through. The county had refused to buy his new stylus design, he said, leaving them with one that does not punch as reliably. Democrats seized on the point. Ahmann also said under questioning that a hand count would be necessary in "very close elections."

Sauls, interested in this point, asked whether the machine card readers were so sensitive that they could see needle pricks. Ahmann said there had been occasions when machines could not read properly punched ballots, and would show different numbers when a recount took place, particularly if the ballots were not properly cleaned of hanging chads before being read. Boies said Ahmann turned out to be the Democrats' best witness, even though he was called by the other side.

Nonvoters and Statistics

Earlier in the day, a statistician brought in by the Bush team criticized an analysis presented on Saturday by Gore's statistician, who had said there were far fewer nonvotes for president recorded in counties using optical voting machines than in counties using punch cards. Democratic lawyers said this demonstrated that it was the voting system that caused the nonvotes by failing to record legitimate votes.

The Bush statistician, Laurentius Marais, said that that was an example of assuming that two things that appeared to be associated with each other were in fact causally related, using the old statistics example of how storks' nests in a town sometimes increase with the number of births. In fact, he said, there were wide variations in the number of nonvotes in counties using optical scanners, just as there were in counties using punch cards, and there was no proof of a relationship between the two.

"There is not enough information to draw any conclusions about a relationship," Marais said. He also said studies have shown that a confusing ballot design could drive voters away from a polling place without voting, citing in particular the same butterfly-ballot design used in Palm Beach County that Democrats have cited as a reason that people voted incorrectly. By the time he was finished, the confusion caused by the Palm Beach ballot had been cited by both sides to make their case.

Barry Richard, making the closing argument for Bush, summarized the now-familiar arguments, saying there was no right under Florida law for a manual recount. "The burden in this case is not on my client," Richard said. "We have a plaintiff seeking to overturn a major election, at least with respect to recounting all the votes. He brought in no evidence to suggest there would have been a difference in the election in Dade County, and the statute doesn't just say a difference in the vote, but also enough of a difference so one can conclude it might change the effect of the election."

Boies devoted his closing argument to the plea that he has been making for the last week — that Sauls simply count the disputed ballots, using a liberal standard of judgment as to the voters' intent. Boies said it no longer mattered whether the votes were counted before or after the certification of Bush's victory by the Florida secretary of state; a contest lawsuit, he said, makes that issue irrelevant, even though it is before the United States Supreme Court. And he reserved for the last word a reminder to the judge that Bush's side had essentially made the same point in a recent appearance before the state's highest court.

"They told the Florida Supreme Court that if there's a problem with this election, Gore and Senator Lieberman ought to challenge it in the contest phase, they ought bring a contest," Boies said. "And the Florida Supreme Court agreed with that. And the Florida Supreme Court said we're going to cut off the certification proceeding so we can get to the contest, and that's where we are now."

Dec. 4, 2000, David Firestone

GORE DIGS IN

WASHINGTON — Al Gore remained determined today to press on with his legal case in Florida, holding a high-level legal strategy session that included Walter E. Dellinger III, the former acting solicitor general of the Clinton administration and a highly respected constitutional scholar.

Today's meeting took on an air of urgency because of the ticking clock, the dwindling of Gore's legal options and the beginning of a potentially decisive week in the courts. Participants said no "fateful" decisions were made at the meeting, but they said they were bracing for a possible setback in at least one Florida court.

And Gore, taking his case again to the court of public opinion, gave every sign in a television interview tonight that he was digging in for at least two more weeks. The states are to choose their electors on Dec. 12, and the electors are to select a president on Dec. 18. In an interview tonight on CBS's *60 Minutes*, Gore said he had given little thought to concession, and admitted to no feelings of anger. "Anger is not — what point would there be to feeling that? I'm concentrating . . ." he said, breaking off in obvious discomfort with the line of questioning.

Gore tried to head off the possibility that Bush could win if the Florida Legislature chose a slate of electors for Bush. "I can't imagine that they would do that," Gore said. Asked if he had set his own deadline for when the contest would be over, Gore showed his resolve. "When the votes are counted," he said. "I think it's going to be completely over with by the middle of December." Asked if that meant Dec. 12, he said: "My expectation is that it will be over on or about then, but expectations have turned out to be not always accurate in this matter."

One of his top advisers, Warren Christopher, said that when the time came Gore would concede graciously, but that time was not now. "It's not over," Christopher said. Participants in the meeting said the team discussed the legal setbacks of Friday, the cases that could be decided in the next few days and sorted through some of Gore's options should the Florida Legislature call a special session this week. The Legislature, dominated by Republicans, is poised to award the state's 25 electors to Bush, even with the final tabulation of votes in doubt, potentially creating constitutional — and political — chaos. Gore's hopes rest on a hand count of nearly 10,000 ballots in Miami-Dade County that were not counted by machine. It is the possibility of Gore's garnering more votes in that hand count that has galvanized Republican leaders to consider a special session, perhaps as early as Wednesday.

The Gore camp is planning a rally for that day in Florida and has begun to try to sow doubts about the impartiality of Bush's brother, Jeb, the governor of Florida, and the potential for conflict of interest if he becomes involved in the process.

Christopher blamed the Bush team for trying to drag out the process in Sauls's courtroom to reduce the time available for a manual count of ballots. "When they name 95 witnesses, and yesterday reduced it to 20, and now down to 7, it certainly seems to me that the matter is going along very slowly," he said. Democratic officials said Gore, who is steeped in the legal maneuvering of his case, made the decision himself to call only two witnesses for his side, in part to speed up the process.

Asked if the Florida Legislature might provoke a constitutional crisis if it named its own slate of electors, even if the tallying of ballots was unresolved, Christopher answered gravely: "That would certainly be a serious mistake on their part. To substitute their will for the will of the voters of Florida, I think, would be very divisive for the country."

Dec. 4, 2000, Katharine Q. Seelye

CHENEY CALLS FOR GORE CONCESSION

WASHINGTON — Dick Cheney called today for Al Gore to concede the presidential election, saying history would regard Gore "in a better light if he were to bring this to a close in the very near future." Speaking on the NBC News program *Meet the Press*, Cheney also said he believed that the nation was on the verge of a recession and needed the stimulus of a tax cut like the one proposed by the Republicans. Both statements seemed designed in part to build public pressure in different ways for an end to Gore's legal challenge of the vote in Florida.

In the same interview, Cheney talked about troubling economic indicators and the importance of a new administration getting to work on them. The political conflict since the election has eaten up so much of the transition period, he said, that there could be damage to the effectiveness of the next administration. "Let's get on with it," said Cheney, the Republican vice-presidential candidate.

Warren Christopher said the vice president had no intention of giving up while the legal challenges in Florida and at the United States Supreme Court were under way. "It's late innings, but it's far from over," Christopher said on the CBS program *Face the Nation*. Cheney, he said, "is trying to hurry history along." "I can assure you that the vice president, when the time comes, will concede in a very gracious way," Christopher said. "He understands his obligations to the people of the country."

Cheney cited "growing evidence" that the economy was slowing abruptly, including declines in automobile sales and corporate earnings, and he asserted that the $1.3 trillion tax cut at the heart of the Bush campaign platform would be both economically appropriate and politically feasible. "We may well be on the front edge of a recession here, and I would hope that would change people's calculations with respect to the wisdom of the kind of tax cut that Governor Bush has recommended," Cheney said.

Cheney's comments about the possibility of a recession were unusual. Few politicians like to be the bearers of bad news or to be seen as pessimists. There have been many signs in the past few weeks that the economy has slowed abruptly after a series of increases in the interest rate by the Federal Reserve and a steep fall in many stock prices. But most economists believe that the economy remains basically healthy and that a slowdown is needed to avert a buildup of inflationary pressures. While there has been increased speculation among analysts about whether a recession might develop next year if the economy continues to decelerate, relatively few economists have predicted an end to what earlier this year became the longest business expansion on record.

Dec. 4, 2000, Richard W. Stevenson

day

27

MONDAY,

DECEMBER 4TH

★ ★ ★ ★ ★

A MAJOR SETBACK FOR GORE, BUSH GETS NO HELP

Judge N. Sanders Sauls rejects every Gore argument, handing him a devastating defeat. Lawyers for Bush hail their victory, while Gore's lawyers say they plan to appeal even while the judge is speaking. Two other cases involving absentee ballots are still in play, but an aura of pessimism pervades the Gore camp after the ruling. Bush maintains a public image of restraint in the wake of his legal victory, but his aides are jubilant. The circuit court ruling in a tiny, crowded Tallahassee courtroom may mark the beginning of the end of the nation's long millennial electoral melodrama. The U.S. Supreme Court finally responds but merely asks for clarification of a previous Florida Supreme Court ruling permitting recounts to continue past a statutory deadline, so Bush gets no federal relief.

FLORIDA JUDGE HANDS GORE A MAJOR DEFEAT

TALLAHASSEE — Sweeping away every legal argument presented by Al Gore, a Florida circuit judge today refused to overturn Bush's victory in the state's presidential election. The decision promised to make Gore's quest for the presidency more difficult than ever.

In an opinion read aloud to a hushed courtroom, N. Sanders Sauls said Gore had failed to prove a "reasonable probability" that the election would have been different if not for problems counting ballots in South Florida. In addition, the only way to properly contest the election, he said, would be to count every ballot in the state of Florida, not just in the three counties where Gore claimed irregularities. "The evidence does not establish any illegality, dishonesty, gross negligence, improper influence, coercion or fraud in the balloting and counting processes," Sauls said.

Gore's lawyers filed a notice that they would appeal the decision to the Florida Supreme Court even before the judge had stopped speaking. They also plan to continue their fight on another front — urging the state's highest court to rewrite an earlier decision that was favorable to Gore in order to comply with a United States Supreme Court ruling handed down today.

"For the first time there's a real sense that this is within our grasp."

— A Bush adviser responding to the court's judgment

But because the Gore team had poured all of its resources and hopes into the final contest decided today, the decision by Sauls made the Supreme Court's decision seem a relatively minor setback. Sauls's decision, the clearest victory yet secured by Bush's legal team, was so broad a refutation of the vice president's contest of the election that it stunned lawyers from both sides.

"This was as complete a victory as I've ever gotten in a trial," said Philip Beck, who interrogated most of the witnesses on behalf of the Bush legal team during the two-day trial that ended late Sunday night. Barry Richard, Bush's lead trial lawyer, said, "Sauls got every point, even one I didn't think of." He would not say what that was.

Some lawyers on the Gore team privately acknowledged that the ruling was a devastating blow, possibly one from which they would not recover. The team has already argued in court that to have any chance at overturning the election, it needed a court to begin the five-day process of counting 14,000 disputed ballots last weekend. Now the earliest they can hope for a ruling from the Florida Supreme Court is Wednesday or Thursday, putting them perilously close to the moment on Dec. 12 when the State Legislature sends Bush's presidential electors to the Electoral College.

Nonetheless, David Boies, Gore's ever-optimistic chief trial lawyer, said he remained hopeful of receiving a positive ruling from the appeal and said there was still time to count the ballots. "It was certainly a very broad ruling," Boies said, immediately after hearing it. "Whether or not you think it is a strong ruling depends on the extent to which you think the ruling is right or not. While we're obviously disappointed in the substantive results we got from Sauls, we do genuinely appreciate and respect the fact that he made that decision now, so that we have meaningful opportunity to appeal to the Florida Supreme Court."

Gore's lawyers argued in particular that Sauls went beyond the language of the Florida statute authorizing election contests in making his ruling. The statute, repeatedly cited by Boies during the trial, says that one of the grounds for a contest is "receipt of a number of illegal votes or rejection of a number of legal votes sufficient to change or place in doubt the result of the election." But the judge quoted a 1982 decision by a Florida appeals court that said the standard of proof in such cases is high. That decision, which denied the contest to a local election said, "It is not enough to show a reasonable possibility that election results could have been altered by the irregularities; a reasonable probability that the results would have been changed must be shown."

In concluding that Gore had failed to meet that standard, Sauls seemed to be dismissing their argument during the case that an initial sample of the disputed ballots in Miami-Dade showed that if the results were extrapolated mathematically to the rest of the county, Gore was gaining enough votes that it was worth counting all of the ballots to see if he would have won. The judge clearly agreed with a statistician presented by the Republicans, who said there was no scientific basis for projecting a victory by Gore based on the small sample, because the sample was mostly of Democratic precincts.

The judge also seemed to be rejecting the Democrats' argument that the several hundred votes for Gore that turned up in the incompleted manual recounts in Miami-Dade and Palm Beach Counties also should be considered as evidence of a potentially wrong outcome in a race where the winning margin was 537 votes. The judge acknowledged that there was voter error and "less than total accuracy" in the punch-card voting machines in Palm Beach and Miami-Dade Counties, which he said the counties had known about for many years. But lacking proof of a reasonable probability of a different outcome, such problems were not enough to overturn the election. He added that the two county election boards did not "abuse their discretion" in deciding not to manually count ballots (as happened in Miami-Dade) or to use a strict standard for judging the intent of voters (as happened in Palm Beach).

By requiring Gore to show that the boards had abused their discretion, the judge used precisely the language that Richard had asked him to employ throughout the trial, though Boies just as persistently argued there was no such language in the Florida statutes.

This argument, which was also raised by several Republican intervenors in the case who protested that their counties were not being recounted, was considered so outlandish by the Gore team that it spent almost no time refuting it during the trial.

In analyzing the opinion, Boies did not say he would have done anything differently during the trial. But he made it clear the team's appeal of the decision would focus on areas where it believes Sauls went beyond the plain statutes. "Remember, the statute says you need only have a sufficient number of votes to change or place in doubt the result of the election," Boies said. "And I don't think anybody can say that the result of the election has not been placed in doubt by the evidence that is there. And that's particularly true when you take into account that he had not even looked at any of the ballots."

Anticipating a possible defeat, Gore's lawyers had already begun working on a possible appeal, as had the Bush team. But the United States Supreme Court decision today, ordering a new opinion in an earlier case about whether Ms. Harris could reject manual counts, presented a new burden for both sides.

The earlier case is all but moot; since Ms. Harris already certified Bush as the winner after a hand count in Broward County, the only practical difference if the hand counts are ruled out are the 393 votes Gore picked up in Broward. But because those votes may still become crucial, both sides want to preserve them and say they will submit briefs on their positions to the Florida Supreme Court on the earlier case. The court announced late today that it would accept 20-page briefs on the matter until 3 p.m. Tuesday.

At the same time, however, both sides will be submitting briefs on the appeal of Sauls's decision. Lawyers for both sides said they would not be surprised if the high court decided to consolidate the cases, holding oral arguments and issuing an opinion on both at the same time. But Republican lawyers said they believe the strength of Sauls's opinion made it possible that the Florida court would not take the case at all.

While Gore's lawyers were dealt a setback on this case, they continue to closely monitor two cases challenging the validity of absentee ballots and scheduled to go to trial on Wednesday. Local Democrats filed the suits, arguing that Republicans had been allowed to improperly amend incomplete applications for absentee ballots that had been rejected by county elections officials. If a judge rules in Gore's favor, the cases could produce a net gain of thousands of votes for Gore, although the Gore team has declined to join their case because winning would require disenfranchising voters.

Dec. 5, 2000, David Firestone

Pessimism on the Vice President's Team

TALLAHASSEE — Several of Al Gore's legal and political advisers and leading Democrats expressed little hope tonight that the Florida Supreme Court would overturn a Leon County Circuit Court ruling, leaving Gore with no more options in his quest for the White House.

Many of these Democrats said that while they had braced themselves for an adverse ruling from N. Sanders Sauls, the decision was more definitive — and dismissive — than they had imagined. "I'm not overly confident," Edward G. Rendell, the general chairman of the Democratic National Committee, said in an interview. "It would be disingenuous to not say we would be in a better position had we won in the court." Asked about Gore's prospects, he said: "I don't want to quantify it. Obviously this makes it more difficult, but not impossible."

While Gore's lawyers were described tonight as frantically drafting a legal brief, one member of the team was even more doubtful than Rendell. "Downhill. Downhill. Downhill," he said of the vice president's case. "We're like an automobile with the brakes that have been disconnected. I'm not saying that this thing couldn't be turned around, but this is not going to be easy, obviously." One of Gore's top political aides put it this way: "People expected we were going to lose with this judge. But it's one thing to expect something — and another to actually experience it."

Many of the Democrats and Gore associates said the developments were the most crushing yet in a turbulent month since the election, and no one was willing to predict flatly that Gore would capture the presidency. Beyond the circuit court ruling here, one Gore lawyer noted that the Supreme Court's more equivocal ruling on a Republican appeal "was not a wipeout" but was a troubling psychological setback because it added to the uncertainty. "The fact that both these decisions were rendered on the same day creates a toxic public relations situation for Gore," he said. Asked for Gore's options beyond the appeal, he added: "There's no place else to go."

William M. Daley, Gore's campaign chairman, did not dispute that there were no options beyond the appeal. "Obviously, the clock is a problem," he said. Describing a conversation he had with Gore tonight, Daley said, "He understands it was a blow, but he also knows that he's got great lawyers." Daley said he was not particularly worried that prominent Democrats would object to the appeal because, no matter what, the whole morass might be over in days.

Mark Fabiani, Gore's deputy campaign manager did not sound as confident but offered a glimmer of hope for his boss. "The worm has turned many times during these tumultuous weeks," he said. "The question is: has the worm expired from exhaustion or does he have one more turn left in him? We're about to find out in the Florida Supreme Court."

Dec. 5, 2000, Richard L. Berke

Bush Takes Restrained Tone

AUSTIN — Publicly, advisers to Bush spoke in muted tones, with measured words, about what happened in Florida today, portraying it not as a victory for Bush but as a matter of justice. There was no celebration, no jubilation.

But privately, aides and advisers to Bush acknowledged that this was a big, big day — and a big, big step down the path toward a final and irrevocable determination that Bush was the next president. At the campaign headquarters here, some workers cheered when they heard the news from Florida. "For the first time," one adviser said, "there's a real sense that this is within our grasp, that it's real. There's a different mood than there was just 24 hours ago."

If Bush felt that way, he was not stepping out to say so or to revel in any way. His one public appearance came before the crucial ruling by N. Sanders Sauls of Leon County Circuit Court, and he projected an image of serenity and emotional distance from the legal developments in Florida. But Bush took ample note of them. His sense of its significance was suggested by his response. Midway through Sauls's televised comments, almost as soon as he first said that there was no credible evidence that a different count would change the election results in Florida, Bush called Karen Hughes, his communications director, and expressed his satisfaction. He also quickly called Donald L. Evans, the chairman of his campaign and perhaps his closest friend.

One adviser said the Bush campaign was carefully tempering its response. "We feel that it's probably better, both politically and in terms of a legal strategy, not, when you win one of these legal cases, to be doing a lot of high fives," the adviser said. Other advisers said they still felt minor stabs of worry, given the action still to come from the Florida Supreme Court and the unpredictability of everything since Election Day. But they clearly saw today as something of a milestone. "Let me put it to you this way," said one Bush adviser. "I think the sun is quickly setting on Al Gore."

Dec. 5, 2000, Frank Bruni

U.S. Justices Send Case Back to Florida High Court

WASHINGTON — The United States Supreme Court avoided a definitive ruling in the Florida election case by stepping back from the brink of disunity and asking the Florida Supreme Court to clarify the basis of its Nov. 21 ruling that permitted recounts to continue past a statutory deadline. The court's unsigned, six-page opinion was unanimous, though the sentiments among the justices on one or more issues in the case almost certainly were not.

The result did not particularly favor either side, though it did add a potentially time-consuming twist to a situation in which the ticking clock is not Al Gore's friend. At the same time, the inconclusive resolution deprived Bush of the Supreme Court victory that many in his camp thought was within his grasp after Friday's argument. As a technical matter, the justices vacated the Florida Supreme Court's decision and sent the case back to that court's jurisdiction for clarification of one statutory and one constitutional point. The justices indicated their concerns with the state court's opinion in an opaque manner that papered over, barely, their own differences.

The Florida court today ordered lawyers for both sides to file briefs by 3 p.m. Dec. 5. The state court could respond very quickly to the justices' decision by adding a few sentences and reissuing its 40-page opinion. It is possible that the United States Supreme Court would then accept a request from Bush to take up the case a second time. But if the state court follows the road map set out for it in the ruling, the case might no longer present a federal question for the justices to review.

In any event, it was clear by the time of the Supreme Court argument on Friday that the legal center of gravity in the case had largely shifted back to the court in Florida, where Gore's vote-counting challenge has moved from the protest phase, which applied before Bush was certified as the winner of the state's 25 electoral votes, to the postcertification contest phase.

In fact, several hours after the Supreme Court's decision was announced, N. Sanders Sauls of Leon County Circuit Court in Tallahassee dealt Gore a major setback by rejecting his request for further recounts.

In seeking clarification from the Florida Supreme Court today, the justices grasped at a suggestion that first emerged during Friday's oral arguments in a comment from Justice Ruth Bader Ginsburg. "I suppose there would be a possibility for this court to remand for clarification," she said during a fast-moving debate over whether in ordering the certification deadline extended for 12 days, the Florida court had invoked the state constitution or had simply engaged in the ordinary, nonconstitutional process of interpreting state law.

The distinction mattered, at least to some justices, because one prong of Bush's legal attack on the Florida Supreme Court decision was based on a reading of a federal constitutional provision that would make it illegitimate for a state court to rely on its state constitution in curbing the legislature's authority to determine how presidential electors should be appointed.

Dec. 5, 2000, Linda Greenhouse

day

28

TUESDAY,

DECEMBER 5TH

★ ★ ★ ★ ★

AL GORE, OPTIMIST

Although he's facing another week of complex legal maneuvering, Al Gore expresses optimism about his contest of the Florida election results. His allies generally support his quest, but some, including Senator Joseph Lieberman, are more cautious. Gore believes that the voting issues will be decided in the Florida Supreme Court, and he focuses on absentee-ballot application suits in two Florida counties where Republican officials added information to incomplete applications. The Florida Supreme Court moves quickly to hear the Gore contest of the presidential election. In federal court, Bush lawyers ask the U.S. Court of Appeals for the 11th Circuit to declare that manual recounts of votes in Florida are unconstitutional. As a result of the controversies in Florida, members of Congress from both parties introduce proposals to modernize American election practices.

COURT DEFEAT LEAVES GORE UNBOWED

WASHINGTON — Unbowed and undeterred, Al Gore declined today to put a time limit on how long he would continue his election contest and suggested instead an expansion of his legal avenues to pursue the White House. He also described himself as optimistic about his chances of prevailing in his month-old political and legal struggle — even after suffering a sweeping defeat in a Florida court on Monday.

Gore said he expected the Florida Supreme Court to be the final arbiter of his situation, and indeed the court scheduled arguments on the appeal for Thursday morning, Dec. 7. But he also suggested that there was more than one case that might come before that court and on which he was pinning his hopes. In particular, Gore dwelled at length on the details of a ballot dispute in Seminole and Martin Counties, suggesting that thousands of votes could be at stake. These cases are to be heard Wednesday.

Whatever the merits of the cases from Seminole and Martin Counties, Gore's eagerness, both today and in an interview Sunday on CBS's *60 Minutes*, to delve into the minutiae of those ballots stood in stark contrast to the posture struck today by his running mate, Joseph Lieberman. Where Gore gave no sign of letting up, Lieberman spoke in more muted tones, even using the language of concession as he thanked Democrats on Capitol Hill for their support. He and Gore, he said, were "proud of the race we ran," a phrase familiar to anyone who has had to concede a loss.

Lieberman, who met with Congressional Democrats this morning, has been under more personal pressure than Gore to acknowledge that the odds are against them. His presence on Capitol Hill, Democratic aides said, gave Lieberman more of an opportunity to be humbled by his colleagues, even as most expressed their continued support of the ticket. But the election of Gore and Lieberman would not be entirely welcome news in the Senate. It would mean Lieberman would have to quit his Senate seat, leaving the governor of Connecticut, a Republican, to appoint a replacement and thus tipping the balance in the chamber to 51-49 in favor of the Republicans. This would undermine the Democrats' current claim to a 50-50 power share with Republicans.

Gore clearly feels wronged by what happened in Seminole and Martin Counties, where, the suits alleged, election officials improperly allowed Republican Party workers to correct absentee ballot applications that otherwise would have been rejected. "More than enough votes were potentially taken away from Democrats because they were not given the same access that Republicans were," Gore said, describing in detail what happened in those counties. He predicted that those cases would also land in the Florida Supreme Court. But, asked how those cases would affect his decision on whether to continue or concede, he replied: "I don't know." Asked if he would "hang on" while they were settled, he said: "Those are hypotheticals on top of hypotheticals, and I'm just not comfortable dealing with a hypothetical like that."

On Sunday, Dec. 3, he had asserted as he has for weeks that the continuing election limbo would be resolved by the middle of December, but he omitted that prediction today. His aides suggested that these suits were likely to be resolved by the end of the week anyway, so any extra time allowed for them was probably moot. Still, he avoided any mention of a deadline in terms of time, only in terms of venue, meaning the Florida Supreme Court would be the end of the line.

As he pursues his appeal, Gore still enjoys the support of Democrats on Capitol Hill. In fact some Congressional Democrats seemed, if anything, to be more adamant in their support than they were the day before. Representatives Peter Deutsch and Corrine Brown, Florida Democrats, told their colleagues about some of the problems in the Florida ballot counting, and some said that these details made them more mad than ever. "It's clear it wasn't great news for Gore yesterday," said Representative Nita M. Lowey, a New York Democrat. "But Corrine Brown repeated the extent of the irregularities that I wasn't aware of. It made someone like me feel like we have a responsibility to move forward with the judicial process."

After a meeting with Lieberman and House Democrats, Representative Richard A. Gephardt of Missouri, the Democratic leader, said, "Al Gore and Joe Lieberman enjoy strong support in our caucus for what they're doing to try to get every vote counted in Florida." Senator Tom Daschle of South Dakota, the Democratic leader, said that Gore "has as much time as he needs to ensure a full and fair recount."

Ron Klain, Gore's former chief of staff and now a top political adviser who is overseeing the Florida legal challenges, cast Gore in almost Churchillian tones. "In some ways, this most difficult moment for Al Gore has turned out to be his finest hour," Klain said on NBC's *Today*.

Dec. 5, 2000, Katharine Q. Seelye

Democrats See Hope in Absentee Ballot Application Trials

TALLAHASSEE—When Michael A. Leach, the Republican Party's regional director here in North Florida, took his laptop computer to the Seminole County elections offices this fall and added missing identification numbers to roughly 2,000 absentee-ballot applications from Republican voters, he was trying to help out George W. Bush in what promised to be a very close election.

But Leach's actions are now the target of a lawsuit, filed by a supporter of Vice President Al Gore, that threatens Bush's certified victory in Florida and could mean Gore's one last chance to become president if the State Supreme Court turns down his own suit seeking to overturn the Florida results. The Seminole suit, which goes to trial here on Wednesday along with a similar one from Martin County, argues that it was illegal to change the county's ballot applications after they had been rejected for the insufficient data, and seeks the discarding of all 15,215 absentee ballots cast there. Those ballots favored Bush by 2 to 1, and so a successful outcome for the suit would mean a net loss of 4,800 votes for him — enough to overturn the results of the election.

Until recently, Gore had kept his distance from the Seminole and Martin suits, which, in calling for disqualification of votes, are largely inconsistent with what has been his chief argument during this month-old post-election challenge: that every vote should be counted. But at a Washington news conference today, Gore spoke extensively about the matter, saying that what happened in

Seminole County, near Orlando, "doesn't seem fair to me" and adding that he expected the case to be decided ultimately by the Florida Supreme Court.

Republicans argue that any infraction involved in their completing the rejected applications was a mere technicality that should not be sufficient to discard thousands of legally cast ballots. They note that both the Democratic and Republican Parties in Florida routinely send thousands of filled-out absentee-ballot applications to party members (who then need only sign them and mail them to elections offices) and that many of those that the Republicans sent out this year simply lacked voter identification numbers, because of a printer's error.

Leach, the Republican official who completed the lacking applications, said in a deposition filed in court here today that he had been instructed by the state party's political director "to go to the Seminole County supervisor of elections office and correct a mistake that the Republican Party of Florida had made on absentee ballot request forms." "I'm a military man, I follow orders," Leach, a 29-year-old veteran of the Air Force, said in that deposition.

The Republicans have suggested that the case is being engineered by the Gore campaign, and have repeatedly tried to highlight the campaign's ties to the plaintiff, Harry Jacobs, a Democratic lawyer. In a deposition given to Republican lawyers, Jacobs said that he donated $50,000 to Democratic candidates this year and that he spent more than $50,000 producing a television commercial criticizing Dick Cheney. Jacobs acknowledged in the deposition that he had spoken about the suit with Mitchell Berger, a lawyer for Gore. But he says the case is being pursued by himself alone, with his own lawyers.

Nikki Ann Clark of Leon County Circuit Court, who is presiding over the case from Seminole County, dealt with that law today at a hearing where lawyers for Bush argued that not all the information that the applicant was supposed to disclose — nine things in all — was mandatory. "In a sense," Clark asked skeptically, "what you're telling me is that the Legislature said the person making the request must disclose these nine things, but don't worry about it if they don't?"

The Republicans have tried to have Clark removed from the case. They note that she served as an aide to a Democratic governor of Florida, Lawton Chiles. And, in a motion for her removal, they argued that Bush's brother Jeb, Florida's current governor, passed her over for appointment to an appellate court. That motion to remove Clark was denied by her, was appealed and was then denied again.

Very few of the facts in this case are in dispute. Indeed, all parties agreed today to sign a stipulation as to basically what happened in Seminole County: The supervisor of elections, Sandra Goard, a Republican, allowed Leach to use her office for some 15 days to add identification numbers to the incomplete ballot applications. Similarly incomplete Democratic applications, having also been rejected, piled up in Ms. Goard's office, with no action taken, she has acknowledged. What is in dispute is whether what the Republicans did is illegal, and if so, what, if anything, can be done about it now.

Richman said that although fewer than 2,000 absentee votes were cast by people whose ballot applications had been altered, there was no way to separate those votes from the absentee votes that were cast from correct applications. So, he said, the court should throw out all 15,215, or at least devise some mathematical formula to alter the vote count to reflect what it should be. To that, Ken Wright, a lawyer for the Florida Republican Party, declared, "The remedy that's being sought is draconian, to take away the votes of 15,000 people."

The case from Martin County is similar. There, Republican workers actually removed incomplete applications from the elections office, then completed them and returned them. The plaintiffs in that case are seeking to have 9,773 absentee ballots discarded; that would result in a net loss of more than 2,000 votes for Bush.

Dec. 6, 2000, Michael Cooper

Florida Supreme Court Moves Quickly to Hear Gore Contest of the Election

TALLAHASSEE — The Florida Supreme Court moved quickly today to set a Thursday hearing for Gore's contest of the presidential election, giving his lawyers what could be their last opportunity to argue the case before the Dec. 12 deadline for naming the state's electors.

The decision to hold another televised hearing before the seven justices raised the possibility that the court could issue a definitive ruling on the case before the weekend. If they rule against Gore, he and his lawyers have suggested that they might not appeal the decision to the United States Supreme Court. If the high court rules in Gore's favor, the following few days could be filled with a frenzied counting of 14,000 disputed ballots from South Florida, which Democratic lawyers say might contain hidden votes for the vice president. Bush's lawyers would almost certainly appeal such a decision to the high court in Washington.

At the same time as both sides were preparing their briefs in the contest case, they also submitted briefs to the Florida Supreme Court today on the ruling handed down by the United States Supreme Court on Monday. Earlier this month, the Florida court had extended the deadline by which the secretary of state had to accept manual recounts from county election boards, but on Monday the United States court vacated that ruling and sent it back to the Florida court to be rewritten.

Gore's legal brief, as expected, urged the Florida court to re-enter its ruling and clarify that it made its decision based on an interpretation of the state's election laws, not the constitution. "This court did not — as the U.S. Supreme Court worried — rely upon the Florida Constitution to circumscribe the Legislature's authority to establish a method for the selection of electors, under the United States Constitution," the Gore brief said. "This court's discussion of the Florida Constitution merely confirmed that its statutory interpretation was consistent with the principles of that Constitution."

Bush's team suggested the court simply drop its ruling and revert to a trial judge's ruling that Secretary of State Katherine Harris was within her rights to certify the election without the manual counts. But Republican lawyers also had another suggestion they said was better: the court should simply turn down Gore's appeal of the contest, and then it would not have to take up the earlier case at all.

If the court is forbidden by the United States Constitution to extend the deadline for the manual counts — which the Bush team argues is the real import of the United States Supreme Court ruling on Monday — then by the same principle, it cannot allow a counting of dimpled ballots in only a few counties, the Bush brief argues. To do so would be to change state election law in the same illegal manner as the earlier ruling, the brief says.

If the court dismisses Gore's appeal of the contest first, the Bush brief says, the earlier case sent back by the Supreme Court in Washington will be moot, because the same Republican electors will be sent to the Electoral College. In that case, says the brief, "judicial economy will be served and this court will avoid the complex federal and constitutional issues implicated in this remanded case. And, of course, the period of uncertainty and instability regarding Florida's participation in the presidential election will be brought to an end and final resolution will be achieved for the 2000 presidential election."

Republican state legislators also filed a brief with the Florida court urging it to drop its earlier ruling and impose the original deadlines for the manual counts. The Legislature, not the court, has the power to choose the presidential electors of the state, the brief said, and such a ruling would allow the state to avoid a confrontation between the two branches.

Dec. 6, 2000, David Firestone

Bush Lawyers Again Urge Federal Court to Reject Florida Recounts

ATLANTA — Lawyers for Bush sought to fortify their legal advantage in Florida today by asking a federal appeals court here to rule that the manual recount of presidential ballots in that state was unconstitutional because it had been conducted selectively in only a few counties. With the election litigants focused mainly on the Florida Supreme Court, today's hearing before the United States Court of Appeals for the 11th Circuit had the feel of a proceeding that might turn out to be moot.

But lawyers for both sides warned that the case could become very significant if the State Supreme Court sided with Gore and overturned Monday's decision by a circuit court judge to uphold the state's certification of Bush as the winner of Florida's 25 electoral votes. In that event, the appellate judges here could provide another line of defense for Bush by invalidating the unfinished manual recounts that reduced Bush's lead in the state to 537 votes.

"I think this case is very important because you don't know what the Florida Supreme Court is going to do," said Theodore B. Olson, the Washington lawyer who represented Bush here today. He added: "No one has won this election as far as I can tell. It's still up in the air."

Chief Judge R. Lanier Anderson III said at the close of today's hearing that the court understood both the import and urgency of the case and would work diligently toward a decision. In today's appeal, which was heard by all 12 judges of the 11th Circuit, Olson asked the court to reverse a Nov. 13 decision by a federal district judge in Miami.

Then, as today, Bush's lawyers argued that the recounts were unconstitutional because they diluted the value of votes that were cast in counties where Gore did not request manual recounts. That dilution, the Bush lawyers maintained, violated the equal protection, due process and First Amendment rights guaranteed by the Constitution. Olson said he was not objecting to manual recounts per se. But he emphasized that neither state law nor the Florida courts have established consistent standards for determining how county canvassing boards are to determine a voter's intent in cases when a chad is not fully detached from a ballot. "That leads to an arbitrary and capricious decision and individualized decision making," Olson argued.

Judge Middlebrooks ruled last month that the dispute more properly belonged in the state courts than in his federal courtroom, and he questioned the substance of the Bush case. Four days later, the 11th Circuit denied the Bush camp's request for an immediate injunction to stop the recounts, but it preserved the right to hear the case on the merits, and that is the case it took up today.

Teresa Wynn Roseborough, a lawyer for the Florida Democratic Party and by extension Gore, argued that the case did not belong in the federal courts so long as state remedies had not been exhausted. She turned the Republicans' dilution argument on its head by maintaining that any potential impact on votes in one county was insufficient reason to not recount votes in another county. "No citizen has the right to insist that another citizen's vote not be counted," she said. Roseborough and other lawyers for the defendants contended that the Bush camp had not established that the recounts posed a threat of irreparable harm, the legal standard for granting the injunction sought by Bush.

Dec. 6, 2000, Kevin Sack

day

29

WEDNESDAY,
DECEMBER 6TH

★ ★ ★ ★ ★

FLORIDA LEGISLATURE DIMS GORE'S HOPES

Gore's lawyers file what they say is his final appeal in his presidential fight, a request to the State Supreme Court to permit counting 14,000 disputed ballots they believe will favor Gore. Despite angry protests from Democrats, Republican leaders of the State Legislature set a special session to appoint presidential electors supporting Bush, asserting their desire to have finality in the election process. In Leon County Circuit Court, trials to disqualify thousands of absentee ballots because of alleged Republican tampering get under way, and a U.S. Appeals Court hands Gore a legal victory by ruling that manual recounts of presidential ballots should not be barred.

LEGISLATORS MOVE ON ELECTORS, COURT SET TO HEAR APPEAL

"On December 12th we may find ourselves in a position that calls for our involvement..."
– John McKay, President Florida Senate

★ ★ ★

TALLAHASSEE — Hours after Al Gore's lawyers filed what they said was his final appeal in his quest for the presidency, the Republican leaders of the Florida Legislature called a special session for Friday to appoint a set of presidential electors who would support George W. Bush.

The Republican legislators said the various unresolved court cases, including Gore's appeal in the Florida Supreme Court to be heard Thursday morning, threatened to replace or "taint" the slate of electors pledged to Bush, who are scheduled to be appointed on Tuesday.

In what amounted to a warning shot fired by one branch of state government toward another, the leaders said the special session would ratify the original Republican electors in the event a court reverses Bush's victory in Florida. "The clock ticketh, and we're not sure how long the Florida Supreme Court will take," said State Senator Jim King, the majority leader.

Democratic lawmakers, who lacked the numbers to block the move, said it was a purely partisan effort orchestrated by Bush and his brother Jeb, the governor of Florida. But Senate President John McKay, a Bush supporter, insisted that the session was designed simply to "ensure that the voters of Florida are not disenfranchised."

If the State Supreme Court agrees to Gore's request to count 14,000 disputed ballots and eventually finds him the winner, the Legislature's move raises the possibility that two sets of presidential electors could be sent to Washington from Florida: one appointed by the court and one appointed by the Legislature. Such a dispute would have to be resolved by Congress, and possibly by the United States Supreme Court.

For the rest of the week, the State Supreme Court will remain the focus of Gore's legal attention. After a broad defeat on Monday, Dec. 4 in the first phase of their lawsuit contesting Bush's victory in Florida, Gore's lawyers filed papers today asking the Florida Supreme Court to count the disputed ballots before time runs out in six days. In almost emotional terms, Gore's lawyers said the court must reject what they called Bush's strategy of delay.

"Now is the last chance for a legal judgment to be rendered in this case," said the 54-page brief, filed at midday. "In but a few more days, only the judgment of history will be left to fall upon a system where deliberate obstruction has succeeded in achieving delay — and where further delays risk succeeding in handing democracy a defeat." The appellate brief argued that the ruling against Gore on Monday by N. Sanders Sauls of Leon County Circuit Court was riddled with errors of fact and law, based on court decisions that have been superseded. The brief even used a Bush legal arguments, accusing Sauls of going so far in rewriting state election law that he violated the federal statute prohibiting changes to the law after an election.

But in their brief, Bush's lawyers said Sauls's decision was "plainly correct," and told the justices they had no choice but to accept his finding that Gore failed to prove the disputed ballots would change the outcome of the election. "The best exercise of this court's discretion, in Florida's interest and the nation's would be to decline to hear this appeal and to bring an end to the many weeks of election discord and uncertainty for all the voters," the brief said. It added that any effort to count ballots in the days left before the state's electors were chosen on Dec. 12 would be futile and unfeasible.

Gore has poured all of his legal resources into this lawsuit, and his lawyers have acknowledged that his appeal of Sauls's strongly worded ruling against him would be difficult. Although the other unresolved court cases could affect the outcome of the race, Gore's legal advisers said they planned no appeal to the United States Supreme Court if the Florida Supreme Court ruled against the vice president. That raised the possibility his contest could end before the weekend, if the court was to rule on Thursday night or Friday.

A ruling in Gore's favor, which the Bush forces would certainly appeal to the United States Supreme Court, would first involve a decision to count the disputed ballots from Miami-Dade and Palm Beach Counties, which remain in the Leon County Courthouse along with 1.2 million others. To save time, Gore's brief urged the Supreme Court to do the counting rather than send the matter back to the trial court.

Gore's brief, using the language of the state statute that permits election contests, said evidence at the trial demonstrated that Bush's certified victory in Florida was based on both illegal votes and the rejection of legal votes. Because the best evidence that legal votes were rejected lies in the disputed ballots, the court must count them. According to the brief, "It simply cannot be the case that a candidate must prove his or her claim in order to get access to the very evidence needed to prove that case. . . To gather the ballots in question, to segregate any subsets to be counted, to determine who should conduct a count, to ascertain what standards govern the count, and to ensure fairness, openness and regularity — all before Dec. 12 comes and goes — is all but entirely unfeasible. And even then, no doubt, the litigation would continue, key federal questions would be unresolved and subject to appeal, and the public's distrust in the ultimate outcome would grow."

Dec. 7, 2000, David Firestone

Bitter Disagreements over Lawmakers' Action

TALLAHASSEE — After hemming and hawing for more than a week about the need to convene a special session of the State Legislature immediately, Florida's Republican Senate president and speaker of the House said today that the pressure of time had forced them to act. Nervous about meeting a deadline of next Tuesday for states to pick electors, and with Al Gore having made remarks indicating that he is not ready to concede, John McKay and Tom Feeney signed a proclamation today convening a special session of the Legislature beginning on Friday.

"On Dec. 12, we may find ourselves in a position that calls for our involvement should there be no finality to the contests that are still pending," McKay said in a joint news conference with Feeney to announce the decision. "And it is possible that there may be more filed before this day is out. It would be irresponsible of us if we failed to put a safety net in place under the current court conditions."

House and Senate Democrats were quick to denounce the move, saying it was more evidence that the Republican-dominated Legislature was taking its marching orders from the campaign of George W. Bush. "The only thing missing from the proclamation was a postmark from Austin, Tex.," said Lois Frankel of West Palm Beach, leader of the House Democrats. "I think it is naive to believe the speaker and the president of the Senate are really calling the shots here." Frankel called the action "ultimately a partisan act that is unnecessary, unfair and unjust."

McKay and Feeney attended a dinner for new House members on Tuesday at which Jeb Bush spoke. But both denied that they had been influenced by the Bush campaign. McKay acknowledged that he had voted for Bush but said his decision to sign the proclamation was not a partisan one. "I embark on a special session not to advocate either position of the two protagonists but as a constitutional officer with a responsibility to represent the best interests of all Floridians."

Feeney dismissed the notion that he was doing the bidding of the Bush campaign by saying he had had "no advice, no guidance, no counsel from either campaign." Saying that the announcement today marked a "very solemn and important occasion," Feeney said he was compelled to call for the special session because "we have a duty to protect Florida's participation in the Electoral College."

The legislation to appoint electors will be a resolution not requiring the governor's signature, avoiding the need for Jeb Bush to take part in the controversial action. The resolution would go before the House and Senate for a first reading on Friday and would be sent to committees on Monday. It would get a second reading on the Senate floor on Tuesday and be voted on on Wednesday.

Dec. 12 is the deadline for states to appoint electors. If election results are still in question after that, the Republicans say, Congress may not recognize them when it formalizes the election in January, making it necessary for the Legislature to act. Republican leaders are expected to reappoint electors who were selected before Election Day and who were certified by Secretary of State Katherine Harris last month.

There were other dynamics behind today's decision, including the deep philosophical divide between the Legislature's conservative leaders and the Florida Supreme Court, dominated by appointees of Democratic governors. The two bodies have clashed bitterly and publicly in recent years, most notably over the Legislature's effort to limit death-penalty appeals. After this effort was thwarted by the State Supreme Court, some Republican legislators even floated the possibility of bringing impeachment proceedings against some of the justices. There has also been talk of expanding the court to allow Jeb Bush to appoint several justices.

Again and again today, even as thousands of Democrats massed in front of the Capitol protesting any intervention by the Legislature, it was clear that Republicans here were worried about the potential fallout of convening a special session. They emphasized their reluctance in choosing this course and spoke of waiting until the very last moment. They insisted that this was about process, not politics, and that the only insurance policy they were concerned about was one that would keep Florida voters from being disenfranchised.

Still, when pressed for a scenario under which the Florida Legislature would ratify Gore's electors, Webster sketched a chain of events that, in terms of probability, was about as likely as winning the lottery and being struck by lightning all at once. He said Gore's slate would be ratified only if he were certified the winner by midnight on Dec. 11, and only then if each of the dozens of lawsuits is concluded — appeals and all — by the same time. "Every case, every appeal," Webster said, flashing a smile that suggested supreme confidence in Bush's prospects.

Dec. 7, 2000, Dana Canedy and David Barstow

24,000 Votes at Stake in Absentee Ballot Trials

TALLAHASSEE — In back-to-back trials, lawyers for George W. Bush urged two Florida judges to resist disqualifying thousands of absentee ballots, even though they acknowledged that Republican workers had been allowed to fix some flawed ballot applications.

One suit, brought by a supporter of Al Gore, seeks to discard 15,000 absentee ballots cast in Seminole County, where Republican workers were allowed to go into the elections office to fix the applications. The other seeks to invalidate the more than 9,000 absentee ballots cast in Martin County, where Republicans were allowed to remove the rejected applications from the elections office, fix them and resubmit them.

Because Bush carried the absentee ballots heavily in both counties, the loss of the votes in either county would be enough to overturn the election results in Florida. Gore's central argument about the Florida election is that every vote should be counted, so the vice president has not joined the suits. But on Tuesday he said he was watching them closely.

The Seminole case was heard for roughly 10 hours today. When it broke for the night at 7, the lawyers for Bush took a brief break before going to a night session called for the Martin trial. The accelerated schedule for the two trials meant that opening arguments in the Martin case were made after 8 tonight. Edward Stafman, a lawyer for the plaintiff, Ronald Taylor, argued that the case involved a local Republican supervisor of elections acting in concert with local Republican officials to achieve a partisan advantage in the election. Daryl Bristow, a lawyer for Bush, asserted that every voter was innocent.

Nikki Ann Clark, who presided over the trial, said at the outset that she would consider two issues: whether the addition of the identification numbers was sufficient cause to throw out the ballots and whether the access the Republicans were granted was favorable treatment that had an effect on the outcome of the election.

The case arose out of a practice common to both the Democratic and Republican parties in Florida. Both parties, in an effort to increase voter turnout, routinely mail out thousands of largely filled-in absentee ballot application forms to voters likely to support their candidates. All the voters have to do, in theory, is complete the forms and send them to their county elections office. But this year a printer's error left the voter identification numbers off thousands of Republican application forms that were returned.

After the Republican Party learned of the error, court papers show, officials asked the election official, Sandra Goard, to allow Michael A. Leach, the north Florida regional director of the state Republican Party, to go to her office and add the missing identification numbers to the rejected ballot applications. She agreed. But while Leach was allowed to fix the applications, no action was taken to fix hundreds of other incomplete ballot applications, and they were not processed.

All told, the lawyers agreed, Leach added identification numbers to at least 2,126 incomplete absentee ballot applications that resulted from the Republican mailing. Those applications resulted in 1,932 absentee votes cast: 1,833 from Republicans, 54 from Democrats and 45 from independents. Since there is a secret ballot, and those votes were added to the rest of the more than 15,000 absentee ballots cast in Seminole County, it is impossible to segregate them and throw them out. So the Democrats argued that all the absentee ballots should be thrown out. But at the trial today, they also offered the judge a third way, suggesting that the 1,932 absentee votes resulting from altered applications could be thrown out according to a mathematical formula estimating how those votes could be expected to have been cast.

The Republican lawyers argued that the act of altering the ballot applications was not enough on its own to alter the outcome of the election. They argued that if Leach had not been allowed to fix the rejected ballot applications, many of the voters would simply have reapplied for ballots or gone to the polls on Election Day.

The lawyer representing Goard said his office conducted an analysis of all the rejected absentee ballot applications that were not altered by Leach. Of the 742 people whose ballot applications were rejected, he said, nearly half received absentee ballots anyway, either because they had already applied for absentee ballots or because they reapplied when they failed to receive one. Of the rest, he said, approximately 80 percent voted at the polls. Of the remaining 70 to 80 people who did not receive absentee ballots and did not go to the polls, he said, many had applications rejected because they did not sign applications, they were not registered to vote or they lived in another county.

Dec. 7, 2000, Michael Cooper

Federal Court Rejects Bush Request to Bar Manual Recounts

ATLANTA — Ruling on narrow grounds, a divided federal appeals court today rejected George W. Bush's request that the manual recount of presidential ballots in Florida be barred, handing Al Gore a badly needed legal victory.

In its 8-to-4 opinion, the United States Court of Appeals for the 11th Circuit here dismissed Bush's claim without ruling on the key question of whether hand recounts in selected counties violated the Constitution's guarantees of equal protection, due process and unfettered speech. It instead determined that Bush had not met the legal standard necessary to receive an injunction, which requires the demonstration of a threat of irreparable injury.

In essence, the court said, Bush could not claim that he would suffer such harm because he had been certified by Katherine Harris as the winner of Florida's balloting and its 25 electoral votes. "Even if manual recounts were to resume pursuant to a state court order," the majority wrote, with a nod to Thursday's hearing on the subject before the Florida Supreme Court, "it is wholly speculative as to whether the results of those recounts eventually place Gore ahead."

The 11th Circuit ruling, Gore aides said today, gives the State Supreme Court a chance to decide whether hand recounts should be ordered in Palm Beach and Miami-Dade Counties without fear of being usurped by the federal courts. "This ruling clears the path for the Florida Supreme Court to move forward with the manual counts that we are requesting," said Doug Hattaway, a Gore spokesman. With Gore trailing Bush in Florida by 537 votes, and with only six days remaining before the state must choose its electors, a revival of the manual recounts apparently is Gore's last hope for winning the presidency.

Theodore B. Olson, the Washington-based lawyer who argued the case for Bush on Tuesday, said no decision had been made about whether to appeal to the United States Supreme Court. But Bush legal advisers said they would be inclined to wait until the State Supreme Court has ruled to see whether a federal appeal is needed. "The court obviously felt that we didn't need its help," Olson said. "And that's somewhat understandable. We tried to persuade the court that these recounts could still matter in terms of the outcome, and the court is suggesting to us that when and if that happens they might be more willing to look at the issues."

Indeed, the judges made it clear that they were not precluding another look at the constitutional issues if political factors change. "In view of the complex and ever-shifting circumstances of the case, we cannot say with any confidence that no live controversy is before us," the majority wrote.

Dec. 7, 2000, Kevin Sack

day

30

THURSDAY,
DECEMBER 7TH

★ ★ ★ ★ ★

FLORIDA HIGH COURT AGAIN HEARS GORE APPEAL

The Florida Supreme Court hears arguments on Gore's bid to overturn a circuit court decision earlier in the week denying manual recounts. In an unusual twist, the Supreme Court is reviewing a decision by N. Sanders Sauls, who was severely rebuked by the court in 1998 for his performance as chief circuit judge in Leon County and then stripped of his title. Elsewhere, arguments conclude in a Florida circuit court on Democratic challenges to absentee ballots in two counties in which Republican officials were allowed to add information to ballot applications; rulings are expected within a few days.

According to a report filed with the I.R.S., Gore's challenge to the Florida election result is financed by many of the same donors who underwrote his presidential bid. The same appears to be true for the Bush camp's battle to end the process now.

FLORIDA JUSTICES ASK POINTED QUESTIONS

TALLAHASSEE — With only 30 minutes to make their final case, lawyers for Al Gore returned today to the Florida Supreme Court to plead his contest of the state's presidential election, but encountered repeated skepticism from several justices about whether the court should get involved at all.

Gore's chief lawyer in the case, David Boies, had to answer questions from five of the seven justices about whether the court had a proper role in the appeal, whether it could legitimately overrule the trial judge who ruled decisively against Gore on Monday, and whether the court could count disputed ballots from only a few counties. Bush's lawyer, Barry Richard, faced intense questioning from two justices about the lower court's refusal to examine the disputed ballots, but left somewhat less battered than Boies.

Boies had barely introduced himself when the chief justice, Charles T. Wells, asked if the court even had the right to hear the appeal. After all, Wells said, the state law says simply that a circuit court can hear contests of elections and does not say whether they can be appealed. The United States Supreme Court, he noted, has given complete power to state legislatures to set election rules.

"Why is not judicial review given to the circuit court and not this court?" he asked. Boies, usually steady on his feet, seemed surprised by the question, which had not come up in the briefs on the case. After a moment's hesitation, he said the United States Constitution certainly did not intend for the legislature to act as a judicial body on election matters, only to set basic laws. The case could be appealed like any other, he said.

But the spirit of the question lingered in the air. In contrast to their demeanor 16 days ago, when they handled a different election challenge from Gore, several justices seemed far more concerned about whether this case truly belonged in their hands, and they struggled with questions of the precise role of the state courts and the legislature in a matter governed by the federal Constitution.

Leander J. Shaw Jr., considered one of the most liberal members of the court, repeatedly asked whether the court was in any position to overrule the findings of fact by the lower court judge, N. Sanders Sauls, who issued a sweeping ruling against Gore's contest on Monday.

"When you put on experts and the judge listens to these experts and then he makes a determination based upon that, normally isn't that a question of fact?" Shaw asked. Yes, Boies responded, but Sauls had both ignored important testimony and misinterpreted the law. He had refused to even look at the 14,000 punch-card ballots that the Democrats believe could reveal votes for Gore if they were manually counted, Boies said, even though the ballots were his side's most important evidence.

Major B. Harding jumped in, asking whether any of Gore's lawyers had tried to show Sauls one of the disputed ballots that had been rejected by a tabulating machine. No, Boies said; they were locked up. "But nobody asked the court for permission to do that or showed him one of those ballots?" Harding asked, implicitly admonishing the Democrats for not having done so. Boies replied, "Not an individual one, although we did tender them in evidence, and we did ask him repeatedly to look at the ballots as part of the evidence."

Two other justices, R. Fred Lewis and Peggy A. Quince, along with Harding, wondered why they were being asked to manually count votes from just two counties, Palm Beach and Miami-Dade, and not from all other counties, or at least those that use punch cards. That position was taken by Sauls, who did not cite any settled law in making that determination, but the justices asked Boies to explain his side's reasoning in picking only two counties, both of which are Democratic strongholds. Boies replied that the losing candidate had the right to decide where to contest the vote, and he pointed out that Bush had turned down an opportunity to have all of the state's ballots manually counted.

The questions from the justices did not necessarily mean they looked harshly at Gore's case. Rather, they seemed to reflect the pressure bearing down on the court from many directions. The court was chastened by the United States Supreme Court this week for an opinion on a related case that did not have a proper legal foundation. Next door, the Republican leaders of the State Legislature have threatened to appoint electors for Bush no matter what the court decides.

Gore's lawyers are demanding that the court not only agree that 14,000 disputed ballots should be counted but also set a procedure for counting them over the weekend, and then declare Gore the winner if the ballots bear that out. If the court does order the ballots counted, Bush's lawyers will file an appeal with the United States Supreme Court within minutes.

These pressures seem to have produced a more fractured court than the one that issued a unanimous opinion last month that the Florida secretary of state had to include manual counts in her certification of the election. Two justices who did not speak during Boies's appearance, Harry Lee Anstead and Barbara J. Pariente, dominated the questioning of Richard, boring in on Sauls's refusal to count the ballots.

"Isn't it highly unusual for a trial court to admit into evidence certain documents that one party claims will be controlling," Justice Anstead asked, "and yet never examine those documents before making their decision?" Richard responded that the Gore team never proved the necessity of doing so, but Pariente interrupted with the language of the state election law, which requires the circuit court "to do whatever is necessary to ensure that each allegation in the complaint is investigated, examined or checked." If that does not mean counting disputed ballots, she asked, what does it mean?

Richard cited a case that left counting to the discretion of county election boards and said the Gore team never convinced Sauls to overrule that discretion. "We had an absolute failure on the part of the plaintiffs here," Richard said. "This court gave the plaintiffs the opportunity to have a trial to prove their case, and it was an absolute failure in the record of this case to establish an abuse of discretion by any of the challenged canvassing boards."

Twice, the justices allowed Richard to sidestep questions about the validity of Judge Sauls's test that Gore had to show a "reasonable probability" that the outcome would change with a recount. But Quince seemed annoyed when Richard said there was no reason to believe that any voter was denied the right to vote because of the voting process, rather than because of the voter's own errors.

"Where in the statute is that standard, that you have to show that a mistake was made through no fault of the voter?" Quince asked. "It seems to me that we've gotten off of what the standard is for showing the rejection of votes." She said she was "really having a problem" with Sauls's reasonable probability standard.

Wells and Pariente asked the only questions about what might be the most pressing logistical issue facing the court if it rules for Gore: how to count the 14,000 ballots in the limited time left. Wells expressed doubt that a remedy for Gore could be completed by Tuesday, and Pariente wondered how it could possibly be done. Boies responded that he believed there was enough time, if the ballots were counted fast enough.

Speaking to reporters after the hearing, W. Dexter Douglass, a Tallahassee trial lawyer working for Gore, elaborated on that plan, saying the clerk of the Leon County Circuit Court had arranged for 25 teams to examine the ballots in the county library, with Republican and Democratic observers for every team. A large group, he said, could go through the ballots in a few days. But Benjamin L. Ginsberg, Bush's general counsel, said a decision to count — particularly if the court decided to count dimpled ballots as votes — would immediately raise federal constitutional issues that his side would take to the United States Supreme Court.

Dec. 8, 2000, David Firestone

SAULS'S DIFFICULT HISTORY WITH FLORIDA HIGH COURT

"I think it was because he wouldn't bend over and kiss their boots."

– Cindy Sauls, the judge's wife

★ ★ ★

TALLAHASSEE — In November 1998, Judge N. Sanders Sauls of Leon County Circuit Court was hauled to the woodshed by the Florida Supreme Court in what many here recall as the most extraordinary professional humiliation in North Florida's recent legal history.

The justices had summoned Judge Sauls to their offices to discuss his performance as chief circuit judge in Leon County and more specifically his efforts to dismiss a court administrator. The justices had been besieged by complaints that Judge Sauls's style was autocratic, and about a courthouse bitterly divided under his leadership. During a tense meeting, they bluntly laid down the law, telling Judge Sauls that he had been arbitrary and unfair, and that things had to change.

That evening when Judge Sauls got home, his wife, Cindy, could see right away that he was livid. "He told me that he could not believe that the Supreme Court justices, of all people, were not interested in the facts," Mrs. Sauls recalled in an interview.

And so the next morning he composed a resignation letter to the Supreme Court, which then promptly stripped him of his title as chief judge with a terse, unanimous order that noted "the continuing disruption in the administration of justice" under Judge Sauls.

"There were a lot of complaints, not only from court personnel but other judges who said he ran the courthouse in an extremely autocratic manner," said Gerald Kogan, a retired Florida Supreme Court justice who participated in the meeting. Mrs. Sauls, a former legal secretary, saw it differently. "I think it was because he wouldn't bend over and kiss their boots," she said.

Today, all but two of the seven justices who demoted Judge Sauls two years ago are reviewing his most important handiwork: a sweeping ruling this week that struck a severe blow to Vice President Al Gore's quest for the White House and could leave Judge Sauls as the man who, in effect, chose the next president of the United States. There is no evidence that this ugly chapter of courthouse factionalism will color the justices' assessment of Judge Sauls's ruling. "They'd treat him as fairly as they'd treat any other judge," Justice Kogan said.

And yet the episode is an example of how the unfolding national political drama is intersecting with the intricate, layered dynamics of a small and clannish legal community.

In this case, Mr. Gore's presidential ambitions have become enmeshed in the history of hard feelings between Judge Sauls, a Democrat and a law-and-order conservative, and the Florida Supreme Court, which in 1997 overturned one of his death sentences, citing the 19-year-old defendant's low I.Q., history of mental illness and abusive childhood. A history buff who can quote from the Federalist Papers and who applies a literalist approach to statutes, Judge Sauls shares the views of leading Republicans who say the Florida Supreme Court is a liberal bench that too often makes new law, his wife and friends said.

Judge Sauls declined to comment for this article. But his wife, eager to counter what she described as a smear campaign by his "enemies" in the liberal wing of Tallahassee's legal and political community, spoke at length after receiving his permission.

And so with Judge Sauls sitting in their living room, Mrs. Sauls stood on their front steps late Wednesday night and launched a passionate defense of her husband. "Loving him and seeing him bashed has been hard," she said, ignoring the chill night air.

She blamed liberal lawyers for ganging up on Judge Sauls to give him a low rating in local bar association polls, and she asserted that liberal bias by The Tallahassee Democrat resulted in unfair coverage of his tenure as chief judge.

In short, Mrs. Sauls described her husband as a man who long ago decided he would rather stand up for his conservative principles than simply go along to make friends, or curry favor with his local newspaper, or win approval from his superiors on the bench. "When you are a man who stands up for what you believe, and you don't pass the buck, you are not always the most admired man," she said.

"My husband," she added, "is not a politician."

But his stubbornness, critics in the legal community said, has contributed to a record of reversals that exceeds that compiled by several of his colleagues on the Leon County Circuit bench. In examining 198 of his cases, appellate courts have reversed him 61 times, according to a search of Lexis, a legal database. Another Leon County Circuit judge, George Reynolds, has been reversed in 28 of 199 cases. A third Leon County Circuit judge, Nikki Ann Clark, who is hearing one of the other cases in the post-election fight, has been reversed in 49 of 219 cases.

Sauls has been repeatedly reversed for taking too narrow an approach with admitting evidence and for punishing defendants too harshly by misinterpreting statutes and sustaining convictions without adequate proof. Likewise, Sauls prides himself in carrying a large caseload, but he has been reversed in several cases for improperly throwing out lawsuits brought by poor people, prison inmates and plaintiffs who don't have lawyers. Appellate judges have criticized him for imposing too strict a standard on filing schedules and other administrative requirements.

Given his record, some members of the Gore legal team now say they feared from the beginning the very result they are now trying to overturn. One Gore lawyer, Dexter Douglass, who has known the judge for decades, said he was concerned from the start that Judge Sauls could not be pushed into acting with the urgency Mr. Gore wanted.

"When we found out it was him, I felt we would have a difficult time," Mr. Douglass said in an interview.

Norman Sanders Sauls, 59, was raised in Monticello, a small town about 35 miles east of Tallahassee in rural Jefferson County. He came from a prominent Democratic family. His father, Clyde, who died when Judge Sauls was a teenager, was the county clerk. His mother, Genevieve Sauls, who died in the late 1970's, ran the county Democratic organization for years.

According to Cindy Sauls, her husband was raised primarily by a black nanny named Ruby Thomas. As a boy, she said, he sometimes referred to his mother as "Mrs. Sauls" and Ms. Thomas as "Mama," and to this day Ms. Thomas remains one of the most important people in Judge Sauls's life, she said. When Ms. Thomas was recently hospitalized, she said, Judge Sauls went to the hospital each morning, noon and night to help feed her, carefully cutting her food and feeding her. "There's a true love there between them," Mrs. Sauls said today.

The Sauls family was an early supporter of Jimmy Carter, whose mother, Lillian, once spent the night at their home during a campaign swing. Genevieve Sauls was also longtime friends with Lawton Chiles, a former Democratic governor and United States senator. According to Judge Sauls's friends, his family's political connections gave him instant access to the good old boy network, a network that helped him, at the age of 37, land a coveted judicial perch as a United States bankruptcy judge for North Florida.

When his term as bankruptcy judge expired in 1986, he sought reappointment but then withdrew that request, court officials said. His wife said he withdrew because their family, with four children to put through private schools, needed more income than he could earn as a judge. In 1993, his youngest daughter, Christine, 16, was killed in an automobile accident, and friends said he visited her grave almost daily in the months after.

By then, he had already rejoined the bench. He was appointed to the Leon County Circuit Court by Gov. Bob Martinez, a Republican.

Today, one of his closest friends and allies is Charles McClure, a former chief judge of the Leon County Circuit who has campaigned for George W. Bush in North Florida, and who has also consulted for the Bush legal team, offering the out-of-town lawyers tips about Sandy Sauls. Judge McClure gives Judge Sauls the highest praise a conservative jurist can get: "He's a strict constructionist."

It is a quality that comes through in his personal life. In the mid-1970's, for example, Judge Sauls argued bitterly over a mere $50 during divorce proceedings from his first wife. Under the divorce agreement, Judge Sauls was supposed to pay his former wife $2,000 to get her resettled. He paid $1,950, but refused to pay the final $50, arguing in court papers that his wife had violated the agreement by keeping a $75 saddle and bridle he had bought for their horse, Sunny.

Similar themes would re-emerge some 20 years later during the dust-up that led to his ouster as chief judge. Ostensibly, the dispute was about a routine personnel matter. When an important family law position opened up in the court, Judge Sauls, overriding a search committee, picked his own candidate, a woman who had less experience than the search committee's choice but who had come recommended by a friend.

Tom Long, the court administrator, objected, and the judge angrily denounced him for insubordination. In searing memos, the judge described Mr. Long's intervention as "uncalled for, unnecessary and highly unprofessional" and issued this stern dictum: "This attitude and conduct must cease at once."

Mrs. Sauls said that she and the judge knew, from the moment he was assigned the Gore contest case by random selection, that all the attention would dredge up the memory of his "heartbreaking" humiliation at the hands of the Supreme Court.

"He said, 'I have it and now I'll do the best I can.' "

He attacked the case in his usual workmanlike manner. After hearing closing arguments late into Sunday night, he came home and kept at it until early Monday. Then he rose at his customary time, 5:30 a.m. At the dining room table, he wrote his opinion in longhand.

Not once did he let on to his wife of 25 years how he intended to rule. She learned of his decision with the rest of the world, she said, watching him proudly from a seat in the courtroom.

Dec. 8, 2000, David Barstow and Somini Segupta

Who's Funding the Recount Fight?

WASHINGTON —Al Gore's challenge to the Florida election result is being financed by many of the same individuals and interests who underwrote his presidential bid, according to a report filed today with the Internal Revenue Service. Mr. Gore received five- and six-figure checks from Hollywood, Wall Street, Silicon Valley and law offices around the country. Many of the donors are among the Democratic Party's biggest recent contributors. The largest single contributor to the recount fund is Steven T. Kirsch, an Internet entrepreneur from Los Altos Hills, Calif. He gave $500,000.

Mr. Kirsch called Florida's vote count a "travesty" and said he had contributed to help finance the legal challenge to the result. "It's obvious to anybody who looks at the statistical data that Gore won the state by a significant margin," Mr. Kirsch said in an interview. "He should have an opportunity to prove that."

The Gore-Lieberman Recount Committee, created the day after the Nov. 7 election, reported that it had raised $3.3 million from Nov. 8 to Nov. 27. The only expenditure in the report is $50,000 paid to the Douglass Law Firm in Tallahassee, one of the firms mounting Mr. Gore's contest to Florida's certification of Gov. George W. Bush as winner of the state's presidential election.

Among the other large donors were Democratic Party stalwarts, including S. Daniel Abraham, founder of SlimFast Foods ($100,000); Stephen L. Bing, a Hollywood producer ($200,000); Peter Buttenwieser, a Philadelphia philanthropist ($50,000); Jane Fonda, the actress ($100,000); Vance K. Opperman, a Minneapolis investor ($100,000); and Jonathan M. Tisch, chairman of Loews Hotels ($50,000).

Julia Payne, a spokeswoman for Gore, said the recount committee had received 1,258 contributions, all but four from individuals. Ms. Payne said 80 percent of the donations were in amounts of less than $200. But she acknowledged that the bulk of the money had come from a handful of large contributions raised by Gore fund-raisers who conducted a money-raising blitz in the early hours after it became clear that the election would turn on the outcome of Florida's disputed vote count.

As of last weekend, the Bush-Cheney Recount Fund had received $3.4 million from more than 11,000 donors. Mr. Bush limits contributions to $5,000. While most of the gifts to the Bush fund are small, more than 500 people have written checks greater than $1,000, according to an analysis by the Center for Responsive Politics. Of these, 73 were from so-called Bush Pioneers, people who have raised at least $100,000 for Bush's presidential campaign.

There were 368 donors who gave the maximum of $5,000, the center found, including Donald J. Carty, head of AMR, the parent of American Airlines; Tom Hicks, owner of the Texas Rangers; Tom Benson, owner of the New Orleans Saints; and Alfred Lerner, chairman of MBNA America Bank.

Dec. 8, 2000, John M. Broder

day

31

FRIDAY,

DECEMBER 8TH

★ ★ ★ ★ ★

FLORIDA SUPREME COURT BACKS RECOUNT

Just when Al Gore's prospects seem dimmest, the Florida Supreme Court once again reverses a lower court and rules 4 to 3 in favor of Gore, ordering the immediate manual recount of thousands of disputed presidential ballots across the state. County election officials and party observers throughout Florida mobilize for the ballot counting while Bush lawyers move for a stay of the decision from the U.S. Supreme Court and ask for an emergency hearing in a U.S. Appeals Court. The Florida court's ruling also adds the new votes from previous recounts, trimming Bush's lead to under 200 votes. Prominent Republicans vow to fight to the end, and Republican leaders in the Florida Legislature push forward with a special session to appoint electors for Bush. The recount is expected to favor Gore, but the final outcome is uncertain. In another case, a U.S. civil rights investigation is set to determine whether minority rights were violated by ballot irregularities.

BUSH'S LEAD BELOW 200 AS FLORIDA SUPREME COURT ORDERS MANUAL RECOUNT

TALLAHASSEE — Al Gore's flagging presidential hopes were suddenly jolted back to life this afternoon when a bitterly divided Florida Supreme Court ordered an immediate manual recount of thousands of ballots across the state.

Wielding its power with a force that neither candidate had fully anticipated, a four-member majority of the seven-member court suddenly erased the growing sense of inevitability that had developed around George W. Bush and set loose what could turn out to be days of confusion and disorder. A judge ordered tonight that the recount of the largest pool of those ballots begin at 8 a.m. Saturday [Dec. 9] and that all recounts conclude by 2 p.m. Sunday. [Dec. 10]

Within an hour of the Supreme Court opinion, election officials around Florida mobilized for a hastily organized recount of ballots on which no vote for president had been officially recorded. In reversing a lower court's decision on Monday that had rejected the Gore campaign's request for a manual recount of disputed ballots, the State Supreme Court said the recount had to go beyond the two counties whose ballots Gore had contested and include all the so-called undervotes — a number estimated at more than 45,000.

"There can be no question that there are legal votes within the 9,000 uncounted votes sufficient to place the results of this election in doubt."

— From the Florida Supreme Court ruling

Just as quickly, lawyers for Bush rushed to the United States Supreme Court to stop the count, filing a request for a stay with Justice Anthony M. Kennedy 31 days after the election, and simultaneously demanding an emergency hearing from the United States Court of Appeals for the 11th Circuit in Atlanta.

In a nine-page request for an injunction from the court of appeals, the lawyers said Bush would "suffer irreparable injury as a result of the unconstitutional Florida manual recounts," and requested that the court prevent any manual recounts from being included in certified vote tabulations.

At the same time, Republican leaders in the State Legislature began efforts to convene a special session that will appoint presidential electors pledged to Bush, no matter what the outcome of the recount is. The move, opposed by Democratic lawmakers, threatens to produce two slates of electors if Gore wins the recount, something that would force a narrowly divided Congress to choose between them.

Such a possibility was envisioned by Charles T. Wells in his dissenting opinion. "Importantly to me, I have a deep and abiding concern that the prolonging of judicial process in this counting contest propels this country and this state into an unprecedented and unnecessary constitutional crisis," he wrote.

To have an impact on the election, the counts must be completed well before Tuesday, when the state's electors will be formally named. The court acknowledged in the opinion that the effort will require a huge amount of work for public officials around Florida this weekend, and raised the possibility that it might not be completed. "We can only do the best we can to carry out our sworn responsibilities to the justice system and its role in this process," the majority opinion said.

The Supreme Court ordered that whichever candidate wins the state after the recount must be awarded Florida's pivotal 25 electoral votes. It also added to the state total the votes for Gore that had been counted in Palm Beach County and 168 from Miami-Dade County, all of which had been earlier rejected by the Florida secretary of state but which the high court said were legal votes.

That reduced Bush's current margin over Gore from 537 to either 154 votes or 193, depending on which side wins a dispute over the number of votes Gore won in Palm Beach County. The decision significantly increased the chances that Gore might find enough votes in the disputed ballots to become the victor.

"Today's ruling by Florida's Supreme Court is an important victory for what has been Al Gore and Joe Lieberman's basic principle since Nov. 7: a full and fair count of all the votes," said Gore's campaign chairman, William M. Daley. "This decision is not just a victory for Al Gore and his millions of supporters; it is a victory for fairness and accountability in our democracy itself."

The court said that N. Sanders Sauls of Leon County Circuit Court employed an excessively high standard in deciding that Gore had not proved the disputed ballots should be counted, accusing him of presenting Gore with "the ultimate Catch-22" in refusing to examine the only evidence that will decide the matter. It ordered that approximately 9,000 ballots from Miami-Dade County that could not be read by a machine be counted by hand, and it said that similar ballots without readable votes be counted in every county in Florida. "There can be no question that there are legal votes within the 9,000 uncounted votes sufficient to place the results of this election in doubt," the court majority wrote. "Thousands of uncounted votes could obviously make a difference."

The Florida Supreme Court usually issues unanimous opinions, and the split within the court reflected the widely differing questions on display in oral arguments on Thursday. In his blistering dissenting opinion, Wells said the majority failed to understand the profound national confusion that would result from allowing a hasty weekend recount of ballots to determine the outcome of a presidential election. "I have to conclude that there is a real and present likelihood that this constitutional crisis will do substantial damage to our country, our state, and to this court as an institution," the chief justice wrote. A separate dissenting opinion signed by Justices Major B. Harding and Leander J. Shaw Jr. said no faith or credibility could be placed in a count conducted under "such chaotic conditions."

Gore's lawyers seized on the court's order that the counting begin immediately, and by 7 p.m. had filed a motion to that effect with the Leon County Circuit Court, where the case originated. Sauls, without explanation, recused himself from any further action on the matter, and the motion was assigned to another judge, Terry P. Lewis, who had ruled in favor of Bush earlier in the day in one of the absentee-ballot cases.

A familiar set of lawyers quickly packed Lewis's courtroom to argue over the standards and procedures to be used in the counting, gathering so quickly that a court reporter had to be found at home to transcribe the proceedings by watching C-Span.

Phil Beck, a lawyer for Bush, said he was concerned not only about what standards would be used in deciding which disputed votes to count, but also about the process of accurately separating the nonrecorded votes from the rest of the votes in each county. "We're very much afraid that if we start willy-nilly segregating these votes, unless they're done the right way, and then counting, we're going to end up with a horrible mess that we'll never be able to put together again," he said. He demanded that a court reporter be assigned to every team of counters, and said the court should use a very strict standard in interpreting dimpled ballots.

Democratic lawyers pressed for a broad interpretation of the high court's voter-intent standard. "We think the court meant immediately when it said immediately," said David Boies. "Hours make a difference here."

Lewis spent an hour considering the arguments of the two sides, and shortly before midnight said he would allow the supervisors of each county's recount to interpret the high court's voter-intent standard on their own, without a detailed instruction on dimples and indentions. The count of the Miami-Dade ballots is scheduled to begin at 8 a.m Saturday, and all the recounts are to conclude by 2 p.m. Sunday. Lewis said he and two other judges from the Leon County Circuit Court would supervise the Miami-Dade County recount. To speed up the process, he said, partisan observers will not be allowed to object to individual ballots, but will have to raise objections later.

In its opinion, the Supreme Court said that a ballot shall be found to have a legal vote if it contains "the clear indication of the intent of the voter." That standard, although vague, has been claimed by Democrats to include dimpled or partially punched holes in punch-card ballots, but the court did not discuss the precise details of what constitutes a vote. The Democratic and Republican Parties immediately mobilized many of the same observers who had watched and argued over the manual count of votes in several Florida counties last month, promising days of disputes over ballots.

The majority opinion, 40 pages in length and signed by Justices Harry Lee Anstead, Barbara J. Pariente, R. Fred Lewis and Peggy A. Quince, all but excoriated Sauls for his legal reasoning in ruling against Gore on Monday. The judge had said that Gore was required to demonstrate a "reasonable probability" that the election would be changed in order to count the votes, but the majority said it was "immediately apparent" that Sauls based that standard on an 1982 case that had since been superseded by the State Legislature.

Echoing the new statute and the language of Gore's lawyers, the opinion said that Gore had only to demonstrate that enough legal votes had been rejected "to place in doubt" the results of the election. The court agreed with Sauls that 3,300 votes that had been evaluated in Palm Beach County need not be recounted, because the county elections board had already determined which ballots contained votes. But the majority said there was no good reason not to count the Miami-Dade ballots, which the elections board stopped counting by hand because it believed it could not make the deadline.

"Although the time constraints are limited, we must do everything required by law to ensure that legal votes that have not been counted are included in the final election results," the opinion said, adding, "Only by examining the contested ballots, which are evidence in the election contest, can a meaningful and final determination in this election contest be made."

The opinion rejected Sauls's assertion that if any ballots are hand counted, all of the state's ballots must be counted. But the court said it was "essential" to count every ballot in the state where a vote was not properly recorded. "This essential principle, that the outcome of elections be determined by the will of the voters, forms the foundation of the election code enacted by the Florida legislature," the opinion said.

Dec. 9, 2000, David Firestone

Angry Republicans Vow Bitter Fight

WASHINGTON — Prominent Republicans, stunned and infuriated by the Florida Supreme Court decision, vowed tonight to mount an intense battle over the presidency and take it to Congress if necessary. But a handful acknowledged for the first time that Al Gore might end up in the White House.

Democratic officials were just as surprised by the court's ruling, and they, too, were poised for political warfare. Many who had seemed ready to give up said tonight that they were newly emboldened and bracing for what could be another long chapter to the drawn-out struggle with George W. Bush.

Republicans, who had started the day expecting to soon hear Gore concede the presidency, again, were particularly rattled by the turn. Even as many in the party sought to discredit the court in Florida by noting that it is controlled by justices appointed by Democrats, several acknowledged for the first time since the election a month ago that they feared that Gore could become the president.

"It was a breathtaking reversal and we're going to fight it," said Tom Cole, chief of staff for the Republican National Committee. "I have no doubt that we will do everything within the law that we can do to resist what we see as an unfair, unjust opinion." He added: "We're moving out of a political crisis to a Constitutional crisis, with very likely competing slates of electors."

Indeed, many Bush supporters who had been measured in their oratory in recent days because they assumed that Gore was on the verge of a concession, sounded like warriors. "This judicial aggression must not stand," Representative Tom DeLay of Texas, the Republican whip, said in a statement. The Florida Supreme Court, he said, "has squandered and violated the trust of the people of Florida in an attempt to manipulate the results of a fair and free election."

Representative Mark Foley, a Florida Republican, said in an interview: "This, obviously, has the potential to be explosive. I think this is outrageous. I'm shocked." For all his willingness to fight, Foley was among the Republicans who, for the first time, entertained the notion that Gore could become the 43rd president. Asked if Gore might become president, Senator Chuck Hagel, Republican of Nebraska, said, "That's very much a possibility. Absolutely."

People close to the Bush campaign said officials in Austin, Tex., had anticipated a Gore withdrawal, and were preparing announcements of appointments to a Bush administration as early as Saturday. Instead, they said, the campaign had suddenly reversed course — and is now prepared for tactics that Bush's advisers had hoped to avoid, like preparing to take the matter to Congress and thus lining up with the Florida Legislature, which is dominated by allies of Bush's brother, Jeb Bush.

Beyond the legal options, Republicans said their strategy to influence public opinion — and politicians who may take up the matter — was to discredit the Florida Supreme Court as controlled by appointees of Democratic governors. Even though it was Bush who filed the first lawsuit in the post-election battle, party officials were already making the case that Gore was seeking extraordinary means through the courts to overturn the results of an election. "It's going to be very hard for Republicans to accept this decision as anything other than liberal, judicial activism gone amok," Cole said. "It's hard to swallow, and particularly difficult when the court was appointed exclusively by Democratic governors."

Democratic officials have said repeatedly that what could save them politically — and give people a renewed sense that Gore's quest was not doomed — would be pictures on the news of people actually counting ballots. They have begun making the case that all they ever wanted was for ballots to be counted fairly. Democrats also said they would depict the Republicans' effort to take the case to the Republican-controlled Florida Legislature as demonstrating that their opponents were driven by partisan politics. "They're attempting to replace the peoples' votes with a partisan Republican vote," asserted one Democratic official, previewing what he said would be party talking points.

Gore campaign officials said their political strategy was buoyed by the fact that the vice president won the popular vote nationally, which does not have any binding effect but gives Gore a psychological edge. "You've always had Gore being the popular-vote winner," said Chris Lehane, a Gore spokesman. "That has given us the moral authority. We now have the legal authority to count the vote."

In his own statement to reporters tonight, William M. Daley, the Gore campaign chairman, quickly voiced the Democratic mantra that the campaign was determined only for votes to be counted — and partisanship kept to a minimum. "All of these matters should be resolved by Florida's independent courts," he said, "not by politicians."

Dec. 9, Richard L. Berke

Ruling Fuels G.O.P. Resolve to Appoint Electors

TALLAHASSEE — Republican legislators here said today's ruling by the Florida Supreme Court made them even more resolved to push forward with a special session to appoint presidential electors for George W. Bush.

With an almost righteous sense of certainty that Bush had won, a legal rationale from conservative scholars and the swagger of street fighters, they vowed to press forward with the legal battle they began just hours before. "The Senate's approach has not altered as a result of the court's action today," John McKay, the Senate president, said in a statement. "We will meet in committee on Monday and begin our first day of full debate on the appropriate manner of selecting the state's electors."

But House and Senate Democrats, who have called the session blatant political manipulation of the system, said they felt a firmer resolve to fight the proceedings. To move forward, the Democrats said, would be to betray Florida's six million voters. Conceding that they lack the numbers to stop their Republican colleagues from ratifying Bush's electors, or even to throw up many procedural obstacles, the Democrats say they will still vigorously argue their points.

"Now this intensifies us, and we'll see them trying harder to protect Bush," said State Representative Lois Frankel of West Palm Beach, leader of the House Democrats. Frankel and the Democratic leadership had warned for days that it would be even more politically destructive for the Legislature to appoint electors if manual recounts showed that Al Gore beat Bush. "We have a constitutional obligation to every Florida voter, and to the nation, to count every vote cast in our state," said Tom Rossin, the Senate Democratic leader.

The Republicans, though, insist that it is more important than ever for them to act because the protracted legal challenges to the election results put Florida in jeopardy of missing the Dec. 12 deadline for states to name electors. Should they miss that deadline, the Republicans say, the state risks being shut out when the Electoral College meets on Dec. 18 to vote for president.

"I am terribly saddened by the Florida Supreme Court's decision today," Tom Feeney, the Republican Speaker of the House, said in a statement. "However, it validates my view that it is an absolute obligation of the Florida Legislature to act to preserve the election law as it existed prior to this election."

Several Republicans expressed outrage at the ruling, which renewed the years of building animosity between them and a Supreme Court filled with Democratic appointees. "What we just saw was the judicialization of our democracy," said Representative Mario Diaz-Balart of Miami. He said the Legislature would still act unless every case and every appeal had been exhausted by Dec. 12 — no matter the outcome of the recounts.

But the development today increases the chances of Florida having two slates of electors — one set by the Legislature supporting Bush and the other by the popular vote supporting Gore. That kind of split has not occurred in more than 100 years.

While the Republicans were quick to dismiss the likelihood of such a scenario, they said even a popular vote in favor of Gore would not deter them if all the legal challenges to the election have not been exhausted by Dec. 12. Even so, if Bush's slim lead in the election dwindles during the recounting, the Republican leadership will have a much tougher time maintaining discipline among a rank and file composed largely of rookie legislators and those whose districts voted for Gore.

And with each new vote Gore picks up, a slate of electors chosen by Bush-faithful politicians becomes a much harder sell to their constituents. Lance deHaven-Smith, a political scientist for Florida State University, said that Republican legislators would surely feel the political pain if the counting proceeds this weekend and the results show Gore either closing or ahead. "Are they really going to say we don't care what the votes are?" he asked. "I think they are going to have a very difficult time if Gore is ahead."

Dec. 9, 2000, Dana Canedy and David Barstow

Gore Loses Both Absentee Ballot Suits

TALLAHASSEE — When the Florida Supreme Court salvaged Al Gore's hopes this afternoon with its ruling to begin recounting votes, he already had two strikes against him. Earlier in the day Gore suffered two setbacks in Leon County Circuit Court, where judges ruled against twin suits filed by his supporters seeking to throw out nearly 25,000 absentee ballots in Martin and Seminole Counties.

While the cases were different, and the judges wrote separate decisions, their findings were roughly the same: while allowing Republicans to fix the ballot applications violated the law, there was no evidence of any intentional wrongdoing or fraud, and the ballots that were cast reflected the will of the people and should not be discarded.

If the ballots, which overwhelmingly favored George W. Bush, had been thrown out, it would have cost Bush enough votes to have lost the election in Florida, and the presidency. So when Terre Cass, the court administrator, announced the rulings this afternoon in the marble rotunda of the courthouse, Bush supporters cheered loudly, and perhaps prematurely, "Na na na na, na na na na, hey hey, goodbye," at Gore's supporters.

In their decisions, the judges in both cases condemned what happened to the absentee ballot requests, but said that it was simply not a grave enough offense to disenfranchise voters. "Although the practices undertaken with regard to the absentee ballot request forms invited strong allegations of wrongdoing and fraud," wrote Judge Nikki Ann Clark, who presided over the Seminole County case, "there was no evidence that the request for ballots or the ballots themselves were tainted, or that the will of the people who voted absentee was thwarted by the involvement of third parties in adding to the ballot request forms."

Judge Terry P. Lewis, who tried the Martin County case, wrote that allowing Republicans to remove the rejected applications from the elections office to fix them "offered an opportunity for fraud and created the appearance of partisan favoritism on the part of the supervisor of elections."

The plaintiffs in both cases, Harry Jacobs, who filed the Seminole County suit, and Ronald Taylor, who filed the Martin County suit, instantly appealed the decisions to the First District Court of Appeal, which sent the cases to the Florida Supreme Court. "There was wrongdoing, and I don't think it was remedied," Jacobs said.

The suit put lawyers from both parties in odd positions. Democrats, who have been arguing in other cases that every vote in Florida should be counted with a lenient reading to determine the will of the voters, found themselves arguing that these absentee ballots should be thrown out. Gore, as a result, declined to join the suit, although he made favorable remarks about it this week. Republicans, who have argued in other cases that only votes cast in strict compliance with the law should be counted, argued that in this case the error with the request forms was a mere technicality that should not keep the votes from being counted.

Both Judge Lewis and Judge Clark included the same citation in their opinions, a 1975 ruling by the Florida Supreme Court that found: "The right to vote is the right to participate; it is also the right to speak, but more importantly, the right to be heard. We must tread carefully on that right or we risk the unnecessary and unjustified muting of the public voice."

Dec. 9, 2000, Michael Cooper

Statement by the Supreme Court of Florida: "The Recount Shall Commence"

"By a vote of 4-3, the majority of the court has reversed the decision of the trial court in part. It has further ordered that the Circuit Court of the Second Judicial Circuit here in Tallahassee shall immediately begin a manual recount of the approximately 9,000 Miami-Dade ballots that registered undervotes.

"In addition, the Circuit Court shall enter orders ensuring the inclusion of the additional 215 legal votes for Gore in Palm Beach County and the 168 additional legal votes from Miami-Dade County.

"In addition, the Circuit Court shall order a manual recount of all undervotes in any Florida county where such a recount has not yet occurred.

"Because time is of the essence, the recount shall commence immediately. In tabulating what constitutes a legal vote, the standard to be used is the one provided by the Legislature: 'A vote shall be counted where there is a clear indication of the intent of the voter.' "

OpEd

The Chaos a Recount Could Bring

The Florida Supreme Court has made its decision, and the country now stares into the abyss. By holding, in a split decision, that all the so-called "undercounted votes" in Florida must be counted, the court has virtually guaranteed that there can be no conclusion to the Florida election story until well after Dec. 12, the date that Congress has fixed for the selection of an incontestable slate of delegates.

As a result, the possibility exists that the Florida Legislature will choose one slate of electors and — if Al Gore's forces win in a statewide recount of the ballots in question — a second slate will eventually be mandated by the courts. There will also be efforts to challenge the legitimacy of both the electors chosen by the Legislature and the hand recount from which any Gore victory might result. It is hard to avoid the conclusion that the country is a long way from an end to this agonizing process.

All this was wholly unnecessary. In its original decision, the Florida Supreme Court required the state Secretary of State to accept any recounted ballots unless they were "submitted so late that their inclusion will preclude Florida's voters from participating fully in the federal electoral process." In other words, in its first decision, the court cited as its highest priority the participation of Florida's electors in the federal election. Now the Florida justices have turned their backs on their own goal, ordering a hand recount of the tens of thousands of undercounted ballots — those on which no votes were recorded — in the Florida presidential contest.

Without action by the Florida Legislature, the delay this recount entails may prevent the state's voters from participating at all in the election of their country's president. We may never know why the Florida court abandoned its original priority; we only know that all of us must now bear the consequences unless a supervening authority steps in.

That authority is the United States Supreme Court, which is now unable to avoid a major role in deciding the outcome of the election. In its order earlier this week, the court seemed to endorse the substance of the argument made by lawyers for George W. Bush — that the United States Constitution, as implemented by federal law, limits the usual discretion of the State Supreme Court to "interpret" Florida statutes in presidential elections.

The United States Supreme Court said that if the Florida Legislature had wanted to make sure that the state's electors were conclusively recognized by Congress, it certainly would not have wanted the Florida Supreme Court to tinker with the exact terms of the Election Code. This suggests that in the face of a contrary federal statute, the Florida Supreme Court might not have even the interpretive powers with respect to state laws that state supreme courts are normally accorded. All of this constituted a fairly blunt shot through the Florida court's intellectual rigging.

But the Florida court apparently could not take the hint, and now the United States Supreme Court must step in. There are ample grounds for it to avert the chaos that the court in Florida has made likely. Among other things, it is not clear, under the language of the Florida statute, that the Florida Supreme Court had jurisdiction to take, and decide, the case. Nor is it clear how the Florida Supreme Court could authorize a statewide recount of the undercounted ballots on the basis of statutory language that does not authorize anything other than full recounts — counting all the ballots that were cast, whether or not they showed presidential votes in the initial machine counting.

It would have been far better for the country and for the justice system generally if the Florida Supreme Court had stayed with its initial view of things — that assuring Florida's participation in the election of the president was its transcendent goal. But since that seemed to conflict with other goals the Florida court may have had in mind, we now have to look to the nation's highest court to bring order out of incipient chaos.

Dec. 9, 2000

By Peter J. Wallison, President Ronald Reagan's counsel in 1986 and 1987 and a resident fellow at the American Enterprise Institute

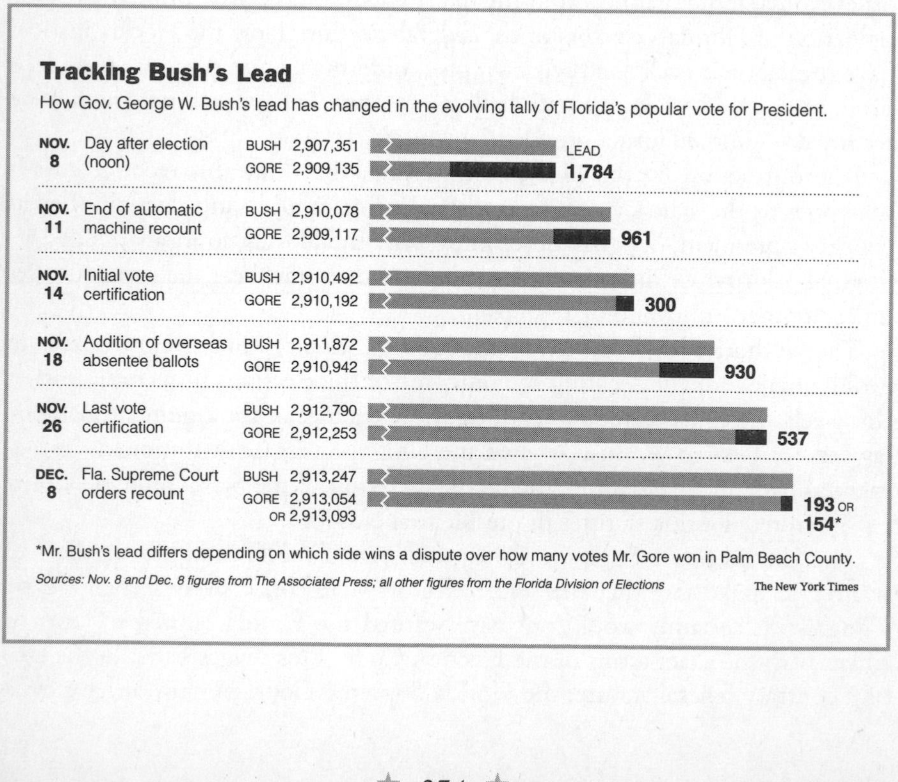

day

32

SATURDAY,

DECEMBER 9TH

★ ★ ★ ★ ★

U.S. SUPREME COURT HALTS THE RECOUNT

Early today, all across Florida, teams of vote counters gather to begin the counting of 45,000 disputed ballots that will finally decide the outcome of the election. In the early afternoon, the U.S. Appeals Court rules that the counting can be done but suddenly at 3 p.m. the U.S. Supreme Court issues a stay to stop it. Democrats are stunned and embittered by the court's action and fear that time will run out on Gore's quest for the presidency, although Gore stays upbeat. Republicans are jubilant. The Supreme Court sets a hearing for Dec. 11 to decide the case. The 5-4 decision granting the stay, requested by Bush, reflects deep divisions between the conservative and liberal wings of the court; Justice Stevens writes a strong dissent to the order. The recount process, supervised by a circuit court judge, is stopped in its tracks. Progress toward the recount is highly variable; some counties were well on their way to completing the tallies, while others had difficulty even beginning. No official reports of partial results are made public, and partisans of both Bush and Gore claim that the results favor their candidate; a Florida Sunshine Law ensures that the disputed ballots will ultimately be counted.

Bitterly Divided High Court Suddenly Steps In

"Count first, and rule upon legality afterwards, is not a recipe for producing election results that have the public acceptance democratic stability requires."

—Justice Scalia

★ ★ ★

WASHINGTON — In a sudden and devastating blow to Al Gore's presidential hopes, the United States Supreme Court voted 5 to 4 today to stop the vote counting that had begun hours earlier in Florida. The court set Monday morning, Dec. 11, for arguments on Bush's appeal of the Florida Supreme Court ruling that ordered manual recounts across the state of ballots that initially showed no vote for president.

With the clock ticking inexorably toward a Dec. 12 deadline for certifying electors, the Supreme Court's order, issued shortly before 3 p.m., could have the effect of erasing the Democrat's chances that the Florida Supreme Court had so dramatically revived barely 24 hours earlier with its 4-to-3 ruling.

Even if by some chance the United States Supreme Court eventually rules in the vice president's favor, the ruling could come too late. While not conceding ultimate defeat, David Boies said today that "if we had world enough and time," a short-term stay would make little difference, but that there was now a "very serious issue" as to whether the vote counting could be finished in time even if the court's eventual ruling allowed it to resume.

Briefs are due at the court at 4 o'clock tomorrow afternoon — two hours after the recount was originally supposed to have been completed — with 90 minutes of argument set for 11 a.m. Monday. Partial returns from the few hours of vote counting before the court intervened showed that Gore was making progress, according to Democrats in Florida, toward erasing his deficit of fewer than 200 votes.

The justices who voted to grant the stay were Chief Justice William H. Rehnquist and his four conservative colleagues: Sandra Day O'Connor, Antonin Scalia, Anthony M. Kennedy and Clarence Thomas. The dissenters were the court's four most liberal members: John Paul Stevens, David H. Souter, Ruth Bader Ginsburg and Stephen G. Breyer.

The bitter division on the court, awkwardly papered over only last Monday with an order to the Florida Supreme Court to clarify an earlier ruling, burst into the open with the action this afternoon. Stevens filed a two-page dissenting opinion, which the other three dissenters joined. "To stop the counting of legal votes, the majority today departs from three venerable rules of judicial restraint that have guided the court throughout its history," Stevens said.

The majority did not issue an opinion in support of its order, but Scalia said he felt obliged to issue a statement in response to the Stevens dissent. "One of the principal issues in the appeal we have accepted is precisely whether the votes that have been ordered to be counted are, under a reasonable interpretation of Florida law, 'legally cast votes,' " Scalia said, adding: "Count first, and rule upon legality afterwards, is not a recipe for producing election results that have the public acceptance democratic stability requires."

Scalia said that "it suffices to say that the issuance of the stay suggests that a majority of the court, while not deciding the issues presented, believe that the petitioner has a substantial probability of success."

On one level, that statement was simple boilerplate: any party seeking a stay from the United States Supreme Court, or any other court, ordinarily has to show a substantial probability of success. But in this case, the granting of the stay demonstrated a probability was likely even higher than "substantial," because any of the five justices in the majority who harbored doubts about the eventual outcome probably would have allowed the vote counting to continue while the court considered the case.

In his dissenting opinion, Stevens said there was a risk that granting the stay was equivalent to deciding this case in favor of Bush. "Preventing the recount from being completed will inevitably cast a cloud on the legitimacy of the election."

Boies said today that the brief the Gore team would file on Sunday, Dec. 10, would argue strongly that the United States Supreme Court should not interfere with a state Supreme Court's interpretation of state law. Throughout this dispute the Democratic legal team has not hesitated to point out the paradox of the Republican side, usually so solicitous of state sovereignty, seeking federal court intervention to stop the recounts. Governor Bush had filed the urgent application for a stay on Friday night, hours after the Florida Supreme Court reversed a lower state court and ordered statewide manual recounting of tens of thousands of ballots.

In his dissenting opinion, Stevens identified three principles he said the order today had violated: respect for rulings by state courts on questions of state law; the cautious exercise of the United States Supreme Court's jurisdiction on matters that largely concern other branches of government; and declining to exercise jurisdiction over federal questions "that were not fairly presented to the court whose judgment is being reviewed." "The majority has acted unwisely," he said.

Under the Supreme Court's rules, a stay requires the votes of five justices and, in addition to a likelihood of success, requires the applicant to show that "irreparable injury" would result unless the court intervened on an emergency basis, without waiting to review the merits of a case. In seeking to meet that standard, Bush's stay application said the Florida Supreme Court ruling "imperils Governor Bush's proper receipt of Florida's 25 electoral votes" by raising "a reasonable possibility that the votes will be called into doubt — or purport to be withdrawn — at a time when the Dec. 12 deadline for naming Florida's electors" would make any later judicial relief futile. In their brief opposing the stay, Gore's lawyers said the assertion that "a candidate for public office can be irreparably harmed by the process of discerning and tabulating the will of the voters" was surprising and "remarkable."

The question of irreparable harm was evidently the question in contention for the justices today. In his concurring statement, Scalia said that "the counting of votes that are of questionable legality does in my view threaten irreparable harm to petitioner," Governor Bush, "by casting a cloud upon what he claims to be the legitimacy of his election."

Stevens, in his dissent, said that while "counting every legally cast vote cannot constitute irreparable harm," there was a danger that the stay itself would cause irreparable harm not only to Gore but "more importantly, the public at large" because, given the deadlines, it would amount to a decision on the merits. "Preventing the recount from being completed will inevitably cast a cloud on the legitimacy of the election," Stevens said. He added: "As a more fundamental matter, the Florida court's ruling reflects the basic principle, inherent in our Constitution and our democracy, that every legal vote should be counted."

The case, Bush v. Gore, No. 00-949, presents obscure statutory and constitutional issues that, while they will form the basis of the eventual decision, will inevitably be overshadowed in the eyes of history by the political import of what occurred today.

Rarely in the United States Supreme Court's modern history have the justices' often-expressed concerns about preserving the court as an institution above and outside of raw politics foundered so visibly. Rarely, if ever, has the court faced such a supercharged political moment across dividing lines of such evident anger and mistrust.

Dec. 10, 2000, Linda Greenhouse

Federal Court Had Just Voted for Recount

ATLANTA—Shortly before the United States Supreme Court suspended the recounting of presidential ballots in Florida, a federal appeals court here ruled that it would not stop the count and denied George W. Bush's request for an emergency hearing on the constitutionality of manual recounts.

Voting 8 to 4, just as it had in denying Bush's request for a ruling against the recounts earlier this week, the United States Court of Appeals for the 11th Circuit declared without comment that it would not grant a rehearing in the case.

At the same time, the court ruled unanimously that the manual recounts could continue until the United States Supreme Court ruled on whether to accept Bush's appeal of Friday's Florida Supreme Court ruling to permit the recounts. But the 11th Circuit judges said the previously certified tally, which gave Bush a 537-vote lead over Al Gore, could not be changed until the United States Supreme Court had decided how to handle the case.

On Wednesday, Dec. 6, the 11th Circuit had ruled that it would not address constitutional concerns raised by Bush because he had not demonstrated that a prospective recount posed any threat of irreparable harm. Such a threat is a key standard for granting the injunction sought by Bush, and the court's majority wrote that Bush could not claim to be irreparably harmed when he had been certified by Florida's Secretary of State as the winner of the state's 25 electoral votes.

But that, Bush's lawyers pointed out in briefs filed late Friday, was before the Florida Supreme Court ordered in its 4-to-3 ruling that a statewide recount should begin immediately. The court decision immediately reduced Bush's lead over Gore in Florida to 154 votes from 537 and raised the possibility that Gore could overtake Bush when tens of thousands of votes were recounted by hand.

"Simply put, there has been a sudden and dramatic change in the core factual assumptions underlying the court's opinion, and plaintiffs' irreparable injury is more immediate and palpable than ever," wrote Theodore B. Olson in a brief filed with the appeals court late Friday night and released this morning. The 11th Circuit judges, who were dispersed around the South, apparently reached their decision today in a conference call.

Dec. 10, 2000, Kevin Sack

TEXT OF SUPREME COURT'S DECISION

Following is the text of the ruling by the United States Supreme Court to halt the hand recount in Florida and set Monday morning for arguments. The vote was 5 to 4. The justices who voted to grant the stay requested by Bush were Chief Justice William H. Rehnquist and Sandra Day O'Connor, Anthony M. Kennedy, Clarence Thomas and Antonin Scalia, who wrote a concurring opinion. John Paul Stevens, David H. Souter, Ruth Bader Ginsburg and Stephen G. Breyer dissented with Stevens writing the dissent.

The Decision

The application for stay presented to Justice Kennedy and by him referred to the court is granted, and it is ordered that the mandate of the Florida Supreme Court is hereby stayed pending further order of the court. In addition, the application for stay is treated as a petition for a writ of certiorari, and the petition for a writ of certiorari is granted. The briefs of the parties, not to exceed 50 pages, are to be filed with the clerk and served upon opposing counsel on or before 4 p.m. Sunday, Dec. 10, 2000. Rule 29.2 is suspended in this case. Briefs may be filed in compliance with Rule 33.2 to be replaced as soon as possible with the briefs prepared in compliance with Rule 33.1. The case is set for oral argument on Monday, Dec. 11, 2000, at 11 a.m., and a total of 1½ hours allotted for oral argument.

(continued on p. 280)

By Justice Scalia, Concurring

Though it is not customary for the court to issue an opinion in connection with its grant of stay, I believe a brief response is necessary to Justice Stevens's dissent. I will not address the merits of this case, since they will shortly be before us in the petition for *certiorari* that we have granted. It suffices to say that the issuance of the stay suggests that a majority of the court, while not deciding the issues presented, believe that the petitioner has a substantial probability of success.

On the question of irreparable harm, however, a few words are appropriate. The issue is not, as the dissent puts it, whether "counting every legally cast vote can constitute irreparable harm." One of the principal issues in the appeal we have accepted is precisely whether the votes that have been ordered to be counted are, under a reasonable interpretation of Florida law, "legally cast votes."

The counting of votes that are of questionable legality does in my view threaten irreparable harm to petitioner, and to the country, by casting a cloud upon what he claims to be the legitimacy of his election. Count first, and rule upon legality afterwards, is not a recipe for producing election results that have the public acceptance democratic stability requires.

Another issue in the case, moreover, is the propriety, indeed the constitutionality, of letting the standard for determination of voters' intent — dimpled chads, hanging chads, etc. — vary from county to county, as the Florida Supreme Court opinion, as interpreted by the circuit court, permits. If petitioner is correct that the counting in this fashion is unlawful, permitting the count to proceed on that erroneous basis will prevent an accurate recount from being conducted on a proper basis later, since it is generally agreed that each manual recount produces a degradation of the ballots, which renders a subsequent recount inaccurate.

For these reasons I have joined the court's issuance of stay, with a highly accelerated timetable for resolving this case on the merits.

By Justice Stevens, in Dissent

To stop the counting of legal votes, the majority today departs from three venerable rules of judicial restraint that have guided the court throughout its history. On questions of state law, we have consistently respected the opinions of the highest courts of the states. On questions whose resolution is committed at least in large measure to another branch of the federal government, we have construed our own jurisdiction narrowly and exercised it cautiously. On federal constitutional questions that were not fairly presented to the court whose judgment is being reviewed, we have prudently declined to express an opinion. The majority has acted unwisely.

(continued on next page)

Time does not permit a full discussion of the merits. It is clear, however, that a stay should not be granted unless an applicant makes a substantial showing of a likelihood of irreparable harm. In this case, applicants have failed to carry that heavy burden. Counting every legally cast vote cannot constitute irreparable harm. On the other hand, there is a danger that a stay may cause irreparable harm to the respondents — and, more importantly, the public at large — because of the risk that "the entry of the stay would be tantamount to a decision on the merits in favor of the applicants." Preventing the recount from being completed will inevitably cast a cloud on the legitimacy of the election.

It is certainly not clear that the Florida decision violated federal law. The Florida code provides elaborate procedures for ensuring that every eligible voter has a full and fair opportunity to cast a ballot and that every ballot so cast is counted. In fact, the statutory provision relating to damaged and defective ballots states that "no vote shall be declared invalid or void if there is a clear indication of the intent of the voter as determined by the canvassing board."

In its opinion, the Florida Supreme Court gave weight to that legislative command. Its ruling was consistent with earlier Florida cases that have repeatedly described the interest in correctly ascertaining the will of the voters as paramount. Its ruling also appears to be consistent with the prevailing view in other states.

As a more fundamental matter, the Florida court's ruling reflects the basic principle, inherent in our Constitution and our democracy, that every legal vote should be counted.

Accordingly, I respectfully dissent.

STUNNED DEMOCRATS ATTACK COURT'S DECISION

WASHINGTON—Expressing disbelief at the United States Supreme Court's order to halt the recount of votes in Florida, several prominent Democrats today said they feared that even if a count resumed, it was nearly impossible to finish it in time for Gore to wrest the White House from Bush.

One after another, Democrats lashed out at the Supreme Court, and in interviews accused justices of inappropriately injecting themselves into the election. "Right now, I'm not optimistic about anything," said Senator Dianne Feinstein of California. "This is the first time I have felt that what is evolving is a morass of uncertainty. It's hard for me to believe that the United States Supreme Court has a role in this. It just increases the polarization. How do we put the bricks together and work for the benefit of this nation?"

Representative Elijah E. Cummings of Maryland said he was stunned. "I just find it incredible," Cummings said. "It shocks the conscience. Scores of

African-Americans and Jews and so many other people have been deprived of their vote being counted. You want to believe that the courts are not politicized but I think the American people have got to begin to wonder what's going on here. "It's extremely disappointing," he added, "not so much for Gore, but for the American people. This is just so much bigger than Gore."

Leading Republicans, meanwhile, were newly jubilant, saying that their overriding objective has been to stop the count. And taking the opposite tack of the Democrats, they criticized the Florida Supreme Court for ordering a recount on Friday. "This is a judicial misadventure of some significant proportion," Gov. Marc Racicot of Montana, a leading backer of Bush, said in Tallahassee, Fla., today about the state court ruling. "It goes even beyond the extraordinary limits of the court's previous attempt to abrogate Florida law. The decision in some respects is naive and in other respects is almost absurd in its expectations of what can be accomplished in a very, very short period of time."

On the other hand, several Democrats upbraided the United States Supreme Court in language that was so harsh that it was reminiscent of the 1960's, when conservatives sought to impeach Chief Justice Earl Warren.

"The court, at least in my eyes, has damaged its credibility," said Senator Bob Kerrey of Nebraska, who had traveled to Florida several days ago to appear on Gore's behalf. "This is not just any court intervening," Kerrey said. "It would be one thing if this were the Warren court. This is the Rehnquist court. That court that has established in case after case the principle of state sovereignty. It's going to put them at odds with their own conclusions in the big Federalism case that's going on." Kerrey said he doubted there was adequate time for the counting to resume — and for Gore to climb back into serious contention. "I don't know how you get them going again," he said.

Dec. 10, 2000, Richard L. Berke

COUNTING STOPPED COLD BY SUPREME COURT ORDER

TALLAHASSEE—Across Florida today, vote counting teams gathered together and geared up, set their machines whirring and began the process of hand-counting the 45,000 ballots set to decide the presidency. Then the United States Supreme Court hit the brakes. From Pensacola to Key West, the entire sprawling enterprise of clerks and judges and observers came to a halt, whipsawing its participants and leaving much of Florida in a winded state of shock.

In county after county, a day that began with elections officials and volunteers removing the seals on the ballot boxes ended with them putting the ballots back inside, and Republicans whooping and cheering. It was an extraordinary day, often marked by confusion and chaos. When it was over, many of those involved gushed emotions of anger, glee and exhaustion. "Just another day in Election 2000," Pam Iorio, the elections supervisor in Hillsborough County, said with a sigh moments after the Canvassing Board shut down its recount.

When the hand-counting was halted about 2:30 p.m., fewer than a dozen counties had completed their work. While aides to Al Gore said that he had picked up nearly five dozen votes on George W. Bush, most of Florida's canvassing boards refused to divulge how far they had gotten and who had received the votes.

In many more counties, the counting had never even begun. Many were still feeding ballots into the machines and waiting for the uncounted ones — the so-called "undervotes" — to come spitting out. In Leon County, election workers were 30 minutes from finishing the recount. The teams of judges counting the roughly 9,000 undervotes from Miami-Dade County had worked their way through nearly half. In Duval County, which contains one of the state's largest pools of uncounted ballots, election workers were running test ballots through the counting machines when the stay was issued.

Across Florida, the recount seemed to proceed on two tracks: Many of the canvassing boards, including those that were tallying ballots cast in Hillsborough and Miami-Dade Counties, proceeded in a mostly businesslike way, with remarkably few problems or partisan clashes. In other counties, bewilderment and inertia prevailed, with elections workers bogged down before they could even start their counting.

In at least two counties in the northern part of the state, elections officials could not get started because they did not have the computer gear they needed to pull the uncounted ballots from the larger pile. In Bradford County, a mostly rural area that contains Florida's state penitentiary, election officials had all but given up. "There's not a whole lot we can do here," said Terry L. Vaughan, supervisor of elections for Bradford County, where the local government lacks the computer software to cull uncounted ballots from the nearly 10,000 votes cast. "We're going to have to regroup. The 'L' in my middle name might as well stand for 'Lost.' "

More than four hours after the deadline ordered by Terry P. Lewis of Leon County Circuit Court had passed for 64 Florida counties to submit their counting plans, only about half had even sent in their plans. Those that did offered an array of plans and guidelines that often seemed to contradict one another. In Bay County, the Canvassing Board informed Lewis in writing that it might ignore his order. In Suwannee County, the Canvassing Board decided that only those ballots that received a unanimous endorsement of the board would be counted. In most other counties, a majority vote was all that was needed. In Hillsborough County, Iorio told the judge that the Canvassing Board there intended to count "hanging chads" even though most counties did not even mention such a standard.

In most places, the ups and downs for Bush and Gore were hardly enough to swing even this tight election. In Escambia County, for instance, Gore picked up three votes. In Collier County, Bush picked up one. But in some of the larger counties, the numbers were big enough to stoke the passions of the candidates' surrogates. "Now you know why this was stopped," said one Democratic observer in Orange County, where the vice president had picked up 18 votes. The observer's voice was nearly drowned out by the cheers and whoops of joyous Republican partisans after the United States Supreme Court's ruling. "Thank God," one Republican observer said. "This is wonderful."

The greatest confusion unfolded in Jacksonville in Duval County, where elections officials believe 4,967 ballots went uncounted by the machines. Volunteers and elections officials there never even started counting. Like their counterparts in Bradford County, election officials in Duval County knew how many undervotes there were; they just could not sort them from the larger pile of 291,000. Computer software was flown up from Miami-Dade County, and election officials here were just beginning the sorting process when word came about the United States Supreme Court's ruling.

In Hillsborough County, preparations for the recount had proceeded smoothly this morning. By 11:15, workers were feeding ballots into machines to segregate those where no vote had been recorded for president. With little debate, the Canvassing Board — two Democrats and a Republican — was in unanimous agreement on which ballots to count (yes to hanging chads) and which ballots to ignore (no to dimples). Six counting teams were ready to go, observers were in place, the first ballots were set to be counted.

Across Tampa Bay, the Pinellas County Canvassing Board had actually counted 227 ballots, a process that yielded two new votes for Bush and one new vote for Gore. In Pinellas, the board had agreed to count some dimples, but not the infamous "rogue dimples" — that is, ballots where all the other candidates were cleanly punched but for the presidential election.

The Leon County supervisor of elections said that the judges had recounted about 4,000 ballots before the action was halted, and that the canvassing boards could discern the voters' intentions on about 160 of them. As in Hillsborough and Pinellas counties, the counting of the Miami-Dade ballots moved at a brisk pace, with teams of judges tallying some 1,000 votes an hour. "I'm not happy about what happened here," said Sancho, an elected Democrat. "I'm an election supervisor, and I like to count votes."

Dec. 10, 2000, Dexter Filkins and Dana Canedy

Florida's Undervote

As of Dec. 9, 2000

County	George W. Bush Votes	George W. Bush Pct.	Al Gore Votes	Al Gore Pct.	Uncounted	Over	Under
Miami-Dade	289,574	46.29	328,867	52.57	28,601	17,851	10,750
Palm Beach	152,964	35.31	269,754	62.27	29,702	19,150	10,604
Broward	177,939	30.93	387,760	67.41	14,611	7,906	6,716
Hillsborough	180,794	50.17	169,576	47.06	9,172	3,641	5,531
Duval	152,460	57.49	108,039	40.74	26,909	21,942	4,967
Pinellas	184,849	46.38	200,657	50.35	8,487		4,226
Marion	55,146	53.56	44,674	43.39	3,345	900	2,445
Collier	60,467	65.59	29,939	32.47	3,184	1,102	2,082
Lee	106,151	57.57	73,571	39.90	4,567		2,054
Sarasota	83,117	51.63	72,869	45.27	3,238	991	1,809
Pasco	68,607	48.05	69,576	48.73	3,917		1,776
Indian River	28,639	57.71	19,769	39.84	1,937	879	1,058
Orange	134,531	48.02	140,236	50.06	2,404	1,438	966
Osceola	26,237	47.11	28,187	50.62	1,684	1,042	642
Sumter	12,127	54.48	9,637	43.29	762	169	593
St. Lucie	34,705	44.50	41,560	53.29	649	112	537
Bay	38,682	65.70	18,873	32.06	663	134	529
Highlands	20,207	57.48	14,169	40.31	1,009	520	489
Volusia	82,368	44.84	97,313	52.98	500	155	448
St. Johns	39,564	65.10	19,509	32.10	558	132	426
Washington	4,995	62.24	2,798	34.86	329	37	292
Brevard	115,253	52.75	97,341	44.55	1,032	755	277
Lake	50,010	56.44	36,571	41.27	3,614	3,114	245
Clay	41,903	72.80	14,668	25.48	153	161	233
Polk	90,310	53.56	75,207	44.60	899	671	228
Alachua	34,135	39.81	47,380	55.25	327	102	225
Seminole	75,790	55.00	59,227	42.98	336	48	219
Nassau	16,408	68.98	6,955	29.24	1,581	1,386	195
Charlotte	35,428	52.96	29,646	44.31	3,156	2,988	168
Citrus	29,801	52.06	25,531	44.60	217	54	163
Manatee	58,023	52.59	49,226	44.61	1,410	1,263	147
Gadsden	4,770	32.38	9,736	66.09	2,073	1,951	122
Hernando	30,658	47.00	32,648	50.05	248		101
Baker	5,611	68.80	2,392	29.33	140	46	94
Jackson	9,139	56.06	6,870	42.14	1,157	1,063	94
Putnam	13,457	51.29	12,107	46.14	168	78	90
Hardee	3,765	60.38	2,342	37.56	408	323	85
Okaloosa	52,186	73.69	16,989	23.99	765	680	85
Monroe	16,063	47.39	16,487	48.64	180	97	83
Taylor	4,058	59.59	2,649	38.90	599	517	82
Columbia	10,968	59.24	7,049	38.07	693	617	76
Franklin	2,454	52.83	2,047	44.07	419	349	70
Flagler	12,618	46.53	13,897	51.25	62	7	55
Levy	6,863	53.92	5,398	42.41	760	708	52
Gulf	3,553	57.79	2,398	39.00	411	363	48
Suwannee	8,009	64.27	4,076	32.71	732	690	42
Bradford	5,416	62.43	3,075	35.45	734	695	40
Hendry	4,747	58.32	3,240	39.81	800	761	39
Liberty	1,317	54.65	1,017	42.20	188	159	29
Hamilton	2,147	54.14	1,723	43.44	389	389	0
DeSoto	4,256	54.48	3,321	42.51	701		
Dixie	2,697	57.79	1,827	39.15	332		
Gilchrist	3,300	61.17	1,910	35.40	288		
Glades	1,841	54.71	1,442	42.85	373		
Jefferson	2,478	43.91	3,041	53.89	573		
Madison	3,038	49.29	3,015	48.92	480		
Wakulla	4,512	52.54	3,838	44.70	422		
Martin	33,972	54.78	26,621	42.93	610		
Escambia	73,171	62.62	40,990	35.08	4,372		
Leon	39,073	37.88	61,444	59.57	181		
Santa Rosa	36,339	72.10	12,818	25.43	365		
Walton	12,186	66.51	5,643	30.80	219		
Okeechobee	5,057	51.32	4,589	46.57	858		
Holmes	5,012	67.77	2,177	29.43	139		
Calhoun	2,873	55.52	2,156	41.66	78		
Lafayette	1,670	66.67	789	31.50	171		
Union	2,332	60.95	1,407	36.77	258		

Breakdown for these counties not available

Source: County canvassing boards

The New York Times

day

33

SUNDAY,

DECEMBER 10TH

★ ★ ★ ★ ★

BUSH V. GORE

As the whole nation waits for tomorrow's U.S. Supreme Court hearing, an eerie calm seems to settle over Washington as well as over Austin and Tallahassee. Even in the New York studios of the major network talk shows the mood is downright civil as most of the candidates' spokespersons and major political party leaders exhort the country to remember that we are a nation of laws. Only the Senate majority leader, Trent Lott, talks about the possible role of the Florida Legislature in naming Bush electors. All agree that the Supreme Court's decision will prove decisive in the final outcome.

Both candidates maintain low profiles with Bush returning to Austin from his ranch and Gore attending church in Washington and hosting several Christmas parties at his home. Late in the afternoon lawyers for both sides file their briefs containing now familiar, but nonetheless bitterly contested arguments about the role assigned to the Supreme Court by the U.S. Constitution in the electoral affairs of the states. Because of the political nature of this case, many legal experts express deep concern that the court is placing its credibility on the line in such a manner that it risks losing the people's respect.

THE BRIEFS ARE FILED

"We have the rule of law in this country. And I have said from the beginning we have to stick with it."

– Representative Richard Gephardt, House minority leader

★ ★ ★

WASHINGTON — With only hours to go before the second Supreme Court argument of the postelection legal battle, the two teams of lawyers threw their best arguments into 50-page briefs, filed simultaneously to meet the 4 o'clock deadline the court set on Saturday [Dec. 9] when it accepted Bush's appeal. The Bush lawyers told the United States Supreme Court today that the vote recount ordered by the Florida Supreme Court on Friday was illegal and unconstitutional, while lawyers for Al Gore maintained that the only real right at issue in the case was "the right of voters to have their ballots counted."

As the competing briefs arrived at the Supreme Court, lawyers and political advocates for the two sides agreed almost universally that the court's decision could well be the final stroke in the long legal struggle. "We are going to follow the dictates of the United States Supreme Court," said James A. Baker III. "You can rest assured on that."

And David Boies, the lawyer who will appear before the court for Gore, said, "If the Florida Supreme Court's opinion is reversed and the United States Supreme Court says no more votes are going to be counted, then that's the end of it."

After weeks in which lawsuits and countersuits proliferated up and down the state and federal courts, this phase of this extraordinary election has now come down to 90 minutes of argument in a case entitled, fittingly and simply, Bush v. Gore. Arguing for Bush will be Theodore B. Olson, who appeared on the Texas governor's behalf in the first Supreme Court argument, on Dec. 1. Joseph P. Klock Jr. will also argue again on the Bush side on behalf of Katherine Harris. Boies, who presented the winning argument in this phase of the case before the Florida Supreme Court last Thursday, will replace Laurence H. Tribe, who argued Gore's cause before the Supreme Court last time and whose name remains as counsel of record on the brief the Gore team filed today. The two lawyers, who argued against each other in a Supreme Court case 13 years ago, have collaborated throughout this case.

THE BUSH ARGUMENT

The Dec. 1 Supreme Court argument, and the justices' subsequent order vacating the Florida Supreme Court decision then at issue, figured prominently in the brief the Bush lawyers filed today attacking the state court's latest ruling. Because the Florida Supreme Court has not yet responded to the justices' Dec. 4 order to clarify the basis for its Nov. 21 decision that extended the deadline for certifying the results of the state's presidential vote, that decision remains vacated, deprived at least temporarily of any legal effect. The Bush brief told the justices today that the Florida court's ruling on Friday nonetheless continued to build on the earlier decision by ordering the inclusion of votes that were counted after the original Nov. 18 certification deadline had expired.

"The court below not only failed to acknowledge that its earlier decision had been vacated," the brief said, "it openly relied on manual recounts that had occurred only because of that opinion." "Such reliance on a prior vacated decision defies this court's mandate and extends the error of the Nov. 21 decision," the Bush lawyers told the court, adding, "Without a single reference to this court's Dec. 4 decision, the majority of the Florida Supreme Court announced sweeping and novel procedures for recounting selected Florida ballots to determine anew the winner of the Nov. 7 presidential election in Florida."

The brief asserted that in ordering the recount, the Florida court committed essentially the same statutory and constitutional errors that caused the justices to vacate the earlier decision: usurping the State Legislature's authority under the United States Constitution to determine the manner of choosing Florida's presidential electors by undertaking a "wholesale revision of Florida statutory law." In addition, the brief said, "the unconstitutional flaws in the Florida Supreme Court's judgment immediately bore further unconstitutional fruit" when the recount decision was carried out on Friday night and Saturday morning. Because neither the State Supreme Court nor the trial court that was supervising the recount set standards for how to assess the various ballot permutations, "the court's newly devised scheme for re-tabulating votes is plainly arbitrary, capricious, unequal and standardless," the Bush brief said. This characterization formed the basis for the brief's argument that the recount violated both the equal protection and due process guarantees of the 14th Amendment.

The Bush lawyers also asserted that the Florida Supreme Court lacked jurisdiction over Gore's appeal of the state circuit court ruling that rejected his suit contesting the certified election results. This assertion represented the third position the Bush side has taken on the jurisdictional question. In argument before the Florida Supreme Court, Barry Richard, representing Bush, said he did not dispute the court's jurisdiction over the appeal.

He then filed a supplemental brief to tell the Florida court that "regardless of whether" state law allowed it to hear the appeal, it did not have authority to grant Gore the relief he sought, namely a recount.

The brief today said that the State Supreme Court "lacked jurisdiction, as a matter of federal law, to enter the judgment" because the source of its appellate jurisdiction was the state constitution rather than state law. Under the Bush side's constitutional theory, which appears to have the support of five Supreme Court justices, Article II of the United States Constitution, in giving state legislatures authority over the electoral process, essentially cuts state courts out of that process.

THE GORE ARGUMENT

The brief filed for Gore maintains that the Bush constitutional and jurisdictional arguments are based on a misreading of Article II and of the Supreme Court's precedents interpreting it. Article II "presupposes the existence of authority in each state to structure the internal processes and organization of each of its governmental branches," the Gore brief said. "Judicial review and interpretation of Florida's election statutes is a necessary legislative assumption," it added.

The Gore lawyers said that in any event it was the Florida Legislature itself that had passed the state constitutional provision governing appellate jurisdiction. The Florida Supreme Court's decision had not made new law. "The law enunciated in the Florida Supreme Court's opinion is the law as it existed on Election Day and long before it," the brief said. The decision did not set multiple standards, but rather "was quite insistent that the counting of ballots must be governed by a single uniform standard: the intent of the voter must control."

Human variation and "some degree of inconsistency" did not create a federal constitutional issue, the brief said, adding, "The only due process right even arguably implicated by this case is the right of voters to have their ballots counted." The brief said it was "worth noting" that the Bush side had argued in favor of counting military absentee ballots that "did not comply with various clear requirements of Florida statutory law."

The Gore lawyers said that to overturn the decision on due process grounds "would do violence both to principles of federalism and to the independence of the judiciary throughout the United States" by holding that "apparently routine judicial acts of statutory construction long thought to involve only questions of state law in fact amount to illegitimate and unconstitutional usurpations of the legislative role."

Dec. 11, 2000, Linda Greenhouse

THE COURT'S CREDIBILITY AT RISK

WASHINGTON — If events unfold over the next few days as now appears likely, the scene at the next Inauguration Day less than six weeks from now will be nothing short of extraordinary. Chief Justice William H. Rehnquist will be administering the oath of office to Gov. George W. Bush, whose election was all but assured by the Supreme Court's last-minute intervention this weekend to stop the Florida vote counting, as the eight other justices, bitterly divided four to four, look on from their front-row seats.

In a way, the court has as much at stake in the playing out of this national drama as either of the politicians whose fate five justices chose on Saturday to take into their hands. With the prospect of bringing an end to the bitter Florida election contest, the justices could not only play the crucial role in validating a winner, but also affect the future makeup of their own court, since the next president may have the chance to select new Supreme Court nominees.

Public response today to the court's action was intense, with much of the debate focused on the propriety of the stay. Terrance Sandalow, a law professor and a former dean of the University of Michigan Law School, said the "balance of harms so unmistakably were on the side of Gore" that the granting of the stay was "incomprehensible." In an interview, Sandalow, a judicial conservative who said he opposed *Roe v. Wade* and supported the 1987 nomination of Robert H. Bork to the Supreme Court, called the stay "an unmistakably partisan decision without any foundation in law."

Charles Fried, a former solicitor general in the administration of President George Bush, who filed a brief today on behalf of the Florida legislative leadership, took an opposite view. It was the Florida Supreme Court's decision to order statewide recounts that was "lawless," Fried said, while the stay "prevents them from garnering the fruits of their lawless behavior."

Eight years ago, riven by debate over whether to uphold or overturn the constitutional right to abortion announced in *Roe v. Wade*, the court faced another moment of institutional crisis, albeit one that had to do with judicial philosophy rather than partisan ideology. On that occasion, three justices, all appointed by Republican presidents, wrote an unusual joint opinion to explain why they had decided to adhere to a precedent that, as an original matter, they might well not have joined.

The court's only real power lies, the three justices wrote in *Planned Parenthood v. Casey*, "in its legitimacy, a product of substance and perception that shows itself in the people's acceptance of the judiciary as fit to determine what the nation's law means and to declare what it demands." It was not always enough, they went on to say, for a decision to have a plausible legal basis. At times when the court is under great pressure, it has to do something more:

"The court must take care to speak and act in ways that allow people to accept its decisions on the terms the court claims for them, as grounded truly in principle, not as compromises with social and political pressures having, as such, no bearing on the principled choices that the court is obliged to make. Thus, the court's legitimacy depends on making legally principled decisions under circumstances in which their principled character is sufficiently plausible to be accepted by the nation."

In concluding that overturning *Roe v. Wade* would cause "profound and unnecessary damage to the court's legitimacy," the three justices concluded: "The court's concern with legitimacy is not for the sake of the court but for the sake of the nation to which it is responsible."

The opinion was signed by Justices Sandra Day O'Connor, Anthony M. Kennedy and David H. Souter. Now with Justices O'Connor and Kennedy having voted on Saturday to stop the vote count, and with Justice Souter having voted in dissent, these onetime allies stand on opposite sides of a gaping divide. And yet the reality that all three expressed so emphatically in 1992 has scarcely changed. In fact, the need for the court to explain its actions in terms the public can understand and accept — even if not agree with — is arguably greater than ever when the court can be perceived as stepping over the fine but nonetheless still distinct line that separates law and politics, immeasurably greater when a narrow majority can be seen as shaping an election that in turn will determine the nature of future Supreme Court appointments.

The majority on Saturday did not explain its decisions to hear the case — the argument is set for Monday morning — or to stop the counting. Justice Antonin Scalia issued a statement in his own name in response to the four dissenters' warning that preventing the counting of votes "will inevitably cast a cloud on the legitimacy of the election." Justice Scalia said it was "the counting of votes that are of questionable legality" that was "casting a cloud," not on the process in general but specifically on what Bush "claims to be the legitimacy of his election."

In other words, the majority's justification for the stay was that if the vote counting proceeded and had appeared to make Al Gore the winner by the time the court could decide the merits of Bush's appeal, the Bush position would be untenable as a political matter even if it prevailed as a matter of law.

That justification put the court in the position of seeming to protect Bush — who has endorsed Justices Scalia and Clarence Thomas, named to the court by his father, as his ideal justices — from whatever uncomfortable truth the uncounted ballots might reveal. The fact that the justices entered the stay with the counting under way and most of it expected to conclude at 2 p.m. on Sunday, gave the court the appearance of racing to beat the clock before an unwelcome truth could come out.

In reprieving Bush from any political embarrassment the vote totals may hold, the majority may have only postponed the governor's problem. Under Florida's expansive "sunshine" law, the ballots will be publicly available for counting by news organizations and others.

Beyond debate is the fact that the court has now placed itself in the midst of the political thicket where it has always most doubted its institutional competence and where as a personal matter the justices have always appeared least comfortable.

Dec. 11, 2000, Linda Greenhouse

★ ★ ★

OpEd

Supreme Court's Incursion Was Not Needed

Who wins the presidential election often alters the Supreme Court, both by determining who appoints new justices and by subtly influencing the court's decisions. But when should the Supreme Court alter who wins an election? That is the question posed by the court's decision this weekend to halt Florida's recount of the ballots.

The last two times the Supreme Court intervened so decisively in the political process were in the mid-1960's, when it announced the requirement of one person, one vote and when the court upheld the Voting Rights Act's re-enfranchisement of black Americans. The concerns that justified those dramatic and rare interventions explain why the current incursion into the political thicket is so ill-advised.

The one person, one vote principle enunciated in 1964 required the reapportionment of virtually every state's legislature and most states' congressional districts. The representatives of grotesquely underpopulated districts would never give up power willingly. The state courts were often powerless to act because the malapportionments were written into state constitutions. Congress itself was malapportioned and not interested in reform. If the Supreme Court did not act, no one else would. The political arteries had hardened. The political process could not cure itself. A judicial bypass was necessary.

It was also necessary in the case of black disenfranchisement. The court needed to step in to guarantee the ability of black voters to vote in places that had barred them from registering, unfairly tossed out their ballots or organized the election system to dilute their voting strength.

The Supreme Court's incursion into the Florida case is entirely different. There was no reason to jump in immediately. Whatever else we might say about Florida, its political system has not been frozen into inaction. The state's judges, elected by Florida citizens, have been sorting out difficult election law questions. The state's legislature has been wrestling with how to ensure that the state's voice will be heard in the Electoral College. It, too, may be acting prematurely. But its jumping the gun is preferable to the Supreme Court's doing so — after all, it remains accountable to the voters. And Congress has been gearing up to fulfill its responsibilities under the Constitution and federal law to ensure an orderly determination of who should be the 43rd president.

Self-government may be messy, time-consuming and partisan. But in the Florida recount case, the political actors are vigorous and functioning. Unless the five justices who voted for the stay reverse course, they are risking much of the court's reputation as a protector of voting rights, since the court's action makes it less likely that every lawful vote will be counted.

They also risk further undermining the legitimacy of this already clouded election. Florida's freedom of information act will make the disputed ballots available for public inspection. The ballots may eventually be examined by the press and civic groups. So one day we may know who got the most votes in Florida. If the Supreme Court's short-circuiting of the recount means that we discover that the wrong man sits in the Oval Office, five justices will have dealt democracy and the court itself a serious blow.

Bush's lead has shrunk steadily — from about 1,700 on election night to perhaps less than 100 when the Supreme Court stepped in to stop the counting. If Bush is to win, ultimately, by one vote, fine. But let that one vote be cast by a Floridian, and not by a justice of the United States Supreme Court.

Dec. 11, 2000

By Pamela S. Karlan, Professor at Stanford Law School

day

34

MONDAY,
DECEMBER 11TH

SUPREME COURT II: SOBER, INTENSE

As the nation's nine Supreme Court justices prepare to hear the arguments in *Bush v. Gore*, thousands gather outside the courthouse to cheer or chant or protest, transforming the block in front of the marble, Corinthian-style building into a national village square. Inside the hearing is fast-paced, with the justices asking very pointed questions of the lawyers for each side. Everyone is aware that the next president will more than likely be determined by the Court's decision.

In Florida the Republican-dominated Legislature realizes this, too, and decides to take the first step toward assuring Bush's election. And in Washington the Gore camp has a federal judge tell *The New York Times* that he believes Justice Clarence Thomas should recuse himself because his wife, Virginia, is working to help a possible Bush administration find qualified people. This revelation, combined with the fact that Justice Scalia's son is a lawyer with Theodore Olson's firm, makes many Democrats skeptical of the whole process.

Hard and Fast Questions From the Highest Court

"Even a dog knows the difference in being stumbled over and being kicked."

– Justice Kennedy to Gore's lawyer about confusing standards in ballot counting

★ ★ ★

WASHINGTON — Members of the Supreme Court's liberal bloc labored visibly today to fashion a compromise that might resolve the case of *Bush v. Gore* and allow the counting of Florida's presidential votes to resume. But it was far from certain by the end of the sober, intense 90-minute session that they had found any customers among the five conservative justices who voted Saturday [Dec. 9] to stop the recount as it was just beginning by order of the Florida Supreme Court.

For the United States Supreme Court, this was the second argument in 10 days to come out of the bitterly disputed Florida election. In contrast to the earlier argument, there was a sense now that time was really running out, for the court as well as the two presidential candidates whose photo finish had driven them into a litigation contest as intense as the campaign itself. Twice, Vice President Al Gore prevailed before Florida's Supreme Court, and twice Gov. George W. Bush persuaded the justices to hear an appeal.

The focus of the argument this time shifted from the constitutional theories that dominated the argument on Dec. 1 to the practicalities of what was actually happening in Florida during the few hours of manual recounts before the United States Supreme Court's 5-to-4 vote to grant Bush's request for an emergency stay. What standards were used to determine the intent of the voters? What were the implications of using different standards for different counties?

It was on this ground that Justices David H. Souter and Stephen G. Breyer struggled to find the outlines of a possible compromise. If differing standards raised questions of fundamental fairness, placing the recount under a constitutional cloud, as Bush's lawyers insisted, then why not just send the case back for imposition of a uniform standard?

The two justices received little help from the two lawyers who argued on the Republican side today, Theodore B. Olson for Bush and Joseph P. Klock Jr. for Katherine Harris. They came into court as likely winners, on the basis of the justices' action on Saturday, and understandably displayed little interest in helping the court do anything but flatly overturn the Florida Supreme Court ruling last Friday that ordered the new recount.

Pressed by Justice Breyer on what a "fair standard" would be for counting punch-card ballots on which a machine had found no vote for president, Mr. Olson replied: "That is the job for a legislature." At a minimum, Mr. Olson said when pressed further, "a penetration of the chad in the ballot, because indentations are no standards at all."

Some canvassing boards in Florida have counted "dimpled chads" as votes under some circumstances, and others have refused to do so. In ordering a statewide manual recount of the "undervotes," those ballots on which tabulating machines did not find a presidential selection, the Florida Supreme Court did not set a standard, and neither did Judge Terry P. Lewis, the circuit court judge in Leon County who was supervising the recount.

Mr. Klock was even more dismissive than his colleague was of the notion that a court might fashion a standard that was not spelled out in the statute. "I don't think the Supreme Court of Florida, respectfully, or any other court can sit down and write the standards that are going to be applied." Asked by Justice Breyer to "take one out of a hat," he also suggested that mere indentations should not count, and then added: "The only problem that we have here is created by people who did not follow instructions" that told voters to be sure to punch completely through the chads on their ballots.

At one point during a long colloquy with Justices Souter and Ruth Bader Ginsburg, Mr. Olson appeared willing to discuss the theoretical possibility of coming up with a statewide standard. At that point, Justice Antonin Scalia jumped into the argument almost as if to make sure that Mr. Olson did not make any unnecessary concessions on the Bush side. "It's part of your submission, I think," Justice Scalia said, "that there is no wrong when a machine does not count those ballots that it's not supposed to count?" In other words, Justice Scalia was reminding Mr. Olson that the Bush position was that undercounts caused by voter error, as opposed to a mechanical malfunction, were not ballots that qualified for counting under any standard.

"That's absolutely correct, Justice Scalia," Mr. Olson said.

"The voters are instructed to detach the chads entirely," Justice Scalia went on, "and the machine, as predicted, does not count those chads where those instructions are not followed, there isn't any wrong."

"That's correct," Mr. Olson said.

Justice Scalia, whose son, Eugene, is a partner of Mr. Olson's at the Los Angeles law firm Gibson, Dunn & Crutcher, has been the most outspoken advocate on the court for Mr. Bush's position. He wrote a separate statement in support of the stay the court granted on Saturday, describing as "irreparable harm" to the Republican nominee the prospect that "the counting of votes that are of questionable legality," presumably for Mr. Gore, would cast a cloud on what Mr. Bush "claims to be the legitimacy of his election."

To have any prospect of emerging from this case with something other than a complete loss, David Boies, Mr. Gore's lawyer, needed to persuade Justices Sandra Day O'Connor and Anthony M. Kennedy that the Florida Supreme Court acted within its authority last Friday when it ordered the manual recount. Neither justice appeared particularly open to persuasion. Justice O'Connor took issue with the argument by Mr. Boies that the Florida Supreme Court had done nothing untoward and was entitled to the deference the justices usually show to state courts.

"You are responding as though there were no special burden to show some deference to legislative choices," Justice O'Connor said. She referred to the clause in Article II of the United States Constitution that gives state legislatures the authority to determine the manner of choosing the state's presidential electors. The Bush argument is that this clause bars state courts from taking action that interferes with the legislative choices.

"In this one context," Justice O'Connor continued, "not when courts review laws generally for general elections, but in the context of selection of presidential electors, isn't there a big red flag up there, 'Watch out'?"

"I think there is in a sense," Mr. Boies replied, "and I think the Florida Supreme Court was grappling with that."

"And you think it did it properly?" Justice O'Connor persisted.

"I think it did do it properly," Mr. Boies replied.

At this point, Justice O'Connor criticized the Florida court directly for not having yet responded to the justices' unanimous order one week ago that vacated an earlier decision that extended the deadline for certifying the presidential vote totals.

"It just seemed to kind of bypass it and assume that all those changes and deadlines were just fine and they could go ahead and adhere to them," Justice O'Connor said, "and I found that troublesome."

Early this evening, the Florida Supreme Court issued a 6-to-1 decision responding to the justices' Dec. 4 order. The state court reinstated the Nov. 21 decision that the justices had vacated, stating that the deadline extension was based not on the Florida Constitution but on state law as interpreted through "longstanding principles of statutory construction." Whether that late-day action from Tallahassee would influence the course of the case in Washington was highly uncertain.

Justice Kennedy, who scowled through much of the argument, engaged in a testy exchange with Mr. Boies about whether the Florida court, in its earlier opinion, had improperly made "new law."

"It wasn't passing a new law," Mr. Boies said. "It was interpreting the existing law."

Justice Kennedy was unpersuaded. "I'm not sure why," he said. "If the Legislature does it, it's a new law, and when the Supreme Court does it, it isn't." Later, Justice Kennedy challenged Mr. Boies to explain whether there was a uniform standard for counting votes in Florida.

Yes, Mr. Boies replied, "the standard is whether or not the intent of the voter is reflected by the ballot."

"That's very general," Justice Kennedy said, adding in an annoyed tone: "Even a dog knows the difference in being stumbled over and being kicked. We know it, yes. In this case what we are concerned with is an intent that focuses on this little piece of paper called a ballot." Under the constitutional guarantee of equal protection, he asked, "could that vary from county to county?"

Mr. Boies, obviously determined not to yield any ground on this line of argument, replied: "I think it can vary from individual to individual."

Later in the argument, Mr. Boies said that the variation in vote-counting standards "is going to have a lot less effect on how votes are treated than the mere difference in the types of machines that are used." He said there were five times as many undervotes in punch-card ballot counties as in optical ballot counties.

"For whatever that reason is," Mr. Boies added, "whether it's voter error or machine problems, that statistic, you know, makes clear that there is some difference in how votes are being treated county by county."

In answer to questions, Mr. Boies said the recount schedule set by the Florida Supreme Court had been a realistic one. A recount could still be completed even now, he said.

But wouldn't there just be more challenges, more appeals, more briefs? Chief Justice William H. Rehnquist wanted to know.

Yes, Mr. Boies said, but the legal teams had the experience to deal with that contingency, having become practiced in how to "do the briefs and have the argument the next day and a decision within 24 hours."

Dec. 12, 2000, Linda Greenhouse

Justices' Queries Reveal Their Chief Concerns

Those Who Voted for the Stay of Counting

Chief Justice William H. Rehnquist largely asked factual questions, apparently to clarify the record. As an example, he noted that one of the dissenting Florida justices said that to review all of the state's undervotes would mean 177,000 ballots needed to be recounted, suggesting that there was not enough time left for a recount. Undervotes are ballots on which votes are registered for some races but not for president. When he asked David Boies, the lawyer for Al Gore, if that was accurate, Boies said that he believed the figure was about 60,000 and that the others were not counted because two choices for president were picked.

Justice Antonin Scalia seemed to try to support the contentions of the Bush side that when voters do not mark their ballots so that their choices are completely obvious —that is, with the chads fully punched out — it is a result of the voter's error, not any problem with the counting. "When the voters are instructed to detach the chads entirely, and the machine, as predicted, does not count those chads, where those instructions are not followed, there isn't any wrong," he said.

Justice Anthony M. Kennedy waited a mere 54 seconds before interrupting Theodore B. Olson, the lawyer for Bush, to ask about his main

(continued on p. 298)

concern. "Can you begin by telling us our federal jurisdiction? Where's the federal question here?" he asked. He waited only about five seconds into the presentation of Mr. Boies to ask the same thing. Justice Kennedy was most concerned about whether the United States Supreme Court had any authority to pass on the Florida court's ruling. He said that the proposition that a state legislature should not be guided by the courts, "seems to me a holding which has grave implications for our republican theory of government."

Justice Sandra Day O'Connor seemed greatly concerned about the argument advanced by Olson that the Florida Supreme Court had no authority to review and pass judgment on the election laws. But in questioning Boies, she expressed a view that perhaps the Florida court did not give sufficient deference to the legislature. "Does that not mean that a court has to, in interpreting a legislative act, give special deference to the legislature's choices insofar as a presidential election is concerned?" she asked. "When courts review laws generally for general elections, but in the context of selection of presidential electors. Isn't there a big red flag up there — watch out?" She also said that she was troubled that "I did not find really a response by the Florida Supreme Court to this court's remand in the case a week ago."

Justice Clarence Thomas did not ask questions at the hearing. He rarely speaks during court hearings and his former clerks and supporters have said that he believes oral arguments are not an efficient way for him to evaluate the cases.

Those Who Voted against the Stay of Counting

Justice John Paul Stevens expressed concern over the idea that Bush's lawyers were arguing that the Florida Supreme Court did not have the authority to review the electoral scheme put into place by the Legislature. He questioned Olson closely about what he said was his view that the Legislature did not specifically authorize such power. "In the context of this case, the justices were saying that they can include the judicial branch, when they wish to do so" but that the Legislature never expressed such an intention, Mr. Olson replied.

Justice Stephen G. Breyer wanted to know from both lawyers what would be a fair system to recount the votes if, in fact, that was the result of all the court rulings. "If it were to start up again, if it were, totally hypothetically, and you were counting just undercounts. I understand that you think that the system that's set up now is very unfair because it's different standards in different places. What, in your opinion, would be a fair standard?" When Olson replied that such decisions were for the Legislature, Justice Breyer pressed again, "But I'd still like to get your opinion,

(continued on next page)

insofar as you could give it." Olson said it would have to, at a minimum, include a standard of penetration of the ballot.

Justice Ruth Bader Ginsburg also pressed the lawyers on what standard should be used in a recount. "Mr. Olson, you have said the intent of the voter simply won't do; it's too vague, it's too subjective. But at least, but at least those words — 'intent of the voter' come from the Legislature. Wouldn't anything added to that be — wouldnt you be objecting much more fiercely than you are now, if something were added to the words that the all-powerful Legislature put in the statute?"

Justice David H. Souter also questioned the contention that the Florida Supreme Court could not review and pass on election standards. He noted that in the law that allows for elections to be contested, the circuit courts are explicitly given authority. He said that unless the Florida Supreme Court had "simply passed the bounds of legitimate statutory construction," he did not see how it was possible to find any federal constitutional problem with the state court's action.

Dec. 12, 2000, David Firestone

Meanwhile, Florida Supreme Court Rewrites Opinion

TALLAHASSEE — A week after the United States Supreme Court told the Florida Supreme Court to rewrite its opinion extending the deadline for manual recounts, the state court did so this evening, restating the earlier opinion in language intended to pass muster in Washington. The new opinion, in a 6-to-1 vote, stated that the Florida Supreme Court was simply interpreting two conflicting election statutes written by the Legislature, not making new law or basing its opinion on the State Constitution. The distinction is important, because the United States Supreme Court has said that only the Legislature is responsible for laws regulating presidential electors.

When it vacated the initial opinion, the United States court said it was concerned that the Florida court might have gone beyond its role of interpreting laws and created something new when it extended the deadlines, in possible violation of federal law prohibiting changing a state's election law after Election Day. The issues in the case are considered largely moot, because Bush won both the original certification of the state's vote and the one extended by the Florida Supreme Court, although by a lesser margin.

In a footnote to today's opinion, the Florida court said that it has been busy working on the contest lawsuit, on which it issued an extraordinary opinion mandating a new set of recounts that were halted the next day by the United States Supreme Court. "We have issued this decision as expeditiously as possible under the foregoing time constraints in order to timely respond to the questions presented by the Supreme Court of the United States in the Dec. 4, 2000, opinion and its remand instructions," the footnote said.

The dissenter, Chief Justice Charles T. Wells, said the majority's timing was bad, and also disagreed with the substance of the opinion. The dissent did not explain why Justice Wells now disagrees with what is functionally identical to the unanimous opinion issued on Nov. 21. Republican lawyers said they, too, disagreed with the opinion, and found the timing suspicious.

"It's curious that less than eight hours after their opinions came in for some rough sledding in the United States Supreme Court, the Florida Supreme Court decided to respond," said Benjamin Ginsberg, Mr. Bush's lawyer. "What they've done is rewrite the whole statutory scheme, putting in deadlines and dimples that didn't exist before, no matter how much they try to rationalize it."

Dec. 12, 2000, David Firestone

Legislature Prepares to Appoint Electors

TALLAHASSEE — One day before federal law calls for each state to settle its presidential contest, Florida's Republican-controlled Legislature moved a step closer to appointing its own slate of electors for George W. Bush. Committees in each chamber passed identical resolutions today superseding the results of Florida's still contested popular vote. The House is set to vote on its measure tomorrow. The Senate is to take up its resolution the following day.

Republicans in both houses said they were prepared to act if the United States Supreme Court did not quickly settle the state's undecided presidential vote. "We have to ensure that the voters of Florida are not disenfranchised," said Senator Don Sullivan, a Republican sponsor of the resolution. "At this moment, it's a great sin to do nothing."

Both committees approved the measure in the form of a resolution that could be enacted without the signature of Gov. Jeb Bush, the brother of the Republican presidential nominee. The dual votes came over the vigorous objections of Democratic legislators and their supporters, who warned of a "constitutional train wreck" if the Republicans moved to seat their own electors. Today's committee votes split nearly along party lines, with one Democratic House member defecting to the Republican side.

Democratic lawmakers, outnumbered in both chambers, accused the Republicans of preparing to circumvent the will of Florida's voters. Many Democrats called the resolution illegal, and hinted at legal action if the Legislature approved the measure. Some called the Republican move unneeded and likely to further complicate the effort to determine a winner in Florida.

"I don't think most people like it when a bunch of politicians go into a room and come out with the next president," said Representative Ken Gottlieb of Miramar, a Democratic member of the committee. Mr. Gottlieb called the effort to create a slate of electors "just an insurance policy to allow a Bush victory."

Republican lawmakers said they had no choice because the uncertainty surrounding the Nov. 7 election threatened to nullify Florida's 25 electoral votes.

The votes followed four hours of mostly partisan testimony from experts and voters, split evenly between those who wanted the Legislature to appoint the electors and those who denounced the undertaking as a stifling of the people's voice.

Hanging above the proceedings was the pending decision by the United States Supreme Court about whether to approve the vote recounts the Florida Supreme Court had ordered on Friday. Several Republican lawmakers said that if the United States Supreme Court nullified the vote recount, they would probably decide against moving forward.

Dec. 12, 2000, Dexter Filkins and Dana Canedy

Those Other Lawsuits Are Still Going On

TALLAHASSEE — Although the eyes of the world were on the United States Supreme Court today, Democrats and Republicans had a few more cards left to play in the Florida court system.

Democrats filed briefs here this morning asking the Florida Supreme Court to overturn the decisions of two lower court judges who decided on Friday not to throw out nearly 25,000 absentee ballots from Seminole and Martin Counties, where Republican workers were improperly allowed to fix Republican ballot request forms that had been rejected. If those ballots were thrown out, it would put Al Gore over the top.

And Republicans looked once more to the issue of overseas absentee ballots, especially from members of the military. They said that if any more recounts were done in Florida, the county canvassing boards should also count overseas absentee ballots using a new, more lenient standard that was ordered by a federal judge in Pensacola on Friday. Those ballots overwhelmingly favored George W. Bush, and he would stand to benefit if more were counted.

But it was unclear what effect, if any, the 11th-hour machinations would have. Bush's lawyers urged the Florida Supreme Court to reject the appeals of both the Seminole and Martin County cases; the court has given no indication of whether it will act.

As supporters of Gore looked to the absentee ballots in those two counties, supporters of Bush looked at the absentee ballots in the rest of the state. On Friday Bush won a partial victory when a federal judge in Pensacola ruled in a lawsuit that Bush had filed contending that seven counties had rejected 337 overseas absentee ballots that should have been counted. The ruling by Judge Lacey A. Collier of Federal District Court could add to Bush's slim lead in the Florida count. Judge Collier rejected several of the Bush camp's arguments for reinstating votes, but agreed in two areas. He ruled that any signed absentee ballots that were rejected solely because they lacked a postmark, or solely because there was no record on file that the voter ever requested such a ballot, should be declared valid votes.

Dec. 12, 2000, Michael Cooper and Richard Pérez-Peña

A Laugh Always Helps

If there was any good humor left in the nation after five weeks of enormous dispute and doubt about its next leader, the Supreme Court was quick to mine that possibility when one of the day's anxious appellants made a factual error and, with all due deference, began misidentifying judges as he pleaded for their sympathy.

"Well, Justice Brennan," said Joseph P. Klock Jr., a lawyer for the Florida secretary of state, as he addressed a question from Justice John Paul Stevens.

Klock instantly realized he had committed a lawyer's nightmare gaffe. "I'm sorry; that's why they tell you not to do that," he apologized amid some light laughter of relief, mindful of a law school dictum against direct address to a judge. But then he did it again.

"Justice Breyer, what I'm saying is," he began to Justice David H. Souter.

"I'm Justice Souter; you've got to cut that out," the judge gently responded.

More laughter nicely filled the hall of justice as Klock replied, "I will now give up."

With a fine sense of timing, Justice Antonin Scalia capped the vaudeville possibilities of the moment: "Mr. Klock, I'm Scalia."

"It will be hard to forget," replied Mr. Klock. And even more laughs punctuated what amounted to an early reading from the court about its disposition. Whatever else the great presidential legal debate deserved to be called — historic, traumatic and all the rest — it at least remained eminently human.

Dec. 12, 2000, Francis X. Clines

day

35

TUESDAY,

DECEMBER 12TH

★ ★ ★ ★ ★

U.S. SUPREME COURT ENDS RECOUNTS

In what appears to be an attempt by the Supreme Court to prevent the presidential election from being decided in Congress, five justices vote to effectively end all the recounts. Although constitutional scholars differ on the fine points, the majority focuses on the law's requirement that every state's electors be chosen by the 12th of December or face the possibility of a challenge in the House of Representatives.

The court's 5-to-4 vote and majority opinion reflect the arguments and positions heard during both hearings and so the outcome is not much of a surprise. The style and tone of the dissenters' written opinions, however, strike most commentators as unusually strong. Justice Breyer calls the decision a "self-inflicted wound that may harm not just the court, but the nation."

Some Democrats urge Gore to concede immediately, but he says he will have a statement tomorrow. According to later reports from his aides, Gore spends the early morning hours on the phone to advisers and lawyers trying to see if there is any loophole that would allow him to press on. His lawyers in Florida work through the night preparing a brief for the Florida Supreme Court.

During the day, however, Florida's high court rules against the Democrats in their suit to throw out thousands of absentee ballots. And for good measure the Florida House of Representatives votes for a slate of electors who could put Bush in the White House.

A Deeply Divided Court Ends the Struggle

"When a court orders a statewide remedy, there must be at least some assurance that the rudimentary requirements of equal treatment and fundamental fairness are satisfied."

– From the Supreme Court's unsigned majority opinion

★ ★ ★

WASHINGTON — The Supreme Court effectively handed the presidential election to George W. Bush tonight, overturning the Florida Supreme Court and ruling by a vote of 5 to 4 that there could be no further counting of Florida's disputed presidential votes.

The ruling came after a long and tense day of waiting at 10 p.m., just two hours before the Dec. 12 "safe harbor" for immunizing a state's electors from challenge in Congress was to come to an end. The unsigned majority opinion said it was the immediacy of this deadline that made it impossible to come up with a way of counting the votes that could both meet "minimal constitutional standards" and be accomplished within the deadline.

The five members of the majority were Chief Justice William H. Rehnquist and Justices Sandra Day O'Connor, Antonin Scalia, Anthony M. Kennedy and Clarence Thomas. Among the four dissenters, two justices, Stephen G. Breyer and David H. Souter, agreed with the majority that the varying standards in different Florida counties for counting the punch-card ballots presented problems of both due process and equal protection. But unlike the majority, these justices said the answer should be not to shut the recount down, but to extend it until the Dec. 18 date for the meeting of the Electoral College. Justice Souter said that such a recount would be a "tall order" but that "there is no justification for denying the state the opportunity to try to count all the disputed ballots now."

The six separate opinions, totaling 65 pages, were filled with evidence that the justices were acutely aware of the controversy the court had entered by accepting Bush's appeal of last Friday's Florida Supreme Court ruling and by granting him a stay of the recount on Saturday afternoon, just hours after the vote counting had begun.

"None are more conscious of the vital limits on judicial authority than are the members of this court," the majority opinion said, referring to "our unsought responsibility to resolve the federal and constitutional issues the judicial system has been forced to confront."

The dissenters said nearly all the objections raised by Bush were insubstantial. The court should not have reviewed either this case or the one it decided last week, they said. Justice John Paul Stevens said the court's action "can only lend credence to the most cynical appraisal of the work of judges throughout the land."

His dissenting opinion, also signed by Justices Breyer and Ruth Bader Ginsburg, added: "It is confidence in the men and women who administer the judicial system that is the true backbone of the rule of law. Time will one day heal the wound to that confidence that will be inflicted by today's decision. One thing, however, is certain. Although we may never know with complete certainty the identity of the winner of this year's Presidential election, the identity of the loser is perfectly clear. It is the nation's confidence in the judge as an impartial guardian of the rule of law."

What the court's day and a half of deliberations yielded tonight was a messy product that bore the earmarks of a failed attempt at a compromise solution that would have permitted the vote counting to continue. It appeared that Justices Souter and Breyer, by taking seriously the equal protection concerns that Justices Kennedy and O'Connor had raised at the argument, had tried to persuade them that those concerns could be addressed in a remedy that would permit the disputed votes to be counted.

Justices O'Connor and Kennedy were the only justices whose names did not appear separately on any opinion, indicating that one or both of them wrote the court's unsigned majority opinion, labelled only *per curiam*, or "by the court." Its focus was narrow, limited to the ballot counting process itself. The opinion objected not only to the varying standards used by different counties for determining voter intent, but to aspects of the Florida Supreme Court's order determining which ballots should be counted.

"We are presented with a situation where a state court with the power to assure uniformity has ordered a statewide recount with minimal procedural safeguards," the opinion said. "When a court orders a statewide remedy, there must be at least some assurance that the rudimentary requirements of equal treatment and fundamental fairness are satisfied."

Three members of the majority — the Chief Justice, and Justices Scalia and Thomas — raised further, more basic objections to the recount and said the Florida Supreme Court had violated state law in ordering it. The fact that Justices O'Connor and Kennedy evidently did not share these deeper concerns had offered a potential basis for a coalition between them and the dissenters. That effort apparently foundered on the two justices' conviction that the midnight deadling of Dec. 12 had to be met.

The majority said that "substantial additional work" was needed to undertake a constitutional recount, including not only uniform statewide standards for determining a legal vote, but also "practical procedures to implement them" and "orderly judicial review of any disputed matters that might arise." There was no way all this could be done, the majority said.

The dissenters said the concern with Dec. 12 was misplaced. Justices Souter and Breyer offered to send the case back to the Florida courts "with instructions to establish uniform standards for evaluating the several types of ballots that have prompted differing treatments," as Justice Souter described his proposed remand order. He added: "Unlike the majority, I see no warrant for this court to assume that Florida could not possibly comply with this requirement before the date set for the meeting of electors, Dec. 18."

Justices Stevens and Ginsburg said they did not share the view that the lack of a uniform vote-counting standard presented an equal protection problem. In addition to joining Justice Souter's dissenting opinion, Justice Breyer wrote one of his own, signed by the three other dissenters, in which he recounted the history of the deadlocked presidential election of 1876 and of the partisan role that one Supreme Court justice, Joseph P. Bradley, played in awarding the presidency to Rutherford B. Hayes.

"This history may help to explain why I think it not only legally wrong, but also most unfortunate, for the Court simply to have terminated the Florida recount," Justice Breyer said. He said the time problem that Florida faced was "in significant part, a problem of the Court's own making." The recount was moving ahead in an "orderly fashion," Justice Breyer said, when "this court improvidently entered a stay." He said: "As a result, we will never know whether the recount could have been completed." There was no need for the court to have involved itself in the election dispute this time, he said, adding: "Above all, in this highly politicized matter, the appearance of a split decision runs the risk of undermining the public's confidence in the court itself. That confidence is a public treasure. It has been built slowly over many years, some of which were marked by a Civil War and the tragedy of segregation. It is a vitally necessary ingredient of any successful effort to protect basic liberty and, indeed, the rule of law itself."

"We do risk a self-inflicted wound," Justice Breyer said, "a wound that may harm not just the court, but the nation."

Justice Ginsburg also wrote a dissenting opinion, joined by the other dissenters. Her focus was on the implications for federalism of the majority's action. "I might join the chief justice were it my commission to interpret Florida law," she said, adding: "The extraordinary setting of this case has obscured the ordinary principle that dictates its proper resolution: federal courts defer to state high courts' interpretations of their state's own law. This principle reflects the core of federalism, on which all agree."

"Were the other members of this court as mindful as they generally are of our system of dual sovereignty," Justice Ginsburg concluded, "they would affirm the judgment of the Florida Supreme Court." Unlike the other dissenters, who said they dissented "respectfully," Justice Ginsburg said only: "I dissent."

Nothing about this case, *Bush v. Gore*, No. 00-949, was ordinary: not its context, not its acceptance over the weekend, not the enormously accelerated schedule with argument on Monday, and not the way the decision was released to the public tonight. When the court issues an opinion, the justices ordinarily take the bench and the justice who has written for the majority gives a brief oral description of the case and the holding. Today, after darkness fell and their work was done, the justices left the Supreme Court building individually from the underground garage, with no word to dozens of journalists from around the world who were waiting in the crowded pressroom for word as to when, or whether, a decision might come. By the time the pressroom staff passed out copies of the decision, the justices were gone.

Dec. 13, 2000, Linda Greenhouse

Gore Still Doesn't Concede

WASHINGTON — In perhaps a fitting coda to a turbulent election night that never seemed to end, the court's verdict was not issued until about 10 p.m., and Gore aides said there would be no concession speech tonight. Just the same, the Bush campaign proceeded with extreme caution, mindful that it appear presumptuous — or unduly triumphant. In a terse statement he read to reporters in Tallahassee, Fla., late tonight, James A. Baker III said Bush and Cheney were "very pleased and gratified" that the court agreed that "there were constitutional problems with the recount ordered by the Florida Supreme Court." Careful not to declare victory, Baker added, "This has been a long and arduous process for everyone on both sides."

Bush's advisers said they wanted to give Gore room to concede before the governor, who was cloistered in the Governor's Mansion in Austin, Tex., publicly proclaimed victory. Gore himself, who collected more popular votes than Bush, and who insisted that a full and accurate recount would show him to be the winner in Florida, remained in his home in Washington with his family. His campaign chairman, William M. Daley, issued a statement describing the complicated ruling and not leaving any hint of a concession that other Gore aides said would be forthcoming. "The decision is both complex and lengthy," Daley said. "It will take time to completely analyze this decision."

Daley said the Gore camp would comment further on Wednesday. But publicly and privately, many Gore intimates said the campaign was effectively over. "He should act now and concede," said Edward G.. Rendell, the general chairman of the Democratic National Committee.

Joe Andrew, the party's national chairman, scrambled to depict Rendell's colleague's comments as premature, saying they were "completely inappropriate, if not, outrageous." Still, most Gore loyalists echoed Rendell, if not publicly.

"I guess that's the end of it," a Gore confidant said.

Aides said Gore participated in a midnight conference call with lawyers and advisers, including David Boies and Daley. Suggesting that a concession is imminent, Mark S. Fabiani, Gore's deputy campaign manager, said, "We'll have a decision by the morning. People are going to sleep on it. It's not going to be a long, drawn-out process."

Shortly after the court's ruling was issued, the pressure was already mounting for Mr. Gore to concede. Democrats expressed concern that the party itself could suffer damage if the vice president continued to fight. "It was both a controversial and a close judgment of the Supreme Court but it was also a final decision, and I hope the people will accept the finality of the judgment," said Senator Robert G. Torricelli, Democrat of New Jersey. "I think George Bush comes to the presidency in very difficult circumstances and it is incumbent on all of us to put the bitterness behind us and help him to succeed. "We've all learned something about our government and Constitution," Mr. Torricelli said. "They are more fragile than we might have imagined."

Dec. 13, 2000, Richard L. Berke

Bush Plays the Strong, Silent Role

AUSTIN — For 35 days George W. Bush has insisted that he won Florida and with it the presidency. But when the Supreme Court appeared to seal his victory late this evening, there was silence from the Governor's Mansion here and Bush's aides quite deliberately avoided any claim of victory.

All day Bush had stayed out of sight, never venturing from his house. But just before 11:30 p.m., Bush's chief legal strategist, James A. Baker III, said he had spoken with the Texas governor and Dick Cheney, his running mate, and described them as "very pleased and gratified" by the court's ruling, and he thanked the Bush legal team as well as the hundreds of volunteers in Florida for their efforts.

But Baker left it open to Al Gore to make the next move. Aides said they would wait to see whether Gore would make a concession announcement, but made it clear that under their reading of the court's opinion, that was now inevitable.

The Gore camp was even more subdued, with no official announcement by the vice president or his staff. But aides and supporters were clearly downcast and in some cases stunned. "It makes you want to call 911 and report a burglary," said Greg Simon, a longtime Gore adviser who has been working in Florida on the recount.

Before Baker's brief comment, Bush's aides here were poring through faxes of the opinion and the lengthy dissents, trying to figure out whether their victory was, in fact, in hand. "We're just reading it like everyone else," said one top aide, speaking in the busy but surprisingly subdued campaign headquarters about eight blocks from Bush's residence. The governor is not expected to say anything in public until Wednesday, and even then, the aide said, may wait for Gore to act first.

Mindy Tucker, a Bush spokeswoman, said, "We are heartened it does mean the Florida Supreme Court has been reversed, and the recount they called for will not happen."

Dec. 13, 2000, David E. Sanger

Gore Backers Lose in Florida Supreme Court

TALLAHASSEE — The Florida Supreme Court this afternoon rejected the appeals of two lawsuits filed by supporters of Al Gore that sought to throw out thousands of absentee ballots from two counties where Republican workers were improperly allowed to fix the ballot requests of their fellow Republicans.

If the Democrats had persuaded the court to invalidate the absentee ballots in Seminole and Martin Counties, it would have cost Bush enough votes to cause him to lose Florida. But the State Supreme Court ruled 6 to 0, with one justice having recused himself, to uphold the opinions of two Leon County

Circuit Court judges who ruled last week that the offenses had not been serious enough to warrant throwing out votes.

But the State Supreme Court went out of its way to criticize the actions of the local elections officials who allowed Republican workers to add missing information to the absentee ballot requests, which otherwise would have been rejected.

"Nothing can be more essential than for a supervisor of elections to maintain strict compliance with the statutes in order to ensure credibility in the outcome of the election," the court wrote in its Seminole County decision, which it said also applied to the Martin County case.

And the court added in a footnote that "the Florida Election Code provides certain penalties for election officials and others who violate the code."

The Bush camp praised the court's decision. "We are gratified by this decision to affirm the reasonable and common sense ruling of the lower court judges," Barry Richard, a lawyer for Bush, said in a statement. "We have believed all along that the law was crystal clear: these legally cast votes should be counted."

But Harry N. Jacobs, the supporter of Gore who filed the Seminole case, said in an interview that he was weighing an appeal to the United States Supreme Court. Jacobs said he was disappointed that Bush's lawyers had been allowed to argue in some elections contests that only votes that were cast in strict compliance with election law should count, while they argued in these cases that a "technicality" should not be enough to invalidate a vote.

Jacobs's main lawyer, Gerald F. Richman, said, "The bottom line is that if people are going to go to the polls to vote, they have to have faith in the integrity of the process."

Dec. 13, 2000, Michael Cooper

day

36

WEDNESDAY,

DECEMBER 13TH

★ ★ ★ ★ ★

GORE FINALLY CONCEDES

Although isolated cries of despair and voices of bitter dissent could be heard after yesterday's Supreme Court decision giving Bush the presidency, today is a day of calm, almost of serenity. After Gore and Bush make well-received, if entirely predictable speeches, most politicians from both sides express relief that the drama is over. This is especially true of members of the U.S. House and the Florida Senate, who would have been involved in making decisions that carried considerable political danger for all concerned. So now an orderly transition begins in the Executive branch and the Legislative branch can prepare for its next session. The only institution that might very well suffer serious damage appears to be the U.S. Supreme Court, even though everyone agrees that it is the only body that could have ended this affair peaceably.

GORE BOWS OUT AND URGES UNITY

WASHINGTON — Al Gore reluctantly surrendered his quest for the presidency tonight, telling the American public that while he was deeply disappointed and sharply disagreed with the Supreme Court verdict that ended his campaign, "partisan rancor must now be put aside."

In a gracious eight-minute televised speech from his ceremonial office next to the White House, Gore said he had telephoned George W. Bush to offer his congratulations. He promised to stand behind Bush, honoring him, for the first time, with the title "president-elect."

"Now the United States Supreme Court has spoken," he said. "Let there be no doubt. While I strongly disagree with the court's decision, I accept it. I accept the finality of the outcome, which will be ratified next Monday in the Electoral College. And tonight, for the sake of our unity as a people and the strength of our democracy, I offer my concession."

The speech was an emotional and political crest for Gore, who had such qualms about giving up his race for the White House, a lifelong goal, that aides said he was on the telephone with them at least until 1:30 this morning, asking about possible legal avenues that the Supreme Court's decision might have left open. He told his advisers that he wanted to sleep on it before making a final decision.

"Our disappointment must be overcome by our love of country."

— Al Gore, conceding the election

Many politicians said Gore's address was as important as the one by Bush that followed. By submerging any bitter feelings and sounding a conciliatory tone, they said, Gore could help reduce the festering tensions between Republicans and Democrats who cling to the belief that their candidate should rightfully claim the White House.

Gore declared that he would "honor the new president-elect and do everything possible to help him bring Americans together." For all his outreach to Bush, Gore dropped several not-so-veiled hints that this might not be his last try. Making clear that he is not about to fade away — or stop fighting — Gore said, "I do have one regret, that I didn't get the chance to stay and fight for the American people over the next four years, especially for those who feel their voices have not been heard. I heard you and I will not forget."

He added: "I've seen America in this campaign and I like what I see. It's worth fighting for — and that's a fight I'll never stop." Over the holidays, he said, he would return to his home state, Tennessee, to spend time to "mend some fences, literally and figuratively." This was Gore's first public nod to his humiliating rejection on Election Day by the state of his forefathers. He spent his summers in Tennessee and represented the state in the Senate for eight years and in the House for eight years before that.

But Gore, who will leave public office for the first time in 24 years, said he did not know what he would do after the vice presidency. "As for what I'll do next," he said, "I don't know the answer to that one yet."

It was arguably the most consequential, and probably the most wrenching speech he has ever delivered because Gore has told friends that he thinks he has a genuine claim to the White House given that he won the popular vote — and believes that more voters in Florida intended to back him.

"Look at the popular vote and add in the fact that they never got votes counted in Florida," one of Gore's senior aides said tonight. "In many ways, he's like a shadow president." In a glancing reference to his popular-vote victory, Gore reached back in history to "many examples of contests as hotly debated, as fiercely fought, with their own challenges to the popular will."

"I know that many of my supporters are disappointed," he said. "I am, too. But our disappointment must be overcome by our love of country."

Reaching out to the man who will be the 43rd president, he said: "President-elect Bush inherits a nation whose citizens will be ready to assist him in the conduct of his large responsibilities. I personally will be at his disposal and I call on all Americans — I particularly urge all who stood with us — to unite behind our next president."

In a tribute to his late father, Albert, whose defeat in his 1970 Senate re-election campaign in Tennessee had devastated father and son, Gore said: "As my father once said, no matter how hard the loss, defeat may serve as well as victory to shake the soul and let the glory out."

By presenting himself as a uniter, Gore also helped himself politically. Several of his close advisers said the vice president was well aware that tonight's prime-time farewell was a critical opportunity for him to leave the American public with a positive image of him that runs counter to the chants in recent weeks from Republicans who decried that he was a "sore loser." That is vital, they said, should he seek a rematch with Bush in 2004.

Dec. 14, 2000, Richard L. Berke and Katharine Q. Seelye

Bush Vows to be President for "One Nation"

AUSTIN — George W. Bush spoke to the nation for the first time as president-elect tonight, declaring that the "nation must rise above a house divided" after one of the closest and most disputed presidential elections in United States history. Speaking from the podium of the Texas House of Representatives, precisely 24 hours after the United State Supreme Court ended a five-week-long dispute by halting a recount of Florida's disputed votes, and thus preserving Bush's razor-thin lead, the 54-year-old governor devoted his entire speech to themes of reconciliation.

"I was not elected to serve one party, but to serve one nation," Bush said. "Whether you voted for me or not, I will do my best to serve your interests," he said, "and I will work to earn your respect."

Bush appeared by turns relaxed and slightly nervous, licking his upper lip as he looked around the large chamber, dominated by a huge Christmas tree and filled with his supporters and staff. "I have a lot to be thankful for," he said in a speech that emphasized only common ground between Democrats and Republicans, and made only glancing references to the disputes that punctuated the campaign and its often bitter aftermath. "I am thankful for America, and thankful that we are able to resolve our electoral differences in a peaceful way."

The choice of locale for his speech underscored the theme: The Texas House is under Democratic control. Bush used the moment to reiterate some of his campaign themes, talking of making "all our public schools excellent," strengthening Medicare and creating a prescription drug benefit for "all of our seniors." He talked of a "broad, fair and fiscally responsible tax relief" a phrase so vague that it could embrace many varieties of tax cuts — and like Gore an hour before him, talked of "common ground."

"During the fall campaign, we differed about details of these proposals but there was remarkable consensus about the important issues before us." He spoke of serving "every race and every background," aware that minorities voted overwhelmingly against him in last month's election. It was not the kind of speech Bush would have delivered had he won the large victory his aides were predicting on election night. He offered nothing to the conservative wing of his party, and evoked none of the cultural issues that often divide the two parties.

Bush is expected to travel to Washington next Tuesday [Dec. 19], aides said, and meet both President Clinton and Vice President Gore. But his transition is already under way, and with tonight's concession by Gore, Bush will now have use of the $5 million transition budget and a large office blocks from the White House. Within days, he is expected to start naming his senior staff and cabinet members.

Though he briefly invoked the words of Abraham Lincoln at the opening of his speech, Bush referred directly to only one of his predecessors, Thomas Jefferson, who took office in a disputed election in 1800. "I will be guided by President Jefferson's sense of purpose," he said, "to stand for principle, to be reasonable in manner, and, above all, to do great good for the cause of freedom and harmony."

"The presidency is more than an honor. It is more than an office," he concluded. "It is a charge to keep." The last phrase was also the title of a book he published at the beginning of the campaign to introduce himself to the American people.

Bush's speech to the nation tonight was no ordinary victory address. After weeks of legal maneuvering and two rapid-fire decisions by the Supreme Court which effectively ended Gore's hopes for a recount on Tuesday night, Bush had much more to accomplish tonight than declaring himself the victor on a typical Election Day.

A man who is at his most uncomfortable with formal addresses in formal settings was called on to give one that he knew would set the tone of his first term. It was a night for perfect pitch and appropriate symbolism, "chiefly the olive branch," one aide said. His words were simple, his rhetoric not as lofty as the speech Gore gave an hour before. In discussions leading up to the drafting of the speech, aides said he had to be humble, while making it clear that other nations and his political opponents at home should not question his command of the office. It is unclear whether he accomplished that goal; his only reference to America's role in the world was a call for bipartisan foreign policy and "a military equal to every challenge, and superior to every adversary."

Dec. 14, 2000, David E. Sanger

Court's Action Brings Confusion, Not Clarity

WASHINGTON — The Supreme Court justices who drove off into the night on Tuesday left behind more than a split decision that ended a disputed presidential election. They also left behind an institution that many students of the court said appeared diminished, if not actually tarnished, by its extraordinary foray into presidential politics. They point to the contradiction between the majority's action in this case and those justices' usual insistence on deference to the states.

The members of the majority appeared at pains to refute any suggestion that the court had intervened unduly by stopping the Florida recount on Saturday or by ruling Tuesday that it could not resume. It was "our unsought responsibility to resolve the federal and constitutional issues" in the case, the majority said in its unsigned opinion. And Justice Clarence Thomas, a member of the 5-to-4 majority, told a group of high school students at the court today that "I have yet to hear any discussion, in nine years, of partisan politics" among the justices.

Be that as it may, the events of the last few days were jarring even for people who pride themselves on being realists rather than romantics about how the court works. One federal judge, a Republican appointee who was a Supreme Court law clerk decades ago, said today that he had long since become accustomed to watching the justices "making it up as they go along." That aspect of the majority opinion, which he called analytically weak and untethered to precedent, did not particularly bother him, he said. "But the very peculiar aspect" of the case, the judge said, was "why they made it up. It just seemed so politically partisan."

The way the court structured and then released its opinion, just before 10 o'clock at night, added to the sense of unease. The justices gave no hint of a reason for the unprecedented late-night release — whether to avoid pushing Florida over the midnight "safe harbor" deadline for immunizing its electors from Congressional challenge, or perhaps out of fear that the explosive and highly divisive decision might leak overnight if the court waited until morning to announce it. No matter. It resulted in an hour or more of frantic confusion that the court did nothing to prevent or alleviate.

While the sight of network correspondents fumbling in the dark on the court plaza to make sense of the decision was deeply unsettling to viewers who urgently wanted to know whether the 2000 election was over, the fault this time was much more the court's than television's. The 65-page document omitted the usual headnote, the synopsis that accompanies opinions and identifies which justices voted on which side.

Furthermore, the opinion was labeled *per curiam*, meaning "by the court," a label used by courts almost exclusively for unanimous opinions so uncontroversial as to not be worth the trouble of a formal opinion-writing process. There was no indication of what the vote actually was. The names of Justices Sandra Day O'Connor and Anthony M. Kennedy, one or both of whom was likely the author, did not appear anywhere on the document.

Unlike the Florida Supreme Court, whose spokesman, Craig Waters, became almost a cult figure for his uninflected but informative announcements of the court's opinions in the election cases, the United States Supreme Court does not authorize its public information staff to make public statements or give any guidance about the decisions.

Since the justices themselves skipped the usual oral announcement of a decision, which takes place in public session in the courtroom and includes the opinion's author summarizing its main points, there was no interpretive guide at all for the correspondents who had to dash off to their waiting cameras. The crux of the *per curiam* opinion, the conclusion that there was no time to conduct any further counting of the votes in Florida, came deep inside and was highlighted neither at the beginning nor at the end.

Among the most baffling aspects of the opinion was its simultaneous creation of a new equal protection right not to have ballots counted according to different standards and its disclaimer that this new constitutional principle would ever apply in another case. "Our consideration is limited to the present circumstances, for the problem of equal protection in election processes generally presents many complexities," the court said.

The justices will not meet again until Jan. 5, the date for their next scheduled conference to review new and pending cases. The passions and pain revealed in Tuesday's opinions will undoubtedly have cooled by then; these are justices who are accustomed to both bitter division — often by the same 5-to-4 alignment — and to moving on to the next case.

But there is something different about *Bush v. Gore* that raises the question about whether moving on will be quite so easy. This was something more than a dispute rooted in judicial philosophy. In fact, as Prof. Suzanna Sherry of Vanderbilt Law School said today, had members of the majority been true to their judicial philosophy, the opinion would have come out differently.

"In the past, the 5-to-4 decisions have been jurisprudentially predictable," Professor Sherry said in an interview. "Some justices are for more federalism, some for less; some for more activism, some for less. Those are not political decisions. By and large, the opinions are consistent with consistent jurisprudential beliefs" and as such present little threat to the court's collegiality.

But in this case, Professor Sherry said, for conservatives "the politics and jurisprudence were in conflict." The conservative justices in the majority set aside their concern for states' rights, for judicial restraint, for limitations on standing, for their usual insistence that claims raised at the Supreme Court level have been fully addressed by the lower courts.

"There is really very little way to reconcile this opinion other than that they wanted Bush to win," Professor Sherry said. Those who oppose the decision, she said, are likely to conclude not only that it was a mistake but "a different kind of mistake, not just that they got the law wrong but that it exposed a different side of the court."

Dec. 14, 2000, Linda Greenhouse

★★★

OpEd

Court May Have Expanded Voting Rights

For the first time in its history, the Supreme Court has declared the winner of an election. And not just any election. For an institution that must conserve its moral capital, the immediate effect of the split decision threatens to harm the public's confidence, a confidence that Justice Stephen Breyer has called "a public treasure." The deeply fractured opinions in *Bush v. Gore* will never fully set to rest charges that the court has compromised its integrity.

Yet though the focus has been on the court's political balance and the majority's halting of the Florida recount, the greater import of this case may be a surprising expansion of voting rights, rather than a contraction.

In an unexpected move, the court announced in its majority opinion a sweeping obligation of the states "to avoid arbitrary and disparate treatment of the members" of the electorate. Seven justices condemned the disturbing, standardless hand recounts in Florida. And in doing so, they have broadened constitutional protections for the right to vote.

The 5-to-4 majority, however, leaped from embracing this powerful principle to making a questionable reading of the federal statutes as requiring the termination of the recounts. This move by the majority is extremely risky.

For most of our nation's history, courts in general have steered clear of any involvement in electoral politics. While the Supreme Court has claimed for itself the role of arbiter of the Constitution, politics has remained the untrod terrain. No matter how contentious a contest, the courts stayed away. Politics was seen as the ultimate poison for institutions whose moral authority came from claims of grander principle.

Only in the 1960's did the Supreme Court declare itself willing to enter the electoral arena. But it did so only when two key preconditions were met. The first was the inability of any other political institution to solve the problem of disenfranchisement of entire segments of the population. The second was the likelihood that the court could establish neutral and clear legal principles that would allow it to deflect charges that it was acting as a partisan body. The court was willing to assess election processes, but declaring who was the winner of a contested election was simply out of bounds.

The court's opinion in *Bush v. Gore* does not meet these standards. The court never explains why it intervened to halt the recounts. After all, if states fail to designate electors in a legally prescribed manner, federal law gives state legislatures the ability to intervene. And the presidential selection act gives Congress the ability to resolve the dispute if there are rival sets of electors claiming to represent a state — as occurred with the Florida, Louisiana and South Carolina delegations in 1876. Nowhere in this scheme is there a role for the court.

Yet by claiming a role in this case, the Supreme Court may have given us an advancement in voting rights doctrine. It has asserted a new constitutional requirement: to avoid disparate and unfair treatment of voters. And this obligation obviously cannot be limited to the recount process alone. The court condemns the fact that "standards for accepting or rejecting contested ballots might vary not only from county to county but indeed within a single county." That criticism surely would apply to the variations in voting machines across Florida, and, for that matter, to similar variations in all other states. The court's new standard may create a more robust constitutional examination of voting practices.

The lasting significance of *Bush v. Gore* is likely to be the reinvigoration of the line of cases from the 1960's that deemed voting a fundamental right. The court's language has now opened the door for constitutional challenges of flawed election methods. The spotlight on Florida revealed just how infirm the operations of elections are. The legacy of this case could be a substantial jolt of justice into the voting arena.

Dec. 14, 2000

By Samuel Issacharoff, professor at Columbia Law School

★ ★ ★

OpEd

NO SURPRISE, IT'S AN ACTIVIST COURT

The Supreme Court has reached out aggressively to solve the nation's election problem, inserting itself into a major political controversy. News commentators and legal experts seemed surprised when the court stepped into this thicket. They shouldn't have been. The Rehnquist Court has been using law to reshape politics for at least a decade. We keep hearing that it consists of "strict constructionists" who (as George W. Bush put it during the debates) oppose "liberal judicial activism." That's because conservative judicial activism is the order of the day. The Warren Court was retiring compared to the present one.

Warren Court activism was largely confined to questions of individual rights, mainly racial equality and the treatment of criminal defendants. The Rehnquist Court has been just as active in this domain. To list a few examples, it has disowned affirmative action, finding no difference between Jim Crow and laws designed to help disadvantaged minorities. It has overturned decades of jurisprudence that protected religious minorities from laws that intruded on their rituals. And it has all but eliminated the right to federal review of state criminal cases.

Individual rights are important, but they actually affect only a small portion of what government does. The real guts of our democracy lie in the system's structure and the way powers are allocated. And here the Warren Court was extremely deferential to other branches of government. Not so the Rehnquist Court, which has abandoned restraint in this area as well.

The court cast aside nearly 70 years of precedent in the area of federalism, holding that Congress cannot use its powers under the Commerce Clause or the 14th Amendment to regulate matters that touch on state interests, unless the court approves. It has declared, among other things, that Congress could not address violence against women, could not impose liability on state governments for age discrimination, could not hold states accountable for violating copyright laws and more.

But perhaps the most audacious instance of judicial activism is the way the court has extended the doctrine of judicial review itself. It was the Warren Court that first clearly established, in connection with school desegregation, that the Supreme Court has the final word about the meaning of the Constitution. Still, that court usually (though not always) gave great weight to the interpretations of other political actors. But the Rehnquist Court has no such inclination. Thus the court struck down the Religious Freedom Restoration Act because it was unwilling to give Congress the authority to provide greater protection to religious minorities than the court itself would give.

Many have viewed the court's actions as aimed at protecting states by limiting the federal government. But the Florida case shows that state governments get no more deference than other branches of government when they run afoul of the court's views of what the law ought to be. Judicial prerogative, it seems, not states' rights, has been at the heart of the Rehnquist Court's docket.

The court's confidence in its own supremacy may have propelled it to try to settle this presidential crisis. And if the court succeeds, the nation may well breathe a sigh of relief, grateful that someone brought this mess to a close. But the court's credibility will surely suffer. And if that diminishes a confidence that has begun to veer toward arrogance, this may not be such a bad thing.

Dec. 12, 2000

By Larry D. Kramer, Professor at New York University School of Law

A Popular Vote Edge for Gore . . .

	George W. Bush REPUBLICAN		Al Gore DEMOCRAT		MARGIN Votes	Pct. points	Electoral votes
TOTAL	**50,456,169**	**(48%)**	**50,996,116**	**(49%)**	**539,947**	**0.516**	
States won by Bush							**271 electoral votes**
Texas	3,799,639	(59%)	2,433,746	(38%)	1,365,893	21.319	32
Florida	2,912,790	(49%)	2,912,253	(49%)	537	0.009	25
Ohio	2,350,363	(50%)	2,183,628	(46%)	166,735	3.546	21
North Carolina	1,631,163	(56%)	1,257,692	(43%)	373,471	12.831	14
Georgia	1,419,720	(55%)	1,116,230	(43%)	303,490	11.749	13
Virginia	1,437,490	(53%)	1,217,290	(44%)	220,200	8.046	13
Indiana	1,245,836	(57%)	901,980	(41%)	343,856	15.771	12
Missouri	1,189,924	(50%)	1,111,138	(47%)	78,786	3.339	11
Tennessee	1,061,949	(51%)	981,720	(47%)	80,229	3.865	11
Alabama	941,173	(57%)	692,611	(42%)	248,562	14.924	9
Louisiana	927,871	(53%)	792,344	(45%)	135,527	7.676	9
Arizona	781,652	(51%)	685,341	(45%)	96,311	6.287	8
Colorado	883,748	(51%)	738,227	(42%)	145,521	8.357	8
Kentucky	872,520	(57%)	638,923	(41%)	233,597	15.129	8
Oklahoma	744,337	(60%)	474,276	(38%)	270,061	21.881	8
South Carolina	786,892	(57%)	566,039	(41%)	220,853	15.961	8
Mississippi	572,844	(58%)	404,614	(41%)	168,230	16.921	7
Arkansas	472,940	(51%)	422,768	(46%)	50,172	5.443	6
Kansas	622,332	(58%)	399,276	(37%)	223,056	20.803	6
Nebraska	433,862	(62%)	231,780	(33%)	202,082	28.992	5
Utah	515,096	(67%)	203,053	(26%)	312,043	40.476	5
West Virginia	336,475	(52%)	295,497	(46%)	40,978	6.323	5
Idaho	336,937	(69%)	138,637	(28%)	198,300	40.525	4
Nevada	301,575	(50%)	279,978	(46%)	21,597	3.546	4
New Hampshire	273,559	(48%)	266,348	(47%)	7,211	1.270	4
Alaska	167,398	(59%)	79,004	(28%)	88,394	31.071	3
Montana	240,178	(58%)	137,178	(33%)	103,000	25.059	3
North Dakota	174,852	(61%)	95,284	(33%)	79,568	27.603	3
South Dakota	190,700	(60%)	118,804	(38%)	71,896	22.733	3
Wyoming	147,947	(69%)	60,481	(28%)	87,466	40.924	3
States won by Gore							**266 electoral votes**
California	4,567,429	(42%)	5,861,203	(53%)	1,293,774	11.798	54
New York	2,403,374	(35%)	4,107,697	(60%)	1,704,323	24.983	33
Pennsylvania	2,281,127	(46%)	2,485,967	(51%)	204,840	4.170	23
Illinois	2,019,421	(43%)	2,589,026	(55%)	569,605	12.012	22
Michigan	1,953,139	(46%)	2,170,418	(51%)	217,279	5.135	18
New Jersey	1,284,173	(40%)	1,788,850	(56%)	504,677	15.834	15
Massachusetts	878,502	(33%)	1,616,487	(60%)	737,985	27.343	12
Washington	1,108,864	(45%)	1,247,652	(50%)	138,788	5.580	11
Wisconsin	1,237,279	(48%)	1,242,987	(48%)	5,708	0.220	11
Maryland	813,827	(40%)	1,144,008	(57%)	330,181	16.329	10
Minnesota	1,109,659	(46%)	1,168,266	(48%)	58,607	2.403	10
Connecticut	561,094	(38%)	816,015	(56%)	254,921	17.481	8
Iowa	634,373	(48%)	638,517	(49%)	4,144	0.315	7
Oregon	713,577	(47%)	720,342	(47%)	6,765	0.442	7
New Mexico	286,417	(48%)	286,783	(48%)	366	0.061	5
Hawaii	137,845	(37%)	205,286	(56%)	67,441	18.329	4
Maine	286,616	(44%)	319,951	(49%)	33,335	5.114	4
Rhode Island	130,555	(32%)	249,508	(61%)	118,953	29.099	4
Delaware	137,288	(42%)	180,068	(55%)	42,780	13.061	3
Vermont	119,775	(41%)	149,022	(51%)	20,247	9.955	3
District of Columbia*	18,073	(9%)	171,923	(85%)	153,850	76.407	2

*One of the district's three electors left her ballot blank.

Postscripts

Looking Back, Looking Ahead

In the days and weeks following the Supreme Court's decision, journalists begin the process of trying to find the hidden reasons behind the final outcome. With hindsight it was clear early on that Gore lost in part because of a few critical decisions he and his lawyers had made at the outset concerning the rules for the recount. But as the weeks passed by, more evidence emerged to show just how active the Republican team in Florida really had been and how fierce their commitment to victory. Speculation about the possible impact weeks of partisan wrangling would have on the president-elect's brother was widespread.An onslaught of articles about the U.S. Supreme Court's role in a political contest kept that issue before the public.

But to many observers the most intriguing postscript to the long election struggle was the announcement by several news organizations that they would undertake a full counting of all 180,000 uncounted Florida ballots. While the result of the election cannot be changed, if it turns out Gore received more votes, the legitimacy of the Bush presidency would surely be continuously challenged, while the impact of such an outcome on the 2002 and 2004 elections could be devastating to the Republicans.

OpEd

This Election's Lesson: Win the Small States

As the protracted election of 2000 plays out, the nation's attention has narrowed again and again: to a few "battleground" states out of 50; then to just one state, Florida; to just a few counties; and even to one county's confusing ballot. But when the lens is broadened again, a deeper reality emerges in the battle of George W. Bush and Al Gore: the bias in the Electoral College toward small states.

Gore won the popular vote, but this time the Electoral College did not fall into line. The small-state bias, not the fate of Florida, helps explain why. States with large populations do get more electoral votes, of course, than those that have relatively few people. Each state gets electoral votes equal to the number of its representatives to the House, which are allocated in proportion to population. But then something else is added: an electoral vote for each senator. And that seemingly small addition has a surprisingly powerful effect. South Dakota's electoral vote, for example, is tripled by the senatorial "add-on" of two electoral votes, while New York's electoral weight is increased by only 6 percent. And so in New York, one electoral vote represents 550,000 people, while in South Dakota it represents 232,000.

Bush generally did well in states with small populations, winning 19 of the 26 states that have fewer than 10 electoral votes each. By winning so many small states, he gained a clear Electoral College advantage. Gore won, for example, 22 electoral votes representing 10.4 million people in Massachusetts and Minnesota. Bush got more — 24 — by winning votes representing only 6.1 million people — spread across six small states.

Or, to look at the numbers another way, first count as a wash the seven small states won by Gore and seven closely comparable small states won by Bush. That leaves Bush winning an additional 12 small states with a total population roughly equal to that of California. From those states, he will receive 73 electoral votes, compared with California's 54. That difference is enough to tilt the outcome of the election.

That difference also violates the principle of one person, one vote that most of us believe in and that, according to a series of Supreme Court decisions in the 1960's, lies at the heart of our democracy. "To say that a vote is worth more in one district than in another would . . . run counter to our fundamental ideas of democratic government," the court announced in 1964. "Legislators," wrote Chief Justice Earl Warren, "represent people, not trees or acres." Yet 18 million people in New York now get 33 electoral votes for the presidency while fewer than 14 million people in a collection of small states also get 33.

Much has been said in recent days about the real or alleged "disenfranchisement" of voters in Florida and elsewhere. As we ponder that critical word, we would do well to keep in mind Justice Warren's conclusion that "the right of suffrage can be denied by a debasement or dilution of the weight of a citizen's vote just as effectively as by wholly prohibiting the free exercise of the franchise."

Those who tout the virtues of the Electoral College should confront the mathematical reality of the inequities they are defending.

Nov. 20, 2000
By Alex Keyssar,
Professor of History and Public Policy at Duke
and author of *The Right to Vote*

INSIDE THE CAMPAIGN: GORE'S HARD STRATEGIC CALLS

Challenging the Count

Clearly it was going to be an important meeting, important enough that Vice President Al Gore thought his running mate, Senator Joseph I. Lieberman, should breach the Sabbath to be there.

It was a Saturday afternoon in November, the first Saturday after the most remarkable election night in American history. Gore and his top aides were meeting at the Naval Observatory, the vice president's official residence, and as the discussion got serious they dispatched Tom Nides, Lieberman's campaign manager, to persuade his boss to join them. He found him at a neighbor's house, enjoying a Sabbath luncheon.

"The veep wants you to come," Nides remembered telling him. "Some tough decisions need to be made and we need to go." Lieberman, a deeply observant Jew, had tried to reassure voters during the campaign that he would bend religious laws prohibiting work on the Sabbath if the national interest was at stake. This meeting, he concluded, would seem to pass the test.

"Can we drive?" asked Nides, a decidedly less observant Jew. He knew the answer before he asked. And so Lieberman and Nides began a two-mile hike to the residence — NavObs as it is known — surrounded by Secret Service agents and trailed by a creeping, five-car motorcade. As they strolled up Wisconsin Avenue, passing motorists honked their horns and rolled down their windows to yell "Go, Joe, go!"

Inside the house, a number of Gore aides and family members had gathered at the dining room table, where two easels with beige butcher paper stood behind the vice president's chair. The issue was whether Gore should join a lawsuit challenging Palm Beach County's butterfly ballot, which the vice president's aides believed had cost him hundreds, if not thousands, of votes and possibly the presidency.

As the discussion proceeded, it became clear that the Gore team would have to fight its post-election battle on several fronts — legal, political and public relations — and that its various strategies would sometimes conflict.

There would be inherent tensions, Gore and his aides realized, among the legal imperative of capturing every Democratic vote in Florida, the communications mission of presenting Gore as reasonable and dignified, and the political goal of keeping supporters on board while buying time for the lawyers.

Those tensions flared repeatedly throughout the next four weeks as the Gore camp searched for a balance. Inevitably, Gore made the final decisions, and at key moments he consistently chose to safeguard his image, sometimes at the expense of legal aggressiveness.

He backed away, for instance, from his lawyers' determination to try to disqualify overseas absentee ballots, many of them cast by members of the armed forces who were presumed to favor Gov. George W. Bush. His guiding principle, Gore said publicly, was to fight for the inclusion of votes, not for their exclusion.

He also ruled against the advisers who urged him to contest improper Republican absentee ballots in Seminole County. That too, Gore reasoned, would undermine his public relations position, though he did not discourage lawsuits filed by supporters challenging the Seminole ballots.

"The lawyers always wanted to be aggressive and do the Seminole thing or the military ballot thing," said William M. Daley, Gore's campaign chairman. "But he had to look at the public relations, at how do you govern if you win, what do you look like. You had those conflicts through this whole thing."

Regarding the butterfly ballots, Democratic field workers were collecting some 8,000 affidavits from confused voters, and Gore's lawyers were eager to litigate. But some in Gore's dining room that first Saturday worried that the proposed remedy — presumably a new vote of some kind — would make him seem unreasonable and extreme, testing the patience of both his partisans and the public.

"He wanted to be striking a reasonable stance," said former Secretary of State Warren Christopher, whom Gore had appointed as his emissary to Tallahassee. "At the same time, he didn't want to compromise legitimate legal issues."

Ever the voice of moderation and propriety, Christopher urged caution. "At the end of this struggle," he said, "I hoped his reputation would be fully intact."

Complicating the decision, several aides said, was Gore's desire to make a public statement that weekend. Except for photo opportunities of him jogging and playing touch football, the vice president had been largely invisible, and completely inaudible, since the day after the election. It was time, Gore believed, to let the country know how he planned to proceed, to plea for patience and to reassure Americans that he was only seeking fairness.

His vehicle, he decided, would be a brief televised speech, delivered on Sunday, Nov. 12, after the pro football games ended. He would tell the country of his proposal to the Republicans: that he would not pursue litigation to challenge voting irregularities — like the butterfly ballots — if Bush would abide by the results of manual recounts, either statewide or in the four counties where Gore had requested them.

Participants in the meeting said Christopher and Daley liked the idea, as did the message gurus, Carter Eskew and Mark D. Fabiani. But Lieberman, among others, thought it was a mistake. As a former Connecticut attorney general, he thought it foolish to foreclose legal options.

"He said, 'Be careful which doors you shut because you may not be able to open them again,' " said one aide in the room.

There were political concerns as well. Frank W. Hunger, Gore's brother-in-law and confidant, worried that such a move should not be made without consulting constituencies with large stakes in Gore's candidacy, like labor and minority groups.

Clearly torn by the dilemma, the vice president decided to sleep on it, and then shelved the speech. Ultimately, he would deliver it Nov. 15, three days after he originally wanted to, in a surprise address timed to coincide with the network news.

By then Katherine Harris had declared she would enforce a Nov. 14 deadline for certifying results from the counties. The legal battle was fully joined, and it was ugly. Gore's campaign press secretary, Chris Lehane, had publicly called Harris "a hack" and "Commissar Harris," drawing critical editorials and a rebuke from the vice president. "This wasn't the communications strategy we agreed on," Gore sternly told one aide.

Now Gore felt he had to make an appearance, call for a more civil tone, and issue his challenge — even if it tied the hands of his lawyers.

"We need to move expeditiously to the most complete and accurate count that is possible," he said that night, standing before a mantel where family photographs had been placed in view of the cameras. "And that is why I propose this evening a way to settle this matter with finality and justice in a period of days, not weeks."

A Breathless Month of Twists

To the surprise of few, the Bush camp brushed that offer aside. But to everyone's wonder, the battle would rage not for days, as Gore had predicted, but for weeks. For Gore and his aides, the next month would be a thrill ride of manic highs and lows. They might be euphoric one day, like Nov. 21, when the Florida Supreme Court ruled that Harris had to accept manual recount tallies, and crestfallen the next, when the Miami-Dade canvassing board abruptly discontinued its recount.

They could be revived from the dead by the electric shock of the Florida Supreme Court order last Friday to resume the recount, only to be shattered on Saturday by the United States Supreme Court's stay. "That Friday night was the first night I slept without a Zantac," said Donna Brazile, Gore's campaign manager. "By Saturday, I was taking a Zantac again."

At the center of the drama was Gore, who stayed largely bunkered at the Naval Observatory while fielding reports from the legal outposts in Tallahassee and South Florida and a makeshift "war room" at the Democratic National Committee.

The weeks were shaped by a continuum of conference calls, e-mails and messages sent by Blackberry, the wireless instant paging system favored by Gore and his aides. "Please make sure that no one trashes the Supreme Court," Gore wrote in an electronic message to Lehane and Fabiani some 25 minutes after it stopped the recount last Saturday. It was a paradox, some Gore aides said, that their high-tech campaign was ultimately done in by Florida's antiquated voting machinery.

Throughout the legal battle, Gore aides and Congressional party leaders like Senator Tom Daschle and Rep. Richard A. Gephardt waged a relentless and largely successful effort to keep leading Democrats on Gore's side. On Nov. 12, the Gore aides began e-mailing twice-a-day briefings to a large group of loyalists. Five days later the computer system crashed. "The technician said we had sent out 1.5 million e-mails," Monica Dixon, Gore's Congressional liaison, said, "and the system wasn't used to it."

From the start of his challenge, Gore faced daunting legal and public relations odds because he had finished behind in the initial Florida count and because the television networks and many newspapers had prematurely declared Bush the winner. Even when court rulings were going his way, the clock was ticking against him.

But through it all, some two dozen aides said in interviews, Gore, a onetime law student, remained deeply engaged, remarkably calm and persistently upbeat, more impressive to many of them as a leader than he had been in the campaign.

He was uncommonly sensitive to the toll on his lawyers and advisers. He twice called the wife of Ronald Klain, one of his top lawyers in Florida, to apologize for keeping him away from home. When Klain could not come home for Thanksgiving, he invited the Klain family to join the Gores.

Gore seemed to take strength, aides said, from his victory in the popular vote and his certainty that he had won the vote in Florida. And early on, he instructed aides that no consideration was to be given to his future prospects.

"I've never been prouder to work for him," said one top aide. "He's been incredibly strong, focused. He's actually been nice. I don't know what's going on inside of him."

In classic fashion, Gore viewed the up-and-down nature of the battle, and the agonizing closeness of various court rulings, as a demonstration of his favorite component of chaos theory: fractals.

"The popular vote was 50-50, the Florida Supreme Court voted 4 to 3, the U.S. Supreme Court voted 5 to 4," Eskew said. "To him, this is all a fractal, the geometric theory that pieces of the whole, regardless of the scale, reflect the universe. He says it all the time."

As in any campaign, there were calibrations along the way. When Gore's speeches were critiqued as disingenuous ("What is at stake is more important than who wins the presidency"), aides scheduled him for television interviews that helped him appear more earnest ("I want to win. I make no bones about it."). When they feared the Bush camp was scoring with its message that votes had been counted and recounted, Gore began comparing uncounted votes to groceries that had not been properly scanned at the checkout counter. They existed. They simply had not been detected.

Gore and top aides raised glasses of Champagne — brought to the residence by Eskew — to toast their second, resuscitating victory in the state Supreme Court. But that moment of celebration was an aberration in the Gore camp's post-election conduct. When Florida's high court ruled in Gore's favor the first time, on Nov. 21, there had been no sustained revelry.

"He just turned to Mrs. Gore and smiled and said, 'Let's get the legal team on the phone,' " recalled Julia Payne, a Gore aide. "There was no high-fiving because he knows how this has gone."

Another Gore aide, asked to characterize Gore's mood during the post-election process, said, "There isn't a mood. It's sort of the absence of a mood."

That is not to say there were not moments of frustration and pain. Some of Gore's children were deeply wounded, according to aides, by the chants of pro-Bush demonstrators outside the residence — "Get out of Cheney's house!" — that echoed through the living quarters.

And when Lieberman addressed members of the House Democratic caucus on Dec. 4, he spoke bitterly of the Miami-Dade canvassing board's decision to stop counting ballots and the Florida Legislature's efforts to circumvent the courts. "There have been moments of real anger," he said, according to one listener.

A Rapid Mobilization

The groundwork for Gore's legal challenge of the balloting in Florida was laid well before any votes were counted. In the week before the Nov. 7 election, Gore's political strategists told Democratic National Committee lawyers that the outcome could be exceedingly close in as many as 20 states. The lawyers, led by D.N.C. general counsel Joseph E. Sandler, collected summaries of recount laws and procedures from each of those states.

"I thought the probability of actually having to worry about it was next to zero," Sandler said.

But near 4 a.m. in the dizzying haze of Nov. 8, Gore had watched Bush's margin in Florida all but vanish and had called Austin to rescind his concession. The vice president's top aides met at the campaign's Nashville headquarters to consider their next moves. Gore, by then awake for nearly 48 hours and with little real sleep for weeks, had retired to his suite at the Loews Vanderbilt Plaza.

Bleary, stunned and emotionally spent, Daley and the others began to construct a plan. Speed would be critical.

Donnie Fowler, a political aide, tapped dozens of campaign workers, many of them backpack-toting "kids," to fly to Tallahassee to help monitor the automatic machine recount Florida mandated in close elections. Klain was placed in charge of the legal effort, and began gathering lawyers from Washington, Nashville and Florida.

Michael Whouley, a strategist, would follow several days later to manage the recount politics. Sandler, now a believer, ripped pages out of a recount manual written by several Democratic lawyers and had dozens of copies made. Someone commandeered Lieberman's campaign plane for the trip to Tallahassee.

Eskew and Daley, without consulting Gore, decided to enlist Christopher, waking him at his home in Beverly Hills, Calif., at 3:30 a.m. Pacific time. It would be important to signal, they sensed, that the campaign had ended and that the next phase would be sober and disciplined, like Christopher himself.

Three hours after taking the call from Daley, Christopher was airborne. Before long, Gore aides saw the slender diplomat, natty in an expensive suit, wheeling his small suitcase down a hotel corridor to the Gore suite.

On the plane to Florida, which left Nashville at about 7:30 a.m. with Klain and the first wave of recount workers, several lawyers took the flight attendant's intercom and began training their election monitors. By state law, they knew from their pre-election research, they would have 72 hours to file any requests for manual recounts.

When the high command gathered in Gore's suite early that afternoon, the two candidates "had sort of a look of wonderment that there was still possibility," Christopher said.

The discussion turned to what Gore should say to explain his determination to challenge the vote. "It was important because of the tone he set," said one adviser in the room. "Two days before, he had been issuing blistering partisan attacks and here he needed to rise to a presidential level."

Aides brought in the "blue goose," as the vice-presidential lectern is known, and planted a forest of American flags behind it. None of the Gore aides imagined that the dispute would take another 35 days to resolve, but Gore suspected enough to issue a warning in his speech. "Because of what is at stake," he said, "this matter must be resolved expeditiously, but deliberately and without any rush to judgment."

A Crucial Early Decision

Once the machine recounts were concluded — reducing Bush's lead from 1,784 votes to a mere 327 — the Gore camp quickly sought manual recounts in four counties where Gore had polled well and where the Democrats contended there had been signs of trouble: Broward, Miami-Dade, Palm Beach and Volusia. Some still hoped to avoid a full-fledged legal war. But that fantasy ended when Bush filed a preemptive federal lawsuit on Nov. 11 — the same Saturday the Gore forces convened at the Naval Observatory — challenging the constitutionality of manual recounts.

Several Gore lawyers and strategists said that little thought was given at the time to requesting a statewide recount. Their attention was focused on the four counties where problems were most apparent, each of which had gone for Gore, and there was little time to collect evidence elsewhere.

They could not be sure whether he would win a statewide recount. And, if anything, they worried that filing for recounts in four counties, instead of the two first contemplated, would draw criticism that they were needlessly prolonging the election. "We had to keep our focus on where our biggest return was, and we couldn't stretch our resources," said one top aide in Florida.

Nearly four weeks later, critics would second-guess that strategy when Judge N. Sanders Sauls of Leon County Circuit Court cited the lack of a statewide recount in ruling against Gore's contest of the certified election results.

Early in the second week of the vote dispute, as Harris declared she would hold to a certification date of Nov. 14, it became clear that the legal battle would take center stage. Klain, Christopher and others decided they needed a prominent trial lawyer and legal spokesman to handle their state court issues.

"Who's the best lawyer in America that we don't have working on this thing?" Klain asked in a phone call to Walter E. Dellinger, a Gore supporter and former United States solicitor general.

They settled on the names of Joel Klein and David Boies, both of whom had been involved in the government's prosecution of the Microsoft Corporation. Klain tried to reach Klein, the former head of the Justice Department's antitrust division, but he was on a plane. Dellinger contacted his former law school classmate Boies, a corporate lawyer known for his quick preparation, agility in the courtroom and good relations with the news media.

Several hours later, by mid-evening on Nov. 13, Boies was flying toward Tallahassee on a private jet with a sheaf of briefing papers in hand. Like many other lawyers on the team, he worked pro bono, paid only with relentless publicity.

By the time Boies arrived, Gore and his aides had essentially established the principle that they would fight vigorously to get every legal vote counted but would not challenge voting irregularities or cases of potential fraud or intimidation.

"Once you decide that, there are not a lot of key decisions along the way," Boies said. "There may be political decisions and public relations decisions about how to describe something. But from a legal perspective, the goal is to get the votes counted and you're driven almost exclusively by that."

Public relations would get in the way the next weekend, however. Unbeknownst to the strategists in Washington, Democratic lawyers in Florida challenged absentee overseas ballots as they were being tabulated on Friday, Nov. 17, including military ballots that appeared to be incorrectly postmarked. While the Democrats maintained that there was no concerted effort to strike military ballots, the Republicans immediately charged that the Gore forces were trying to disenfranchise men and women in uniform.

When Eskew woke to the news on Nov. 18, he realized it was a fiasco in the making. "That was one time when our legal strategy wasn't in synch with our p.r.," he said. "Generally, this has been a well-run campaign, but it's being run in three centers by people who haven't had a day off in two years, and we missed some things."

Some Washington aides primarily concerned with Gore's politics urged quick action to stave off more damage. Surrogates were dispatched to make the case that the Republicans were selling a phony issue. But Lieberman, in a Sunday appearance on NBC's *Meet the Press* went much further, urging state officials to "give the benefit of the doubt" to military votes.

"He probably made more policy on that show than he was supposed to," said an aide.

The team in Florida was stunned by what it saw as a very public rebuke. "It was a body blow to a lot of people in Tallahassee," said a top Florida strategist. "He sort of helped put us on the defensive."

As Thanksgiving week began, Fabiani acknowledged in a memorandum to Daley that "the Republicans have scored on the issues of military absentee ballots and on the seemingly endless nature of the recount process." To counter those problems, he outlined a communications plan that would emphasize "allowing the will of the people to be reflected" and the related message that the Republicans were "employing every delaying tactic possible."

Fabiani's memo detailed a plan that left little to chance in a crusade to "create news relentlessly, especially news that is televised." He suggested ways to plant stories in *The New York Times* and prescribed "a strict schedule of two televised press events each day," including a Thanksgiving-eve visit to a homeless shelter.

While there, Fabiani wrote in his script, "Gore wanders over to the cameras and gives a statement so we have sound from him over the holiday." That is essentially what Gore did as he unloaded boxes of food. "We don't have to count these boxes, do we?" he asked with a grin.

The communications task had been easier the week before, Fabiani wrote, "when our focus was squarely on the partisan manipulation of the process by the Florida secretary of state." Indeed, Fabiani said in an interview that Harris became an inviting target and that he had "argued very vigorously that we needed an enemy."

Fabiani said that when Harris emerged as a key player, Gore asked him, "What do we know about her?" He said he responded that Harris was a partisan and co-chairwoman of the Bush Florida campaign. "Why aren't we getting that out?" Gore demanded, according to Fabiani.

Fabiani said that attacking Harris was "the right thing to do, and it worked." He added: "I felt we needed to do something to delegitimize her because if we let people perceive her as a figure of authority," the Gore cause would suffer.

The Gore team also devoted significant effort to lobbying top newspaper and newsmagazine editors and TV news executives. Gore made two rounds of phone calls, once when he feared Harris would certify the Florida results on Nov. 18 — after the tabulation of absentee ballots — and again when she was about to certify on Nov. 26. The vice president explained the rationale behind his continuing court fight, implicitly encouraging the editors and executives not to join Harris in declaring Bush the winner.

A Final Strategy Dispute

Soon there would be another dilemma exposing the friction within the Gore camp. In filing a contest to overturn Harris's certification of the Florida results, Gore had to decide whether to challenge only the counting of votes, or also irregularities like the absentee ballot problems in Seminole County.

In what seemed a clear violation of state law, elections supervisors in Seminole County had allowed Republican officials to write missing voter identification numbers on absentee ballot applications. The more aggressive members of the Gore team, particularly those in Florida like Whouley and Klain, supported including the Seminole case.

But Daley and Christopher, among others, again urged caution. Having stated repeatedly that his goal was to count the votes, Gore would seem a hypocrite to call for discounting them, they argued. There were more meetings and conference calls the last weekend of November. Again, image prevailed.

"He said, 'What happened in Seminole is probably the closest thing to fraud that we have, but I'm also disturbed by the remedy,' " Eskew recalled, referring to Gore. " 'I empathize with these other cases and support them. But I have to look ahead at how I become president and the consequences of that.' "

The contest, of course, would fail after being rejected by Judge Sauls, revived by the Florida Supreme Court last Friday, and killed once and for all by the United States Supreme Court on Tuesday. Even then, tensions would persist. As his lawyers in Tallahassee quixotically prepared yet another brief, Gore slept Tuesday night on his dilemma. Would the country, and the judgment of history, indulge one more appeal?

By sunrise, his decision was clear, and he spent Wednesday in a living room at NavObs, fielding condolence calls and writing a speech. There was discussion about whether he should utter the word "concession." "Some people felt very passionately that this word should not be used," said one aide. "But he never really considered not using it because he didn't want to be grudging."

After delivering the concession speech shortly after 9 p.m. Eastern time, Gore took an appreciative call from former President Bush. But he did not watch the speech by the president-elect that followed his at around 10 p.m., aides said; Gore chose instead to mingle with about 100 friends, aides and family members who had gathered under a white tent at his residence for a hastily planned party.

As the evening ran late, one guest, Jon Bon Jovi, the rock singer and a Gore fundraiser, expressed dissatisfaction with the band and asked if he could call some friends. Near midnight, they arrived: Stevie Wonder, Tom Petty and others. They played for hours, joined at times by Tipper Gore on drums.

Before the party broke up near 3 a.m., the Gores spent much of the night dancing, happy to be together, according to attendees. "You got the sense of a guy who felt good about the way he exited," said one aide, "but who also felt a sense of release."

Dec. 15, 2000, Kevin Sack

Gore's Critical Mistake: Failure to Ask for a Statewide Recount

TALLAHASSEE — In the inevitable second-guessing that followed Al Gore's defeat at the hands of the United States Supreme Court, his failure to ask the Florida courts for a manual statewide recount has emerged as one in a series of pivotal legal miscalculations that may have doomed his 35-day battle.

While acknowledging the clarifying benefits of hindsight, these lawyers and professors said that this failure unnecessarily raised constitutional obstacles that made it far more difficult for Florida's courts to fashion a timely remedy that the Supreme Court might have found tolerable. That error, they said, had been compounded by an earlier misstep by Gore's lawyers — a decision to seek more time to complete the first phase of the counting process. That decision, one on which even Gore's lawyers disagreed, greatly shortened the time available in the second phase to seek a statewide manual recount.

"He has nobody to blame but himself," said Thomas W. Merrill, a professor of law at Northwestern University, who criticized the Gore campaign for elevating hardball tactics — seeking immediate hand recounts in Democratic strongholds — over a strategy of demanding that all votes be counted regardless of the political consequences.

"It had the appearance of being manipulative," Merrill said. "It had the appearance of making it look as if he didn't want a level playing field. I think it seeped into the way the judicial system perceived things."

The decision by the court tonight also suggested that Gore's lawyers might well have argued against the inflexibility of the Dec. 12 cut-off date for naming Florida's electors to the Electoral College. It also suggested that Gore's principal lawyer, David Boies, erred in failing to respond to a clear invitation from several justices to define more precisely how counters should evaluate voter intent in examining ballots.

Lawyers who followed the court case said today that they were most struck by Gore's decision not to formally petition the Florida courts for a manual statewide recount. Instead, Gore had only made the offer to Bush in a televised address nearly a month ago. Bush rejected the offer, and Gore's lawyers never once pursued it in court even though they were invited to do just that during oral arguments before the Florida Supreme Court. Boies said the vice president would "accept" a statewide recount, but added, "We are not urging that upon the court."

Gore's lawyers, explaining what happened, said that in the first chaotic days after the election there was a palpable political nervousness about appearing too indiscriminate in seeking manual recounts, and there was also a practical need, given logistical difficulties, to concentrate legal firepower on those counties where the chances of getting manual recounts offered the highest likelihood of success.

Later, as today's deadline approached for naming Florida's electors, Gore's lawyers were reluctant to push hard in any court for a statewide recount, they said. To propose so huge an undertaking, they feared, would only provide Bush's lawyers with unlimited possibilities for delaying tactics. "We were reluctant to get involved in anything that could slow us down," Dexter Douglass, one of Gore's lawyers, said. "Our focus was on moving our winnable case."

Still, in defending their overall strategy, Gore's lawyers noted that any number of crucial decisions were made on the fly, often with incomplete information, often at the edge of exhaustion, and always under the pressure of crushing deadlines. Under such conditions, they said, miscalculations were inevitable, and entirely human. None of the Gore lawyers, for example, anticipated the extent to which judges at every level would dwell on their failure to formally seek a manual statewide recount.

One of the first was Judge N. Sanders Sauls of Leon County Circuit Court, who, in dismissing Gore's lawsuit contesting Florida's certified results, faulted Gore's lawyers for not seeking a statewide manual recount. To properly contest a statewide election, he ruled, Gore was obligated to ask for "a review and recount of all ballots in all the counties in this state."

The Florida Supreme Court reversed Judge Sauls. But it, too, agreed that it was "absolutely essential" to count every ballot where there was a concern that tabulation machines had failed to detect a presidential vote. Douglass and other Gore lawyers said they never dreamed, given the shortness of time, that the Florida Supreme Court would order a statewide manual recount of some 45,000 ballots.

The topic came up again on Monday during oral arguments before the United States Supreme Court, where several justices raised questions about how a recount could be conducted in a way that guaranteed all voters equal protection under Florida's election laws. In a question to Boies, Chief Justice William H. Rehnquist asked whether the Florida Supreme Court ordered a broader recount than Gore requested because the Florida court "thought that to do just what he wanted would be unfair."

"I think that's right," Boies replied.

The decision not to pursue a statewide manual recount in court didn't simply raise unforeseen objections from judges. There was also a price to be paid on the public relations front. Just as they did when Democratic lawyers tried to disqualify hundreds of military absentee ballots, Republicans quickly branded

Gore a hypocrite for proclaiming his desire to count every vote as his lawyers were seeking hand recounts in select Democratic strongholds.

Ben Ginsberg, a senior lawyer for the Bush team, said that Gore's lawyers pursued an intellectually dishonest course to further one overriding goal: finding enough Democratic votes to overcome Bush's lead.

"Going statewide, they're really not sure they can win," Ginsberg said. "Their overall mistake," he added, "is being so hypocritical about what they were asking for. When I was talking about goal-oriented, that has exposed their hypocrisy a good deal. They haven't been able to sustain as a legal matter what they were talking about at press conferences. That hurt them in court."

Since Election Day, there have been two distinct points at which Gore had the opportunity to ask for comprehensive hand recounts. The first came during the so-called protest phase, a 72-hour window after the election when candidates can petition county canvassing commissions to conduct manual recounts. The Gore team sought recounts in four of Florida's 67 counties — Broward, Palm Beach, Volusia and Miami-Dade — all of which, it so happened, had voted for Gore.

One member of the Gore legal team, insisting on anonymity, said that the decision was dictated by practical realities as much as anything else. There was only so much time, he said, and only so many lawyers, and Gore and his closest advisers were still sorting through overall strategy questions. "We knew absolutely there were big problems with those four counties, and so we went there," he said. "Had we known more about other counties, we would have gone there, too. But we didn't. It might have looked partisan, but it wasn't."

Joshua Rosenkranz, president of the Brennan Center for Justice at New York University's School of Law, defended the early push for limited recounts in Democratic counties as a reasonable position given the known facts at the time. "What they were trying to do was limit their recounts where they thought they had the vote," Rosenkranz said. "And that was not a dumb strategy, back when they made that decision. I think it didn't dawn on anyone that recounts in some counties and not others would be considered an equal protection violation. That was a theory that sort of emerged."

Far more questionable, he said, was the decision to ask the Florida Supreme Court to extend the deadline for completing manual recounts before the results were certified by Florida's secretary of state. As he and several other legal experts noted, by successfully extending the protest period by eight days, Gore necessarily cut eight days from the time available to him to contest the certified results.

Worst still, they said, in extending the protest period, the Florida Supreme Court and the Gore campaign became embroiled in new time-consuming arguments about whether the Florida justices had usurped power delegated to legislatures by the United States Constitution.

"The first strategic judgment was asking for an extension of the deadline for protests, which launched this whole barrage of judicial criticism that the

Florida Supreme Court ultimately was changing the rules," Rosenkranz. "Looking back on it, my hunch is that the protest ended up not redounding to Gore's benefit, and that they wish they hadn't done it. This is a classic trade-off between law and politics. What was driving that was, 'Oh my God, whatever you do, don't allow the secretary of state to certify a winner.' It was palpable the moment she certified it."

Dec. 13, 2000, David Barstow and Adam Nagourney

BOIES'S CONCESSION ON "DEADLINE" PROVED FATAL

Back on Nov. 20, during what would be the first of a series of historic oral arguments, the chief justice of the Florida Supreme Court turned to David Boies and asked a question. In that exchange, Boies made a pivotal concession that, in retrospect, helped bring the vice president's defeat in the legal war for White House. The chief justice, Charles T. Wells, mentioned the date Dec. 12. He wondered whether battles over the Florida vote "have to be finally determined by that date," and asked, "Do you agree with that?"

Boies looked up. "I do your honor," he said.

That concession began a chain of legal events that ended with the conclusion by a majority of the justices of the United States Supreme Court on Tuesday — Dec. 12 — that time had simply run out. Florida recounts could not go on after that date, the justices said, even if they could be conducted constitutionally.

Yesterday, legal experts of differing political persuasions said the skirmish over what came to be called "the deadline" proved decisive. But some of them said that under federal law, at least, it was not a deadline, but merely advice by Congress to states about how to assure that their voters' choice for president would be honored.

"It is a promise by Congress that if you do three things a state's electors will be conclusive in Congress" should some other slate claim to be the real one, said John C. Yoo, a conservative constitutional law professor at the University of California at Berkeley.

To win what has been called the Dec. 12 "safe harbor," states must name electors; must do so under rules enacted before Election Day, and must resolve any contests over who the electors are by six days before the meeting of the Electoral College, which is to meet on Dec. 18.

The United States Supreme Court's majority opinion on Tuesday did not say Dec. 12 was a federal deadline. Instead, the majority said that was what Florida law provided. There is no provision of Florida law specifying a Dec. 12 deadline. But the majority of the justices in Washington said the Florida Supreme Court had held that the State Legislature meant to gain the "safe harbor" protection for Florida's electors. The four justices in the minority suggested that Florida law provided no such thing. And yesterday, legal experts said that central conclusion of the majority was a debatable legal point. "The problem with that is it is not clear that's what the Florida Supreme Court would say the law of Florida is," said Philip P. Frickey, a constitutional law expert at the University of California at Berkeley.

For the Florida Supreme Court to reach that conclusion in the presidential battle, Professor Frickey said, it would have to decide that Florida law said it was more important to obtain the "safe harbor" protection than it was to complete a recount to see which candidate had won.

But some experts said it was reasonable for the justices to conclude the Florida Supreme Court had decided the Legislature meant to get all election contests completed in time to assure that Florida's electoral votes would be counted.

"The way they read the Florida Supreme Court decisions is not inevitable, but it is quite justifiable," said Daniel H. Lowenstein, an election law expert at the University of California at Los Angeles.

The evidence for that view of Florida law can be traced back to Boies's concession about the "deadline" back on Nov. 20. For a while after that argument, the idea of a Dec. 12 deadline slipped from notice. That may have been because Chief Justice Wells, apparently its primary proponent on the Florida court, agreed to go along with a unanimous ruling that ordered recounts in three heavily Democratic counties be included in Florida's tally. But by Dec. 8, when the Florida court made its next major decision, the court had been bruised by a reversal from the justices in Washington. The justices in Washington had taken notice of the "safe harbor" law and seemed to, in their words, "counsel against" taking any action that would result in Florida losing any benefit the Legislature might have intended from an early completion of election contests.

On Dec. 8, the Florida justices split bitterly, with Chief Justice Wells filing his own angry dissent. By then, the dissenting Florida justices suggested they were concerned about the "safe harbor" issue. But Boies's agreement that there was a deadline meant even the justices who did not think there was a true deadline were undercut by one of the chief adversaries in the case.

In the Dec. 8 ruling, the four-justice majority fended off the issue. The majority opinion said the four were "cognizant" of it. In a footnote, they said they were doing their best in light of the "looming deadlines." It is apparently those references that convinced the majority in Washington this week that "the Supreme Court of Florida has said that the Legislature intended" to establish a Dec. 12 deadline.

But after Boies's exchange with Chief Justice Wells on Nov. 20, the Florida Supreme Court seemed, simply, confused about the deadline issue, said L. Kinvin Wroth, dean of Vermont Law School, who wrote a law review article about the "safe harbor" law's operation in the 1960 presidential election. The footnote reference to the "looming deadline" may have reflected that confusion. If so, Wroth said, the majority of the Washington justices may have been wrong when they concluded that Florida law required that counting could not continue past Tuesday.

"The presidency," Wroth said, "is being decided on the basis of a confused situation in which the Florida court, almost inadvertently, spoke as though the Florida Legislature had intended to have any contest proceeding complete by Dec. 12."

The majority of the Washington justices, Wroth said, "played 'gotcha' with that."

Dec. 14, 2000, William Glaberson

Inside the Campaign: G.O.P.'s Depth Outdid Gore's Team in Florida

MIAMI — If Al Gore wants to appreciate the forces that defeated him in Florida over the last six weeks, he need not look much beyond the scene on December 18th in the Senate chamber in Tallahassee: Gov. Jeb Bush and the state's entire Republican leadership presiding in triumph as Florida's 25 electoral votes were finally delivered to George W. Bush.

The ceremony was more than a celebration of Bush's ascent to the White House. It was a display of the depth and complexity of the political forces Gore confronted here in Florida. And it demonstrated the extent to which Gore was up against far more than the presidential nominee of the Republican Party. Gore may have had some reason to feel that he was fighting the government of Florida itself.

From the morning after the election, Jeb Bush took an intense and passionate interest in the battle to make his brother president, according to interviews with several state and Republican officials, notwithstanding his effort to strike a low public profile. He offered detailed guidance to his brother's lawyers on how to navigate the political thicket that was South Florida, providing information and insight about local officials who could determine his brother's political future.

He enlisted his own campaign lawyer, Barry Richard of Tallahassee, to be the chief Florida lawyer on his brother's legal team, and he recruited dozens of volunteers to move into the disputed counties in the days after the election, Republican officials said. And within 24 hours after Election Day, six of the Florida governor's senior political operatives took unpaid leaves to join the effort against Gore, dealing with everything from answering routine press calls to briefing out-of-town lawyers on Florida election law. Bush's acting general counsel, Frank Jimenez, was the one who telephoned Richard to request his services.

"I couldn't bear the thought of sitting behind my desk doing nothing while this situation played itself out around me," Jimenez said.

The Democrats also mobilized intensively and relentlessly, but they had fewer levers of power. At every street corner demonstration and counting hall, it seemed that they were outnumbered, outshouted and outorganized by Republicans. The state's two leading Democrats, Senator Bob Graham and Attorney General Robert A. Butterworth, all but disappeared for long stretches of the contest.

Jeb Bush, in his annual year-end interview with Florida Statehouse reporters this week, again portrayed himself as mostly detached from the effort that got his brother to the White House. He said he paid close attention to the fight only in the first week after Election Day, then "increasingly less, to the point where I was really completely out of it."

But the extent to which both the state Republican Party and the government offices it controlled in Florida assisted in Bush's post-election success was suggested this week in interviews with party operatives across the state and in Washington, with lawyers and with aides to Jeb Bush and President-elect Bush.

While the Republicans were widely known to have a coordinated strategy in Florida, the reach of the national party's connection all the way down to minor county party affiliates is now becoming even clearer. Local and state officials described in interviews a web of activity — from seminars on ballot challenges and election law to the distribution of cheap cameras to collect evidence — as new indicators of how sophisticated their efforts were.

The state Republican Party, which is run by Al Cardenas, a lawyer who has been a close ally of Jeb Bush's for 22 years, turned overnight into a full-fledged operative arm of the Bush effort. It turned over all three floors of its red-brick headquarters to Bush's lawyers and strategists, led by James A. Baker III, the former secretary of state, and Benjamin L. Ginsberg, the general counsel for the Bush campaign.

Thirty state party employees who were to have been laid off after Election Day were put at the round-the-clock service of the Bush campaign, doing everything from legal research to fetching food and laundry for Bush's team.

In at least 42 counties, Republican lawyers with ties to the state party were pressed into service, Cardenas said. In an orchestrated daily campaign, state legislators and local elected officials called radio stations, using airwaves to denounce any hint of a victory by the Gore forces and to broadcast the party "talking points" that were sent several times a day by e-mail. Republican workers in the state's 67 counties, many of whom viewed this as a personal test of Jeb Bush, moved into the counties that were at the fulcrum of the dispute, faxing and e-mailing daily updates about what was taking place on the ground to the presidential campaign headquarters in Austin.

"As a local chairman, my ability to call on 40, 50, 60 volunteers in a short period of time, and to have them down there quick to help out, was quite an asset," said Paul Bedinghaus, the Florida Republican Party treasurer and the Pinellas County chairman. "The Democrats couldn't match that."

In Tallahassee, Katherine Harris, the secretary of state who served both as the state's chief elections officer and the co-chairwoman of Bush's campaign, hired a battery of outside lawyers to defend her rulings on what, if any, recounts would be permitted — lawyers paid with taxpayers' money.

And finally, Bush had a fire wall: The State Legislature, a Republican bedrock, which Bush's advisers quickly determined could provide them the last line of protection should that prove necessary. Bush's lawyers, in researching the Constitution and federal election law, came across language that might allow the Legislature to, in effect, supersede the election and appoint its own slate of electors. And when the Florida Supreme Court issued one of a series of rulings that went against Bush on Nov. 21, Baker held a midnight news conference where he very deliberately noted this power afforded to state legislators. The Republican leaders got the message and made plans to call a session.

The Bushes, without question, had their own partisan obstacles to confront in the state of Florida, including Democrats who controlled some of the important canvassing boards in South Florida and a State Supreme Court dominated by justices appointed by Democratic governors. Bush benefited from Gore's legal miscalculations, in particular, his failure to aggressively pursue a statewide, rather than selective recount, with uniform standards for counting ballots.

Finally, and not incidentally, participants at every level of the effort to defend Bush from Gore's onslaught invariably described their work as a moral crusade that, if aggressive, crossed no lines and broke no laws as it sought to halt what many described as an illicit bid for power by Gore.

"We were fighting for our lives, and we were fighting for a righteous cause," said Marjorie Kincaid, the Republican chairwoman in Hillsborough County.

Democrats these days speak with a certain respectful awe about the persistence, ferocity and scope of the Republican Party's mobilization, citing, for example, how local party workers at one point staked out virtually every court clerk's office to act as an early warning system for surprise motions or orders.

"The Bush strategy was fight everything everywhere all the time," said John D.C. Newton, a Tallahassee lawyer who worked on Gore's legal team here. "There were deadlines, and they were short, and as long as they kept fighting, the official record said they were ahead."

A Single Goal: Fighting to Maintain a Razor-Thin Lead

Baker and his team of lawyers arrived within 48 hours after the polls had closed, plunging immediately into a tumultuous and anxious environment. The Texas governor's lead over Gore had dropped to 327 votes as the state's 67 counties conducted a mandatory post-election machine recount. And Gore had quickly moved to seize the political advantage, pressing for a more thorough count of the votes.

"There was great concern that we were behind the eight ball on the P.R. kind of thing," said Bedinghaus, the state party treasurer. "We got a lot of calls locally, saying: 'You guys are rolling over. Why aren't you out there?' "

Baker and his aides moved into the state party headquarters, which is named after the first president named Bush, and seized on the goal that would govern their actions in the courts and the political arena: To block a recount. The overriding concern, one senior Bush aide said, was that any tally putting Gore even fleetingly in the lead, especially since the vice president was carrying the popular vote nationwide, would be politically devastating for Bush.

From the start, Bush's advisers kept an eye on the clock, appreciating the extent to which legal deadlines played to their benefit, and the advantage of exploiting opportunities to slow down the proceedings. And they swiftly decided to aggressively present to the nation and, not incidentally, to federal and state judges who were watching the counts on television, an image of Florida in chaos. They did that not only by alerting reporters to genuine episodes of discord, but also by organizing their own demonstrations, then complaining about the chaos that resulted. These images underscored Baker's warnings, in his televised appearances, that the nation was growing alarmed at the spectacle in Florida.

Republican "observers" were dispatched in teams to disputed counties, told to aggressively monitor the counts and to steer the news media to episodes where there was evidence of disagreement. Party officials directed this effort with two daily conference calls, at 7 a.m. and 10 p.m.

The Bush campaign arranged three-hour election law seminars in Tampa, to instruct Florida Republicans and others who came from out of state on the intricacies of the state's election law and open meetings law, including detailed instructions on how to challenge a ballot.

State Republicans handed out disposable cameras to document episodes of questionable vote counting, and even "evidence bags" to gather disputed chads. At times, those props served to encourage a carnival atmosphere.

Bush's ability to marshal these forces was in no small part a tribute to the strength the Republican Party in Florida enjoys with his brother in power. It also reflects the changing political demographics of this state where, like in much of the rest of the South, the Democratic Party is in decline. And Democrats here do not have the advantage of a strong labor movement that might otherwise have provided Gore with the troops needed to counter the Republicans.

The loyalty to Bush in the state that elected his brother is, even Democrats say, much more intense than that shown toward Gore. "We'd call people all night to have them there the next day and nobody got mad that we woke them up or anything," said Kincaid, the Hillsborough County Republican chairwoman.

A Principal Player: A Neutral Stance, a Common Effort

As secretary of state, Harris was in a position to use her broad discretion over the conduct of state elections to shape the outcome of the race.

Harris promised that she would carry out her duties in a neutral fashion. To emphasize the point, she retained Steel, Hector & Davis, a major Tallahassee law firm traditionally associated with prominent Florida Democrats.

Joseph P. Klock Jr., managing partner of the firm, said in a interview this week that Harris remained true to her neutrality pledge. "Some clients," Klock said, "will tell you, 'This is where I want to go, take me there.' She did not do that once. She said, 'Show me the law.' "

Over the 36 days it took to settle the Florida election, Harris made a series of crucial decisions, and each one, without exception, helped Bush and hurt Gore. She told county canvassing boards they lacked the discretion to conduct manual recounts — recounts Gore desperately wanted. She enforced strict counting deadlines, just as Bush wanted, and then, contradicting an earlier directive from her office, she advised counties to apply a liberal standard for counting absentee ballots, a move that helped Bush pick up hundreds of critical votes.

"She was clearly trying to get as many of these votes in as she could, whether or not they met the criteria, and so was the Bush campaign and the Republican Party," said Bob Rackleff, a Democrat on the Leon County canvassing board.

In courtrooms across the state, her formidable team of lawyers relentlessly opposed the Gore campaign at every step. Besides her own legal staff, Klock's firm placed 29 lawyers and 11 paralegals at Harris's disposal.

These lawyers, billing Florida's taxpayers $175 an hour, pulled out all the stops, routinely clocking 16-hour days, sometimes working in shifts to crank out briefs 24 hours a day, sometimes sleeping on conference tables. They rented a private plane to fly to Washington for arguments in the United States Supreme Court. So far, Klock's firm has submitted bills for $627,280 in legal work and $54,986 in expenses.

No matter the courtroom, the Gore legal team, as high-powered as it was with David Boies, the man who took on Microsoft, as its leader, faced a potent tag team of private Bush lawyers and public Harris lawyers. The Harris and Bush lawyers, reinforcing each other's arguments, eating up precious court time, each focused on the single, shared goal of preventing recounts.

"The most harmful thing was the stops and starts caused by the elections decisions from Harris's office," said Newton, the Gore lawyer. "There were too many days when nobody counted, and in those early days, every little bump hurt. We'd get past one hurdle, then face another, and another, and another. Every time we turned around there was another obstacle."

Richard, the senior lawyer for the Bush campaign in Florida, drew a blank when asked to cite a single argument or action by Harris that hurt Bush. There was, he said after a pause, perhaps one minor argument by the Harris lawyers that displeased Bush lawyers. "I can't remember what it was."

Richard said the Bush campaign cautioned that the legal team should keep a careful distance from Harris, partly to avoid accusations of improper coordination. But mainly, he said, the Bush team worried that efforts to influence her might backfire. "They didn't want to offend her," he said.

Klock recalled things differently, saying that Harris was under substantial pressure from the Bush team.

"The campaign people wanted to be able to communicate with her," he said.

And while Harris first barred him and his firm from having contact with the Bush campaign, she later authorized cooperation "on limited matters," Klock said. As a result, the leading Harris and Bush lawyers had several strategic conversations, he recalled.

The cooperation included routine legal housekeeping matters, like coordinating witness depositions, and involved sharing some legal strategy, Klock said. The Harris lawyers, for example, were given advance word on which witnesses the Bush campaign planned to call in one crucial hearing. In turn, the Harris team told the Bush lawyers which issues would be argued before the United States Supreme Court.

Klock said there was nothing untoward about this cooperation, calling it a common practice for litigants who share the same basic legal stance in a case. But he also said that when the Harris lawyers did something that displeased the Bush campaign, they might hear about it. His lawyers would get wind that major state party figures were calling, upset at any indication that Harris was not sticking the Republican line. "Anything that was inconsistent with that, they didn't want to see," Klock said.

Klock said he tried to convey neutrality. "We don't have a horse in this race," he would tell judges and reporters alike. The courts did not quite agree. The Florida Supreme Court, for example, rejected his request for the secretary of state to be given a separate allotment for oral arguments. The justices said his time would have to come off the Republican clock.

At times, partisan emotions seeped into Harris's office. She was angered by Democratic attacks, and she drew comfort from sympathy calls from her prominent Republican friends. Indeed, the Republican loyalists in her office initially viewed with suspicion the advice from Klock and the other Democratic lawyers. "In the beginning we had the sense we were in the enemy camp," said Klock, who, despite his party affiliation, is also a friend of Jeb Bush and several of his major donors. "Everyone was nice," he said, "but there's nice, and then nice."

The Strategy: A Stream of Protests, Endless Arguments

From the beginning, Ginsberg, the Bush campaign counsel, said, the Republicans were seeking only to guard against abuses in a state where, he argued, there were no uniform rules on how to count a ballot and where Democrats were pushing for standards that would favor Gore.

That said, the effect was to slow the count and in many cases stop it. David Leahy, the nonpartisan election supervisor in Miami-Dade County, said his board was barraged with "objections and challenges and arguments," the vast majority brought by Republicans.

In Broward County, the head of the canvassing board, Judge Robert W. Lee, said: "Suddenly, I would get an envelope stuffed with 50 challenged ballots, and when I looked at them, almost all of them had been plainly marked. This just wasn't a good-faith effort to count votes.

"The first time I asked one of the Republican volunteers to explain to me what he was doing, and he told me he didn't have to say anything to me. I had a deputy remove him from the building. I wasn't going to tolerate delays."

Indeed, Bush's supporters were, by their own account, tireless in coming up with ways, they said, to block the unfair counting of votes. In Broward, they complained that chewing gum could be used to surreptitiously remove chads from questionable ballots.

The executive director of the New York Republican State Committee, J. Brendan Quinn, one of hundreds of Republicans who were flown in from around the country, said he saw a counter "eating the chads off the table" and shouted out his objection.

More subtle forces were employed by the Republicans as well. State party leaders said they recruited Republican celebrities, like Bob Dole, Gov. Christie Whitman of New Jersey and Gov. George E. Pataki of New York, to increase pressure on counting officials.

Charles Lichtman, a Democratic lawyer, said that when Gov. John Engler of Michigan attended a Broward County meeting, he spent an hour staring directly at the lone Republican on that canvassing board, Robert Rosenberg, a county judge, while Bob Dole, the former Republican candidate for president, stood over him. "They were really glaring at him," said Lichtman. "I think they wanted to make sure that on close calls, Judge Rosenberg would side with them." Judge Rosenberg declined a request for an interview.

In Orange County, the state Republican chairman, Lew Oliver, used out-of-towners to act as the bad cops toward his own canvassing board. "They were colleagues and friends and two circuit court judges, and I knew better than to go up against them," Oliver said of the board. When firmer measures were needed, "I traded my position for someone from out-of-town to be bad cop," Oliver said. "And they'd be threatened with being thrown out of the room."

In many ways, all the forces of mobilization converged in Miami, on the day before Thanksgiving, when the Miami-Dade canvassing board abruptly shut down its manual count, in the very county where Gore's advisers believed he could win the election. The extent of Republican organization was on display here. Two Republican members of Congress had gone on the radio urging listeners to head for the county government center and join the protest. A recreational vehicle, turned up by Bush's campaign, was set up outside to provide a stream of fresh T-shirts and placards to the hundreds of demonstrators who chanted and yelled in the very room where the votes were being counted.

The canvassing board headed upstairs to perform the manual recount. Even from there, Leahy said, he could hear the shouts and the pounding on the doors and windows below. When the board returned downstairs, Leahy noted that many of the demonstrators were the same Republicans who had been methodically filing ballot protests over the previous two days.

Leahy said he was not swayed by the tumult but instead was made weary by a realization that it would be impossible to count the disputed ballots in time for a deadline set by the court. The board ended the counting, a moment — as much as the United Supreme Court decision that would come two weeks later — that Gore's supporters later said marked the real end of his campaign for the White House.

Dec. 22, 2000, Adam Nagourney and David Barstow

Election Dispute Casts Cloud on Jeb Bush's Future

TALLAHASSEE — Gov. Jeb Bush of Florida was once such a political smash that fans would mob him at events, begging for autographs. Democrats predicted that he would coast to re-election in 2002. And Republicans thought their governor's influence would only be enhanced if his older brother reached the White House. They even speculated that Jeb Bush would reward his key supporters by sending them to Washington to collect presidential appointments.

That was before Nov. 7.

Now, more than any other politician in America except the two nominees themselves, Jeb Bush finds himself bruised by this presidential election despite his best efforts not to be drawn into the vortex early on. Republicans say they are bracing for a bloody political brawl over the next two years because Democrats in Florida now consider Bush vulnerable and have begun plotting to oust him in 2002.

Beyond Florida, Bush, of course, is no longer talked about as a likely future president. And for Bush to even dream of moving up, he first has to contend with the political firestorm surrounding him at home.

"In my community, if you just mention Jeb Bush's name, you get scowls on people's faces," said State Representative Christopher L. Smith, a Democrat from Fort Lauderdale who endorsed Bush in 1998 and who has since turned on him.

Aside from the partisan complaints, Democrats and Republicans alike now seem worried that Florida has become a laughingstock, with commentators on television chat shows endlessly deriding the state as "Flori-duh." Plenty of the anger and plenty of the disappointment seems directed at the Florida governor himself.

"He hurts like a brother seeing the trials of his own flesh and blood," said Gov. Frank Keating of Oklahoma. "He's got to be tired. He's got to be stressed. There's a sense of frustration and disquiet as a result of 28 days of uncertainty. This is his brother, whose potential presidency hangs in the balance. There is a flesh and blood investment here."

Aside from the personal aspects, the political toll for Bush is significant. Republicans accuse him of not being sufficiently energetic in helping his brother win Florida outright over Vice President Al Gore. Democrats accuse him of rigging the process to get his brother elected, whether acting on his own or through political allies including Katherine Harris, the secretary of state, Tom Feeney, the House speaker, and John McKay, the Senate president.

"I'm expecting a holy war in Florida in 2002," said Representative Joe Scarborough, a Republican from Pensacola. "And Jeb's the hot button that Democrats are going to be pushing over the next four years, claiming that W.'s brother helped him win the presidency because he was governor of Florida."

But Scarborough said that Republicans, in turn, were just as energized. "Republicans will line up behind Jeb regardless of whether they thought he should have done more, or less, during the campaign," he said, "because things have degenerated to an 'us versus them' scenario."

Bush's predicament is not just in Florida. Asked whether Bush had a future in national politics, Gov. Bob Taft of Ohio, a Republican, replied, "That's a tough one. I'm sure he's not thinking about that now."

It is extremely premature, certainly, to write Jeb Bush's political obituary. The latest polls show that he remains relatively popular. The Democrats have yet to settle on a candidate to challenge him in 2002. And if George W. Bush does become president, he could help his brother win favor by lavishing attention on this state.

While he is largely staying clear of the news media, outwardly, at least, Jeb Bush is trying mightily to survive the presidential morass. At a dinner with newly elected legislators here on Tuesday, where he appeared with Governor Keating, Bush gamely joked about the interminable campaign.

Still, many Republicans say they are unnerved not only by the prospect of a backlash if Bush becomes president, but by the fact that vital Democratic constituencies like blacks and Jews turned out in huge numbers for Gore. Many Democrats say that showing was not so much borne out of affection for the vice president but out of anger at Jeb Bush, particularly among minorities. "We had record turnout in minority districts such as mine," Smith, the state representative, said. "I would say 40 percent of it was for Gore and 60 percent against Bush — and most of that was against Jeb Bush."

Smith said that while he disapproved of Bush's handling of the post-election developments, he gave up on the governor out of disdain for his One Florida initiative. Bush proposed that a year ago to end racial preferences in university admissions and some public contracts. It was intended to head off an even more controversial ballot measure, but instead stirred up passions among African-Americans. Now, minorities may be even more emboldened because they think the Republicans tried to stop them from voting in the presidential election.

"I'm not one of those conspiracy theorists who says this election is Jeb's fault," Smith said. "But people are looking for someone to pin this on — and he's the perfect target."

One high-level Democratic Party operative here from Washington said he could already envision the mass mailing his party could send out to galvanize Democrats in 2002: "You say in a piece of mail, 'How can you vote for Jeb Bush, who disenfranchised your vote for Al Gore and Joe Lieberman last time?' "

Asked about such Democratic warnings, Richard Bond, a former Republican national chairman who is close to the Bush family, said, "If Democrats are trying to make some cause out of Jeb Bush for trying to win the presidency for his brother, my message would be, 'Bring it on, baby,' because the Florida Republican Party is energized like I've never seen."

The notion of Bush as the target is a particularly unexpected turn because he went out of his way to avoid being visible during the presidential campaign. He said in an interview last summer that his emphasis would be on tending to his state. Many other Republican governors were far more visible in stumping for George W. Bush.

When asked about his brother's support during the campaign, George W. Bush joked that he told Jeb "the turkey at Thanksgiving might be a little chilly if things don't work out." That remark has led to numerous political cartoons of Jeb dining at the children's table at Thanksgiving.

In the immediate wake of the unsettled election, Jeb Bush again tried to stay on the sidelines, at least publicly, by recusing himself from the state's Elections Canvassing Commission.

But he thrust himself into the fray and endorsed plans by Republican legislators to name a set of electors. In making that high-profile move, Bush seemed to invite his detractors to say he was unduly trying to help his brother; some Republicans surmised that Bush decided to curry favor with party loyalists whose support he needs in 2002 — and, of course, to help his brother.

"Jeb has been temperate in his response," said Ken Connor, a lawyer here who Bush defeated in the 1994 Republican primary for governor and who was just named president of a conservative group, the Family Research Council.

"He's shown remarkable restraint," Connor said. "But it's safe to say that Jeb's in for a rough ride for the next two years."

Al Cardenas, the Republican Party chairman in Florida, insisted that he was not too worried about Bush because people should focus on the long term. "In the year 2002, you will have much less voter turnout, which will significantly favor Republicans," Cardenas said. "And you'll have a popular Republican governor facing re-election."

For better or for worse, Cardenas added, Jeb Bush's future was tied to his brother. "If his brother gets elected, that's a new dynamic," he said. "If his brother does well, or not, that will have an effect on Jeb."

For all the Democrats' threats against Bush, most agree, at least at this early stage, that the most potent challenge would come from Senator Bob Graham, who has served as governor before. But it is hardly clear that Graham wants to be governor again. Other possible candidates, like Robert A. Butterworth, the state attorney general, are not viewed by many Democrats as apt to muster adequate financial and political support to defeat Bush, who is highly successful at raising money.

Bush's predicament is all the more difficult because he was the brother who most of his family (including his mother) and friends thought was the most likely to become president.

But, in a pivotal turn of events, Bush lost his bid for governor in 1994 — and George W. won his in Texas, setting the stage for his presidential drive. Even now, people who are close to both say that Jeb Bush has a far more impressive command of the issues.

It was not supposed to be this way. In an interview in his office here in July, Bush, an earnest politician who lacks his brother's back-slapping talents, discussed how he relished staying clear of the spotlight and preferred the nitty-gritty of policy.

"One of the great things about the job," Jeb Bush said, "is I don't have to think too much about the politics. I didn't run to be a politician. I ran to serve."

Dec. 8, 2000, Richard Berke

LEGAL SCHOLARS QUESTION SUPREME COURT'S ROLE

In the national spotlight as it has not been in many years, the United States Supreme Court gave the country a decision that seemed to end one man's quest for the presidency while exposing itself to unusually harsh criticism.

The critique of the court began almost at the level of comedy when the country stopped for a minute to try to figure out exactly what the complicated package of opinions really said — and had some trouble deciphering the court's reasoning. The criticism quickly grew among some constitutional law experts who said the decision was one that seemed almost to have laid a trap for the Florida Supreme Court and, in the process, closed down the possibilities for further recounts.

The majority declared that the Florida Supreme Court's method of conducting recounts was constitutionally flawed, but it also said that there was no longer any time to repair the constitutional problem.

"I think the reaction will be immediate outrage by Democrats, glee by Republicans and, in the long run, increased cynicism about the courts," said Michael C. Dorf, a professor of constitutional law at Columbia Law School.

Barry Friedman, a constitutional law professor at New York University School of Law, said the majority of the justices seemed concerned with a Dec. 12 deadline that some legal experts have said was not really a deadline at all.

"It is remarkable," Professor Friedman said, "that the Supreme Court decided for the State of Florida that the Dec. 12 deadline was more important than finding the will of the voters."

Randall Bezanson, a constitutional law expert at the University of Iowa, said there was a "certain strange ironic twist" to the decision because it was based on the United States Supreme Court's determination that the Florida Legislature intended all election contest battles to be completed by Dec. 12, the date under federal law when election contests are to be completed.

That federal law says that if a state makes its final selection of electors by Dec. 12, that decision will be considered definitive if there is a battle later in Congress.

But Professor Bezanson said the United States Supreme Court based its decision in part on the previous decisions of the Florida Supreme Court, which the justices in Washington had overturned. Some constitutional law scholars said that was an odd end to the gargantuan legal struggle because the United States Supreme Court itself appeared to have contributed to that time problem. The week before the case decided last night, the Supreme Court had sent back to the Florida Supreme Court a different case in the election legal battle.

That case, some of the experts noted, simply asked the judges on Florida's highest court to explain the legal basis used in its earlier decision. But the Supreme Court did not then suggest, as it did last night, that the recounts Florida was conducting were constitutionally flawed because different standards were being used in different counties.

"I would compare this to someone seeing someone drowning in the sea," said Jack M. Balkin, a constitutional law professor at Yale Law School. "And then that person said, 'Wait, I'll save you.' And then says, 'I changed my mind,' and then swims back to shore."

The legal scholars said it would take days to sort out their reactions to the justices' opinions.

But in the first few minutes, as the country waited for clarity, the experts, along with everyone else, tried to understand telegraphed phrases repeated by television reporters.

There was the decision. But what was it? "The case is remanded for further proceedings not inconsistent with this opinion." As it turned out, according to several legal experts, that remand was likely to be a fairly empty proceeding because the United States Supreme Court did not leave the Florida Supreme Court much room to consider anything in that proceeding.

Dec. 13, 2000, William Glaberson

Two Media Groups Move To Examine Florida Votes

After weeks of negotiations, the organized effort by news organizations to examine uncounted Florida ballots has resulted in two independent projects. A consortium of eight news organizations, including *The New York Times*, *The Washington Post*, *The Wall Street Journal*, the Tribune Company and CNN, announced yesterday that they had retained the National Opinion Research Center to examine and report its findings on an estimated 180,000 overvotes and undervotes across the state.

Another effort, led by *The Miami Herald* and joined yesterday by *USA Today*, has been examining undervotes by county for more than three weeks. Several efforts to get the groups to join forces foundered on questions like which ballots to count, how many counters there should be and how the group would be governed.

But even in its bifurcated form, the media effort to examine the Florida ballots is one of the largest joint projects ever mounted in a business where competition is acute and exclusive reports are among the most highly prized features. The three major television networks declined to participate.

It is also a project that was shunned by the country's largest accounting firms, who rejected the news organizations' requests that they serve as the independent third party doing the actual examination of the ballots.

"All of us at the outset were surprised that we were even engaged in these discussions with people we historically compete against," said John Broder, the Washington editor of *The New York Times* and a spokesman for the larger consortium of news organizations. "The initial reluctance was overcome by the cost of the effort, which we now estimate will run in excess of $500,000, and the sheer logistical challenge of arranging to examine ballots in 67 counties in a large state."

Republicans yesterday offered muted criticism of the effort, focusing on the issues of the difficulty of finding a single standard to use for such a project and the confusion that could result from a review that might cast doubt on the legitimacy of George W. Bush's election.

"I think there is some question about whether this will simply add confusion upon confusion," Ken Lisaius, responding to a call to Bush's transition office, said. "There are some concerns about how some of these groups — either one of the two — are going about this. About whether they're looking at everything they need to look at if they want a complete and accurate assessment of the situation."

Methodology was the central issue in the breakdown of talks between *The Herald*, which has retained the accounting firm BDO Seidman to examine the ballots, and the larger consortium, which also includes The Associated Press, *The Los Angeles Times*, which is owned by the Tribune Company, *The Palm Beach Post* and *The St. Petersburg Times*.

For one thing, The *Herald*'s original plan called for an examination of 60,000 undervotes, or ballots not counted because no presidential choice was discerned in the original counting. The consortium — in particular representatives of *The Wall Street Journal* — insisted that 120,000 overvotes, or ballots uncounted because more than one presidential choice was recorded, also be included. For another, the Seidman group allotted one person in each county to examine the ballots as presented by county elections officials. The National

Opinion Research Center will commit three examiners to the process.

The research center was hired after several accounting firms, including KPMG, declined to participate. David Nestor, a spokesman for PricewaterhouseCoopers L.L.P., said yesterday, "We see very little value in another unofficial vote tally that in any case would not change the outcome of the election and at worst would only serve the cause of bitterness and acrimony."

But Dan Keating, the database editor of *The Washington Post*, said unofficial tallies were not the object. "Our absolute purpose was to build the definitive historical archive of these records with statistical validity and social science methodology and utter transparency," he said.

The ballot examiners from the National Opinion Research Center, which is based at the University of Chicago, will fill out questionnaires that divide ballots into categories. In counties with punch-card voting, for instance, the categories will include blank ballots, ballots with chads entirely punched out, and a variety of intermediate situations: dimples, dimples through which light is visible, misaligned punches and so on. The final database will be made available to anyone interested.

"We are hiring a highly respected independent research firm with no agendas and asking them to do a double- or triple-blind procedure so it is not subject to biases or errors by a single counter," said Alan Murray, the Washington Bureau chief of *The Wall Street Journal*. "That is as close as anyone will get to describing what's on those disputed ballots."

Martin Baron, *The Herald*'s executive editor, said that since his organization took steps to examine ballots, he was called by Joseph Lelyveld, the executive editor of *The New York Times*, and Leonard Downie Jr., the executive editor of *The Post*, each suggesting collaboration. No agreement came from these talks. Later discussions between the publishers of *The Times* and *The Post*, Arthur Sulzberger Jr. and Boisfeuillet Jones Jr., and P. Anthony Ridder, chief executive of Knight Ridder, *The Herald*'s parent company, also came to naught.

"We felt that *The Miami Herald* as the largest paper in the state of Florida should do this story," Baron said. "This was a project we should run; we shouldn't just be a bit player in a consortium of every large news organization in America where our role would be very unclear, to say the least."

Jan. 10, 2001, Felicity Barringer

Appendix

Text of Supreme Court Ruling in Bush v. Gore Florida Recount Case

Following is a slightly edited version of the Supreme Court's decision that there could be no further counting of Florida's disputed presidential ballot. The vote in *Bush v. Gore* was 5-to-4. It is not clear who wrote the majority opinion, but Chief Justice William H. Rehnquist wrote a concurring opinion in which Justices Antonin Scalia and Clarence Thomas joined. Justices John Paul Stevens, David H. Souter, Ruth Bader Ginsburg and Stephen G. Breyer wrote dissents in which various justices joined.

On Dec. 8, 2000, the Supreme Court of Florida ordered that the Circuit Court of Leon County tabulate by hand 9,000 ballots in Miami-Dade County. It also ordered the inclusion in the certified vote totals of 215 votes identified in Palm Beach County and 168 votes identified in Miami-Dade County for Vice President Albert Gore Jr., and Senator Joseph Lieberman, Democratic candidates for president and vice president. The Supreme Court noted that petitioner, Gov. George W. Bush asserted that the net gain for Vice President Gore in Palm Beach County was 176 votes, and directed the Circuit Court to resolve that dispute on remand. The court further held that relief would require manual recounts in all Florida counties where so-called undervotes had not been subject to manual tabulation. The court ordered all manual recounts to begin at once. Governor Bush and Richard Cheney, Republican candidates for the presidency and vice presidency, filed an emergency application for a stay of this mandate. On Dec. 9, we granted the application, treated the application as a petition for a writ of certiorari, and granted certiorari.

The proceedings leading to the present controversy are discussed in some detail in our opinion in Bush v. Palm Beach County Canvassing Board. On Nov. 8, 2000, the day following the presidential election, the Florida Division of Elections reported that petitioner, Governor Bush, had received 2,909,135 votes, and respondent, Vice President Gore, had received 2,907,351 votes, a margin of 1,784 for Governor Bush. Because Governor Bush's margin of victory was less than "one-half of a percent . . . of the votes cast," an automatic machine recount was conducted under Section 102.141(4) of the election code, the results of which showed Governor Bush still winning the race but by a diminished margin. Vice President Gore then sought manual recounts in Volusia, Palm Beach, Broward, and Miami-Dade Counties, pursuant to Florida's election protest provisions. A dispute arose concerning the deadline for local county canvassing boards to submit their returns to the secretary of state. The secretary declined to waive the Nov. 14 deadline imposed by statute. The Florida Supreme Court, however, set the deadline at Nov. 26. We granted certiorari and vacated the Florida Supreme Court's decision, finding considerable uncertainty as to the grounds on which it was based. On Dec. 11, the Florida Supreme Court issued a decision on remand reinstating that date. On Nov. 26, the Florida Elections Canvassing Commission certified the results of the election and declared Governor Bush the winner of Florida's 25 electoral votes. On Nov. 27, Vice President Gore, pursuant to Florida's contest provisions, filed a complaint in Leon County Circuit Court contesting the certification. He sought relief pursuant to Section 102.168(3)(c), which provides that "receipt of a number of illegal votes or rejection of a number of legal votes sufficient to change or place in doubt the result of the election" shall be grounds for a contest. The circuit court denied relief, stating that Vice President Gore failed to meet his burden of proof. He appealed to the First District Court of Appeal, which certified the matter to the Florida Supreme Court.

Accepting jurisdiction, the Florida Supreme Court affirmed in part and reversed in part. The court held that the circuit court had been correct to reject Vice President Gore's challenge to the results certified in Nassau County and his challenge to the Palm Beach County Canvassing Board's determination that 3,300 ballots cast in that county were not, in the statutory phrase, "legal votes."

The Supreme Court held that Vice President Gore had satisfied his burden of proof under Section 102.168(3)(c) with respect to his challenge to Miami-Dade County's failure to tabulate, by manual count, 9,000 ballots on which the machines had failed to detect a vote for president ("undervotes"). Noting the closeness of the election, the court explained that "on this record, there can be no question that there are legal votes within the 9,000 uncounted votes sufficient to place the results of this election in doubt." A "legal vote," as determined by the Supreme Court, is "one in which there is a clear indication of the intent of the voter." The court therefore ordered a hand recount of the 9,000 ballots in Miami-Dade County. Observing that the contest provisions vest broad discretion in the circuit judge to "provide any relief appropriate under such circumstances," the Supreme Court further held that the circuit court could order "the supervisor of elections and the canvassing boards, as well as the necessary public officials, in all counties that have not conducted a manual recount or tabulation of the undervotes . . . to do so forthwith, said tabulation to take place in the individual counties where the ballots are located." The Supreme Court also determined that both Palm Beach County and Miami-Dade County, in their earlier manual recounts, had identified a net gain of 215 and 168 legal votes for Vice President Gore. Rejecting the circuit court's conclusion that Palm Beach County lacked the authority to include the 215 net votes submitted past the Nov. 26 deadline, the Supreme Court explained that the deadline was not intended to exclude votes identified after that date through ongoing manual recounts. As to Miami-Dade County, the Court concluded that although the 168 votes identified were the result of a partial recount, they were "legal votes that could change the outcome of the election." The Supreme Court therefore directed the circuit court to include those totals in the certified results, subject to resolution of the actual vote total from the Miami-Dade partial recount.

The petition presents the following questions: whether the Florida Supreme Court established new standards for resolving presidential election contests, thereby violating Article II, Section 1, clause 2, of the United States Constitution and failing to comply with 3 U.S.C. Section 5, and whether the use of standardless manual recounts violates the equal protection and due process clauses. With respect to the equal protection question, we find a violation of the equal protection clause.

The closeness of this election, and the multitude of legal challenges which have followed in its wake, have brought into sharp focus a common, if heretofore unnoticed, phenomenon.

Nationwide statistics reveal that an estimated 2 percent of ballots cast do not register a vote for president for whatever reason, including deliberately choosing no candidate at all or some voter error, such as voting for two candidates or insufficiently marking a ballot. In certifying election results, the votes eligible for inclusion in the certification are the votes meeting the properly established legal requirements.

This case has shown that punch-card balloting machines can produce an unfortunate number of ballots which are not punched in a clean, complete way by the voter. After the current counting, it is likely legislative bodies nationwide will examine ways to improve the mechanisms and machinery for voting.

The individual citizen has no federal constitutional right to vote for electors for the president of the United States unless and until the state legislature chooses a statewide election as the means to implement its power to appoint members of the Electoral College. This is the source for the statement in McPherson v. Blacker that the state legislature' s power to select the manner for appointing electors is plenary; it may, if it so chooses, select the electors itself, which indeed was the manner used by state legislatures in several states for many years after the framing of our Constitution. History has now favored the voter, and in each of the several states the citizens themselves vote for presidential electors. When the state legislature vests the right to vote for president in its people, the right to vote as the legislature has prescribed is fundamental; and one source of its fundamental nature lies in the equal weight accorded to each vote and the equal dignity owed to each voter. The state, of course, after granting the franchise in the special context of Article II, can take back the power to appoint electors.

The right to vote is protected in more than the initial allocation of the franchise. Equal protection applies as well to the manner of its exercise. Having once granted the right to vote on equal terms, the state may not, by later arbitrary and disparate treatment, value one person's vote over that of another. It must be remembered that "the right of suffrage can be denied by a debasement or dilution of the weight of a citizen' s vote just as effectively as by wholly prohibiting the free exercise of the franchise."

There is no difference between the two sides of the present controversy on these basic propositions. Respondents say that the very purpose of vindicating the right to vote justifies the recount procedures now at issue. The question before us, however, is whether the recount procedures the Florida Supreme Court has adopted are consistent with its obligation to avoid arbitrary and disparate treatment of the members of its electorate.

Much of the controversy seems to revolve around ballot cards designed to be perforated by a stylus but which, either through error or deliberate omission, have not been perforated with sufficient precision for a machine to count them. In some cases a piece of the card — a chad — is hanging, say by two corners. In other cases there is no separation at all, just an indentation. The Florida Supreme Court has ordered that the intent of the voter be discerned from such ballots. For purposes of resolving the equal protection challenge, it is not necessary to decide whether the Florida Supreme Court had the authority under the legislative scheme for resolving election disputes to define what a legal vote is and to mandate a manual recount implementing that definition. The recount mechanisms implemented in response to the decisions of the Florida Supreme Court do not satisfy the minimum requirement for non-arbitrary treatment of voters necessary to secure the fundamental right. Florida's basic command for the count of legally cast votes is to consider the "intent of the voter." This is unobjectionable as an abstract proposition and a starting principle. The problem inheres in the absence of specific standards to ensure its equal application. The formulation of uniform rules to determine intent based on these recurring circumstances is practicable and, we conclude, necessary.

The law does not refrain from searching for the intent of the actor in a multitude of circumstances; and in some cases the general command to ascertain intent is not susceptible to much further refinement. In this instance, however, the question is not whether to believe a witness but how to interpret the marks or holes or scratches on an inanimate object, a piece of cardboard or paper which, it is said, might not have registered as a vote during the machine count. The factfinder confronts a thing, not a person. The search for intent can be confined by specific rules designed to ensure uniform treatment. The want of those rules here has led to unequal evaluation of ballots in various respects. As seems to have been acknowledged at oral argument, the stan-dards for accepting or rejecting contested ballots might vary not only from county to county but indeed within a single county from one recount team to another. The record provides some examples. A monitor in Miami-Dade County testified at trial that he observed that three members of the county canvassing board applied different standards in defining a legal vote. And testimony at trial also revealed that at least one county changed its evaluative standards during the counting process. Palm Beach County, for example, began the process with a 1990 guideline which precluded counting completely attached chads, switched to a rule that considered a vote to be legal if any light could be seen through a chad, changed back to the 1990 rule, and then abandoned any pretense of a per se rule, only to have a court order that the county consider dimpled chads legal. This is not a process with sufficient guarantees of equal treatment. An early case in our one person, one vote jurisprudence arose when a state accorded arbitrary and disparate treatment to voters in its different counties. The court found a constitutional violation. We relied on these principles in the context of the presidential selection process in Moore v. Ogilvie, where we invalidated a county-based procedure that diluted the influence of citizens in larger counties in the nominating process. There we observed that "the idea that one group can be granted greater voting strength than another is hostile to the one man, one vote basis of our representative government."

The State Supreme Court ratified this uneven treatment. It mandated that the recount totals from two counties, Miami-Dade and Palm Beach, be included in the certified total. The court also appeared to hold sub silentio that the recount totals from Broward County, which were not completed until after the original Nov. 14 certification by the secretary of state, were to be considered part of the new certified vote totals even though the county certification was not contested by Vice President Gore. Yet each of the counties used varying standards to determine what was a legal vote. Broward County used a more forgiving standard than Palm Beach County, and uncovered almost three times as many new votes, a result markedly disproportionate to the difference in population between the counties. In addition, the recounts in these three counties were not limited to so-called undervotes but extended to all of the ballots. The distinction has real consequences. A manual recount of all ballots identifies not only those ballots which show no vote but also those which contain more than one, the so-called overvotes. Neither category will be counted by the machine. This is not a trivial concern.

At oral argument, respondents estimated there are as many as 110,000 overvotes statewide. As a result, the citizen whose ballot was not read by a machine because he failed to vote for a candidate in a way readable by a machine may still have his vote counted in a manual recount; on the other hand, the citizen who marks two candidates in a way discernable by the machine will not have the same opportunity to have his vote count, even if a manual examination of the ballot would reveal the requisite indicia of intent. Furthermore, the citizen who marks two candidates, only one of which is discernable by the machine, will have his vote counted even though it should have been read as an invalid ballot. The State Supreme Court's inclusion of vote counts based on these variant standards exemplifies concerns with the remedial processes that were under way.

That brings the analysis to yet a further equal protection problem. The votes certified by the court included a partial total from one county, Miami-Dade. The Florida Supreme Court's decision thus gives no assurance that the recounts included in a final certification must be complete. Indeed, it is respondent's submission that it would be consistent with the rules of the recount procedures to include whatever partial counts are done by the time of final certification, and we interpret the Florida Supreme Court's decision to permit this. This accommodation no doubt results from the truncated contest period established by the Florida Supreme Court in Bush I, at respondents' own urging. The press of time does not diminish the constitutional concern. A desire for speed is not a general excuse for ignoring equal protection guarantees.

In addition to these difficulties the actual process by which the votes were to be counted under the Florida Supreme Court' s decision raises further concerns. That order did not specify who would recount the ballots. The county canvassing boards were forced to pull together ad hoc teams comprised of judges from various circuits who had no previous training in handling and interpreting ballots. Furthermore, while others were permitted to observe, they were prohibited from objecting during the recount.

The recount process, in its features here described, is inconsistent with the minimum procedures necessary to protect the fundamental right of each voter in the special instance of a statewide recount under the authority of a single state judicial officer. Our consideration is limited to the present circumstances, for the problem of equal protection in election processes generally presents many complexities.

The question before the court is not whether local entities, in the exercise of their expertise, may develop different systems for implementing elections. Instead, we are presented with a situation where a state court with the power to assure uniformity has ordered a statewide recount with minimal procedural safeguards. When a court orders a statewide remedy, there must be at least some assurance that the rudimentary requirements of equal treatment and fundamental fairness are satisfied. Given the court's assessment that the recount process under way was probably being conducted in an unconstitutional manner, the court stayed the order directing the recount so it could hear this case and render an expedited decision. The contest provision, as it was mandated by the state Supreme Court, is not well calculated to sustain the confidence that all citizens must have in the outcome of elections. The state has not shown that its procedures include the necessary safeguards. The problem, for instance, of the estimated 110,000 overvotes has not been addressed, although Chief Justice Wells called attention to the concern in his dissenting opinion.

Upon due consideration of the difficulties identified to this point, it is obvious that the recount cannot be conducted in compliance with the requirements of equal protection and due process without substantial additional work. It would require not only the adoption (after opportunity for argument) of adequate statewide standards for determining what is a legal vote, and practicable procedures to implement them, but also orderly judicial review of any disputed matters that might arise. In addition, the secretary of state has advised that the recount of only a portion of the ballots requires that the vote tabulation equipment be used to screen out undervotes, a function for which the machines were not designed. If a recount of overvotes were also required, perhaps even a second screening would be necessary. Use of the equipment for this purpose, and any new software developed for it, would have to be evaluated for accuracy by the secretary of state, as required by Florida Statutes, Section 101.015.

The Supreme Court of Florida has said that the legislature intended the state's electors to "participate fully in the federal electoral process," as provided in 3 U.S.C. Section 5.

That statute, in turn, requires that any controversy or contest that is designed to lead to a conclusive selection of electors be completed by Dec. 12. That date is upon us, and there is no recount procedure in place under the state Supreme Court's order that comports with minimal constitutional standards. Because it is evident that any recount seeking to meet the Dec. 12 date will be unconstitutional for the reasons we have discussed, we reverse the judgment of the Supreme Court of Florida ordering a recount to proceed. Seven justices of the court agree that there are constitutional problems with the recount ordered by the Florida Supreme Court that demand a remedy.

The only disagreement is as to the remedy.

Because the Florida Supreme Court has said that the Florida Legislature intended to obtain the safe-harbor benefits of 3 U.S.C. Section 5, Justice Breyer's proposed remedy — remanding to the Florida Supreme Court for its ordering of a constitutionally proper contest until Dec. 18 — contemplates action in violation of the Florida election code, and hence could not be part of an "appropriate" order authorized by Florida Statutes, Section 102.168(8).

None are more conscious of the vital limits on judicial authority than are the members of this court, and none stand more in admiration of the Constitution' s design to leave the selection of the president to the people, through their legislatures, and to the political sphere. When contending parties invoke the process of the courts, however, it becomes our unsought responsibility to resolve the federal and constitutional issues the judicial system has been forced to confront. The judgment of the Supreme Court of Florida is reversed, and the case is remanded for further proceedings not inconsistent with this opinion.

Pursuant to this court's Rule 45.2, the clerk is directed to issue the mandate in this case forthwith.

It is so ordered.

CHIEF JUSTICE REHNQUIST
with Justice Scalia and Justice Thomas concurring

We join the per curiam opinion. We write separately because we believe there are additional grounds that require us to reverse the Florida Supreme Court's decision.

We deal here not with an ordinary election, but with an election for the president of the United States. In Burroughs v. United States, we said: "While presidential electors are not officers or agents of the federal government, they exercise federal functions under, and discharge duties in virtue of authority conferred by, the Constitution of the United States. The president is vested with the executive power of the nation. The importance of his election and the vital character of its relationship to and effect upon the welfare and safety of the whole people cannot be too strongly stated."

Likewise, in Anderson v. Celebrezze, we said: "In the context of a presidential election, state-imposed restrictions implicate a uniquely important national interest. For the president and the vice president of the United States are the only elected officials who represent all the voters in the nation."

In most cases, comity and respect for federalism compel us to defer to the decisions of state courts on issues of state law. That practice reflects our understanding that the decisions of state courts are definitive pronouncements of the will of the states as sovereigns. Of course, in ordinary cases, the distribution of powers among the branches of a state's government raises no questions of federal constitutional law, subject to the requirement that the government be republican in character. But there are a few exceptional cases in which the Constitution imposes a duty or confers a power on a particular branch of a state's government. This is one of them.

Article II, Section 1, Clause 2, provides that "each state shall appoint, in such manner as the Legislature thereof may direct," electors for president and vice president. Thus, the text of the election law itself, and not just its interpretation by the courts of the states, takes on independent significance. In McPherson v. Blacker, we explained that Article II, Section 1, Clause. 2, "conveys the broadest power of determination" and "leaves it to the Legislature exclusively to define the method" of appointment. A significant departure from the legislative scheme for appointing presidential electors presents a federal constitutional question.

3 U.S.C. Section 5 informs our application of Article II, Section 1, Clause 2, to the Florida statutory scheme, which, as the Florida Supreme Court acknowledged, took that statute into account. Section 5 provides that the state's selection of electors "shall be conclusive, and shall govern in the counting of the electoral votes" if the

electors are chosen under laws enacted prior to Election Day, and if the selection process is completed six days prior to the meeting of the electoral college. As we noted in Bush v. Palm Beach County Canvassing Board:

"Since Section 5 contains a principle of federal law that would assure finality of the State' s determination if made pursuant to a state law in effect before the election, a legislative wish to take advantage of the 'safe harbor' would counsel against any construction of the election code that Congress might deem to be a change in the law."

If we are to respect the Legislature's Article II powers, therefore, we must ensure that post-election state-court actions do not frustrate the legislative desire to attain the "safe harbor" provided by Section 5.

In Florida, the Legislature has chosen to hold statewide elections to appoint the state's 25 electors. Importantly, the Legislature has delegated the authority to run the elections and to oversee election disputes to the secretary of state, and to state circuit courts. Isolated sections of the code may well admit of more than one interpretation, but the general coherence of the legislative scheme may not be altered by judicial interpretation so as to wholly change the statutorily provided apportionment of responsibility among these various bodies. In any election but a presidential election, the Florida Supreme Court can give as little or as much deference to Florida's executives as it chooses, so far as Article II is concerned, and this court will have no cause to question the court' s actions. But, with respect to a presidential election, the court must be both mindful of the Legislature's role under Article II in choosing the manner of appointing electors and deferential to those bodies expressly empowered by the Legislature to carry out its constitutional mandate.

In order to determine whether a state court has infringed upon the Legislature's authority, we necessarily must examine the law of the state as it existed prior to the action of the court. Though we generally defer to state courts on the interpretation of state law, there are of course areas in which the Constitution requires this court to undertake an independent, if still deferential, analysis of state law. [. . .]

This inquiry does not imply a disrespect for state courts but rather a respect for the constitutionally prescribed role of state legislatures. To attach definitive weight to the pronouncement of a state court, when the very question at issue is whether the court has actually departed from the statutory meaning, would be to abdicate our responsibility to enforce the explicit requirements of Article II.

Acting pursuant to its constitutional grant of authority, the Florida Legislature has created a detailed, if not perfectly crafted, statutory scheme that provides for appointment of presidential electors by direct election. Under the statute, "votes cast for the actual candidates for president and vice president shall be counted as votes cast for the presidential electors supporting such candidates." The legislature has designated the secretary of state as the "chief election officer," with the responsibility to "obtain and maintain uniformity in the application, operation and interpretation of the election laws."

The state Legislature has delegated to county canvassing boards the duties of administering elections. Those boards are responsible for providing results to the state elections canvassing commission, comprising the governor, the secretary of state and the director of the division of elections. ("The election process . . . is committed to the executive branch of government through duly designated officials all charged with specific duties. . . . The judgments of these officials are entitled to be regarded by the courts as presumptively correct . . .")

After the election has taken place, the canvassing boards receive returns from precincts, count the votes, and in the event that a candidate was defeated by 0.5 percent or less, conduct a mandatory recount. The county canvassing boards must file certified election returns with the Department of State by 5 p.m. on the seventh day following the election. The elections canvassing commission must then certify the results of the election.

The state Legislature has also provided mechanisms both for protesting election returns and for contesting certified election results. Section 102.166 governs protests. Any protest must be filed prior to the certification of election results by the county canvassing board. Once a protest has been filed, "the county canvassing board may authorize a manual recount." If a sample recountconducted pursuant to Section 102.166(5) "indicates an error in the vote tabulation which could affect the outcome of the election," the county canvassing board is instructed to: "(A) Correct the error and recount the remaining precincts with the vote tabulation system; (B) Request the Department of State to verify the tabulation software; or (C) Manually recount all ballots." In the event a canvassing board chooses to conduct a manual recount of all ballots, Section 102.166(7) prescribes procedures for such a recount.

Contests to the certification of an election, on the other hand, are controlled by Section 102.168. The grounds for contesting an election include "receipt of a number of illegal votes or rejection of a number of legal votes sufficient to change or place in doubt the result of the election." Any contest must be filed in the appropriate Florida circuit court, and the canvassing board or election board is the proper party defendant. Section 102.168(8) provides that "the circuit judge to whom the contest is presented may fashion such orders as he or she deems necessary to ensure that each allegation in the complaint is investigated, examined or checked, to prevent or correct any alleged wrong and to provide any relief appropriate under such circumstances." In presidential elections, the contest period necessarily terminates on the date set by 3 U.S.C., Section 5 for concluding the state's "final determination" of election controversies.

In its first decision, Palm Beach Canvassing Board v. Harris, the Florida Supreme Court extended the seven-day statutory certification deadline established by the Legislature. This modification of the code, by lengthening the protest period, necessarily shortened the contest period for presidential elections. Underlying the extension of the certification deadline and the shortchanging of the contest period was, presumably, the clear implication that certification was a matter of significance: The certified winner would enjoy presumptive validity, making a contest proceeding by the losing candidate an uphill battle. In its latest opinion, however, the court empties certification of virtually all legal consequence during the contest, and in doing so departs from the provisions enacted by the Florida Legislature. The court determined that canvassing boards' decisions regarding whether to recount ballots past the certification deadline (even the certification deadline established by Harris I) are to be reviewed de novo, although the election code clearly vests discretion whether to recount in the boards, and sets strict deadlines subject to the secretary' s rejection of late tallies and monetary fines for tardiness. Moreover, the Florida court held that all late vote tallies arriving during the contest period should be automatically included in the certification regardless of the certification deadline (even the certification deadline established by Harris I), thus virtually eliminating both the deadline and the secretary's discretion to disregard recounts that violate it. Moreover, the court's interpretation of "legal vote," and hence its decision to order a contest-period recount, plainly departed from the legislative scheme. Florida statutory law cannot reasonably be thought to require the counting of improperly marked ballots. Each Florida precinct before Election Day provides instructions on how properly to cast a vote; each polling place on Election Day contains a working model of the voting machine it uses; and each voting booth contains a sample ballot. In precincts using punch-card ballots, voters are instructed to punch out the ballot cleanly: "After voting, check your ballot card to be sure your voting selections are clearly and cleanly punched and there are no chips left hanging on the back of the card."

No reasonable person would call it "an error in the vote tabulation," or a "rejection of legal votes," when electronic or electromechanical equipment performs precisely in the manner designed, and fails to count those ballots that are not marked in the manner that these voting instructions explicitly and prominently specify. The scheme that the Florida Supreme Court's opinion attributes to the Legislature is one in which machines are required to be "capable of correctly counting votes," but which nonetheless regularly produces elections in which legal votes are predictably not tabulated, so that in close elections manual recounts are regularly required. This is of course absurd. The secretary of state, who is authorized by law to issue binding interpretations of the election code, rejected this peculiar reading of the statutes. The Florida Supreme Court, although it must defer to the secretary's interpretations, rejected her reasonable interpretation and embraced the peculiar one. [. . .]

The scope and nature of the remedy ordered by the Florida Supreme Court jeopardizes the "legislative wish" to take advantage of the safe harbor provided by 3 U.S.C., Section 5. Dec. 12, 2000, is the last date for a final determination of the Florida electors that will satisfy Section 5. Yet in the late afternoon of Dec. 8 — four days before this deadline — the Supreme Court of Florida ordered recounts of tens of thousands of so-called "undervotes" spread through 64 of the state's 67 counties. This was done in a search for elusive — perhaps delusive — certainty as to the exact count of six million votes. But no one claims that these ballots have not previously been tabulated; they were initially read by voting machines at the time of the election, and thereafter reread by virtue of Florida' s automatic recount provision. No one claims there was any fraud in the election. The Supreme Court of Florida ordered this additional recount under the provision of the election code giving the circuit judge the authority to provide relief that is "appropriate under such circumstances."

Surely when the Florida Legislature empowered the courts of the state to grant "appropriate" relief, it must have meant relief that would have become final by the cut-off date of 3 U.S.C., Section 5. In light of the inevitable legal challenges and ensuing appeals to the Supreme Court of Florida and petitions for certiorari to this court, the entire recounting process could not possibly be completed by that date. Whereas the majority in the Supreme Court of Florida stated its confidence that "the remaining undervotes in these counties can be [counted] within the required time frame," it made no assertion that the seemingly inevitable appeals could be disposed of in that time. Although the Florida Supreme Court has on occasion taken over a year to resolve disputes over local elections, it has heard and decided the appeals in the present case with great promptness. But the federal deadlines for the presidential election simply do not permit even such a shortened process. [. . .]

It significantly departed from the statutory framework in place on Nov. 7, and authorized open-ended further proceedings which could not be completed by Dec. 12, thereby preventing a final determination by that date.

For these reasons, in addition to those given in the per curiam, we would reverse.

A DISSENT

By Justice Stevens joined by Justices Ginsburg and Breyer

The Constitution assigns to the states the primary responsibility for determining the manner of selecting the presidential electors. When questions arise about the meaning of state laws, including election laws, it is our settled practice to accept the opinions of the highest courts of the states as providing the final answers. On rare occasions, however, either federal statutes or the federal Constitution may require federal judicial intervention in state elections. This is not such an occasion.

The federal questions that ultimately emerged in this case are not substantial. Article II provides that "each state shall appoint, in such manner as the legislature thereof may direct, a number of electors." It does not create state legislatures out of whole cloth, but rather takes them as they come — as creatures born of, and constrained by, their state constitutions. Lest there be any doubt, we stated over 100 years ago in McPherson v. Blacker that "what is forbidden or required to be done by a state" in the Article II context "is forbidden or required of the legislative power under state constitutions as they exist." In the same vein, we also observed that "the state's legislative power is the supreme authority except as limited by the constitution of the state." The legislative power in Florida is subject to judicial review pursuant to Article V of the Florida Constitution, and nothing in Article II of the federal Constitution frees the State Legislature from the constraints in the state Constitution that created it. Moreover, the Florida Legislature's own decision to employ a unitary code for all elections indicates that it intended the Florida Supreme Court to play the same role in presidential elections that it has historically played in resolving electoral disputes. The Florida Supreme Court's exercise of appellate jurisdiction therefore was wholly consistent with, and indeed contemplated by, the grant of authority in Article II.

It hardly needs stating that Congress, pursuant to 3 U.S.C., Section 5, did not impose any affirmative duties upon the states that their governmental branches could "violate." Rather, Section 5 provides a safe harbor for states to select electors in contested elections "by judicial or other methods" established by laws prior to the Election Day. Section 5, like Article II, assumes the involvement of the state judiciary in interpreting state election laws and resolving election disputes under those laws. Neither Section 5 nor Article II grants federal judges any special authority to substitute their views for those of the state judiciary on matters of state law.

Nor are petitioners correct in asserting that the failure of the Florida Supreme Court to specify in detail the precise manner in which the "intent of the voter," Florida Statute Section 101.5614(5) is to be determined rises to the level of a constitutional violation. We found such a violation when individual votes within the same state were weighted unequally, but we have never before called into question the substantive standard by which a state determines that a vote has been legally cast. And there is no reason to think that the guidance provided to the fact-finders, specifically the various canvassing boards, by the "intent of the voter" standard is any less sufficient — or will lead to results any less uniform — than, for example, the "beyond a reasonable doubt" standard employed everyday by ordinary citizens in courtrooms across this country.

Admittedly, the use of differing substandards for determining voter intent in different counties employing similar voting systems may raise serious concerns. Those concerns are alleviated — if not eliminated — by the fact that a single impartial magistrate will ultimately adjudicate all objections arising from the recount process. Of course, as a general matter, "the interpretation of constitutional principles must not be too literal. We must remember that the machinery of government would not work if it were not allowed a little play in its joints." If it were otherwise, Florida's decision to leave to each county the determination of what balloting system to employ — despite enormous differences in accuracy — might run afoul of equal protection. So, too, might the similar decisions of the vast majority of state legislatures to delegate to local authorities certain decisions with respect to voting systems and ballot design. Even assuming that aspects of the remedial scheme might ultimately be found to violate the Equal Protection Clause, I could not subscribe to the majority's disposition of the case. As the majority explicitly holds, once a state legislature determines to select electors through a popular vote, the right to have one's vote counted is of constitutional stature. As the majority further acknowledges, Florida law holds that all ballots that reveal the intent of the voter constitute valid votes. Recognizing these principles, the majority nonetheless orders the termination of the contest proceeding before all such votes have been tabulated. Under their own reasoning, the appropriate course of action would be to remand to allow more specific procedures for implementing the legislature's uniform general standard to be established.

In the interest of finality, however, the majority effectively orders the disenfranchisement of an unknown number of voters whose ballots reveal their intent — and are therefore legal votes under state law — but were for some reason rejected by ballot-counting machines. It does so on the basis of the deadlines set forth in Title 3 of the United States Code. But, as I have already noted, those provisions merely provide rules of decision for Congress to follow when selecting among conflicting slates of electors. They do not prohibit a state from counting what the majority concedes to be legal votes until a bona fide winner is determined. Indeed, in 1960, Hawaii appointed two slates of electors and Congress chose to count the one appointed on Jan. 4, 1961, well after the Title 3 deadlines. Thus, nothing prevents the majority, even if it properly found an equal protection violation, from ordering relief appropriate to remedy that violation without depriving Florida voters of their right to have their votes counted. As the majority notes, "a desire for speed is not a general excuse for ignoring equal protection guarantees." Finally, neither in this case, nor in its earlier opinion in Palm Beach County Canvassing Bd. v. Harris, did the Florida Supreme Court make any substantive change in Florida electoral law. Its decisions were rooted in long-established precedent and were consistent with the relevant statutory provisions, taken as a whole. It did what courts do — it decided the case before it in light of the Legislature's intent to leave no legally cast vote uncounted. In so doing, it relied on the sufficiency of the general "intent of the voter" standard articulated by the State Legislature, coupled with a procedure for ultimate review by an impartial judge, to resolve the concern about disparate evaluations of contested ballots. If we assume — as I do — that the members of that court and the judges who would have carried out its mandate are impartial, its decision does not even raise a colorable federal question.

What must underlie petitioners' entire federal assault on the Florida election procedures is an unstated lack of confidence in the impartiality and capacity of the state judges who would make the critical decisions if the vote count were to proceed. Otherwise, their position is wholly without merit. The endorsement of that position by the majority of this court can only lend credence to the most cynical appraisal of the work of judges throughout the land. It is confidence in the men and women who administer the judicial system that is the true backbone of the rule of law. Time will one day heal the wound to that confidence that will be inflicted by today's decision. One thing, however, is certain. Although we may never know with complete certainty the identity of the winner of this year's presidential election, the identity of the loser is perfectly clear. It is the nation's confidence in the judge as an impartial guardian of the rule of law. I respectfully dissent.

A DISSENT

By Justice Souter

(With Justice Breyer joining, and with whom Justice Stevens and Justice Ginsburg join with regard to all but the third section.)

[. . .]As will be clear, I am in substantial agreement with the dissenting opinions of Justice Stevens, Justice Ginsburg and Justice Breyer. I write separately only to say how straightforward the issues before us really are.

There are three issues: whether the State Supreme Court's interpretation of the statute providing for a contest of the state election results somehow violates 3 U.S.C., Section 5; whether that court' s construction of the state statutory provisions governing contests impermissibly changes a state law from what the state's Legislature has provided, in violation of Article II, Section 1, Clause 2, of the national Constitution; and whether the manner of interpreting markings on disputed ballots failing to cause machines to register votes for president (the undervote ballots) violates the equal protection or due process guaranteed by the Fourteenth Amendment. None of these issues is difficult to describe or to resolve.

The 3 U.S.C., Section 5 issue is not serious. That provision sets certain conditions for treating a state's certification of presidential electors as conclusive in the event that a dispute over recognizing those electors must be resolved in the Congress under 3 U.S.C., Section 15.

Conclusiveness requires selection under a legal scheme in place before the election, with results determined at least six days before the date set for casting electoral votes. But no state is required to conform to Section 5 if it cannot do that (for whatever reason); the sanction for failing to satisfy the conditions of Section 5 is simply loss of what has been called its "safe harbor." And even that determination is to be made, if made anywhere, in the Congress.

The second matter here goes to the State Supreme Court's interpretation of certain terms in the state statute governing election "contests;" there is no question here about the state court' s interpretation of the related provisions dealing with the antecedent process of "protesting" particular vote counts, which was involved in the previous case, Bush v. Palm Beach County Canvassing Board.

The issue is whether the judgment of the state Supreme Court has displaced the state Legislature' s provisions for election contests: is the law as declared by the court different from the provisions made by the Legislature, to which the national Constitution commits responsibility for determining how each state's presidential electors are chosen?

Bush does not, of course, claim that any judicial act interpreting a statute of uncertain meaning is enough to displace the legislative provision and violate Article II; statutes require interpretation, which does not without more affect the legislative character of a statute within the meaning of the Constitution. What Bush does argue, as I understand the contention, is that the interpretation of Section 102.168 was so unreasonable as to transcend the accepted bounds of statutory interpretation, to the point of being a nonjudicial act and producing new law untethered to the legislative act in question.

The starting point for evaluating the claim that the Florida Supreme Court's interpretation effectively rewrote Section 102.168 must be the language of the provision on which Gore relies to show his right to raise this contest: that the previously certified result in Bush's favor was produced by "rejection of a number of legal votes sufficient to change or place in doubt the result of the election."

None of the state court's interpretations is unreasonable to the point of displacing the legislative enactment quoted. As I will note below, other interpretations were of course possible, and some might have been better than those adopted by the Florida court's majority; the two dissents from the majority opinion of that court and various briefs submitted to us set out alternatives. But the majority view is in each instance within the bounds of reasonable interpretation, and the law as declared is consistent with Article II.

The statute does not define a "legal vote," the rejection of which may affect the election. The State Supreme Court was therefore required to define it, and in doing that the court looked to another election statute, dealing with damaged or defective ballots, which contains a provision that no vote shall be disregarded "if there is a clear indication of the intent of the voter as determined by a canvassing board." The court read that objective of looking to the voter's intent as indicating that the Legislature probably meant "legal vote" to mean a vote recorded on a ballot indicating what the voter intended.

It is perfectly true that the majority might have chosen a different reading. But even so, there is no constitutional violation in following the majority view; Article II is unconcerned with mere disagreements about interpretive merits.

The Florida court next interpreted "rejection" to determine what act in the counting process may be attacked in a contest. Again, the statute does not define the term. The court majority read the word to mean simply a failure to count. That reading is certainly within the bounds of common sense, given the objective to give effect to a voter's intent if that can be determined.

A different reading, of course, is possible. The majority might have concluded that "rejection" should refer to machine malfunction, or that a ballot should not be treated as "rejected" in the absence of wrongdoing by election officials, lest contests be so easy to claim that every election will end up in one. There is, however, nothing nonjudicial in the Florida majority' s more hospitable reading.

The same is true about the court majority' s understanding of the phrase "votes sufficient to change or place in doubt" the result of the election in Florida. The court held that if the uncounted ballots were so numerous that it was reasonably possible that they contained enough "legal" votes to swing the election, this contest would be authorized by the statute. While the majority might have thought (as the trial judge did) that a probability, not a possibility, should be necessary to justify a contest, that reading is not required by the statute's text, which says nothing about probability.

Whatever people of good will and good sense may argue about the merits of the Florida court' s reading, there is no warrant for saying that it transcends the limits of reasonable statutory interpretation to the point of supplanting the statute enacted by the "legislature" within the meaning of Article II.

In sum, the interpretations by the Florida court raise no substantial question under Article II. That court engaged in permissible construction in determining that Gore had instituted a contest authorized by the state statute, and it proceeded to direct the trial judge to deal with that contest in the exercise of the discretionary powers generously conferred by Florida Statute Section 102.168(8), to "fashion such orders as he or she deems necessary to ensure that each allegation in the complaint is investigated, examined or checked, to prevent or correct any alleged wrong, and to provide any relief appropriate under such circumstances."

As Justice Ginsburg has persuasively explained in her own dissenting opinion, our customary respect for state interpretations of state law counsels against rejection of the Florida court's determinations in this case. [. . .]

I can conceive of no legitimate state interest served by these differing treatments of the expressions of voters' fundamental rights. The differences appear wholly arbitrary. In deciding what to do about this, we should take account of the fact that electoral votes are due to be cast in six days. I would therefore remand the case to the courts of Florida with instructions to establish uniform standards for evaluating the several types of ballots that have prompted differing treatments, to be applied within and among counties when passing on such identical ballots in any further recounting (or successive recounting) that the courts might order.

Unlike the majority, I see no warrant for this court to assume that Florida could not possibly comply with this requirement before the date set for the meeting of electors, Dec. 18.

Although one of the dissenting justices of the State Supreme Court estimated that disparate standards potentially affected 170,000 votes, the number at issue is significantly smaller. The 170,000 figure apparently represents all uncounted votes, both undervotes (those for which no presidential choice was recorded by a machine) and overvotes (those rejected because of votes for more than one candidate). But as Justice Breyer has pointed out, no showing has been made of legal overvotes uncounted, and counsel for Gore made an uncontradicted representation to the court that the statewide total of undervotes is about 60,000. To recount these manually would be a tall order, but before this court stayed the effort to do that the courts of Florida were ready to do their best to get that job done. There is no justification for denying the state the opportunity to try to count all disputed ballots now. I respectfully dissent.

A DISSENT
By Justice Ginsburg

(With whom Justice Stevens joins, and with whom Justice Souter and Justice Breyer join as to the first part.)

The chief justice acknowledges that provisions of Florida's election code "may well admit of more than one interpretation." But instead of respecting the state high court's province to say what the state's election code means, the chief justice maintains that Florida's Supreme Court has veered so far from the ordinary practice of judicial review that what it did cannot properly be called judging. My colleagues have offered a reasonable construction of Florida's law. Their construction coincides with the view of one of Florida's seven Supreme Court justices. I might join the chief justice were it my commission to interpret Florida law. But disagreement with the Florida court's interpretation of its own state's law does not warrant the conclusion that the justices of that court have legislated. There is no cause here to believe that the members of Florida's high court have done less than "their mortal best to discharge their oath of office," and no cause to upset their reasoned interpretation of Florida law.

This court more than occasionally affirms statutory, and even constitutional, interpretations with which it disagrees. For example, when reviewing challenges to administrative agencies' interpretations of laws they implement, we defer to the agencies unless their interpretation violates "the unambiguously expressed intent of Congress." We do so in the face of the declaration in Article I of the United States Constitution that "all legislative powers herein granted shall be vested in a Congress of the United States."

Surely the Constitution does not call upon us to pay more respect to a federal administrative agency's construction of federal law than to a state high court's interpretation of its own state's law. And not uncommonly, we let stand state-court interpretations of federal law with which we might disagree.

Notably, in the habeas context, the court adheres to the view that "there is no intrinsic reason why the fact that a man is a federal judge should make him more competent, or conscientious or learned with respect to federal law than his neighbor in the state courthouse." (The Teague doctrine validates reasonable, good-faith interpretations of existing precedents made by state courts even though they are shown to be contrary to later decisions.") "There is no reason to assume that state court judges cannot and will not provide a 'hospitable forum' in litigating federal constitutional questions."

No doubt there are cases in which the proper application of federal law may hinge on interpretations of state law. Unavoidably, this court must sometimes examine state law in order to protect federal rights. But we have dealt with such cases ever mindful of the full measure of respect we owe to interpretations of state law by a state' s highest court. In the contract clause case, General Motors Corporation v. Romein, for example, we said that although "ultimately we are bound to decide for ourselves whether a contract was made," the court "accords respectful consideration and great weight to the views of the state's highest court."

And in Central Union Telephone Co. v. Edwardsville, we upheld the Illinois Supreme Court' s interpretation of a state waiver rule, even though that interpretation resulted in the forfeiture of federal constitutional rights. Refusing to supplant

Illinois law with a federal definition of waiver, we explained that the state court' s declaration "should bind us unless so unfair or unreasonable in its application to those asserting a federal right as to obstruct it."

In deferring to state courts on matters of state law, we appropriately recognize that this Court acts as an " 'outsider' lacking the common exposure to local law which comes from sitting in the jurisdiction." That recognition has sometimes prompted us to resolve doubts about the meaning of state law by certifying issues to a state's highest court, even when federal rights are at stake. ("Warnings against premature adjudication of constitutional questions bear heightened attention when a federal court is asked to invalidate a state's law, for the federal tribunal risks friction-generating error when it endeavors to construe a novel state act not yet reviewed by the state's highest court.") Notwithstanding our authority to decide issues of state law underlying federal claims, we have used the certification devise to afford state high courts an opportunity to inform us on matters of their own state's law because such restraint "helps build a cooperative judicial federalism."

Just last Term, in Fiore v. White, we took advantage of Pennsylvania's certification procedure. In that case, a state prisoner brought a federal habeas action claiming that the state had failed to prove an essential element of his charged offense in violation of the due process clause.Instead of resolving the state-law question on which the federal claim depended, we certified the question to the Pennsylvania Supreme Court for that court to "help determine the proper state-law predicate for our determination of the federal constitutional questions raised."

The chief justice's willingness to reverse the Florida Supreme Court's interpretation of Florida law in this case is at least in tension with our reluctance in Fiore even to interpret Pennsylvania law before seeking instruction from the Pennsylvania Supreme Court. I would have thought the "cautious approach" we counsel when federal courts address matters of state law, and our commitment to "building cooperative judicial federalism," demanded greater restraint. Rarely has this court rejected outright an interpretation of state law by a state high court. Fairfax's Devisee V. Hunter's Lessee, N.A.A.C.P. v. Alabama and Bouie v. City of Columbia, cited by the chief justice, are three such rare instances. But those cases are embedded in historical contexts hardly comparable to the situation here. Fairfax's Devisee, which held that the Virginia Court of Appeals had misconstrued its own forfeiture laws to deprive a British subject of lands secured to him by federal treaties, occurred amidst vociferous states' rights attacks on the Marshall Court. The Virginia court refused to obey this court's Fairfax's Devisee mandate to enter judgment for the British subject's successor in interest. That refusal led to the court's pathmarking decision in Martin v. Hunter's Lessee. Patterson, a case decided three months after Cooper v. Aaron, in the face of Southern resistance to the civil rights movement, held that the Alabama Supreme Court had irregularly applied its own procedural rules to deny review of a contempt order against the N.A.A.C.P. arising from its refusal to disclose membership lists. We said that "our jurisdiction is not defeated if the nonfederal ground relied on by the state court is without any fair or substantial support." Bouie, stemming from a lunch counter "sit-in" at the height of the civil rights movement, held that the South Carolina Supreme Court' s construction of its trespass laws — criminalizing conduct not covered by the text of an otherwise clear statute — was "unforeseeable" and thus violated due process when applied retroactively to the petitioners.

The chief justice's casual citation of these cases might lead one to believe they are part of a larger collection of cases in which we said that the Constitution impelled us to train a skeptical eye on a state court's portrayal of state law. But one would be hard pressed, I think, to find additional cases that fit the mold. As Justice Breyer convincingly explains, this case involves nothing close to the kind of recalcitrance by a state high court that warrants extraordinary action by this court. The Florida Supreme Court concluded that counting every legal vote was the overriding concern of the Florida Legislature when it enacted the state's election code. The court surely should not be bracketed with state high courts of the Jim Crow South.

The chief justice says that Article II, by providing that state legislatures shall direct the manner of appointing electors, authorizes federal superintendence over the relationship between state courts and state legislatures, and licenses a departure from the usual deference we give to state court interpretations of state law.

The framers of our Constitution, however, understood that in a republican government, the judiciary would construe the Legislature's enactments. In light of the constitutional guarantee to States of a "Republican Form of Government," Article IV, Section 4, Article II can hardly be read to invite this court to disrupt a state's republican regime. Yet the chief justice today would reach out to do just that. By holding that Article II requires our revision of a state court's construction of state laws in order to protect one organ of the state from another, the chief justice contradicts the basic principle that a state may organize itself as it sees fit. Article II does not call for the scrutiny undertaken by this court.

The extraordinary setting of this case has obscured the ordinary principle that dictates its proper resolution: Federal courts defer to state high courts' interpretations of their state's own law. This principle reflects the core of federalism, on which all agree. "The framers split the atom of sovereignty. It was the genius of their idea that our citizens would have two political capacities, one state and one federal, each protected from incursion by the other."

The chief justice's solicitude for the Florida Legislature comes at the expense of the more fundamental solicitude we owe to the Legislature's sovereignty.

Were the other members of this court as mindful as they generally are of our system of dual sovereignty, there would affirm the judgment of the Florida Supreme Court.

I agree with Justice Stevens that petitions have not presented a substantial equal protection claim. Ideally, perfection would be the appropriate stand for judging the recount. But we live in an imperfect world, one in which thousands of votes have not been counted. I cannot agree that the recount adopted by the Florida court, flawed as it may be, would yield a result any less flair or precise than the certification that preceded that recount.

Even if there were an equal protection violation, I would agree with Justice Stevens, Justice Souter and Justice Breyer that the court's concern about "the Dec. 12 deadline," is misplaced. Time is short in part because of the court's entry of a stay on Dec. 9, several hours after an able circuit judge in Leon County had begun to superintend the recount process. More fundamentally, the court's reluctance to let the recount go forward, despite its suggestion that "the search for intent can be confined by specific rules designed to ensure uniform treatment," ultimately turns on its own judgment about the practical realities of implementing a recount, not the judgment of those much close to the process.

Equally important, as Justice Breyer explains, the Dec. 12 "deadline" for bringing Florida's electoral votes into 3 U.S.C., Section 5's safe harbor lacks the significance the court assigns it. Were that date to pass, Florida would still be entitled to deliver elector votes Congress must count unless both Houses find that the votes "had not been . . . regularly give." The state identifies other significant dates (specifying Dec. 18 as the date electors "shall meet and give their votes"); Section 12 (specifying "the fourth Wednesday in December" this year, Dec. 27, as the date on which Congress, if it has not received a state's electoral vote, shall request the state secretary of state to send a certified return immediately. But none of these dates has ultimate significance in light of Congress's detailed provisions for determining, on "the sixth day of January," the validity of electoral votes.

The court assumes that time will not permit "orderly judicial review of any disputed matters that might arise." But no one has doubted the good faith and diligence with which Florida election officials, attorneys for all sides of this controversy, and the courts of law have performed their duties. Notably, the Florida Supreme Court has produce two substantial opinions within 29 hours of oral argument. In sum, the court's conclusion that a constitutionally adequate recount is impractical is a prophecy the court's own judgment will not allow to be tested. Such an untested prophecy should not decide the presidency of the United States.

I dissent.

A DISSENT

By Justice Breyer

(With Justice Stevens and Justice Ginsburg joining for all but the third and fourth paragraphs, and Justice Souter joining for the second, third and fourth paragraphs only.)

The court was wrong to take this case. It was wrong to grant a stay. It should now vacate that stay and permit the Florida Supreme Court to decide whether the recount should resume.

The political implications of this case for the country are momentous. But the federal legal questions presented, with one exception, are insubstantial.

The majority raises three equal protection problems with the Florida Supreme Court's recount order: first, the failure to include overvotes in the manual recount; second, the fact that all ballots, rather than simply the undervotes, were recounted in some, but not all, counties; and third, the absence of a uniform, specific standard to guide the recounts. As far as the first issue is concerned, petitioners presented no evidence, to this court or to any Florida court, that a manual recount of overvotes would identify additional legal votes. The same is true of the second, and, in addition, the majority's reasoning would seem to invalidate any state provision for a manual recount of individual counties in a statewide election.

The majority's third concern does implicate principles of fundamental fairness. The majority concludes that the equal protection clause requires that a manual recount be governed not only by the uniform general standard of the "clear intent of the voter," but also by uniform subsidiary standards (for example, a uniform determination whether indented, but not perforated, "undervotes" should count). The opinion points out that the Florida Supreme Court ordered the inclusion of Broward County's undercounted "legal votes" even though those votes included ballots that were not perforated but simply "dimpled," while newly recounted ballots from other counties will likely include only votes determined to be "legal" on the basis of a stricter standard. In light of our previous remand, the Florida Supreme Court may have been reluctant to adopt a more specific standard than that provided for by the Legislature for fear of exceeding its authority under Article II. However, since the use of different standards could favor one or the other of the candidates, since time was, and is, too short to permit the lower courts to iron out significant differences through ordinary judicial review, and since the relevant distinction was embodied in the order of the state's highest court, I agree that, in these very special circumstances, basic principles of fairness may well have counseled the adoption of a uniform standard to address the problem. In light of the majority's disposition, I need not decide whether, or the extent to which, as a remedial matter, the Constitution would place limits upon the content of the uniform standard.

Nonetheless, there is no justification for the majority's remedy, which is simply to reverse the lower court and halt the recount entirely. An appropriate remedy would be, instead, to remand this case with instructions that, even at this late date, would permit the Florida Supreme Court to require recounting all undercounted votes in Florida, including those from Broward, Volusia, Palm Beach and Miami-Dade Counties, whether or not previously recounted prior to the end of the protest period, and to do so in accordance with a single-uniform substandard.

The majority justifies stopping the recount entirely on the ground that there is no more time. In particular, the majority relies on the lack of time for the secretary to review and approve equipment needed to separate undervotes. But the majority reaches this conclusion in the absence of any record evidence that the recount could not have been completed in the time allowed by the Florida Supreme Court. The majority finds facts outside of the record on matters that state courts are in a far better position to address. Of course, it is too late for any such recount to take place by Dec. 12, the date by which election disputes must be decided if a state is to take advantage of the safe harbor provisions of 3 U.S.C., Section 5.

Whether there is time to conduct a recount prior to Dec. 18, when the electors are scheduled to meet, is a matter for the state courts to determine. And whether, under Florida law, Florida could or could not take further action is obviously a matter for Florida courts, not this court, to decide.

By halting the manual recount, and thus ensuring that the uncounted legal votes will not be counted under any standard, this court crafts a remedy out of proportion to the asserted harm. And that remedy harms the very fairness interests the court is attempting to protect. The manual recount would itself redress a problem of unequal treatment of ballots. As Justice Stevens points out, the ballots of voters in counties that use punch-card systems are more likely to be disqualified than those in counties using optical-scanning systems. According to recent news reports, variations in the undervote rate are even more pronounced. Thus, in a system that allows counties to use different types of voting systems, voters already arrive at the polls with an unequal chance that their votes will be counted. I do not see how the fact that this results from counties' selection of different voting machines rather than a court order makes the outcome any more fair. Nor do I understand why the Florida Supreme Court's recount order, which helps to redress this inequity, must be entirely prohibited based on a deficiency that could easily be remedied.

The remainder of petitioners' claims, which are the focus of the chief justice's concurrence, raise no significant federal questions. I cannot agree that the chief justice's unusual review of state law in this case, is justified by reference either to Art. II, Section 1, or to 3 U.S.C., Section 5.

Moreover, even were such review proper, the conclusion that the Florida Supreme Court's decision contravenes federal law is untenable. While conceding that, in most cases, "comity and respect for federalism compel us to defer to the decisions of state courts on issues of state law," the concurrence relies on some combination of Article II, Section 1, and 3 U.S.C., Section 5 to justify the majority's conclusion that this case is one of the few in which we may lay that fundamental principle aside. The concurrence's primary foundation for this conclusion rests on an appeal to plain text: Article II, Section 1's grant of the power to appoint presidential electors to the state "Legislature." But neither the text of Article II itself nor the only case the concurrence cites that interprets Article II, McPherson v. Blacker, leads to the conclusion that Article II grants unlimited power to the legislature, devoid of any state constitutional limitations, to select the manner of appointing electors. Nor, as Justice Stevens points out, have we interpreted the Federal constitutional provision most analogous to Article II, Section 1 — Article I, Section 4 — in the strained manner put forth in the concurrence. The concurrence's treatment of Section 5 as "informing" its interpretation of Article II, Section 1, is no more convincing. The chief justice contends that our opinion in Bush v. Palm Beach County Canvassing Board, in which we stated that "a legislative wish to take advantage of Section 5 would counsel against" a construction of Florida law that Congress might deem to be a change in law, now means that this court "must ensure that post-election state court actions do not frustrate the legislative desire to attain the 'safe harbor' provided by Section 5." However, Section 5 is part of the rules that govern Congress's recognition of slates of electors. Nowhere in Bush I did we establish that this court had the authority to enforce Section 5. Nor did we suggest that the permissive "counsel against" could be transformed into the mandatory "must ensure." And nowhere did we intimate, as the concurrence does here, that a state court decision that threatens the safe harbor provision of Section 5 does so in violation of Article II. The concurrence's logic turns the presumption that legislatures would wish to take advantage of Section 5's "safe harbor" provision into a mandate that trumps other statutory provisions and overrides the intent that the legislature did express.

But, in any event, the concurrence, having conducted its review, now reaches the wrong conclusion. It says that "the Florida Supreme Court's interpretation of the Florida election laws impermissibly distorted them beyond what a fair reading required, in violation of Article II." But what precisely is the distortion? Apparently, it has three elements. First, the Florida court, in its earlier opinion, changed the election certification date from Nov. 14 to Nov. 26. Second, the Florida court ordered a manual recount of "undercounted" ballots that could not have been fully completed by the Dec. 12 "safe harbor" deadline.

Third, the Florida court, in the opinion now under review, failed to give adequate deference to the determinations of canvassing boards and the secretary. To characterize the first element as a "distortion," however, requires the concurrence to second-guess the way in which the state court resolved a plain conflict in the language of different statutes. In any event, that issue no longer has any practical importance and cannot justify the reversal of the different Florida court decision before us now.

To characterize the second element as a "distortion" requires the concurrence to overlook the fact that the inability of the Florida courts to conduct the recount on time is, in significant part, a problem of the court's own making. The Florida Supreme Court thought that the recount could be completed on time, and, within hours, the Florida Circuit Court was moving in an orderly fashion to meet the deadline. This court improvidently entered a stay. As a result, we will never know whether the recount could have been completed.

Nor can one characterize the third element as "impermissible distorting" once one understands that there are two sides to the opinion's argument that the Florida Supreme Court "virtually eliminated the secretary's discretion."

The Florida statute in question was amended in 1999 to provide that the "grounds for contesting an election" include the "rejection of a number of legal votes sufficient to . . . place in doubt the result of the election." And the parties have argued about the proper meaning of the statute's term "legal vote." The secretary has claimed that a "legal vote" is a vote "properly executed in accordance with the instructions provided to all registered voters." On that interpretation, punch-card ballots for which the machines cannot register a vote are not "legal" votes. The Florida Supreme Court did not accept her definition. But it had a reason. Its reason was that a different provision of Florida election laws (a provision that addresses damaged or defective ballots) says that no vote shall be disregarded "if there is a clear indication of the intent of the voter as determined by the canvassing board" (adding that ballots should not be counted "if it is impossible to determine the elector's choice"). Given this statutory language, certain roughly analogous judicial precedent, e.g., Darby v. State ex rel. McCollough, and somewhat similar determinations by courts throughout the nation, the Florida Supreme Court concluded that the term "legal vote" means a vote recorded on a ballot that clearly reflects what the voter intended. That conclusion differs from the conclusion of the secretary. But nothing in Florida law requires the Florida Supreme Court to accept as determinative the secretary's view on such a matter. Nor can one say that the court's ultimate determination is so unreasonable as to amount to a constitutionally "impermissible distortion" of Florida law. The Florida Supreme Court, applying this definition, decided, on the basis of the record, that respondents had shown that the ballots undercounted by the voting machines contained enough "legal votes" to place "the results" of the election "in doubt." Since only a few hundred votes separated the candidates, and since the "undercounted" ballots numbered tens of thousands, it is difficult to see how anyone could find this conclusion unreasonable — however strict the standard used to measure the voter's "clear intent." Nor did this conclusion "strip" canvassing boards of their discretion. The boards retain their traditional discretionary authority during the protest period. And during the contest period, as the court stated, "the canvassing board's actions during the protest period may constitute evidence that a ballot does or does not qualify as a legal vote." Whether a local county canvassing board's discretionary judgment during the protest period not to conduct a manual recount will be set aside during a contest period depends upon whether a candidate provides additional evidence that the rejected votes contain enough "legal votes" to place the outcome of the race in doubt. To limit the local canvassing board's discretion in this way is not to eliminate that discretion.

At the least, one could reasonably so believe. The statute goes on to provide the Florida circuit judge with authority to "fashion such orders as he or she deems necessary to ensure that each allegation . . . is investigated, examined or checked, . . . and to provide any relief appropriate." The Florida Supreme Court did just that. One might reasonably disagree with the Florida Supreme Court's interpretation of these, or other, words in the statute. But I do not see how one could call its plain language interpretation of a 1999 statutory change so misguided as no longer to qualify as judicial interpretation or as a usurpation of the authority of the state Legislature. Indeed, other state courts have interpreted roughly similar state statutes in similar ways..

I repeat, where is the "impermissible" distortion?

Despite the reminder that this case involves "an election for the president of the United States," no pre-eminent legal concern, or practical concern related to legal questions, required this court to hear this case, let alone to issue a stay that stopped Florida' s recount process in its tracks. With one exception, petitioners' claims do not ask us to vindicate a constitutional provision designed to protect a basic human right. Petitioners invoke fundamental fairness, namely, the need for procedural fairness, including finality. But with the one "equal protection" exception, they rely upon law that focuses, not upon that basic need, but upon the constitutional allocation of power. Respondents invoke a competing fundamental consideration — the need to determine the voter' s true intent. But they look to state law, not to federal constitutional law, to protect that interest.

Neither side claims electoral fraud, dishonesty or the like. And the more fundamental equal protection claim might have been left to the state court to resolve if and when it was discovered to have mattered. It could still be resolved through a remand conditioned upon issuance of a uniform standard; it does not require reversing the Florida Supreme Court. Of course, the selection of the president is of fundamental national importance. But that importance is political, not legal. And this court should resist the temptation unnecessarily to resolve tangential legal disputes, where doing so threatens to determine the outcome of the election.

The Constitution and federal statutes themselves make clear that restraint is appropriate. They set forth a road map of how to resolve disputes about electors, even after an election as close as this one. That road map foresees resolution of electoral disputes by state courts. But it nowhere provides for involvement by the United States Supreme Court. To the contrary, the Twelfth Amendment commits to Congress the authority and responsibility to count electoral votes. A federal statute, the Electoral Count Act, enacted after the close 1876 Hayes-Tilden presidential election, specifies that, after states have tried to resolve disputes (through "judicial" or other means), Congress is the body primarily authorized to resolve remaining disputes.

The legislative history of the act makes clear its intent to commit the power to resolve such disputes to Congress, rather than the courts:

"The two Houses are, by the Constitution, authorized to make the count of electoral votes. They can only count legal votes, and in doing so must determine, from the best evidence to be had, what are legal votes . . . The power to determine rests with the two Houses, and there is no other constitutional tribunal."

The member of Congress who introduced the act added:

"The power to judge of the legality of the votes is a necessary consequent of the power to count. The existence of this power is of absolute necessity to the preservation of the government. The interests of all the States in their relations to each other in the federal union demand that the ultimate tribunal to decide upon the election of president should be a constituent body, in which the states in their federal relationships and the people in their sovereign capacity should be represented."

"Under the Constitution who else could decide? Who is nearer to the state in determining a question of vital importance to the whole union of states than the constituent body upon whom the Constitution has devolved the duty to count the vote?"

The act goes on to set out rules for the congressional determination of disputes about those votes. If, for example, a state submits a single slate of electors, Congress must count those votes unless both Houses agree that the votes "have not been . . . regularly given." If, as occurred in 1876, one or more states submits two sets of electors, then Congress must determine whether a slate has entered the safe harbor of Section 5, in which case its votes will have "conclusive" effect. If, as also occurred in 1876, there is controversy about "which of two or more of such state authorities . . . is the lawful tribunal" authorized to appoint electors, then each House shall determine separately which votes are "supported by the decision of such state so authorized by its law." If the two Houses of Congress agree, the votes they have approved will be counted. If they disagree, then "the votes of the electors whose appointment shall have been certified by the executive of the state, under the seal thereof, shall be counted."

Given this detailed, comprehensive scheme for counting electoral votes, there is no reason to believe that federal law either foresees or requires resolution of such a political issue by this court. Nor, for that matter, is there any reason to that think the Constitution's framers would have reached a different conclusion. Madison, at least, believed that allowing the judiciary to choose the presidential electors "was out of the question." The decision by both the Constitution's framers and the 1886 Congress to minimize this court's role in resolving close federal presidential elections is as wise as it is clear.

However awkward or difficult it may be for Congress to resolve difficult electoral disputes, Congress, being a political body, expresses the people' s will far more accurately than does an unelected court. And the people' s will is what elections are about. Moreover, Congress was fully aware of the danger that would arise should it ask judges, unarmed with appropriate legal standards, to resolve a hotly contested presidential election contest. Just after the 1876 presidential election, Florida, South Carolina, and Louisiana each sent two slates of electors to Washington. Without these states, Tilden, the Democrat, had 184 electoral votes, one short of the number required to win the presidency. With those states, Hayes, his Republican opponent, would have had 185. In order to choose between the two slates of electors, Congress decided to appoint an electoral commission composed of five senators, five representatives, and five Supreme Court justices. Initially the commission was to be evenly divided between Republicans and Democrats, with Justice David Davis, an independent, to possess the decisive vote. However, when at the last minute the Illinois Legislature elected Justice Davis to the United States Senate, the final position on the Commission was filled by Supreme Court Justice Joseph P. Bradley.

The commission divided along partisan lines, and the responsibility to cast the deciding vote fell to Justice Bradley. He decided to accept the votes by the Republican electors, and thereby awarded the presidency to Hayes. Justice Bradley immediately became the subject of vociferous attacks. Bradley was accused of accepting bribes, of being captured by railroad interests, and of an eleventh-hour change in position after a night in which his house "was surrounded by the carriages" of Republican partisans and railroad officials. Many years later, Professor Bickel concluded that Bradley was honest and impartial.

He thought that "the great question" for Bradley was, in fact, whether Congress was entitled to go behind election returns or had to accept them as certified by state authorities," an "issue of principle." Nonetheless, Bickel points out, the legal question upon which Justice Bradley's decision turned was not very important in the contemporaneous political context. He says that "in the circumstances the issue of principle was trivial, it was overwhelmed by all that hung in the balance, and it should not have been decisive."

For present purposes, the relevance of this history lies in the fact that the participation in the work of the electoral commission by five justices, including Justice Bradley, did not lend that process legitimacy. Nor did it assure the public that the process had worked fairly, guided by the law. Rather, it simply embroiled members of the court in partisan conflict, thereby undermining respect for the judicial process. And the Congress that later enacted the Electoral Count Act knew it. This history may help to explain why I think it not only legally wrong, but also most unfortunate, for the court simply to have terminated the Florida recount. Those who caution judicial restraint in resolving political disputes have described the quintessential case for that restraint as a case marked, among other things, by the "strangeness of the issue," its "intractability to principled resolution," its "sheer momentousness, . . . which tends to unbalance judicial judgment," and "the inner vulnerability, the self-doubt of an institution which is electorally irresponsible and has no earth to draw strength from." Those characteristics mark this case.

At the same time, as I have said, the court is not acting to vindicate a fundamental constitutional principle, such as the need to protect a basic human liberty. No other strong reason to act is present. Congressional statutes tend to obviate the need. And, above all, in this highly politicized matter, the appearance of a split decision runs the risk of undermining the public' s confidence in the court itself. That confidence is a public treasure. It has been built slowly over many years, some of which were marked by a Civil War and the tragedy of segregation. It is a vitally necessary ingredient of any successful effort to protect basic liberty and, indeed, the rule of law itself. We run no risk of returning to the days when a president (responding to this court's efforts to protect the Cherokee Indians) might have said, "John Marshall has made his decision; now let him enforce it!" But we do risk a self-inflicted wound — a wound that may harm not just the court, but the nation.

I fear that in order to bring this agonizingly long election process to a definitive conclusion, we have not adequately attended to that necessary "check upon our own exercise of power," "our own sense of self-restraint." Justice Brandeis once said of the court, "The most important thing we do is not doing." What it does today, the court should have left undone. I would repair the damage done as best we now can, by permitting the Florida recount to continue under uniform standards. I respectfully dissent.

Index

absentee ballots (see also "overseas ballots")
disputes over, 98-99, 118, 146-47, 162-62, 188-89, 244-45, 253-54, 301
Ackerman, Bruce, 186, 196, 204
African-Americans
election complaints, 36-38, 91-92
Ahmann, John, 230, 231
Anderson, R. Lanier 248
Anstead, Harry Lee (Judge), 117, 258, 267
Armey, Dick, 141
Article II (U.S. Constitution), 151, 204-5, 208, 210, 211-214, 288-9, 296

Backus, Jenny, 31, 102, 109, 134, 139
Baker, James A. III, 8, 9, 16, 29, 30, 40, 41, 42, 49, 53, 54, 71, 86, 95, 127, 128, 129, 140, 165, 166, 167, 287, 307, 308, 337, 338, 339
Profile, 21-23
ballots (see "absentee ballots," "butterfly ballot," "dimpled ballots," "military ballots," "Palm Beach ballots")
undervotes, by ballot type, 191
Bartlit, Fred H., 163
Begala, Paul, 113
Boies, David, 69, 72, 116, 143, 154, 160, 170, 171, 187, 188, 193, 216, 226, 227, 267, 276, 277, 298, 307, 328, 331, 332, 340
concession on deadline, 334-36
at Florida Supreme Court, 256-59, 294-97
at Leon County trial, 221-24, 228-32, 235-38
Profile, 75-76
at U.S. Supreme Court, 287, 295-97
Brace, Kimball, 223
Brazile, Donna, 4, 324
Brevard County, 96, 102, 112, 190
Breyer, Stephen G., 205, 206, 294, 295, 298, 302, 303, 304, 305, 306, 316
dissenting opinion, 305-6
queries, 298
briefs (see "legal briefs")
Broward County, 130
election problems, 51-53
plans recount, 51
reconsiders recount, 74-75
rejects recount, 65
tempers flare, 145-46
Brown, Corrine, 244
Brutus, Phillip, 38
Buchanan, Patrick J., 10, 11, 12, 18, 32, 34, 36, 50, 51, 81, 82, 91, 152
Burton, Charles E., 44, 50, 51, 73, 89, 105, 159, 166, 171, 172, 224
Bush camp (see "G.O.P." and "Republican Party")
Bush, George P., 6
Bush, George W.
claims victory, 164, 166-67
declared winner, 2
inside the campaign, 336-43
lawsuits, federal, 39-42, 247-48
lawsuits, 138-39
lawyers stall, 192-94
lead shrinks, 28, 29, 264-65
plans transition, 178-79
plays strong role, 308
restrained tone, 239-40
sticks to script, 80-81
sends Baker, 9
tracking his lead, 174-274
urges Gore to concede, 28-29
victory speech, 312-14

Bush, Jeb
backs Legislature's plan, 195-96
cloud on Future, 343-45
ready to sign bill, 181-82
Bush v. Gore, 286-90
butterfly ballot, 10-13, 28, 34-35, 49, 51, 64, 67, 74, 81-83, 91, 118, 119, 123, 131, 152, 153, 178, 215, 216, 231, 322, 323, 324
Butterworth, Robert A., 73, 90, 104, 116, 123, 337, 346
Byrd, Johnny, 106, 155, 161, 184, 185, 201
Byron, David, 38, 66

Caesar, Mitch, 29
Card, Andrew, 30, 167, 179
Carlton, Lisa, 155, 185, 196
Carvin, Michael A., 117
chads, 43, 48, 62-63, 122, 135, 173, 198, 200, 221-23, 230-31, 280, 283-4, 295, 297, 339
in Broward County, 51, 107-9, 117, 130, 145
dimpled, 44-45
eating, 104-5
and Florida Supreme Court, 125
hanging, 45, 47
illustration, 90
judge OKs, 93, 95-96
in Miami-Dade County, 109, 130
in Palm Beach County, 50, 64, 89, 130, 158
Cheney, Dick, 8, 30, 41, 132, 167, 180, 209, 263, 307-8, 326
asks Gore to concede, 233-34
on Gore's obstinacy, 179
has heart attack, 136-37
Christopher, Warren, 9, 16, 40, 41, 54, 60, 63, 71, 72, 232, 233, 234, 323, 324, 327, 328, 330
Profile, 21-23
Clark, Nikki Ann (Judge), 245, 253, 261, 271, 272
Clay County, 97, 98
Clinton Administration
denies money to Bush, 180
Coffey, Kendall, 30, 193
Cole, Tom 268, 269
Collier, Lacey A., 301
Cummings, Elijah E., 281

Daley, William M., 4, 15, 18, 30, 33, 54, 70, 86, 239, 266, 269, 307, 323, 324, 326, 327, 329, 330
Daschle, Tom, 23, 24, 36, 179, 244, 325
Datavote, 191
rate of undervotes, 191
DeGrandy, Miguel A. 105, 121
DeLay, Tom, 77, 83, 84, 268
Democrats
attack plan on certification, 153-54
denounce certification, 164-66
hope in absentee ballots, 244-46
hope in dimpled ballots, 128-29
losing heart, 147-48
seek manual recounts, 31-33
stunned by U.S. Supreme Court, 281-82
tell of statewide problems, 17-20
weigh legal battle, 31-33, 35-36
Dershowitz, Alan M., 63, 91, 113
Deutsch, Peter, 156, 244
dimpled ballots, 128-29, 158-60
Dole, Bob, 31, 57, 155, 342
Douglass, W. Dexter 61, 87, 194, 230, 259, 261, 263, 332
Dowd, Matthew, 5
due process, 83, 150, 194, 248, 255, 288, 289, 304
Duval County
ballot problems, 91-92

Election Data Services, 190, 223
elections, past, 13
Electoral College
becomes issue, 23-25
final votes, 319
Lesson of election (*OpEd*), 321-22
Safeguard of Federalism (*OpEd*), 25-26
Unfair (*OpEd*), 26-27
Electoral votes, final, 319
Electoral Count Act (1887), 186
Engler, John, 155, 342
equal protection, 53, 150, 199, 248, 255, 288, 296, 304, 305, 306, 315, 332, 333
Escambia County, 283
Evans, Donald L., 15, 240

Fabiani, Mark D., 6, 35, 239, 307, 324, 325, 329
Face the Nation, 53, 234
Feeney, Tom, 106, 113, 154, 155, 181, 182, 184, 251, 252, 270, 344
Feinstein, Dianne, 281
Fleischer, Ari, 44, 49, 54, 57, 64, 123, 153
Florida House of Representatives (see also "Florida Legislature"), 303

Florida Legislature
backing Bush suit, 154-55
considering options, 139-40
court decision fuels resolve, 270
Democrats complain, 185-86
moves to assure Bush win, 183-85
plan to bypass courts, 195-96
plays a dangerous game (*OpEd*), 203-4
prepares to appoint electors, 300
special session plans, 197, 201, 249-51
Florida Senate (see also "Florida Legislature"), 201, 249, 310
Florida Supreme Court
backs recounts, 125, 126-27
bars certification, 93-95
Court should take charge (*OpEd*), 123-24
Democratic oasis, 87-88
hearing on recounts, 116-17, 256-59
Justices went too far (*OpEd*), 130-31
moves quickly on Gore contest, 246-47
rebuke of Judge Sauls, 259-62
rejects absentee ballot suits, 309
rejects Gore appeal, 215-16
rules for recounts, 85-87, 94, 265-68
Frankel, Lois, 106, 180, 182, 185, 202, 203, 252, 270
Fried, Charles (*OpEd*), 25-26, 291

Gadsden County, 174
Galey, Fred, 96, 102, 112
Gelber, Dan, 184, 185
Geller, Joe, 135
General Services Administration, 180
Ginsberg, Benjamin L., 216, 222, 229, 259, 300, 333, 337, 341
Ginsburg, Ruth Bader, 205, 206, 241, 276, 279, 295, 304
dissenting opinions, 306, 366-69
queries, 298
questions, 210
Goard, Sandra, 54, 55, 99, 118, 161, 245, 254
G.O.P. (see also "Republican Party")
launches legal attacks, 137-38
on military ballots, 162-63
questions Bush campaign, 56-58
stalls, 197-99
Gore, Al
appeals for faster count, 192-94
challenges Harris, 87
concedes, 310-12
contests election, 175-78
critical mistake, 331-34
defeat , 235-39
digs in, 232-33
fights on many fronts, 152-53
inside the campaign, 322-331
legal challenge, 142-43
loses absentee suits, 271-72
loses appeal for immediate count, 215-16
loses Miami suit, 142-43
modest gains in Broward, 155-56
popular vote, 1, 14, 319
refuses to concede, 307-8, 164-66
remains optimistic, 242-44
retracts concession, 3-4
sends Christopher, 9
speech stuns G.O.P., 79-80
Leon County trial, 221-24
and U.S. Supreme Court, 144-45
Gore camp (see "Democrats")
Gregory, Rodney G., 92
Grossman, Richard, 224

Hancock, Paul F., 116, 206
hand recounts (see "recounts, manual")
Harding, Major B., 116, 117, 257, 266
Harris, Katherine
adheres to deadline, 59-61
attacks on, 103-4, 113
certifies vote, 164-65
declares Bush winner, 164-66
Profile, 113-14
rejects recounts, 77-79, 172
sets deadline, 69-72
statement, 76
takes charge, 59-62
Hastings, Alcee L., 37
Hengartner, Nicholas, 223, 224
Hillsborough County, 162, 190, 282, 283, 284, 338, 339
Holtzer, Bernard, 34
Holzendorf, Betty S., 202, 203
Hughes, Karen P., 15, 63, 240
Jackson, Jesse 20, 64, 135, 153, 209
Jacobs, Harry 54, 55, 99, 118, 245, 272, 309
Justice Department, 17, 37, 75, 180, 217, 222, 328

Kane, Charles, 189
Kennedy, Anthony M., 205, 206, 265, 276, 279, 290, 294, 295, 296, 297, 298, 304, 305, 315
queries, 297-98
Kerrey, Bob, 282
King, Jim, 250
King, Shirley, 154, 173, 174
Klock, Joseph P., 87, 116, 117, 226, 287, 294, 295, 302, 340, 341

Labasky, Ronald, 163, 176
Larry King Live, 136
Leach, Michael, 162, 244, 245, 254
Leahy, David C., 112, 135, 341, 342, 343
Leahy, Patrick J., 141
Lee, Robert W., 17, 65, 74, 155, 342
legal battle lines, 109-111
legal briefs, 109-111, 287-89
Lehane, Chris, 41, 120, 269, 297, 324, 325
Leon County, 97, 98, 162, 163, 170, 171, 228, 284
Leon County Circuit Court, 249
trial about recount, 221-27, 228-32, 235-38
LePore, Theresa, 10, 11, 13, 18, 20, 21, 34, 49, 50, 151, 172
Lewis, Doug, 43, 45
Lewis, John, 209
Lewis, R. Fred, 257, 267
Lewis, Terry P. (Judge), 61, 66, 69, 70, 71, 75, 85, 86, 93, 94, 131, 266, 267, 272, 283, 295
Lieberman, Joseph I. (Joe)
attacks Florida legislature, 202
on military ballots, 111-13
Limbaugh, Rush, 89
Lott, Trent, 141, 179, 286

manual recounts (see "recounts, manual")
Martin County, 188, 189, 243, 244, 246, 253, 271, 272, 301, 309
McKay, John, 154, 155, 181, 182, 184, 249, 250, 251, 252, 270, 344
McKinnon, Mark, 5, 155
McPherson v. Blacker, 208
Meet the Press, 233, 329
Miami-Dade County
halts recount, 133-34
protest in 134-35
Miami Herald, 348, 349
Middlebrooks, Donald M., 40, 53, 62, 248
military ballots
Bush lawsuits, 138-39
Democrats end fight, 123
disputes over, 101-2, 162-63
Lieberman statement, 111-13
Miller, John A., 74, 75, 95

N.A.A.C.P., 37
Nassau County, 154, 161, 170, 173, 174, 175, 176, 177, 224
furor over missed votes, 173-74
New York Times
election night, XXX
interview with Gore, 168-69
part of consortium, 348-49
poll (with CBS), 67
recount estimates, 172
voting machine analysis, 189-91

O'Connor, Sandra Day, 205, 206, 207, 210, 276, 279, 290, 295, 296, 298, 304, 305, 315
queries, 298
questions, 210
Okaloosa County, 97, 162
Olson, Theodore B., 63, 206, 207, 208, 248, 255, 279, 287, 293, 297, 298
Profile, 218-19
at U.S. Supreme Court, 206-8, 210, 294-95
OpEd Articles
on Electoral College, 23-25, 25-26, 321-22
on Florida Legislature, 203-4
on Florida Supreme Court, 123-24, 130-31
on recounts (danger of), 273-74
on U.S. Supreme Court, 156-57, 291-92
optical ballot scanners, 189, 190, 223, 224, 231
rate of undervotes, 191
Orange County, 97, 98, 102, 162, 190, 283, 342
Overseas ballots (see also "Military ballots")
Bush winning, 100, 101
furor over, 96-98
ruling for, 123
overvotes, 12, 35, 348, 349
county-by-county, 285

Palm Beach County, 130
ballot flap, 130
chads in, 43-45
prior complaints, 90-91
recount begins, 48-51, 88-89
recount slows, 104-5
street protests, 20-21
Palm Beach County Canvassing Board
approves recount, 48-51
plans for recount, 63-64
votes for recount, 73-74
Pariente, Barbara J. 258, 259, 267
Pasco County, 162
per curiam 305, 315
Pinellas County, 13, 20, 32, 98, 190, 198, 215, 284, 337

Planned Parenthood v. Casey, 290
Poe, Bob, 34, 55, 101, 147
Polk County, 102, 162
poll, *Times*/CBS, 67
popular vote, final, 319
Pozzuoli, Edward J. 52, 108
Presidential Transition Act, 180
Price, David E. 84
punch-card ballots, 40, 44, 45, 63, 90, 105, 110, 134, 147, 152, 173, 189, 190, 221, 222, 223, 224, 229, 230, 237, 257, 267, 294, 297, 304, 349

Quince, Peggy A., 117, 257, 258, 267

Racicot, Marc (Gov.), 108, 281
Recount begins, 8-9
Recount, manual
 could bring chaos (*OpEd*), 273-74
 debate in court, 115, 116-17
 Florida court backs, 126-27, 264-68
 funding of, 263
 Gore gains 466 votes, 158-59
 standards debate, 119-20
 trial (see "Leon County Circuit Court" and "Sauls, N. Sanders")
 U.S. Supreme Court halts, 275, 276-81, 282-83
Rehnquist, William H., 205, 207, 208, 276, 279, 282, 289, 297, 304, 332
 final opinion, 356-60
 queries, 297
Rendell, Edward G. (Ed), 238, 239, 307
Reno, Janet, 17, 37
Republicans
 ace in the hole, 106
 attack chads, 107, 108-9
 attack Gore's suit, 197-99
 corrected absentee applications, 54-55
 jeer at Broward recount, 155-56
 protest in Miami, 134-35
 threaten to challenge electors, 141
 stalling tactics, 197-99
 vow fight of recount rulings, 127-28, 268-69
Richard, Barry, 177, 187, 193, 199, 222, 224, 226, 227, 229, 231, 236, 257, 258, 288, 309, 336, 340
Ridge, Tom (Gov.), 2
Robbins, Peggy, 189
Roberts, Carol A., 35, 50, 73, 89, 172
Roberts, L. Clayton, 12, 60, 65, 73, 90, 104
Roe v. Wade, 290
Roseborough, Teresa Wynn, 248
Rosenberg, Robert 155, 342
Ross, Dale, 155
Rossin, Tom, 184, 186, 202, 203, 270
Rove, Karl, 2, 5, 15, 57, 58
Safire, William, 7
Sauls, Cindy, 259, 260, 262
Sauls, N. Sanders (Judge), 176, 192, 198, 199, 200, 215, 216, 233, 240, 241, 250, 251, 256, 257, 258, 259, 260, 261, 262, 266, 267, 268, 328, 330
 decides against Gore, 235-38
 earlier criticism of, 259-62
 orders transfer of ballots, 193-94
 refuses to count ballots, 186-88
 trial on disputed ballots, 221-27, 228-32, 235-38
 weighs competing standards, 225-27
Scalia, Antonin, 144, 205, 207, 208, 211, 276, 277, 278, 279, 291, 293, 295, 297, 302, 304, 305
 answers Stevens, 276-77
 concurring statement, 279-80
 queries, 297
 questions, 211
Scalia, Eugene, 293, 295
Schooley, Jeffrey, 189
Schwarzkopf, H. Norman, 101
Section 5 (Title 3), 150, 151, 207, 208, 211-214
 consequences of, 213-214
 meaning of, 213
Seminole County, 16, 48, 54, 55, 93, 115, 118, 158, 161, 162, 178, 188, 189, 243, 244, 245, 253, 254, 271, 272, 301, 309, 323, 330
 Absentee ballot dispute, 98-99
Shaw, Leander J., 257, 266
Siegel v. LePore, 151
Smith, Emma, 188, 189
"Snippy,", Safire on, 7
Souter, David H., 207, 208, 276, 279, 290, 294, 295, 299, 302, 304, 305, 306
 dissenting opinion, 305-6
 queries, 299
special master, 171, 175, 176, 177, 216
special session, 128, 139, 141, 155, 175, 181-182, 183-186, 192, 195-197, 201-203, 232, 233, 249-251, 252, 253, 264, 265, 270, 344

Stevens, John Paul, 208, 275, 276, 277, 278, 279, 280, 298, 302, 304, 306
dissents on decisions, 277, 280-81, 304-5
Sunshine Law, 65, 275, 291
sunshine rule, 50
Supreme Court, Florida (see "Florida Supreme Court")
Supreme Court, U.S. (see "U.S. Supreme Court")
Sweeney, John, 119, 120

Thomas, Bill, 83
Thomas, Clarence, 185, 207, 276, 279, 291, 293, 298, 304, 305, 314
wife's conflict of interest, 293
Title 3 (U.S. Code), 106, 150, 151, 207, 212, 214
Torricelli, Robert G., 15, 23, 36, 308
Tribe, Laurence H., 23, 24, 63, 137, 138, 140, 144, 207, 208, 211, 287
Profile, 217-218
at U.S. Supreme Court, 207-8
Tucker, Mindy, 101, 308
undervotes, 35, 49, 73, 183, 265, 272, 282, 283, 284, 295, 297, 348, 349
county-by-county, 285
rate, by ballot type, 191

Unger, Jason 97, 198, 333
U.S. Court of Appeals
rejects Bush suit, 255
rules in favor of recount, 278-79, 382
U.S. Supreme Court
activist court (*OpEd*), 317-18
agrees to hear Bush case, 150, 151-52
credibility at risk, 289-91
ends recounts, 303, 304-7
excerpts of first hearing, 210, 211
halts recounts, 275, 276-81
historic moment at, 205-8
incursion not needed (OpEd), 291-92
justices' questions, 297-99
may expand voting rights (OpEd), 316-17
right to take case (OpEd), 156-57
scholars question role of, 346-47
second hearing, 293, 294-97
sends case back to Florida, 240-41
text of final ruling, 350-76

Volusia County, 16, 18, 19, 28, 29, 31, 38, 59, 61, 63, 64, 72, 82, 104, 174, 198, 215, 327
recount finds new votes, 65-66
vote tallies
by Florida county, 285
final nationwide,
Votomatic, 90
illustration, 46, 47
rate of undervotes, 191

Wall Street Journal, 106, 348, 349
Washington Post, 114, 348, 349
Waters, Craig, 126, 315
Weisman, Robert, 12, 33, 34
Weldon, Dave, 83
Wells, Charles T. (Chief Justice, Florida Supreme Court), 257, 259, 266, 299, 334, 335
dissent on recount, 265
Williams, Robert 154
Wilson, Jamie 188

Yoo, John 157, 185, 334

Zack, Stephen 106, 222, 230